Sport in Urban England

Sport in Urban England

Middlesbrough, 1870–1914

Catherine Budd

LEXINGTON BOOKS
Lanham • Boulder • New York • London

Published by Lexington Books
An imprint of The Rowman & Littlefield Publishing Group, Inc.
4501 Forbes Boulevard, Suite 200, Lanham, Maryland 20706
www.rowman.com

Unit A, Whitacre Mews, 26-34 Stannary Street, London SE11 4AB

British Library Cataloguing in Publication Information Available

Library of Congress Cataloging-in-Publication Data

Names: Budd, Catherine.
Title: Sport in urban England : Middlesbrough, 1870-1914 / by Catherine Budd.
Description: Lanham, Maryland : Lexington Books, [2016] | Includes
    bibliographical references and index.
Identifiers: LCCN 2017000791 (print) | LCCN 2017005777 (ebook) | ISBN
    9781498529433 (cloth : alk. paper) | ISBN 9781498529440 (Electronic)
Subjects: LCSH: Sports—England—Middlesbrough—History.
Classification: LCC GV605.7.M54 B84 2016 (print) | LCC GV605.7.M54 (ebook) |
    DDC 796.09428/53—dc23
LC record available at https://lccn.loc.gov/2017000791

Printed in the United States of America

To my grandparents who each played many roles in Middlesbrough's history—trade unionist, teacher, cricketer, cinema manager, shopkeeper, usherette, librarian, Wren.

Contents

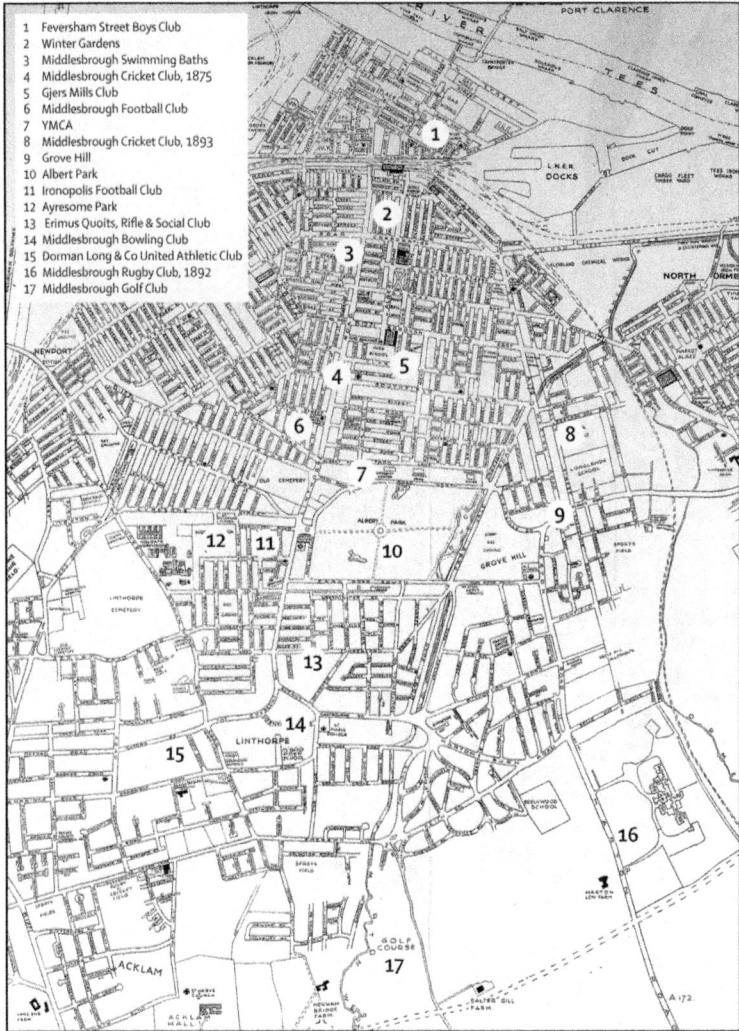

1   Feversham Street Boys Club
2   Winter Gardens
3   Middlesbrough Swimming Baths
4   Middlesbrough Cricket Club, 1875
5   Gjers Mills Club
6   Middlesbrough Football Club
7   YMCA
8   Middlesbrough Cricket Club, 1893
9   Grove Hill
10 Albert Park
11 Ironopolis Football Club
12 Ayresome Park
13 Erimus Quoits, Rifle & Social Club
14 Middlesbrough Bowling Club
15 Dorman Long & Co United Athletic Club
16 Middlesbrough Rugby Club, 1892
17 Middlesbrough Golf Club

Map of Middlesbrough, 1935.
Teesside Archives, CB/M/E/1/44.

List of Tables

Acknowledgments

First and foremost, I need to thank Neil Carter and Dilwyn Porter, the supervisors of the PhD from which this book was developed. Their support, encouragement and advice during the writing of my thesis and plans for this book was invaluable.

Secondly, my thanks to Brian Hill and Eric Kuntzman at Lexington Books who have helped me through every step of the publishing process.

I would also like to thank my academic friends and colleagues who have supported this book from the outset—Brad Beaven, Tony Collins, David Dee, Jeff Hill, Richard Holt, Rob Lake, Malcolm MacLean, Tony Mason, Martin Polley, Ben Roberts, Duncan Stone, Matt Taylor, Tosh Warwick and Jean Williams.

Thanks are due to a number of individuals who allowed me to consult archival material—Anthony Emmerson (then at Middlesbrough Football Club), Graeme Moir (Middlesbrough Bowling Club), Jonathan Still (River Tees Watersports Centre) and David Hunter (Middlesbrough Golf Club).

Finally, my greatest thanks go to my family and friends, whose encouragement has never faltered throughout my prolonged endeavours to complete this book. It is finally finished.

Introduction

During the second half of the nineteenth century, Middlesbrough was heralded as a model Victorian town; the result of the enterprise, endeavor and hard work of its inhabitants. It was "smoke-dried, iron-bound, enterprising, wealth-making, [and] utilitarian,"[1] and fluctuations to its economy aside, portrayals of the expanding town changed very little in the mid to late nineteenth century. The town prided itself on "its enterprise, financial success and municipal growth," and its identity was "rooted in its industry, its urban-ness, its novelty and its survival."[2] The development of sport in Middlesbrough was greatly influenced by the industrial setting, urban expansion, and by the mass migration of workers to the district. The lack of a landed, upper class and the existence of a large working-class population, with the associated problems that this brought to the town, led Middlesbrough to present itself as a town with aspirations to middle-class values. Yet despite the desire to create a moral and decorous society, during much of this period workers' leisure time was not catered to, and their own efforts to fill this time often led them instead to the public house. Opportunities to participate in spectator sports did gradually increase, and because of the strength of the amateur ethos and the characteristics that sports such as cricket and football hoped to encourage, sport offered a way of civilizing the populace.

The period covered in this book witnessed the expansion of both spectator and participant sports, but although there already exists a substantial historiography of British sport in the Victorian and Edwardian periods, that for Middlesbrough in comparison is very small. This is despite the assertions in the nineteenth century that the town was both economically important and occupied a unique place in English history. Much of the literature on the town relates to its economic and industrial history; there are considerable gaps in the existing historiography with regards to the

1

social and cultural history of the town, and this examination of its sporting past fills a gap both in the existing literature on the town, but just as crucially, in the history of urban England.

As well as providing a case study of urban sporting history, this book challenges or questions a number of existing ideas. First, it has been claimed by a number of historians that from the last quarter of the nineteenth century, the physical withdrawal of Middlesbrough's elite was accompanied by a marked decrease in their influence and philanthropic activity. This book suggests that the number of roles occupied in sporting organizations by members of the elite indicates that their withdrawal has been overstated. Secondly, Middlesbrough is characterized as being dominated by working-class, disorderly leisure, but it will be shown that when it came to the town's sport, it was the domain of the respectable lower-middle and middle classes. Third, the view that the North unreservedly embraced professional football and the payment of players in sport more generally is challenged. By examining the town's first attempt to establish a professional football club, the strength of opinion in favor of amateurism is evidenced. Finally, this book explores the idea that football provided a vehicle for civic pride and the formation of local identities. By examining the place of football in Middlesbrough and the roles played by the town's smaller clubs, the links between sport and identity is explored.

In 1983 Walton and Walvin called for the themes of the history of leisure to be tested at the local level in order to provide a more informed and contextually aware synthesis. They noted that at that point, case studies had been patchy geographically with most urban and industrial environments having been neglected thus far.[3] More than ten years later, Holt stated that there was a lack of good studies of sport in the cities of the Industrial Revolution, despite there already being equivalent studies for American cities.[4] More recently Bailey suggested that local studies are capable of revealing "the considerable diversity of working class leisure well past the supposed inception of its massification." Bailey argued that local studies challenge the representation of a homogenous working class in the late nineteenth century. Furthermore, the study of local and regional identities demonstrates the diversity of working-class cultures "in the face of standardizing pressures" from education, the press, and commercialized leisure. Such case studies allow for an investigation of the effects of leisure on different communities and classes and demonstrate the "staggered rhythm" of continuity and change.[5] Likewise Hill has suggested that case studies are capable of demonstrating variations in society such as the pace of change, the timings of the adoption of particular sports, and the behavior of different social groups.[6]

There are a number of case studies whose focus is similar to that of this book—sport in an urban environment, the impact of economic development, the influence of class structures on the provision of sport, the role of rational recreation, the position of local elites, working-class cultures— and thus give the case study of Middlesbrough further context. Such case studies make it possible to identify and explore the unique elements of this town's sporting history. Crump's study of recreation in Leicester also examined the demands of social reformers and the use of sport as a form of social control.[7] Beaven's examination of Coventry considered issues of rational recreation and its failure, the problems associated with male leisure and ideas of citizenship.[8] His study follows the changing patterns of leisure from that offered by rational recreationists to the growth of mass commercial leisure, alongside issues relating to the suburbanization of towns. He argued that workingmen showed "a remarkable propensity to manipulate the entertainment offered to coincide with their own cultural preferences."[9] Metcalfe's research on the mining villages of East Northumberland also examined the role played by the workers in their leisure activities, exploring the relationship between such activities and the villages' economic and social structures.[10] Metcalfe stated that a number of meanings were ascribed to sports—self-improvement, entertainment, promotion of community, tradition—which are also seen in Middlesbrough's own sporting culture. Meller's study of Bristol looked at the provision of facilities by local government, the efforts to "civilize" the poor, and the impact of religion and temperance, and outlined the attempts by elites to "improve the social environment of the city."[11]

As well as similar studies elsewhere in England, Middlesbrough can also be examined alongside local case studies in Wales, Scotland, and Ireland. Like Middlesbrough, Merthyr Tydfil has been described as "the quintessential 'frontier town," "its development being "determined by the exigencies of the iron industry."[12] Through an examination of its culture and spaces, Croll documented the efforts by Merthyr Tydfil's elite to both civilize the town and build a civic landscape, through the regulation of drinking and of public spaces, and by controlling working-class leisure. McDowell's work on Scottish football indicates that there are a number of parallels between the development of the sport there and in Middlesbrough.[13] By examining the influence of work and of employers and industrialists, attitudes toward amateurism and professionalism, and the growth of the game and of clubs, he locates football's place within Scottish society and examines the relationship between football and identity. Similarly, Tranter's examination of sport in central Scotland indicates a number of parallels between those involved in local clubs, particularly when looking at the motivations of patrons and sponsors.[14]

The importance of regional case studies is demonstrated in Curran's work on Donegal. Although this is, in his words, a "peripheral Irish county,"[15] its distance from the main conurbations draws immediate parallels with Middlesbrough. Curran examines the influences on the growth of a variety of sports, both British and local pre-codified games, and in doing so demonstrates the importance of local conditions in determining rates of development. Similarly, although Westmeath differs from Middlesbrough in its economic and political history, there are also similarities between the sporting histories of the two places.[16]

For more than fifty years the starting point for any history of Middlesbrough has been Asa Briggs's essay, "Middlesbrough: The growth of a new community." First published in 1963, it was reproduced in its entirety in A. J. Pollard's edited volume *Middlesbrough: Town and Community 1830–1950* in 1996.[17] That Briggs's essay was published without any reassessments or additions has allowed his account to become *the* history of Middlesbrough with little reevaluation. His arguments have remained unchallenged, and a number of his assertions are tested in this book. Briggs suggested that the interest in Middlesbrough's history lay in "the speed with which an intricate and complex economic, social, and political sequence was unfolded." He described the town's unplanned expansion, the decline in involvement of the ironmasters and the increasing influence in local politics of a "shopocracy." Briggs argued that as the size of local industry increased, "the contribution of employers to the life of the community outside the factory was inevitably curtailed."[18] Furthermore, he claimed that the subsequent generations of ironmasters and managers did not share the "feelings of the older generation about the links which bound them to the town."[19]

A study of the history of Middlesbrough's sport will in fact demonstrate the important role played by members of the town's elite in the development of clubs and organizations. Briggs's long-standing contention that the town's elite retreated from the town and its inhabitants has been restated by other historians. Hadfield has examined the attitudes of the town's ironmasters and their role in local government. Like Briggs, he concluded that they took part in few philanthropic activities, arguing that the ironmasters "remained largely wrapped up in their own affairs," and "exhibited a singular lack of interest" in seeing their workers provided for.[20] Orde's work on the Pease family has shown that despite the financial interests the Middlesbrough Owners had in the town, they were not concerned with its development.[21] Rowe has also pointed out that throughout the region, when urban leaders moved out of their towns, it became "very easy to do nothing about them."[22] In contrast, Warwick has recently argued that Middlesbrough's elite continued to play an active role in the town, via a range of political, cultural, and phil-anthropic activities.[23] A major theme of this case study is the significant and recurrent involvement of a considerable number of the town's elite in sporting organizations, which would suggest that the notion of with-drawal has been overstated. Ironmasters and industrialists continued to be associated with clubs and leagues throughout the period, and this indicates that clubs looked to such individuals as representatives of the existing hierarchy of the town. That members of the elite accepted the positions suggests that they regarded such roles as part of their wider responsibilities to the community.

Much of the existing literature on northeast England has seen Middles-brough receive far less attention than Tyneside, Newcastle, or Sunderland, despite the importance ascribed to the town in the nineteenth century. An example of this is McCord's article, "Some Aspects of Change in the Nineteenth-Century North East" which, despite the title, only details eco-nomic developments in Tyneside and Newcastle.[24] This can be explained in part by Middlesbrough's place both within the Northeast and as part of North Yorkshire. Rowe has discussed the problems associated with defining the region, suggesting that some of Teesside may have stronger ties with agricultural North Yorkshire than to the industrial heartlands of the Northeast. He argued that even though Middlesbrough developed at the southern end of the region, due to "dictates of industrial logic" a partly rural North Riding was subsequently included with Northumber-land and Durham.[25] Lancaster, who in asking whether the Northeast can be described as a particularly distinctive region, failed to find a place for Middlesbrough or Teesside in it, paying little attention to either place, ignoring the nationally important industries to be found there.[26]

Much of the history written about Middlesbrough has concentrated on the economic development of the town. In 1971 Rowe pointed out that the Northeast had been neglected by economic historians,[27] following which Rowe and McCord examined the development of various industries in the region, but only skimmed the service of the area's social history.[28] A recent addition to Middlesbrough's historiography is the work by Yasu-moto, who stated that the town offers "one of the richest fields within which to study those forces operating and interplaying in the making of modern British urban society," as well as a case study of "a rapidly form-ing urban identity."[29] Furthermore, Hudson has argued that Middles-brough offers a "particular . . . window through which to view wider process of industrial/urban growth and the varieties of local and regional exceptionalism during the long industrial revolution."[30]

It is only relatively recently that aspects of Middlesbrough's social history have been examined, though such research demonstrates that it is impossible to divorce the town's history from its industry. Such work shows the influence that the town's economy and urban development had on determining the shape of Middlesbrough's society and the population more generally, as was the case with regards to the town's sport. Taylor argued that Middlesbrough's "reputation for lawlessness has given it a distinctiveness that sets it apart" from many other British towns, but that it had been the intention of the town's founders to "create a morally, as well as a physically ordered society."[31] This book demonstrates how these two conflicting aspects of Middlesbrough society influenced the ways in which sport developed. Stubley's research documents the concerns of the church in Middlesbrough, suggesting that the main interests of the clergy were peoples' morals and the effects of industrialization rather than social reform. Stubley has also described the provisions made by the church for the working classes and attitudes toward temperance. The existence of a number of church-based sports clubs and organizations, and the accompanying rhetoric, does suggest a concern about the behavior of the working classes.[32] Linda Polley's discussion of Middlesbrough's urban and suburban growth offers another perspective on the town's social development and related problems. Her work allows for comparisons between the areas inhabited by the workers and those populated by their employers and managers. She has documented the suburban expansion of the town, showing how business connections were reflected in the physical connectedness of individuals' homes.[33] Recent research by Roberts and Warwick on civic ritual and elite withdrawal respectively, have sought to reassess existing ideas on Middlesbrough's history, and indicate an increased interest in the history of the town.[34]

It is evident that there remain a number of gaps in the existing histories of Middlesbrough, and until now the history of the town's sport has been virtually unwritten. Huggins has briefly described the development and growth of sport, increasing commercialization, and the divide between middle-class respectable leisure and more disreputable working-class pursuits. He stated that in the 1860s and 1870s there was a "strengthening of independent, respectable middle class leisure forms," after which however, the town was "dominated by commercial leisure forms which placed a premium on short-term, immediate excitement."[35] Huggins concluded that working-class forms of leisure came to dominate, offering a diversion from the realities of working life.[36] Though Huggins placed a great deal of emphasis on commercialized leisure in general, it is clear that apart from football, there was in fact little commercial sport in Middlesbrough.

A number of themes dominate this study of Middlesbrough's sport. Firstly, the particular class structure of the town—the influence of the elite, the dominance of sport by a small middle class, and the large working population demonstrate that class was key to the development of sport. A clear distinction was made between the sports and clubs of the workers and those of their masters, but participant or spectator sports were nevertheless popular with much of the population. In addition, the involvement of the town's elite and middle classes as club presidents and vice-presidents meant that sport could be used to underline or define an individual's position in local society. Secondly, given Middlesbrough's industry and large working class, the role of the workplace emerges as an important related theme. This is most clearly demonstrated by the increasing number of large sports clubs of the various works, and the provision of sports days and other events, as well as in the smaller clubs whose roots could be found in places of work. Third, it is clear from studying the growth of Middlesbrough's sporting culture that football quickly became the most popular sport in the town. Often at the expense of other sports and smaller football clubs, the town's preeminent team drew large crowds and dominated newspapers' sports pages. It has been suggested that sport, and football in particular, enabled people to create and strengthen their local identity. This book examines the extent to which this was the case in Middlesbrough. Furthermore, it also looks at different overlapping identities and loyalties, demonstrating the complexities of local and regional identities. A final key theme is the growth of clubs. A huge number of clubs, organizations, and associations existed whose origins are to be found in a range of backgrounds.

This book places Middlesbrough's sporting history firmly within existing work on the history of sport, both furthering our understanding of the cultural, social and political history of the town and of England in general. Huggins argues that Victorian sporting culture "provided a crucial way in which class was articulated in the nineteenth century." The middle classes regarded amateur sport as a tool for "personal, communal and national virtue," but it was also a form of entertainment and a means of socializing.[37] This can often be seen to be the case among the middle class in Middlesbrough, particularly with regards to the number of social events associated with some clubs. Huggins has suggested that the role of the middle classes has not received the attention it deserves.[38] The role of this group in Middlesbrough is crucial to understanding the growth of clubs and organizations, and it is this group that enabled sport to flourish. An examination of the town's middle class will therefore add to our understanding of their input in sport in general. Bailey suggested that although Victorian sport offered new opportunities to members of the middle class, this was not necessarily met with unanimous approval as some sports had "a disturbing impact on middle-class sensibilities," as demonstrated by Middlesbrough's first attempt at professional football.[39] Holt argues that the new professional middle classes were nevertheless

willing to invest in clubs or become directors, and "achieve the prominence and respect he felt his wealth entitled him to," and this can also
be demonstrated by the continued input of Middlesbrough's elite and
middle classes as club officials.[40]

In Middlesbrough, there were only limited opportunities for members
of the working class to participate in sport. Jones suggested that some
members of the working class adapted middle-class sports and incorpo-
rated them into their own culture, often leading to separate working-class
sports and organizations.[41] Bailey has outlined the ways in which the
working class "realized the freedoms of modern leisure amid the unique
complex of opportunities and constraints" of society, as well as the role of
rational recreationists,[42] and Huggins argues that for the skilled working
class, sport provided access to "self-esteem and higher community standing."[43] It has been suggested by Hill that "the control of people's leisure
could never be entirely separated from the improvement of their minds,"
as attempts to improve leisure was connected to the need to "civilize"
the workers.[44] This is evidenced by the formation of the Cleveland and
Middlesbrough Athletic Institute, though the fact that this was only short-
lived may suggest a rejection of such attempts to "civilize."

Football was undoubtedly the most popular sport in Middlesbrough,
and this study will explain how and why this became the case. The
popularity of the sport is evidenced in the increasingly large numbers of
spectators that watched Middlesbrough FC play, the crowds that turned
out to celebrate victories for this and other clubs, and the reaction of
the public and press to developments in the game. The first attempt to
establish a professional football club in Middlesbrough provides a case
study in which to test the debates surrounding the sport's development.
The subsequent progress of Middlesbrough FC and the growth of smaller
clubs and local leagues will add to the existing historiography of football.
An examination of football in Middlesbrough answers James and Day's
request for more local or regional studies of the sport. Such research allows for a greater understanding of the various factors that influenced
the development of football, as James and Day suggest that the complex
nature of football's emergence demonstrates that it would be ill-advised
to use just one explanation.[45]

While accounting for football's success, this book also accounts for the
failure of rugby to find a permanent place in Middlesbrough's sporting
culture. Collins suggests that football came to dominate over rugby in
some parts of England because of its place as "a truly national sport,"
football's more open style of play, and because it was "a game of all the
classes."[46] The last two reasons were both given for the lack of success for
rugby in Middlesbrough. In addition, Dunning and Sheard have argued
that the game's "roughness" made it more appealing to some groups,

but that this aspect of the game may also have disadvantaged rugby when attempting to find favor with muscular Christians. The diffusion of football was assisted by the church, schools, and the workplace, but rugby clubs were far more socially exclusive, as is demonstrated by those involved in Middlesbrough Rovers Rugby Club.[47] That Middlesbrough identified more strongly with the football-playing north-east than with Yorkshire (where rugby was more popular) also contributed to the failure of Middlesbrough rugby,[48] and further demonstrates the complexity of Middlesbrough's regional identity. The popularity of football in the town is demonstrated by the number of football clubs in Middlesbrough—increasing from two in 1878 to forty-four eight years later; in contrast, the number of rugby clubs decreased from just three to one.[49]

It has been argued that sport, and football in particular, played a key role in the formation of local identities. This study will ascertain the extent to which individuals identified with particular clubs or teams and how this affected local identities, or indeed whether sport was simply a means of entertainment and escape from work. Holt argues that team sports were capable of inculcating a strong sense of local identity in spectators, as clubs and teams were able to represent both place and pride.[50] Williams suggests that supporting a club was "an expression of a town identity,"[51] and Huggins states that sport "provided one way of facilitating and renewing strong community allegiances and loyalties." He points out that during a time of mass migration, sport supplied a new focus for old rivalries between towns and regions.[52] Given that the vast majority of Middlesbrough's population were new arrivals to the town, the assertion that sport could assist in the creation of local loyalties can be examined.

As well as helping to form a local identity, sport could also contribute to the formation of a larger regional identity, as is demonstrated by the support for football teams in the Amateur Cup from elsewhere in the region or district. Mason argues that rather than contributing to a northern identity, football served to strengthen local loyalties,[53] but Russell argues that sport provided "a powerful means of expressing a body of supposed northern values" and facilitated the "expression and construction of a range of personal and collective northern identities."[54]

It has been claimed by a number of historians that football in particular helped to form local identities. This book assesses the extent to which this was the case in Middlesbrough, and whether the celebrations of football teams' victories can also be regarded as celebrations of the town. Holt suggests that football's ability to express "a sense of civic pride and identity" contributed greatly to the sport's appeal to the working classes, and that by following a team within the national league, people could assert their "membership of the city."[55] Furthermore he argues that football provided a means by which "men could come to terms with the reality of the

late Victorian city."[56] Similarly, Beaven claims that football allowed workingmen to foster "a sense of place and belonging." He attributes this to the
process of socialization and citizenship that was taking place in growing
cities as football developed. Indeed, he argues that for working-class men,
football *defined* their citizenship.[57] Mason has stated that football helped
to develop and reinforce local consciousness, not only for those who attended matches but also through conversations and press coverage, the
latter being particularly important in relaying opinion on local football in
Middlesbrough.[58] It has been suggested by Fishwick that the fortunes of a
football club "were commonly taken as reflecting the vitality and prosperity of the locality itself," and in a town effected by economic vicissitudes,
football can be located within Middlesbrough's development.[59]

Clubs are central to the development of Middlesbrough's sports, and as
Szymanski has stated, the tradition of forming clubs and associations was
fundamental to the growth of sport; all modern-day sports owe their existence to the "hierarchical systems of clubs and governing federations." As
is shown to be the case in Middlesbrough, Szymanski points out that club
development was led by the middle classes as they were able to share
the running costs.[60] Hill stresses the role of voluntary associations in the
growth of sport, and Vamplew states that clubs "enabled people with a
common purpose to come together," and secure a location for "participation and sociability."[61] As the example of Middlesbrough demonstrates,
increases in middle-class involvement meant that clubs spread out from
town centers and pubs, and in to suburbia, acting, as Lowerson states,
as instruments of "social differentiation and arbiters of public custom."[62]
Furthermore, such suburban or exclusive clubs allowed members of the
professions to climb the "social ladder."[63]

The first chapter of this book outlines the establishment and early history of Middlesbrough, its rapid growth and the expansion of its industry,
and the rhetoric that extolled the town's development. This is followed in
the second chapter by an examination of the early forms of leisure available to the population. Besides the public house and parks, there was little
organized leisure for most members of the working class. In comparison,
this period saw an increase in the formation of middle-class clubs and organized sports, some of which attracted relatively large crowds. The popularity of sports days among a cross section of society is also demonstrated.

By examining Middlesbrough Football Club between 1885 and 1894,
the third chapter acts as a case study for the development of football and
the debates that surrounded the professionalization of the sport. This
chapter demonstrates the popularity of the sport, the expectations of the
public and press, and the role of the middle class in Middlesbrough FC.
The formation of a professional club, Ironopolis, was accompanied by
initial success, greater working-class involvement as well as increased

expenditure, but ultimately ended in failure. This chapter demonstrates the strength of amateurism in the town and the arguments that were generated in the press over the payment of footballers.

Chapter 4 documents the expansion of Middlesbrough's sporting culture, taking into account the detrimental effects the popularity of football and the town's continued growth had on the progress of some clubs. This chapter shows the key role played by the middle class and identifies a great number of individual participants and club officials, and in doing so demonstrates that there were few instances of working-class sport. The chapter details a range of sports that experienced varying degrees of success, from cycling to baseball, and also shows that there was little commercial or professional sport. An attempt at rational recreation is demonstrated by the formation of the Cleveland and Middlesbrough Athletic Institute. In documenting the sporting opportunities available to the female population, it will be shown that women's limited leisure opportunities were only available to the middle classes.

The fifth chapter demonstrates the ways in which the growth of Middlesbrough's lower-middle class was reflected in sports clubs. The increase in cross-class and lower-middle-class clubs is viewed alongside elite organizations like the boating and golf clubs. This chapter details the important formation and developments in workplace-based sports clubs with large numbers of working-class members, as well as the formation of church-based organizations. The fluctuating popularity of cricket is evidenced, including the disbanding of the town's principal club. In contrast, some new sports involved a degree of commercialization, and other sports were promoted because of their health-giving aspects. This chapter demonstrates further that although an increased number of sporting activities were regarded as acceptable for women, sport remained closed off to working-class women.

The final chapter demonstrates the place of football in Middlesbrough's sporting culture. The role played by the sport is shown by the reaction in the town to victories in the FA Amateur Cup, and by the column inches generated during Middlesbrough FC's progress as a professional, Football League club. Furthermore, reaction to the club's scandals demonstrates the importance attributed to the club by many. That football was firmly entrenched in the town's sporting landscape is further shown by the great number of smaller clubs and variety of leagues in existence throughout the town and district.

NOTES

1. L. Praed, *History of the Rise and Progress of Middlesbrough* (Newcastle, 1863), p. 4.

2. L. Polley, "To Hell, Utopia and Back Again: Reflections on the urban landscape of Middlesbrough," in T. Faulkner, H. Berry and J. Gregory (eds.), *Northern Landscapes: Representations and realities of north-east England* (Woodbridge, 2010), p. 238.

3. J. K. Walton and J. Walvin, "Introduction," in J. K. Walton and J. Walvin (eds.), *Leisure in Britain, 1780–1939* (Manchester, 1983), pp. 3–4.

4. R. Holt, "Sport and History: The state of the subject in Britain," *Twentieth Century British History* 7, 2 (1996), pp. 235–236.

5. P. Bailey, "The Politics and Poetics of Modern British Leisure," *Rethinking History* 3, 2 (1999), pp. 146–147, p. 154.

6. J. Hill, "British Sports History: A post-modern future?," *Journal of Sport History* 23, 1 (1996), p. 5.

7. J. Crump, Amusements of the People: The provision of recreation in Leicester, 1850–1914, unpublished PhD thesis, University of Warwick, 1985.

8. B. Beaven, *Leisure, Citizenship and Working-Class Men in Britain, 1850–1945* (Manchester, 2005).

9. Beaven, *Leisure, Citizenship and Working-Class Men*, p. 39.

10. A. Metcalfe, *Leisure and Recreation in a Victorian Mining Community: The social economy of leisure in North-East England, 1820–1914* (Abingdon, 2006).

11. H. E. Meller, *Leisure and the Changing City, 1870–1914* (London, 1976), p. 72.

12. A. Croll, *Civilizing the Urban: Popular culture and public space in Merthyr, c.1870–1914* (Cardiff, 2000), p. 1.

13. M. L. McDowell, *A Cultural History of Association Football in Scotland, 1865–1902: Understanding sports as a way of understanding society* (Lewiston, New York, 2013).

14. N. L. Tranter, "The Patronage of Organised Sport in Central Scotland, 1820–1900," *Journal of Sport History* 16, 3 (1989), pp. 227–247.

15. C. Curran, Why Donegal Slept: The development of Gaelic Games in Donegal, 1884–1934, unpublished PhD thesis, De Montfort University, 2012, p. 3.

16. T. Hunt., The Development of Sport in County Westmeath 1850–1905, unpublished PhD thesis, De Montfort University, 2005.

17. A. Briggs, *Victorian Cities* (London, 1963); A. Briggs, "Middlesbrough: The growth of a new community," in A. J. Pollard (ed.), *Middlesbrough: Town and Community 1830–1950* (Stroud, 1996).

18. Briggs, "Middlesbrough," p. 23, p. 30.

19. Briggs, "Middlesbrough," p. 16.

20. D. W. Hadfield, Political and Social Attitudes in Middlesbrough 1853–1889: with especial reference to the role of the Middlesbrough ironmasters, unpublished PhD thesis, Teesside Polytechnic, 1981, pp. 356–358.

21. A. Orde, *Religion, Business and Society in North-East England: The Pease family of Darlington in the nineteenth century* (Stamford, 2000), p. 29.

22. D. J. Rowe, "The North-East," in F. M. L. Thompson (ed.), *Cambridge Social History of Britain, 1750–1950: Regions and communities* (Cambridge, 1990), p. 462.

23. T. Warwick, "Middlesbrough's Steel Magnates: Business, Culture and Participation: 1880–1934," unpublished PhD thesis, University of Huddersfield, 2014.

24. N. McCord, "Some Aspects of Change in the Nineteenth-Century North East," *Northern History* 31 (1995), pp. 241–266.

25. Rowe, "The North-East," p. 417.

26. B. Lancaster, "The North East, England's Most Distinctive Region?," in B. Lancaster, D. Newton and N. Vall (eds.), *An Agenda for Regional History* (Newcastle, 2007).

27. D. J. Rowe, "The Economy of the North-East in the Nineteenth Century: A survey," *Northern History* 6 (1971), pp. 117–147.

28. N. McCord and D. J. Rowe, "Industrialisation and Urban Growth in North-East England," *International Review of Social History* 22 (1977), pp. 30–64.

29. M. Yasumoto, *The Rise of a Victorian Ironopolis: Middlesbrough and regional industrialization* (Woodbridge, 2011), p. xi, p. 188.

30. P. Hudson, "Review of 'The Rise of a Victorian Ironopolis: Middlesbrough and regional industrialization,'" *Cultural & Social History* 10, 1 (2013), p. 156.

31. D. Taylor, "Conquering the British Ballarat: The policing of Victorian Middlesbrough," *Journal of Social History* 37, 3 (2004), pp. 755–771.

32. P. Stubley, "Churchmen in a Late Victorian Town," *Theology* 83, 695 (1980), pp. 346–354; P. Stubley, *Industrial Society and Church: Middlesbrough 1830–1914* (Bognor Regis, 2001).

33. L. Polley, *The Other Middlesbrough: A study of three 19th century suburbs* (Middlesbrough, 1993); L. Polley, "Housing the Community, 1830–1914," in Pollard (ed.), *Middlesbrough: Town and Community.*

34. B. K. O. Roberts, Civic Ritual in Darlington and Middlesbrough in Comparative Perspective, c.1850–1953, unpublished PhD thesis, Teesside University, 2013; Warwick, "Middlesbrough's Steel Magnates."

35. M. J. Huggins, "Leisure and Sport in Middlesbrough, 1840–1914" in Pollard (ed.), *Middlesbrough: Town and Community*, pp. 128–129.

36. Huggins, "Leisure and Sport in Middlesbrough," pp. 150–151.

37. M. Huggins, *The Victorians and Sport* (London, 2004), p. 21, pp. 31–35.

38. M. Huggins, "Second-Class Citizens? English middle-class culture and sport, 1850–1910: A reconsideration," *International Journal of the History of Sport* 17, 1 (2000), pp. 1–35.

39. P. Bailey, "'A Mingled Mass of Perfectly Legitimate Pleasures': The Victorian middle class and the problem of leisure," *Victorian Studies* 21, 1 (1977), p. 8.

40. R. Holt, *Sport and the British: A modern history* (Oxford, 1989), p. 114.

41. S. G. Jones, *Sport, Politics and the Working Class: Organised labour and sport in inter-war Britain* (Manchester, 1988), chapter 2.

42. P. Bailey, *Leisure and Class in Victorian England: Rational recreation and the contest for control, 1830–1885* (London, 1978), pp. 5–6.

43. Huggins, *The Victorians and Sport*, p. 43.

44. J. Hill, *Sport, Leisure & Culture in Twentieth-Century Britain* (Basingstoke, 2002), p. 167.

45. G. James and D. Day, "The Emergence of an Association Football Culture in Manchester, 1840–1884," *Sport in History*, 34, 1 (2014), pp. 49–74; G. James and D. Day, "FA Cup Success, Football Infrastructure and the Establishment of Manchester's Footballing Identity," *Soccer & Society* 16, 2–3 (2015), pp. 200–216.

46. T. Collins, *Rugby's Great Split: Class, culture and the origins of rugby league football* (Abingdon, 2006), pp. 144–147.

47. E. Dunning and K. Sheard, *Barbarians, Gentlemen and Players: A sociological study of the development of rugby football* (Abingdon, 2005), pp. 119–121.

48. For the geographical spread of football and rugby see A. Harvey, *Football: The first hundred years—the untold story* (Abingdon, 2005), chapter 7.

49. M. Huggins, "The Spread of Association Football in North-East England, 1876–90: The Pattern of Diffusion," *International Journal of the History of Sport* 6, 1 (1989), p. 300.

50. R. Holt, "Heroes of the North: Sport and the shaping of regional identity," in J. Hill and J. Williams (eds.), *Sport and Identity in the North of England* (Keele, 1996), pp. 138–139.

51. J. Williams, "'One Could Literally Have Walked on the Heads of the People Congregated There': Sport, the town and identity," in K. Laybourn (ed.), *Social Conditions, Status and Community 1860-c.1920* (Stroud, 1997), p. 125.

52. Huggins, *The Victorians and Sport*, p. 192, chapter 8.

53. T. Mason, "Football, Sport of the North?," in Hill and Williams (eds.), *Sport and Identity*, p. 50.

54. D. Russell, *Looking North: Northern England and the national imagination* (Manchester, 2004), p. 240.

55. Holt, *Sport and the British*, pp. 166–168.

56. R. Holt, "Football and the Urban Way of Life in Nineteenth-Century Britain," in J. Mangan (ed.), *Pleasure, Profit, and Proselytism: British Culture and Sport at Home and Abroad, 1700–1914* (London, 1988), p. 81.

57. Beaven, *Leisure, Citizenship and Working-Class Men*, p. 74, p. 79.

58. T. Mason, *Association Football and English Society 1863–1915* (Brighton, 1981), p. 234.

59. N. Fishwick, *English Football and Society, 1910–1950* (Manchester, 1989), p. 26

60. S. Szymanski, "A Theory of the Evolution of Modern Sport," *Journal of Sport History* 35, 1 (2008), p. 3. He also argues that when the working classes found themselves excluded, they were able to form their own associations instead, Szymanski, "A Theory of the Evolution of Modern Sport," pp. 3–8.

61. Hill, *Sport, Leisure & Culture*, p. 137; W. Vamplew, "Theories and Typologies: A historical explanation of the Sports Club in Britain," *International Journal of the History of Sport* 30, 14 (2013), p. 1569.

62. J. Lowerson, *Sport and the English Middle Classes 1870–1914* (Manchester, 1993), pp. 96–98.

63. Holt, *Sport and the British*, pp. 110–114.

ONE

"This Smoky Ironopolis of Ours"[1]

The Economic and Social Development of Middlesbrough

When William Gladstone (the then Chancellor of the Exchequer) visited Middlesbrough in 1862 he proclaimed,

> This remarkable place, the youngest child, as I may call it, of England's enterprise . . . 'tis I think possible that you are destined to become, as you already are, one of the first in energy and rapidity of progress, so you are destined to become also in the extent of your operations and the vastness of your resources, one of the very first among those commercial and industrial communities of England which have contributed so much to the strength and safety of the Empire. . . . I believe it is but an infant compared with what it is destined to become hereafter. It is an infant, but it is an infant Hercules.[2]

Within a few years of Middlesbrough's establishment as a port in 1830, it had grown from a hamlet into a celebrated industrial metropolis. It was the epitome of Victorian industry, the personification of enterprise and modernity, a town which had "won a name without a history . . . and commands the attention of statesmen."[3] The town had expanded rapidly to become crucial to Britain's economy and was regarded as "an addition to the riches of the world. . . . It's very name comes down upon the imagination with the thud of a forging hammer."[4] Though the town could not boast of "ancient and valuable institutions," greater pleasure was taken in "seeing those institutions rising up in the midst of us, by our own industry and exertions."[5]

The 527 acres that formed the original hamlet of Middlesbrough, had been purchased for £35,000 in 1829 by the Owners of the Middlesbrough Estate who intended to develop it into a railway town to transport coal.[6] It was the discovery of iron ore in the nearby Eston Hills that initiated the town's rise to prominence. The subsequent establishment and expansion of the iron industry was coupled with an inevitable dramatic increase in the population. From a village of 150 inhabitants in 1831, the population had increased to 39,284 in 1871, reaching 55,934 ten years later.[7] Although in-migration was crucial in maintaining industrial progress and success, Middlesbrough had not been built to accommodate such numbers of workers, and as the town grew "its original spacious center was quickly turned into an unhealthy, overcrowded and neglected slum." The utilitarian nature of the town meant that there were high levels of poverty and ill-health, but this was regarded as the price to be paid for progress and prosperity.[8] The Middlesbrough Owners had envisaged a town of only five thousand, designed with "some uniformity and respectability," but instead there were comparisons with the American frontier due to the continuing immigration from almost every county of England and Wales.[9] The town subsequently displayed problems of social cohesion and segmentation, particularly relating to rootlessness and alienation.[10] The respectability that had been hoped for became increasingly difficult to attain and Taylor suggests that though the Owners and many of the early ironmasters had "sought to create an ordered and decorous society," this was at odds with "the habits and values of the ever-increasing number of working class people." In 1841, 40 percent of the male population were aged twenty–forty, many of whom had arrived in the town without their families, and had to adjust to this "coarse and demanding environment." Middlesbrough found it difficult to shake off the image of an unforgiving, working-class, frontier town, with an ethos of hard work and hard play, and disproportionately high levels of crime.[11] Leonard attributes the lack of law and order as much to "an inadequate system of local government as from inhabitants wishing to live without the law," and Polley has suggested that early Middlesbrough was a relatively "well-ordered and regulated environment for anyone adventurous enough to accept the challenge of living there."[12] Importantly, there was also a distinct imbalance in class composition with no landed class and only a small middle class, who eventually "moved out into whichever suburban neighbourhood was appropriate to their means and social status."[13]

By the 1870s Middlesbrough's industry was producing more than a third of the national output of iron ore, worth more than £1 million, and contributed a quarter of Britain's export of pig iron.[14] Hugh Gilzean Reid, the editor of the *North-Eastern Daily Gazette*, outlined the international importance of the town's iron,

> It furnishes railways to Europe; it runs by Neapolitan and Papal dungeons; it startles the bandit in his haunts in Cicilia; it crosses the wild jungles of Africa; it streaks the prairies of America; it stretches over the plains of India; it surprises the Belochees . . . every articulation in its burnished body bears throughout remotest lands the stamp of the industrious and energetic hands of Middlesbrough.[15]

Almost half of the population of the town was employed in the manufacturing industry, of which a third worked in iron and steel. The dependence on a narrow industrial base left the town at the mercy of both national and international fluctuations in trade, and while the output of iron on Teesside increased during the 1870s, its actual value failed to grow at the same rate.[16] The boom in the industry was followed soon after by a fall in demand, and an increase in the use of steel. Not only was local iron ore unsuitable for conversion into steel, the ironmasters were slow (and initially reluctant) to address the problem. Despite this, that the town was able to recover was regarded as further proof that the town's leaders were "men of energy and foresight."[17] However, the steel industry could not reach the levels of prosperity experienced by the town's iron trade. In the coming decades Middlesbrough's industry and population continued to be at the mercy of fluctuations in the trade cycle.

The town had been founded on ambition and optimism, with the ironmasters dominating the town and determining its success. They were described with reverence and respect, and controlled both industry and local politics, but by the early 1880s, prominent members of the community were beginning to despair of Middlesbrough's progress. The founders moved away from the center of the town, and it is suggested that neither their descendants nor the managerial class that followed them had the same desire for political or civic involvement. As Briggs argued, "improvements had depended for so long on the paternalism either of the Owners or of the ironmasters that once their influence was removed the zest for improvement was reduced." Similarly, Hadfield has suggested that the vast majority of ironmasters "remained largely wrapped up in their own affairs," while Turner states that the ironmasters only took part in municipal affairs when their own business interests were at stake.[18] Middlesbrough's previously "small and recognisable hierarchy of businessmen" was gradually replaced by "a more intricate economic and social structure" which included those in professional and clerical occupations.[19] Indeed from the 1870s, the "intermediate social classes" became increasingly important in local politics. Only two of the town's eighteen mayors between 1893 and 1912 belonged to the traditional group of large manufacturers.[20] In 1872, there had been ten ironmasters and seven shopkeepers on the council, but by 1912 this had changed to only one ironmaster and fifteen shopkeepers.[21]

The celebration of the town's jubilee in 1881 (a year late) was "designed primarily as a public relations exercise," and it was hoped that it would renew interest in the area and its industries and allow Middlesbrough's unique history to be recounted in the press. The town was held up as "a model of public and private prosperity, and as stable a fabric of social happiness and national grandeur, as the world has ever seen."[22] Reid, like many others, applauded the town's founders, and suggested that there existed a harmonious relationship with the people of the town in spite of the difficulties the workers were experiencing; the town's history afforded "a striking example of the associative principle." The "thought and capital of one man, or a few men, led to the establishment of a blast-furnace; but thought and capital . . . were not sufficient in themselves: skilled labour was required to turn them to productive account."[23] Despite the celebrations and the accompanying confident, idealistic rhetoric, three years later the town was still to recover from the latest trade depression. However, one Alderman noted that in the town's brief history "they had passed through season[s] of great prosperity and the reverse" and with "perseverance, and industry, and courage hoped that they might yet weather the storm."[24]

The following chapter explores the growth of sport and leisure within this industrial environment and alongside an ever-growing working-class population. What opportunities were available for the town's inhabitants to participate in sport? Did the development of sport in Middlesbrough follow the same patterns as in other towns in Britain? This exploration of Middlesbrough's early sport and leisure will also examine how the continued urban expansion of the town impacted on sport and will consider whether the town's class structure was reflected in its sporting organizations.

NOTES

1. *Cleveland News, Ayton, Broughton, Bilsdale, Hutton and Swainby Record, Yarm and Stokesley Advertiser* (hereafter *Cleveland News*), 5th July 1884.

2. *The Times*, 11th October 1862.

3. H. G. Reid, *Middlesbrough and its Jubilee: a history of the iron and steel industries, with biographies of pioneers* (Middlesbrough, 1881), p. 1.

4. L. Praed, *History of the Rise and Progress of Middlesbrough* (Newcastle, 1863), pp. 3–4.

5. William Fallows quoted in A. Briggs, "Middlesbrough: The growth of a new community," in A. J. Pollard (ed.), *Middlesbrough: Town and Community 1830–1950* (Stroud, 1996), p. 5.

6. The Middlesbrough Owners were Joseph Pease (merchant), Edward Pease (merchant), Thomas Richardson (bill broker), Henry Birkbeck (banker), Simon Martin (banker), and Francis Gibson (brewer)—W. Lillie, *The History of Middlesbrough* (Middlesbrough, 1968), pp. 48–49.

7. W. Lillie, *The History of Middlesbrough* (Middlesbrough, 1968), pp. 473–474.

8. L. Polley, "To Hell, Utopia and Back Again: Reflections on the urban landscape of Middlesbrough," in T. Faulkner, H. Berry and J. Gregory (eds.), *Northern Landscapes: Representations and realities of north-east England* (Woodbridge, 2010), p. 230; J. Turner, "The Frontier Revisited: Thrift and fellowship in the new industrial town, c.1830–1914," in Pollard (ed.), *Middlesbrough: Town and Community*, p. 82.

9. E. G. Ravenstein, "The Laws of Migration," *Journal of Royal Statistical Society* XLVIII (June 1885), pp. 214–216; D. Taylor, "Bearbrass or Ballarat? Asa Briggs' Middlesbrough and the Pattern of Nineteenth Century Urbanisation," *Journal of Regional and Local Studies* 22, 2 (2003), pp. 4–5.

10. M. Yasumoto, *The Rise of a Victorian Ironopolis: Middlesbrough and regional industrialization* (Woodbridge, 2011), p. 1.

11. Taylor, "Bearbrass or Ballarat?," p. 5; D. Taylor, "Melbourne, Middlesbrough and Morality: Policing Victorian 'new towns' in the old world and the new," *Social History* 31, 1 (2006), p. 18; Turner, "The Frontier Revisited," p. 84.

12. J. W. Leonard, Urban Development and Population Growth in Middlesbrough 1831–71, unpublished PhD thesis, University of York, 1975, p. 250; Polley, "To Hell, Utopia and Back Again," p. 237.

13. Polley, "To Hell, Utopia and Back Again," p. 230; With reference to the town's small middle class, Yasumoto notes that 85 percent of the working population were employed in manufacturing, and only 10 percent worked in the commercial sector—Yasumoto, *The Rise of a Victorian Ironopolis*, p. 195.

14. I. Bullock, "The Origins of Economic Growth on Teesside 1851–81," *Northern History* 9 (1974), p. 84.

15. Reid, *Middlesbrough and its Jubilee*, p. 1.

16. Bullock, "The Origins of Economic Growth on Teesside," pp. 84–87; D. Taylor, "The Infant Hercules and the Augean Stables: A century of economic and social development in Middlesbrough c.1840–1939," in Pollard (ed.), *Middlesbrough: Town and Community*, pp. 61–62.

17. W. H. Burnett, *Middlesbrough and the District: Being notes, historical, industrial, scientific* (Middlesbrough, 1881), p. 16.

18. Briggs, "Middlesbrough," pp. 15–17; D. W. Hadfield, Political and Social Attitudes in Middlesbrough 1853–1889: With especial reference to the role of the Middlesbrough ironmasters, unpublished PhD thesis, Teesside Polytechnic, 1981, p. 356; Turner, "The Frontier Revisited," pp. 106–107.

19. L. Polley, *The Other Middlesbrough: A study of three nineteenth century suburbs* (Middlesbrough, 1993), p. 43.

20. The ironmaster Hugh Bell and chemical manufacturer Samuel Sadler.

21. Briggs, "Middlesbrough," p. 16; Lillie, *The History of Middlesbrough*, p. 339; This confirms Doyle's suggestion that the growing influence of shopkeepers "reflected their increasing social, economic and political relevance in an urban sphere shaped by consumption, modernity and spatial change"—B. Doyle, "Rehabilitating the Retailer: Shopkeepers in urban government, 1900–1950," in S. Couperus, C. Smit, and D. J. Wolffram (eds.), *In Control of the City: Local elites and the dynamics of urban politics, 1800–1960* (Leuven, 2007), p. 43.

22. Joseph Cowen MP, quoted in *Bulmer's History, Topography and Directory of Yorkshire 1890* (Ashton-on-Ribble, 1890), p. 262; T. Nicholson, "'Jacky' and the Jubilee: Middlesbrough's creation myth," in Pollard (ed.), *Middlesbrough: Town and Community*, p. 33.

23. Reid, *Middlesbrough and its Jubilee*, pp. 5–7.

24. Alderman Matthew George Collingwood in *Cleveland News*, 17th May 1884.

Two

An Emerging
Sporting Culture, c. 1870–1884

EARLY FORMS OF LEISURE

In Middlesbrough, an individual's access to leisure was very much determined by their class and the amount of free time at their disposal.[1] The nature of heavy industry often meant working twenty-four-hour-long shifts, and it was suggested in 1865 that employers should "grant time to the workingmen to read the books and enjoy the parks." A letter to the *Middlesbrough Exchange* in 1869 pointed out that workmen were unable to "enjoy the physical and religious benefits of the Sabbath."[2] Furthermore, the Middlesbrough Temperance Society argued that the "intellectual, moral and religious elevation of the people has not been in proportion to the material progress of the town."[3] Exclusive members-only organizations were formed such as the Cleveland Club (established in 1868). With annual subscriptions of more than £10, the use of its rooms was confined to "a society of gentlemen connected with each other by a common bond of professional acquaintance." Similarly the Erimus Club (founded in 1873) was "chiefly intended for gentlemen connected with the iron and coal trades," with annual subscriptions of five guineas. In comparison, the ironmaster Henry Bolckow opened a workingmen's club in 1873 which had a quarterly subscription of 2s and offered opportunities for "rational and civilising pleasures."[4] Parks offered some of the first opportunities for the workers to partake in recreation. Though a small park had already been laid out in between two railways lines at the docks,[5] in 1859 the *Middlesbrough Weekly News & Cleveland Advertiser* stated that,

> The want is felt by all classes in the town [for a park]. No place is so badly provided for in the recreative department as ours. Sickly-looking youth and pallid manhood would receive a boon indeed by the establishment of some recreative institution or the enclosure of some ground where cramped limbs

might be exercised, and the mind be dragged from the everlasting monotony around us.

When Bolckow announced his intention to buy land for a park in 1864, the same newspaper thought that "of all [the] gifts that could have been imagined this will confer the greatest happiness on the greatest number of inhabitants."[6] At the opening of Albert Park in 1868, the Archbishop of York stated that he hoped it would be "a place of innocent and healthful recreation" that would "diminish intemperance."[7] The park included a croquet land, bowling green, a maze, cricket, and exhibition and archery grounds, providing space "for out-door recreation of all kinds," while drinking, swearing and brawling were prohibited.[8]

It had been noted as early as 1863 that there was a keen interest in sport in Middlesbrough. Landor Praed remarked that, "on the day of a [horse] race, a crowd of workmen may be found in the market-place, marking up their betting-books, just as they congregate in the Haymarket or in St. Bride's passage in London." Indeed it was reported that at a horse race at nearby High Leven, "a great amount of money depended upon the result . . . the bulk of the money going from Middlesbrough."[9] However, the *Middlesbrough Weekly News & Cleveland Advertiser* suggested in 1859 that the workingman ought to spend "a great deal of his spare time to enlighten and instruct the mind," rather than on "the gratification of his purely animal nature."[10] Nevertheless, an attempt to introduce horse racing to Middlesbrough one Monday afternoon in 1875 proved popular. The five races had been "most anxiously looked for," and the event attracted a "large concourse of people . . . the grand-stand and every available inch of vantage ground was taken up."[11] By the early 1880s the local press were reporting on a diverse number of sports, many of which were becoming increasingly associated with gambling. An editorial in the *North-Eastern Daily Gazette* argued that as long as the aristocracy partook in gambling, "so long will the working man claim the privilege of posting his shilling at Stockton [races]."[12] The *Northern Echo* argued that although it was perfectly acceptable "that the natives of different localities should be proud of the proficiency in a manly and healthy pursuit of the men they produce," the practice of betting was leaving "its evil impress on every grade of society." The newspaper concluded that this led "the moralist to look askance upon many pursuits [that are] otherwise innocent and hearty."[13]

THE GROWTH OF ORGANIZED SPORT

It is against a backdrop of economic boom and bust, and within the town's working class–dominated social structure that Middlesbrough's sporting culture developed and opportunities to partake in leisure gradually increased. From the middle of the nineteenth century, forms of rational recreation were emerging to counter less respectable activities. The physical conditions of Middlesbrough were thought to breed intemperance and immorality, and the Middlesbrough Temperance Society was formed just four years after the town was established. However, the efforts of temperance groups were met with little permanent success.[14] In 1873 Middlesbrough was described as "godless, gambling, [and] tipsy," alcohol remaining central to the culture of the town's working-class men, there being few alternate forms of leisure.[15] Indeed Vamplew points out that in the industrial city, drink "provided an escape from the monotony and regimentation of work and from the squalor of the urban environment."[16] As Bailey has argued, while working-class leisure was increasingly recognized as necessary, it was felt that "without moral vigilance its practice would threaten the priorities of work and social discipline."[17] Therefore, sport was used as a means of creating a healthy and orderly workforce, often acting simultaneously as a form of social control, and as a means of offering an opportunity for like-minded middle-class gentlemen to socialize together. From the 1860s, Britain experienced a sporting revolution, and Vamplew suggests that one of the reasons that the working classes were so accepting of new leisure opportunities was that these were not offered in opposition to their traditional activities, but instead were able to accommodate or tolerate drinking and gambling.[18] A number of factors have been identified (rising incomes, increased spending power and free time, transport improvements, urbanization, the growth of the middle class and entrepreneurs) that together laid the foundations for the growth of commercial spectator sport, all of which are evidenced in the development of sport in Middlesbrough. In addition, because Middlesbrough was a young, immigrant town it did not possess indigenous working-class sports or pastimes of its own,[19] though those new arrivals to the town may have brought their own sporting traditions with them. The town did not possess an aristocracy or upper class, and did not have an established amateur tradition to contend with before professional, commercial sport could come to the fore. However, it is clear that some members of Middlesbrough's elite embraced, albeit later than elsewhere, amateur sport and its ethos, as a counter to the pastimes of the town's unruly working class.

A number of competitive sports developed in Middlesbrough, some attracting considerable crowds, such as cricket, football, and rowing. While cycling and rowing drew large numbers of spectators for professional contests, most sports adhered to the tenets of amateurism, and there were few opportunities for members of the working class to participate. Cricket was well established in Middlesbrough by the mid-1870s, the first team having been founded more than thirty years earlier by the Mechanics' Institute.[20] In 1875 Middlesbrough Cricket Club (established in the mid-1850s) were able to open a new ground at a cost of around £1,000, evidently with some commercial interests and profits in mind; it included a "grand pavilion . . . which, having an open front, can be used either as a grandstand or a dancing saloon." There was also a high wall "so that they who wish to see a good game will be compelled to pay for the privilege," and one side of the ground was to be fitted with seats to allow ladies to watch in comfort.[21] Many of the club officials were members of the town's elite, and the presence of two ironmasters (William Randolph Innes Hopkins as president and Alfred C. Downey as vice president) contradicts the notion of elite withdrawal (though it is unclear how much actual input such officials had in the club). Other officials included a doctor, an ironworks manager, and a watchmaker and jeweler.[22]

Such was the standing of the game in the town that a match against a Middlesbrough & District Eighteen was included in a tour by an Australian Eleven in 1880. The interest in the sport for spectators was evidenced as the match was well attended on all four days and the Australians visited the town again two years later, completing a victory over Yorkshire in front of a crowd of around three thousand. The *Weekly Exchange* noted that, "Middlesbrough itself turned out almost to a man to witness the tournament and during the afternoon the streets have worn an almost deserted appearance."[23]

In the early 1880s cricket remained the preserve of the middle classes in Middlesbrough. In 1881 the president and captain of the cricket club was a solicitor and coroner who was said to have "assisted the club both with his time and purse." The deputy captain and one of the secretaries were accountants, the treasurer was a banker, and committee members included two clerks, and an iron and lumber merchant.[24] In contrast, the club's professionals during this period were a cricket outfitter, an ironworks laborer, and a joiner. That these players had other jobs suggests that the money they were paid from playing cricket only supplemented their regular income, but also indicates that the players were able to spare the time away from work. It is safe to assume that for many workingmen, it would have been almost impossible to take the necessary time off from work to play cricket; it was after all (in theory) a game "played solely for its own sake, and of which honor is the only prize."[25] The following account of a cricket match in 1882 between Constable Burton in the Yorkshire Dales (more than thirty miles away) and Middlesbrough, demonstrates the relaxed attitude of those playing as well as the amount of time spent away from the town,

Starting by the first train (6.30) the party arrived safely at their journey's end . . . having beguiled the time, some with the usual packet of books, provided on all such occasions, and the morning papers. After strolling leisurely down from the station, admiring the scenery, passing through the little village of Constable Burton . . . they arrived at Burton Hall . . . where breakfast was waiting for them . . . The party wandered through the woods and gardens and green and hot houses, admiring the fruits and flowers, till the time fixed for starting, when a march was made to the scene of action about 10.30.[26]

In comparison, Ironopolis Cricket Club (founded in 1880) was based in Eston next to the ironworks. It was noted in the press that "some of its most promising bats have not been able to devote that time to its interests which they would have desired," presumably due to a lack of leisure time. However, details of their matches show that this club was also able to employ the same professional as Middlesbrough.[27]

The number of cricket matches reported in the local press increased as the game maintained its popularity; as the *Daily Exchange* stated, there was "scarcely a club which does not possess a strip of perfectly level sward where wickets can be pitched."[28] Aside from the bigger, more important games of the day, the reporting of many cricket matches consisted solely of a final score, and it is difficult to accurately identify the origins of many clubs or teams, or the backgrounds of players. The names of most clubs suggest their origins are to be found in location, though the names of some clubs suggest roots in the church or the workplace. For example, of the thirty-seven cricket matches reported in the *North-Eastern Daily Gazette* on 23rd June 1884, only nine team names suggest origins in a place of worship, and only four team names place the club definitively within the workplace.[29] Nevertheless a game between the foremen of two steelworks was described as "the cricket match of the season," there being a crowd of nearly one thousand present. The match was evidently taken very seriously, it being reported that both teams had been in training for three weeks, with the result that "the Middlesbrough men had no chance whatever with the heroes of the Steelworks."[30] In contrast the *North-Eastern Daily Gazette* reported on the "annual match amongst the youths who are home from school on their holidays," where the teams were captained by a solicitor and an ironmaster, and two years later a game between a team of clowns from a visiting circus and members of the Royal Antedeluvian Order of Buffaloes was reported on. Drawing a large crowd of two thousand, "the fielding of the clowns attracted considerable attention, inasmuch as they turned somersaults, and performed various other feats of the ring during the course of play."[31]

Though a relatively new game to Middlesbrough in comparison to cricket, football was already beginning to establish itself in the early 1880s as one of the more popular spectator sports in the town and quickly "got its hold of the people."[32] The number of football clubs on Teesside increased from nine in 1877–78 to thirty-five by 1880–81,[33] and the number of spectators watching the town's principal team, Middlesbrough Football Club (founded in 1876), grew so much that the club was forced to move its games from a local park to the grounds of the cricket club on Linthorpe Road. It was felt that football "brought out the best points in a young man's character, especially when he was associated with young men of his own class." Football offered "the means of employing leisure time profitably and pleasantly, keeping young men from bad associations," therefore making it an ideal game for the men of Middlesbrough.[34] Although the origins of the sport and a number of clubs owed their existence to alumni of public schools, it soon became apparent that football "belonged to the people not to any public school."[35] That the sport rapidly attracted large numbers of spectators was at odds with the game's original amateur principles. As Holt points out, spectatorism was regarded as "no more than mindless fanaticism, obstinate and arbitrary partisanship devoid of sense, morality or self-restraint."[36] Those members of the middle classes who favored the game were of the opinion that football could improve character, that it gave the working classes a valid pastime, and that it could also help to bring different classes together.[37] Though the *Northern Athlete* suggested that football in Middlesbrough was cross-class, as it brought together men "of every grade, from the prosperous iron master to the humblest riveter,"[38] in the early 1880s the administration of Middlesbrough FC was in the hands of the middle class—the president was a chemical manufacturer, the captains were clerks, and the secretary was an accountant.[39]

Increases in both local interest and in the standards of the game can be gauged in the local press, which devoted an increasing number of column inches to the sport and reported it in ever greater detail. An estimated 2,500 spectators watched the Sheffield Association Challenge Cup tie between Middlesbrough and nearby rival Redcar in October 1880.[40] In 1881 the Cleveland Football Association was formed with a cup competition beginning a year later. Middlesbrough went on to beat Redcar in the first five finals, and the resulting rivalry between the two clubs helped to generate interest in the sport. In 1882, the final attracted one thousand spectators including various Middlesbrough dignitaries and industrialists. Ending in a draw, it was said to be "the most scientific display of football which has ever been seen in the district."[41] After Middlesbrough won the replay, the *Weekly Exchange* reported on the growing interest in the game,

During the past week the final tie has been an absorbing topic of conversation in the iron town and adjacent villages, and partizan [sic] feeling ran very high. Every scrap of news relative to the training and composition of the respective teams was eagerly seized upon and discussed. . . . To attempt to describe the play is well-nigh impossible, the intensest [sic] spirit of rivalry affecting both players and spectators alike, and the match will long be remembered and fought peacefully in words over and over again.[42]

In 1884 the final was played at Redcar and attracted between three thousand and five thousand spectators. After Middlesbrough's victory the club's president remarked that, "every member who took part in the competition and won those extraordinary series of matches, would wear these [winning] medals on his manly bosom, remembering the part he had to take and the manly fellows he had to beat in order to win."[43]

In 1884 the club was growing so rapidly as to necessitate the construction of a new grandstand at their Linthorpe Road ground.[44] The *Cleveland News* commended the club on the newly built stand as it would satisfy "a much-felt want, and will no doubt tend to the further patronage of a pastime that is becoming ever more and more in favour."[45] However, the cost resulted in so much debt that the club debated withdrawing from the Sheffield Association Cup as they could not afford the travel expenses to the semifinal. The popularity of the sport was demonstrated in an editorial in the *Daily Exchange* which expressed dismay at the decision to withdraw. It was suggested that a victory in the cup would be valued by spectators and that the public would "readily contribute to free the club from the responsibility of incurring further debt, in order that they might have a fair chance of bringing to Middlesbrough the high honor which a cup victory would gain."[46] This statement proved correct as the prospect of withdrawal prompted donations "from the humble but useful sixpence to a sovereign," but the club "told them to keep their money, the offers of which had afforded much gratification as proving the hold of the club on a kind but critical public," and proceeded in the competition.[47]

There were many other smaller football clubs in existence, whose origins would appear to be similar to the local cricket teams discussed above. Published results also included second teams and junior sides, and like cricket, much of the reporting on smaller football teams consisted of limited details. Some of those involved with South Bank Football Club (formed in 1868) can be identified, and the officials of this club were similar in background to those of Middlesbrough FC. In 1883 the president was a doctor, the vice-presidents included a clerk, an ironworks manager, a civil engineer, and a Catholic priest, and the secretary was a clerk. Their birthplaces included Scotland, Ireland, Wales, Leicestershire, and Lancashire.[48]

Like the roots of both cricket and football in Middlesbrough, those of Middlesbrough Rovers Rugby Club would also appear to be middle class. The club's president was a doctor, and the club's captain from 1881–1884 was a solicitor.[49] However, while football flourished, rugby's popularity declined as clubs struggled to attract spectators. In 1878 there had been three rugby clubs and two football clubs in Middlesbrough, but by 1884 there were four rugby clubs and forty-five football clubs.[50] In 1882 the principal rugby teams in the town, Middlesbrough Rovers and Tees Wanderers, met in front of "a good attendance" despite the game taking place at the same time as a home game for Middlesbrough FC against Redcar.[51] Reports of fixtures for both Rovers and Wanderers continued to be reported in the press, albeit with rugby referred to as "the old-fashioned game," a notion that no doubt contributed to the game's decline in a town that prided itself on its modernity.[52] Middlesbrough Rovers were watched by a sizeable crowd of one thousand for a Yorkshire County Challenge Cup tie in 1884, and a month later Middlesbrough Football Club had a much bigger crowd of between three thousand and five thousand for the Cleveland Cup final.[53]

The reasons for rugby's comparative lack of support are unclear. The *Cleveland News* covered the difficulties of Middlesbrough Rovers with some interest in 1884. The newspaper wondered whether the reason that no new clubs were being formed was because of "the difficulty experienced by beginners understanding the very many points required to be known by a player under this code." Rugby was thought to be "uninteresting to a spectator who imagines it to consist chiefly of scrimmages and running with the ball." Though the club "had its interests well and substantially looked after by a gentleman who is a staunch supporter of out-door sport," Rovers struggled to find a ground on which to play. The *Cleveland News* surmised that should the club succeed in obtaining one, "no doubt the Rugby game will be clearer exemplified and become much more popular." It was also reported that Rovers were "going on a different tack to what they have hitherto done, and are opening their club out more for new members." It was noted that though expenses had been steep, "these have been cheerfully borne by the players, and the public of Middlesbrough have never yet been asked in any way to help it pecuniarily."[54] It is safe to assume that despite this "opening out" of the club, the playing membership was still largely middle class; team members in the early 1880s included four clerks, a solicitor, a mechanical engineer, and a gas manager's assistant.[55]

After a deal with the cricket club to use their field fell through, Rovers were left without a ground, and the *Cleveland News* stated that "much sympathy is felt for the rejected club and their supporters."[56] The newspaper evidently regarded the game particularly favorably, often devoting more column inches to rugby than to football. In October 1884 there appeared a report of Rovers' home game against Northern of Newcastle-upon-Tyne. Though there were only two hundred to three hundred supporters present, this was thought to be "a sign that the 'carrying game' is becoming more popular in the town." The *Cleveland News* was pleased to note that "the play was void of all roughness, and the two teams seemed to leave the field as sound in body and limb as they entered it, which is something to mark in favor of the Rugby rules."[57]

As was the case with cricket, football, and rugby, both in England generally and in Middlesbrough in particular, amateur rowing was dominated by the local elite, though the sport did coexist alongside popular professional competitions. Dominated by members of the middle class, rowing clubs emphasized good behavior and high standards, and were often socially exclusive. Regattas were the only public demonstrations of the merits of the sport, which at the same time offered respectable entertainment, which Middlesbrough still lacked. Indeed in 1878 the *Daily Gazette* hoped that occasional rowing events would be held in Middlesbrough "giving the public something wherewith to be entertained."[58]

The Middlesbrough Amateur Boating Club was formed in 1866 with a naval architect as president. A boathouse was erected at a cost of £86, and a trainer was appointed from April to October for 30s a week. Membership was exclusive with annual subscriptions, entrance fees, and the mandatory purchase of expensive club uniforms, which constituted "white flannel trousers, white flannel jerseys bound with blue braid, and diamond pattern flannel cap in red, white and blue, and for full dress pea jacket, with club buttons, white straw hat, black ribbon, edged with gold, and the initials of the club MABC in gold."[59] In the mid-1870s the club's officials were upper-middle and middle class (see table 2.1).

The first Tees Amateur Regatta was held in August 1874, established "under the auspices of the nobility and gentry of the district, and heartily nurtured by gentlemen well known as ardent supporters of aquatic amusements." Advance tickets for the enclosure were priced at 1s and the banks of the river were subsequently "crowded with spectators." The fees for entering the seven events ranged from 7s 6d for the canoe steeplechase ("one mile over land and water") to £2 2s for the Tees ("for gentleman amateurs") and Ironmasters cups.[60] The *Northern Echo* pointed out that the regatta was only open to amateurs, races by "ships' boats, fishing cobles and other craft . . . were conspicuous by their absence," and suggested that in the future such races should be included "as a means of varying the sport," as races would have been opened up to workingmen.[61]

The costs involved in participating in rowing kept membership numbers low,[62] and it was felt by some that the sport was not as popular as it ought to be. In 1875 one member stated that he was disappointed that a town the size of Middlesbrough devoted only one day a year to rowing. He thought "it was a standing disgrace" that these proponents of muscular Christianity "could not give one half day to a regatta."[63] In 1877 the club's secretary stated that he had found it difficult to get subscriptions from ironmasters "who were always ready to give in prosperous times,"

Table 2.1. Middlesbrough Amateur Boating Club officials, 1875[1]

	Role	Occupation	Address	Place of birth	Servants
John Thomas Belk	Vice president	Solicitor and coroner	Park Villas, Middlesbrough	Pontefract, Yorkshire	5
Raylton Dixon	Vice president	Shipbuilder	Oatlands, Marton Road, Middlesbrough	Newcastle	5
James Harris	Deputy lieutenant	Sail manufacturer	Grove Hill, Middlesbrough	Middlesbrough	2
William C. Park	Treasurer	Bank cashier	5 Victoria Terrace, Kirkleatham	Scotland	None (lodger)
Bernhard Samuelson	Vice president	MP for Banbury, Ironmaster	56 Princes Gate, London	Germany	3
John George Swan	Vice president	Ironmaster	Upsall Hall, Upsall	Long Benton, Northumberland	6
John R. Winpenny	Secretary	Secretary of Middlesbrough Exchange Company	85 Grange Road West, Middlesbrough	Barnard Castle, County Durham	1

[1] 1871 and 1881 census; *Daily Gazette*, March 2, 1875

and a year later the *Daily Gazette* suggested that given the depression in trade, it would not have been surprising if the club had "gone the way of many men and some institutions of this once thriving borough," and folded. The newspaper hoped that the club would continue as "the sports of the district are none too numerous," indicating that there was still a desire for more leisure and entertainment opportunities.[64] At the annual meeting of the club in 1883, there were only fifty ordinary members, and at the regatta a year later there were complaints about the organization of the event. The races had not finished until eight o'clock and the *Cleveland News* complained that no band had been provided "to wile away the tedious hours," so that "spectators gradually thinned off, and very few were left to witness the final contests."[65]

"Following the example of other districts," the Middlesbrough Bicycle Club was formed in 1877 and had twenty members within a few weeks. As was the case with the other clubs already identified, this club also benefited from the patronage of members of Middlesbrough's elite. The first president was John Gjers (a Swedish ironmaster) followed later by Sadler and Dixon (though it was reported that the latter "did not ride"),[66] and the club's officials included two further ironmasters and other individuals with middle-class occupations. Four of the officials lived in the suburban and affluent Southfield Villas, giving a further indication of the exclusivity of the club (see table 2.2).

By 1881 the club had eighty members, and its own premises with smoking and reading rooms, and a billiard table that acted as a means of "keeping them together in the winter months."[67] Cycling's increasing popularity was evidenced at the fourth northeastern bicycle meet held in Middlesbrough in 1882. More than 260 cyclists from twenty-three clubs across the region cycled through the town, ending at Gunnergate Hall in Marton to be met by Raylton Dixon, who proclaimed that the procession "had given the people of Middlesbrough satisfaction and much gratification."[68]

Despite the assertion of the president of the National Cyclists' Union that cycling "opened out a new and very enjoyable form of recreation to a class of the community whose means of enjoyment are by no means too numerous," it required time and money to partake in events such as that described above, and the poorest residents of the town were inevitably excluded.[69] Advertisements from 1883 and 1884 in the *North-Eastern Daily Gazette* for secondhand bicycles show a range in prices. For example, one bicycle which had been "scarcely ridden" was for sale for £13, another was advertised for £10 10s, and other secondhand bicycles ranged from £2 10s to £4 10s.[70] An advertisement for R. W. Huggins & Co stated that the company had "genuine bargains at extremely low prices," and prices ranged from £2 15s to £11. Another advertisement for Young's Bicycle Repository included boys' bicycles for £2 15s, and adult bicycles from £3 10s to £11 10s.[71]

Table 2.2. Middlesbrough Bicycle Club officials, 1877[1]

	Role	Occupation	Address	Place of birth	Servants
John Gjers	President	Ironmaster	2 Southfield Villas, Middlesbrough	Sweden	3
Frederick Angus	Committee	Iron trade salesman	76 Church Street, Middlesbrough	Darlington, County Durham	None
John Dunning	Vice president	Ironmaster and timber merchant	11 Southfield Villas, Middlesbrough	Yorkshire	2
Lawrence Farrar Gjers	Captain	Mechanical engineer	2 Southfield Villas, Middlesbrough	Middlesbrough	3
William Hanson	Vice president	Ironmaster	6 Southfield Villas, Middlesbrough	County Durham	4
William King	Secretary	Retired draper	Southfield Grove, Middlesbrough	Marske, Yorkshire	3
John G. Lincoln	Committee	Solicitor	45 Grange Road West, Middlesbrough	Yorkshire	1
William H. Pluse	Committee	Clerk	22 Peacock Street, Middlesbrough	Hunsworth, County Durham	1

[1] 1881 census; *Daily Gazette*, April 23, 1877

There was little public provision of leisure at this time, though the public swimming baths were opened in October 1884. The *North-Eastern Daily Gazette* thought this facility was long overdue, suggesting that the baths would be of benefit to workingmen,

> The nature of the work in which the great majority of the inhabitants are engaged, the absence of a safe and suitable place for bathing in the river, and the frequent occurrence of persons being drowned whilst bathing from dangerous spots on the bank, are circumstances that point plainly enough to the necessity of providing Public Baths.[72]

The baths also involved elements of exclusivity and exclusion. One Alderman proposed that in order that the baths "be made as popular as possible," on one day a week only 1d should be charged. He hoped that the baths would "not be kept for the exclusive use of the 'upper ten.'" It was decided that 1d would be charged on Saturdays, 6d was charged on the day the pool was filled with fresh water, 4d on the following day, and 3d for the remaining days. On the second Saturday that the baths were open it was reported that 1,500 people visited.[73] An amateur swimming club was formed in September 1884 (a month before the baths opened) with a civil engineer and secretary of the North Riding Infirmary appointed secretary.[74] The club proposed to have exclusive use of the baths for one afternoon and one evening per week. The *Daily Exchange* published a letter from 'SWMR' who complained that the club was asking too much. The writer claimed that "in time we shall find a large majority coming to the public baths after a day's work and seeing a placard with the word 'Private,'" and hoped that the Sanitary Committee would "think before they will cripple the opportunities for bathing of the working and schooling population."[75]

PROFESSIONAL SPORT

Professional rowing had long been a popular spectator sport, particularly on the Tyne and Thames, and in the mid-nineteenth century it provided a means of satisfying "the needs of many for some form of excitement and entertainment," as well as supplying some of the first popular sporting heroes. Indeed it is suggested that in the mid-nineteenth century professional rowing contests were taking over the sport; matches that had initially been promoted by amateurs became dominated by professionals.[76] Though by the 1880s the heyday of professional rowing was all but over, contests took place on the Tees attracting large numbers of spectators. In early 1875 two races were held between a local rower and a competitor from Sunderland for £25 and £20. At the first race a steamboat was "literally crammed with spectators" and thousands lined the river for both races. A similar race took place later that year, which again "excited great interest."[77] In 1880, the *South Durham & Cleveland Mercury* reported on a "boat handicap" which had been organized by the former professional English champion Robert Boyd "for the purpose of encouraging rowing on the Tees." Fifty-eight competitors were watched by 250 spectators on a specially chartered steamboat, as well as thousands along the course.[78]

Two years later Boyd raced against the Australian champion Elias Laycock on the Tees, and this contest attracted a huge amount of local interest, providing an opportunity to explore notions of local identity and expressions of civic pride. This is particularly important to note as Boyd, like much of the town's population, was not from Middlesbrough (having been born in Gateshead) but still "belonged" to the town. Boyd was praised in the local press for insisting that the race take place in Middlesbrough rather on the more popular Thames or Tyne courses; the *Daily Exchange* stated that "some natural jealousy has been evinced by the Tyneside people," and the *North-Eastern Daily Gazette* regarded the race as the start of "a new chapter in the history of the Tees," with the result that the town's name "will be once more prominently brought to the front." The editor of the *Daily Exchange* wrote that,

> The boat race to be rowed today has its intrinsic interest, but to dwellers on the banks of the Tees there is associated with that the feeling that a Teessider is one of the competitors, and that this is the first occasion on which the Tees has been honoured with, what may almost be deemed, a champion course upon its waters . . . It would be hypocrisy also on our part did we not own up to the hope that our townsman may carry off the honours.[79]

Local newspapers did not try to hide their bias for Boyd, "our own local celebrity," in the almost daily reporting on race preparations.[80] In contrast, the *Newcastle Courant* thought it strange that Boyd, a "Tynesider," had proposed that the race be held on the Tees, and that because of the choice of river the match was "singularly deficient in interest so far as betting was concerned."[81]

The crowd at the race was estimated at 80,000–100,000, and included those who "would not be seen on a race course, and who certainly take no interest in [sport] as a trade or profession." The *Newcastle Courant* conceded that there was "a more extraordinary and numerous congregation of sightseers" than had ever been seen for a race on the Tyne. Special trains were arranged from as far away as London and Edinburgh, many local works were suspended, and the town became "lively and gay with holiday folk." One dockyard charged 3d to watch the race from their premises, or 6d from a stationary steamer (with proceedings being donated to charity), and another boat charged £1. *The Times* reported that "daring and eager spectators" utilized "ships' masts, the tops of blast furnaces, and the roofs of works" to view the race.[82] Unfortunately for the Tees, Laycock won the race by a considerable margin, and took the prize money of £200. Nevertheless it was felt that Boyd had "successfully brought the Tees to the front . . . and has advertised it all over the world as a suitable arena for aquatic contests."[83]

Like rowing, amateur recreational cycling coexisted alongside prize-giving competitions. In 1880 a six-day contest for both amateurs and professionals was organized by George Waller, a professional cyclist. It took place on a specially built platform with a first prize of £50 and a gold medal for professionals, the winner being the cyclist who covered the greatest distance in twelve hours. The event "attracted a number of first-class bicyclists" and a large crowd including six thousand spectators on the penultimate day. Prizes were also handed out for the amateur contest—a ten-guinea clock, a tea service, and a case of knives and forks.[84] Waller organized a similar event the following year, and was praised for having "done so much to encourage this which is undoubtedly the most enjoyable and fascinating sport ever taken up by the young generation." The *North-Eastern Daily Gazette* reported that there were large numbers of spectators, and proclaimed that there "may occasionally be heard some exclamation expressive at once of surprise and alarm" from the crowds as the cyclists raced around the track.[85] Again, prizes were handed out to both professionals and amateurs. The amateur winners received a salad bowl, a biscuit box, and a cruet stand, and the professional cyclists received a gold watch and £3, a gold medal and £3, and a silver medal and £2.[86] With races drawing increasingly large crowds, the *North-Eastern Weekly Gazette* felt able to proclaim that "there are few places in England where bicycling as a sport is so highly popular as at Middlesbrough."[87]

AMATEUR SPORTS DAYS

The amateur sports days held by a variety of clubs appear to have been hugely popular, offering a rare day of entertainment for many men and women. These events often attracted many competitors from Middlesbrough and further afield who were able to win prizes, and were reported on at length in the local press. In 1875 the *Daily Gazette* reported that sports were included at three separate galas as part of the Whitsuntide festivities, which "afforded [an] opportunity of recreation for the masses" and included footraces, quoits, and gathering stones.[88] Middlesbrough Cricket Club first held an amateur sports day in 1878, and spectators included members of the town's establishment. The event included hurdle, flat, walking and bicycle races, long jump, and throwing a ball at a wicket, all for prizes ranging in value from £1 1s to £7 7s.[89] At the club's event two years later, it was reported that not only were there "numerous ladies" in the pavilion, but that "all points of vantage were crowded with spectators."[90] Similarly in 1881, the sports day of Middlesbrough Bicycle Club on the cricket field saw the pavilion filled, and one side of the field was also "uncomfortably crowded."[91] The cricket club's two-day event in 1882 attracted between five thousand and six thousand on the first day, and four thousand on the second. As well as a number of bicycle, hurdle, and flat races, it also included "shooting galleries, swings, round-abouts, booths, and stalls for the sale and barter of every conceivable commodity," suggesting that the event was more than a sports day, offering a day of both leisure and entertainment for attendees. Indeed, boys from the workhouse and the industrial school were permitted to watch the cricket club's event in 1884.[92] However, such events could become too heavily influenced by the working classes. At an event in 1885, the obstacle race was viewed as "simply disgraceful," as it left one competitor with the shirt torn off his back. Noting the range of people present, the *Daily Exchange* pointed out that "the roughs quickly proved that it was more in their line than that of the occupants of the pavilion, by breaking ground so as to enjoy the performance a little closer."[93] One race was criticized when it became apparent that the object was to *entertain* the spectators "without a due regard to the comparative merits of the competitors," but there were no such objections to the giving of prizes at these "amateur" events. At the cricket club's event in 1884 prizes varied from a marble clock for the winners of the 120 yards and quarter-mile flat races, to £5 5s for the one-mile flat race. There was also a "consolation race" for those who had failed to win their own races, for which an egg stand was awarded for first place and a traveling bag for second.[94] Ironopolis Cricket Club's first event was held in 1883 over two consecutive Saturdays in April, and as well as the usual flat and bicycle races, included a sack race, a quoits handicap, a "half-hour go-as-you-please," and a metal carriers' race[95] with a prize of a pair of trousers for first place, and a ham for the runner-up.[96] Such days were regarded as just rewards for the hard work undertaken during the week. The editor of the *Daily Exchange* remarked upon this and pointed out that sports days were attended by both workers and ironmasters,

> Nowhere do people work harder than in that iron workshop, known throughout the world as Middlesbrough, and nowhere is there a stronger reason for such sports as we had on Saturday. It was a pleasant sight indeed to behold not only "the beauty and the chivalry" of the capital of Cleveland, but the ironmasters, the ironworkers, and even the soft-handed quill-drivers of the counting-houses turn out for the afternoon to enjoy, with the proper manly feeling, such manly sports.[97]

CONCLUSION

Though amateur sports days did enable the people of the town to come together, it is also clear that such inclusive events were rare. The town was referred to as a growing colony, populated by a "pleasure-loving" young population, and there was recognition by some that a gap existed between those who were able to play sport at their leisure and those with no such opportunities. Editorials in the *North-Eastern Daily Gazette* in 1881 pointed out that there was "a crowd of growing boys in our midst who are too poor to pay for their physical training," and suggested that public facilities in the park would be invaluable to them. Such facilities would "draw poverty stricken and stunted children from their hovels."[98] In 1883 an announcement was made that a public gymnasium was to be built in Albert Park. This was met with no small amount of opposition from some councillors and from the *Daily Exchange,* which suggested that the gymnasium acted as "such a focus for all the 'roughs' of the neighbourhood, that it greatly detracts from the rural simplicity which pervades nearly every other part of the park."[99] In contrast, an editorial in the *North-Eastern Daily Gazette* stated that opponents to the gymnasium did not,

> really know what sort of humanity it is that hides its ill-shapen form down the courts and alleys. . . . No cricket or football or aquatics for them. They have no money to pay for club fees, and if they had it would be all the same. The clubs would not have them.[100]

There was however, a growing belief that the *right* types of sport were capable of refining the working classes, and that employers could use sport to reinforce the notion that they had the interests of the workers at heart. This idea was expressed by the *Cleveland News* in 1884,

> For some years past the love for manly out-door sports has been gradually growing in this district, as evidenced by the manner in which football or cricket matches are attended, and it is to the credit of the leading manufacturers and other wealthy gentlemen of the district that they have, by giving liberal prizes, done a good deal to elevate the character of athleticism, and to encourage young men to compete for supremacy in healthy exercises away from the influences of the gambling mania.[101]

However, another underlying feature of editorials in the local press was the fear that sport also had the ability to accentuate the uncivilized nature of the workers, bringing to the fore those characteristics of sport that ran counter to the amateur ethos. This is particularly apparent in opinions on gambling. As the *Cleveland News* stated, "If football is to be made a matter of betting, and spiteful feeling, and nothing of the chivalrous or heroic to enter into it, the game will scarcely take a hold on the public mind."[102]

The development of sport in Middlesbrough in the 1870s and early 1880s was heavily influenced by the class structure in the town. Middlesbrough's small middle class dominated as sporting administrators and participants just as they did as employers and politicians. It is clear that there were an increasing number of opportunities for the town's middle class to take part in sport, and to play and socialize together. This is in direct contrast to the decidedly limited options for participation for the poorer members of the town's population. Given the money that was required to participate in many organized sports, and the cost associated with joining a club, it is not surprising that during the period examined here the only involvement available for most people was spectating. If the town was an infant sporting Hercules, it was one which did not favor the majority of its populace. It is evident that the role of money in sport was slowly increasing and that there was a growing audience for sporting events. The popularity of football among the working classes and the uneasy relationship with professionalism will be examined in the following chapter.

NOTES

1. Portions of this chapter were originally published as "'A healthy stimulating sport and an exhilarating pastime': Middlesbrough's amateur and recreational football clubs, c.1880–1914," *Soccer History* 32 (2014), pp. 7–13.

2. Quoted in M. Huggins, "'Fashionable Watering Place' or 'Popular Resort': Residential visitors and day trippers to Redcar and Coatham, 1865–90," *Journal of Regional and Local Studies* December 1983, p. 59; S. Metcalf, "Albert Park: A place for the recreation of the people," *Bulletin of the Cleveland and Teesside Local History Society* 38 (Spring 1980), p. 17.

3. Quoted in M. Huggins, "Leisure and Sport in Middlesbrough, 1840–1914," in A.J. Pollard (ed.), *Middlesbrough: Town and Community, 1830–1950* (Stroud, 1996), p. 130.

4. Cleveland Club Rules and Regulations, U/CLB 1/1, Teesside Archives; A. Briggs, "Middlesbrough: The growth of a new community in Pollard (ed.), *Middlesbrough: Town and Community*, p. 15; *Kelly's Directory of Middlesbrough, 1885* (London, 1885), p. 133; 'Erimus," latin for 'We shall be," is Middlesbrough's motto.

5. Jowsey Park was described by the *Darlington & Stockton Times* in 1856 as "delightful a retreat and pleasure ground as in this part of the country," though in 1889 the *North-Eastern Weekly Gazette* suggested that it had been "a murky paradise" to juveniles—N. Moorsom, *The Story of Middlesbrough Dock in Greater Middlehaven* (Middlesbrough, 2006), p. 45.

6. Quoted in N. Moorsom, *Middlesbrough's Albert Park—History, heritage and restoration* (Barnsley, 2002), pp. 17–20.

7. Quoted in Metcalf, "Albert Park," p. 17.

8. *Kelly's Directory of Middlesbrough, 1885*, p. 133; Metcalf, "Albert Park," p. 20; Moorsom, *Middlesbrough's Albert Park*, p. 80, p. 104; D. Taylor, *Policing the Victorian Town: The development of the police in Middlesbrough c.1840–1914* (Basingstoke, 2002), p. 28.

9. *Evening Gazette*, 2nd December 1872; L. Praed, *History of the Rise and Progress of Middlesbrough* (Newcastle, 1863), p. 22.

10. Quoted in R. Humphreys, "Spending Leisure Time in Teesside During the mid-Nineteenth Century," *Bulletin of the Cleveland and Teesside Local History Society* 24 (Spring 1974), p. 5.

11. *Daily Gazette*, 1st February 1875; *Northern Echo*, 2nd February 1875. Patrons of the race included Henry W. F. Bolckow MP, Frederick Milbank MP, Bernhard Samuelson MP, Viscount Helmsley MP and John G. Swan (ironmaster).

12. *North-Eastern Daily Gazette*, 9th November 1881.

13. *Northern Echo*, 3rd April 1882.

14. Huggins, "Leisure and Sport in Middlesbrough," pp. 129–130.

15. Huggins, "Fashionable Watering Place," p. 59; Taylor, *Policing the Victorian Town*, p. 72.

16. W. Vamplew, *Pay Up and Play the Game: Professional sport in Britain, 1875–1914* (Cambridge, 1988), pp. 45–46.

17. P. Bailey, *Leisure and Class in Victorian England: Rational recreation and the contest for control, 1830–1885* (London, 1978), pp. 88–94.

18. R. Holt, *Sport and the British: A Modern History* (Oxford, 1989), pp. 148–151; Vamplew, *Pay Up and Play the Game*, p. 70.

19. This point is made about the town in general by Yasumoto who states that the town was "inadequately provided with fixed or disposable old endowments and legacies, whether spiritual, physical of institutional, from the past," and thus people had to fill that vacuum themselves—M. Yasumoto, *The Rise of a Victorian Ironopolis: Middlesbrough and regional industrialisation* (Woodbridge, 2011), p. 107.

20. The Mechanics' Institute Cricket Club had were three levels of membership with subscription of 2s, 1s 6d, and 1s for the season. The first rules of the club stated that "all improper language and the use of intoxicating drinks be strictly prohibited," while "no matches shall be allowed to be made for money"—Middlesbrough Mechanic Institute, Rules for Cricket Club 1849, U/MI/6, Teesside Archives.

21. *Daily Gazette*, 12th March, 18th May 1875; *Middlesbrough Weekly News & Cleveland Advertiser*, 21st May 1875, quoted in R. Baker, *Iron and Willow: A History of Middlesbrough CC, volume one 1855–1911* (Middlesbrough, 1989), pp. 45–46.

22. 1871 and 1881 census; *Daily Gazette*, 12th March 1875; *Northern Echo*, 8th March 1877.

23. *Northern Echo*, 8th July 1880; *Weekly Exchange*, 22nd July 1882.

24. *North-Eastern Daily Gazette*, 2nd November 1881.

25. Anon, "Cricket," *Quarterly Review* 158 (1884), p. 467.

26. *Weekly Exchange*, 19th August 1882.

27. *Middlesbrough Weekly News & Cleveland Advertiser*, 7th October 1882, quoted in Baker, *Iron and Willow*, p. 68; *North-Eastern Daily Gazette*, 15th August 1884.

28. *Daily Exchange*, 15th June 1882.

29. *North-Eastern Daily Gazette*, 23rd June 1884—Church clubs: St John's, Stockton Primitive Union, All Saints, South Stockton (St Paul's), South Stockton Wesleyans, St Peter's, Stockton Wesleyans, St John's (Shildon), St Paul's (Spennymoor); Clubs originating in the workplace: Stockton Wholesale Traders, Stockton Traders 2nd, Durham Training College, Hartlepool Schoolmasters. Note that none of these clubs were based in Middlesbrough. Other work-based clubs mentioned in 1884 include Jordison & Co (printers and publishers), North-Eastern Daily Gazette, Watchmakers, Hatters, English Butchers—*Cleveland News*, 5th July, 27th September 1884; *Daily Exchange*, 18th September 1884.

30. Bolckow Vaughan v Cleveland—*Cleveland News*, 26th July 1884.

31. *Daily Exchange*, 4th July 1882; *North-Eastern Daily Gazette*, 29th August 1884; *Cleveland News*, 13th September 1884.

32. *Sports Gazette*, 2nd November 1912.

33. M. Huggins, "The Spread of Association Football in North-East England, 1876–90: The Pattern of Diffusion," *International Journal of the History of Sport* 6, 1 (1989), p. 301.

34. Alderman and ironmaster John Dunning, *Daily Gazette*, 7th February 1881.

35. Indeed, Middlesbrough's captain, Oswald Henry Cochrane, was educated at Uppingham and Oxford—*Middlesbrough Rugby Union Football Club Eightieth Anniversary 1872–1952* (Middlesbrough, 1952), p. 9; Holt, *Sport and the British*, p. 86

36. Holt, *Sport and the British*, p. 145.

37. T. Mason, *Association Football and English Society 1863–1915* (Brighton, 1981), pp. 223–229.

38. *Northern Athlete*, 10th October 1883, quoted in P. Dixon, N. Garnham, and A. Jackson, 'Shareholders and Shareholding: The case of the football company in late Victorian England," *Business History* 46, 4 (2004), p. 515.

39. *North-Eastern Daily Gazette*, 13th September 1881.

40. *Middlesbrough Daily Exchange*, 18th October 1880; *Northern Echo*, 18th October 1880.

41. *Weekly Exchange*, 18th March 1882.

42. *Weekly Exchange*, 8th April 1882.

43. *Cleveland News*, 12th April, 17th May 1884.

44. *North Star*, 21st January 1884; *Weekly Gazette*, 5th May 1883; The new stand had room for three hundred spectators and standing room for a further one hundred, the club having 265 members in 1883.

45. *Cleveland News*, 16th February 1884.

46. *Daily Exchange*, 15th February 1884.

47. *Daily Exchange*, 21st February 1884.

48. 1881 census; *North-Eastern Daily Gazette*, 25th September 1883.

49. 1881 census; *Middlesbrough Rugby Union Football Club*, p. 9.

50. Huggins, 'The Spread of Association Football," p. 300.

51. *Weekly Exchange*, 25th March 1882; This clash was repeated later in the year, Rovers playing at home to Darlington West End, and Middlesbrough FC played Redcar at the Linthorpe Road ground—*Northern Echo*, 23rd October 1882.

52. *Weekly Exchange*, 25th November 1882.

53. *Cleveland News*, 15th March 1884.

54. *Cleveland News*, 27th September, 4th October 1884.

55. 1881 census; *Middlesbrough Rugby Union Football Club*, p. 9; *Daily Gazette*, 10th January 1881.

56. *Cleveland News*, 4th, 11th October 1884.

57. *Cleveland News*, 25th October 1884.

58. *Daily Gazette*, 3rd June 1878.

59. 1861 census; *Sports Gazette*, 5th August 1905.

60. *Daily Gazette*, 10th, 12th August 1874; *Northern Echo*, 8th August 1874.

61. *Northern Echo*, 12th August 1874; The London Rowing Club also differentiated between "gentlemen amateurs" and "tradesmen" amateurs, and stipulated that the "barriers between them were not broken down"—M. Huggins, *The Victorians and Sport* (London, 2004), p. 56.

62. In 1876 the club had eighty-seven members—*Daily Gazette*, 14th March 1876.

63. *Daily Gazette*, 27th April 1875.

64. *Daily Gazette*, 3rd June 1878; *Weekly Gazette*, 2nd June 1877.

65. *Cleveland News*, 31st May, 16th August 1884; *Weekly Gazette*, 24th March 1883.

66. R. Goodall, Cycling in North Yorkshire and South Durham, 1869–1914, unpublished MA thesis, Teesside Polytechnic, 1988, p. 18; *Daily Gazette*, 29th March, 23rd April 1877.

67. *North-Eastern Daily Gazette*, 22nd August 1881.

68. *North-Eastern Daily Gazette*, 30th May 1882; A year later the same event attracted three hundred participants, and included races with prizes as high as £10 10s—*North-Eastern Daily Gazette*, 15th May 1883.

69. Viscount Bury, "Cycling and Cyclists," *Nineteenth Century* 17 (1885), p. 92.

70. *North-Eastern Daily Gazette*, 26th January, 26th April, 13th October 1883, 10th March, 17th April 1884.

71. *North-Eastern Daily Gazette*, 10th June, 2nd September 1884.

72. *North-Eastern Daily Gazette*, 11th September 1884.

73. *North-Eastern Daily Gazette*, 8th October, 4th November 1884.

74. *Kelly's Directory of Middlesbrough, 1885*, p. 138, p. 181; *Northern Echo*, 18th September 1884.

75. *Daily Exchange*, 18th September 1884.

76. E. Halladay, *Rowing in England: A social history—the amateur debate* (Manchester, 1990), p. 15, chapter 1 passim; N. Wigglesworth, *A Social History of English Rowing* (London, 1992), p. 71, chapter 4 passim.

77. *Daily Gazette*, 22nd February, 8th March, 21st June 1875.

78. *South Durham & Cleveland Mercury*, 18th September 1880.

79. *Daily Exchange*, 4th May, 3rd July 1882; *North-Eastern Daily Gazette*, 30th June 1882.

80. *Daily Exchange*, 6th May 1882. Examples of reporting on Boyd's physical preparations, including racing and meals—*North-Eastern Daily Gazette*, 13th, 18th, 19th, 22nd, 23rd May, 23rd June 1882.

81. *Newcastle Courant*, 7th July 1882. Only two years earlier the *Newcastle Daily Journal* had stated that Boyd was a product of "Tyneside's spirit of boat rowing which is inbred with the people"—quoted in Wigglesworth, *A Social History of English Rowing*, p. 77.

82. *Daily Exchange,* 3rd July, 4th July 1882; *Newcastle Courant,* 7th July 1882; *Northern Echo,* 3rd July 1882; *The Times,* 4th July 1882.

83. *Daily Exchange,* 4th July 1882.

84. *Northern Echo,* 28th September, 2nd, 4th October 1880.

85. *North-Eastern Daily Gazette,* 19th, 21st September 1881.

86. *North-Eastern Daily Gazette,* 19th September 1881.

87. *North-Eastern Weekly Gazette,* 13th October 1883.

88. *Daily Gazette,* 18th May 1875.

89. *Daily Gazette,* 19th August 1878.

90. *Daily Gazette,* 21st June 1880.

91. *Daily Gazette,* 22nd August 1881.

92. *North Star,* 16th June 1884; *Weekly Exchange,* 15th April 1882.

93. *Daily Exchange,* 19th June 1882.

94. *Cleveland News,* 21st June 1884; *Daily Exchange,* 19th June 1882; *Northern Echo,* 16th June 1884.

95. For which each competitor carried a pig of iron on their back.

96. *North-Eastern Daily Gazette,* 30th April 1883; *Northern Echo,* 30th April, 7th May 1883; *Weekly Exchange,* 12th May 1883.

97. *Daily Exchange,* 19th June 1882.

98. *Cleveland News,* 21st February 1885; *North-Eastern Daily Gazette,* 9th, 28th November 1881.

99. Indeed, a few months later a committee was set up to consider better ways of managing the gymnasium—N. Moorsom, *Middlesbrough's Albert Park—History, heritage and restoration* (Barnsley, 2002), p. 109.

100. *North-Eastern Weekly Gazette,* 14th July 1883.

101. *Cleveland News,* 21st June 1884.

102. *Cleveland News,* 12th April 1884.

THREE

"A Noble Game Became Degraded"[1]

The Rise and Fall
of Professional Football, 1885–1894

By the mid-1880s the popularity of football was increasing across England, and it had become the main spectator sport in Middlesbrough.[2] Football attracted ever larger crowds but as professionalism took hold of many clubs across the country, those in charge of football in Middlesbrough hoped to stem the tide. This chapter acts as a case study of the early development of professional football. It will trace the progress of professionalism in the town, outlining the debates that took place in the local press both for and against the payment of players, will detail those involved in the town's two principal clubs, Middlesbrough and Ironopolis, and examine the relationship between the two. Why and how did football become so popular with spectators? Why was a professional club formed and why did it fail?

By 1885 thirty-one local associations across the country were affiliated to the Football Association, and by 1888 one thousand clubs were affiliated.[3] The introduction of the FA Cup was important to the growth of football, with local associations imitating the knock-out competition with their own contests. Initially dominated by public school-based teams in London, by the early 1880s the competition was national in scope; the 1883–84 competition had 101 entrants. In 1883 the amateur team Old Etonians were beaten in the final by Blackburn Olympic (a team of workingmen), a result regarded as a major watershed in football's history.[4] One critic suggested in 1889 that "for better or for worse cups and cup ties are the life and soul of the Association game," so much so that cups had "turned the game into more of a business than a sport."[5] Large attendances were now commonplace and with this came a need for teams to obtain the best players possible. Professionalism was legalized by the FA in 1885, providing "a clear and distinct line to define unpaid from paid."[6] Though money was becoming increasingly important to the game, at the beginning of the period "the pursuit of wealth did not characterize the game;" rather club directors and committees were willing to forgo profits in exchange for results on the pitch.[7] The Football League was formed three years later, providing a "reliable and permanent fixture list" to the twelve member clubs and producing more competitive football.[8] The League was an immediate financial success, and the journalist James Catton stated that it had "galvanised the dry bones of club football into life." Indeed the average match attendance in the Football League's first season was 4,600.[9] Crowds continued to increase and although the majority of spectators were working class, clubs recognized the need to cater to their wealthier supporters, building pavilions with more expensive reserved sections. How did football in Middlesbrough fit in with these changes to the game? How did the growing commercialism affect local football?

THE GROWTH OF MIDDLESBROUGH FC

While smaller clubs still thrived across Middlesbrough and Teesside (new clubs were "rapidly springing into notice and public favour" according to the Cleveland Association),[10] they could not compete with the town's foremost team. Middlesbrough Football Club could now frequently draw crowds in the thousands due to their ability to attract some of the better teams from England and Scotland to their ground. Expectations were growing and an increasing amount of importance was placed on winning. For example, ahead of Middlesbrough's fourth round FA Cup tie against Old Etonians in January 1885, a letter to the *Cleveland News* urged the players to prepare properly to avoid defeat—"if the players leave off tobacco, reduce the liquor supply, take walking exercise in the evening, and follow the old maxim of 'Early to bed etc,' this will go a long way towards winning the game."[11] Furthermore it was hoped that in order "to satisfy the desires of football supporters in the district," "much more important engagements [would be] entered into than any which have hitherto been recorded on the Middlesbrough list of fixtures."[12] The club was financially secure, and with a balance in hand of over £45 in 1885 one committee member suggested that the club needed to "devise some method of spending their money."[13]

In the summer of 1886, Middlesbrough FC amalgamated with Middlesbrough St John's FC, giving the club more footballers to choose from. By now Middlesbrough FC had 550 members, and with thirty-one fixtures arranged for the coming season, was in an "exceptionally good" financial position. So much so that the committee could afford, and in recognizing that the players were assets to the club felt it necessary, to take out insurance on the team.[14] That the club could boast of such economic comforts, did not reflect the situation in the rest of the town with fluctuations in trade meaning that at times no new work was being taken on at the collieries, iron, or steelworks.[15] Nevertheless, at the start of the season, crowds of three thousand still attended the first- and second-round FA Cup ties at the Linthorpe Road ground.[16] Fixtures had been arranged with many of Britain's foremost clubs, leading the *Northern Review* to congratulate the committee "on the wise disposal of their funds." However, by the end of the season the club had suffered a record number of defeats, and the *Northern Review* now claimed that the actions of the committee were "often distinguished rather for caprice than judgement, and more for novelty than consistency."[17] At Middlesbrough's AGM in 1887, the secretary conceded that the club's record was poor in comparison to previous seasons, but pointed out that,

> the committee had endeavoured to cater for the large body of the members by bringing, at a very large expense, some of the leading clubs of Lancashire and Scotland . . . he trusted [that] members would consider the high class clubs the team had met, and how in some cases they had upheld the prestige of the district by making results worthy of the foremost clubs.[18]

The committee could justifiably feel that the season had been a success in other areas. Membership had increased to 750 and subscriptions had also increased by 50 percent on the previous year.[19] The football ground had been improved which was "a great boon to the spectators, and had fully recompensed the club for the outlay." Match receipts totaled more than £457, and despite expenditure of around £600, the club still had a balance of more than £77.[20]

At the beginning of the 1887–1888 season, supporters gathered to watch Middlesbrough players in a practice match, and the *Northern Review* speculated over the composition of the team—"Was Miller likely to get a school near Middlesbro' after Christmas? Was the Parson's [Rev E. J. Wilson] leg strong again? Did anyone know anything about a new left wing forward who was said to have come to act as Scripture Reader at one of the churches?" Though it is difficult to identify many of the players, this quote suggests that a proportion of the players had middle-class occupations. Furthermore, it was also reported that Percy Sadler,[21] the son of Lieutenant Colonel Samuel Sadler (club president, alderman, and chemical manufacturer) was a promising half back for the club. The occupations of four other players can be identified—a publican, a commercial traveler and two solicitors, and although players' occupations were relatively varied, the educated middle classes dominated. In contrast, four players were also imported from outside of Teesside, including the professional of Sheffield Cricket Club, George Waller.[22]

By November 1887, membership stood at 1,100[23] and the FA Cup third-round tie against Sunderland attracted a crowd of 5,000. Special attention had been given to the training of the team ahead of the tie, though the committee regretted that they had "found it was impossible to obtain the services of a professional trainer without destroying the amateur status of the club." Instead, five committee members volunteered to "undertake the arduous duties of trainers." Players were advised by this committee to have "little salt, less sugar, no pastry, no fat meat, no suppers, two meals a day . . . no baccy, no beer etc." Not being paid to adhere to such demands however, it was thought that "there is not one man of the lot who would bind himself to the whole of these rules."[24] The game ended in a draw, and the committee evidently placed a great deal of importance on the result, as they accompanied the team to the replay at Sunderland, each taking charge of a player "who will not be allowed to exert himself in the slightest degree, until placed upon the field." Two thousand Middlesbrough supporters reportedly travelled by train to Wearside, but they arrived after half the game had already been played.[25] Middlesbrough faced Old Foresters at home in the following round and in front of a crowd of eight thousand, defeated them by four goals to nil.[26] Defeat in the next round to Crewe Alexandra was attributed to substandard players, and the *South Durham & Cleveland Mercury* suggested that new players were required—"if this is not done, and done at once, the future of the club will be a simple history of gradual degeneracy." 'Off-side' in the *Northern Echo* agreed, stating that in the case of two or three players, "their football days are over."[27] Furthermore, despite winning the Cleveland Cup for the sixth time in seven years in 1888, "Off-side" still felt that "the team is not [the] success which the high standing of the club should demand."[28] Evidently the club agreed that improvements could be made and, reflecting the evolving but unplanned training methods of the day, it was reported that one committee member had invented the "Football Playing Board," the aim being to drive a ball through a sprung door on a board. This would "teach forwards to shoot with precision, weight, and alacrity, thereby depriving backs of an advantage they have had hitherto, owing to the forwards stopping or placing the ball before shooting." Unfortunately despite promising "a revolution in goal getting . . . after many vicissitudes and alterations, it has resolved itself into a bill-sticking board."[29]

AMATEURISM VERSUS PROFESSIONALISM AND THE FORMATION OF IRONOPOLIS FC

Though the payment of players had been sanctioned by the Football Association in 1885, there was still considerable opposition to professionalism. The *Saturday Review* was disappointed to have to report that professionals meant "combination and passing had replaced skill and dash,"[30] and Arthur Budd (a member of the Rugby Football Union committee) argued that the introduction of professional football had led to "corrupt-ibility, disrepute, and sometimes absolute decay . . . the extinction of the amateur, the exclusion of native talent and the seduction by pecuniary inducement of players." Opposing payment for "broken time," Budd suggested that if a player "cannot afford the leisure to play a game, he must do without it."[31] In contrast William Suddell, the manager of Preston North End FC, argued that professionalism would improve football as "men who devote their entire attention to the game are more likely to be-come good players than the amateur who is worried by business cares."[32] It is suggested that the payment of players was supported by the FA in order to control professionalism but also to enable the organization to retain its power and influence, albeit at the expense of the amateur clubs.[33]

At the start of the season in September 1888, discussions on profes-sionalism began in Middlesbrough. In the *Northern Review*, 'Rambler,' a member of Middlesbrough FC,[34] considered the merits of professional-ism. Prior to this point, the issue had been mentioned very little in relation to football in the local press, other than to object to the use of professionals in the game in general. 'Rambler' suggested that,

> It is no use disguising the fact that the clubs who are attempting to exist on purely amateur lines are seriously handicapped by the importing clubs. I do not want to see the day when the clubs in this district seek assistance from professional ranks, but I can't help seeing that the current is turning in that direction. Will the amateurism of Middlesbrough, Stockton and Darlington stand constant beating by Sunderland, Newcastle East End, West End, and other local clubs?[35]

A month later 'The Tout,' also writing in the *Northern Review*, was more vociferous in his distaste for professionalism, stating that he would "rather see the [Middlesbrough] club at the bottom of the list than win matches with the aid of foreigners, who have no sympathy with us as a club; who play for their pecuniary benefit." However, he also called for the rules to be altered to allow a player to be refunded for loss of earn-ings while playing in a match. He reasoned that this had not been carried out already because "many of our football legislators are gentlemen, or employed in offices, therefore have never a day's pay stopped," and were unable to sympathize with footballers.[36] Indeed the Football Associa-tion was dominated by leisured gentlemen, members of the professions, and public school alumni who subscribed to the notion that sports were played for fun.[37]

When it was reported in 1888 that South Bank FC had become the first club in Cleveland to register a professional player, 'Rambler' reiterated his opinion on such players stating, "I feel sorry it should have been found necessary." The writer was quick to state that the player would in fact not receive any remuneration and had already asked to be reinstated as an amateur.[38] The advantages of bringing in new players were recognized but the payment of individuals was regarded as an unfortunate side effect of this. Such was the desire for the team to succeed, that in early 1889 'Rambler' suggested that Middlesbrough should begin importing players—"Seeing that we have no local talent sufficiently good, rather than let the club sink, will it not be better to look afield for . . . steady men who in return for work at their own trade, will devote Saturday afternoons to football." However, at the same time 'Rambler' was also of the opinion that importation "savours too much of 'pot-hunting' matches to be won by hook or crook," which would lead to a "morbid unhealthy desire to win." Standards of play were thought to be slipping and the desire to win so great that it was suggested that the club needed to "do as our neighbours, and sink for a season the high principles which have previously guided the club" in order to ensure that the supporters did not "fall away like chaff in the hour of humiliation and defeat."[39]

Following a defeat at home to Stockton in January 1889, a series of letters were published in the *North-Eastern Daily Gazette* and *Northern Echo*, commenting on the quality of the play and the price of admission. The correspondence that was published demonstrates the ever growing interest in football as well as the debates on the pros and cons of professionalism. It also shows the role football played in the lives of many people. The first letter, from John Wilkinson and his "fellow workmen," complained that Middlesbrough were the only club in the area that charged 6d for "ordinary" matches, and the "third-rate football . . . [that] juniors would be ashamed of" was not worth such a steep fee.[40] Another letter agreed that it was "a shame to ask working men who are not members of the club to pay 6d," and suggested that either prices should be lowered, or standards of play increased. The author of this letter was not opposed to importation,

> Now that the game is so much thought of here, and right well patronised, if we cannot depend upon native talent, then by all means let us have some of these stray Scotchmen who can be picked up so easily by our neighbours. Has the noble game, now that it has got such a hold on the public, to die out, and have we to dwindle into a fourth rate club after all our grand achievements? In conjunction with hundreds of others, I say no.[41]

Shortly afterward, a letter was published from a member of the club pointing out the contradiction in desiring both a reduction in the cost of admission and funds for new players. However, the author did agree that it was not the cost but "the quality of the entertainment provided that has evoked the representative growl" in the newspaper. By bringing good teams to play at Middlesbrough, the committee had "educated us to a point of appreciation of the beauties of the game to which the present team . . . has not attained."[42] The author of the final letter to the *Gazette* reminded the committee that as "caterers for the public amusement," they had a "duty to perform to the outsiders who contribute so largely to the financial success of the club" rather than thinking solely of the "privileges and comforts of the members."[43] A letter from "A Working Man" in the *Northern Echo* argued that "witnessing a struggle between teams worthy of each other, and who play to win, excites in the breast healthy, manly, and altogether refreshing feelings and affords an enjoyment that in this dull, weary, work-a-day time I could ill afford to lose." Under the name "Referee," another letter demonstrated the strength of feeling among those who favored amateurism. It stated that while football was "a healthy, noble, manly pastime," there were a number of aspects that should be changed,

> So long as men are paid for being footballers; so long as men are imported from other parts of the country and work found for them . . . because they are footballers; so long as there is the "gate"; so long as publicans are ground-keepers [sic]; so long as the headquarters . . . is at a public house, and the landlord can offer inducements to win; so long as there is any remuneration for playing football . . . so long as these palpable evils are permitted to associate themselves with football, so long will many people . . . condemn football and everybody associated with it.[44]

The professionalism debate appeared to have come to a head in April 1889 when the *North-Eastern Weekly Gazette* reported that a handbill had been distributed among spectators at Middlesbrough's last game of the season stating,

> Wanted, 1,000 members to attend the annual meeting to vote for the payment of all players, and also to support the nomination for the committee of those gentlemen who intend to try and place the club in the position it once occupied in the football world, and in the North of England in particular. Support them, and by doing so you will promote good football.

The newspaper thought it probable that the majority of the membership would withdraw from the club to form a professional side, but the AGM a month later was described as "one of the liveliest, but one of the most harmonious."[45] The first half of this statement might be regarded as something of an understatement, as the seven hundred attendees reportedly applauded, groaned, and heckled the speakers. A proposal for the payment of players received the most attention. John Wood suggested that players be paid a fixed sum per match, larger if the game was won, in addition to expenses for matches away from home,

> the time had come for them to import a few good men into the team, and find them work in the town. They wanted respectable men, and he did not think there would be any difficulty in obtaining them and finding them work. It had become an absolute necessity for something to be done.

The proposal was seconded but others vehemently disagreed. A Mr Dodds contended that "so soon as they started paying players from a distance then would the peace and harmony of the club be broken." William H. Thomas, the club's treasurer, suggested that if the proposition was carried, "it would result in the formation of an amateur club in the town to compete with the professionals." A Mr. Kedward agreed, arguing that the importation of players would mean the club "would at once lose their good name as gentlemanly players, for if they paid a man to win he would win at no matter what cost." The proposal was defeated.[46]

As is shown in table 3.1, most of those running the club had professional, middle-class occupations, and others were lower-middle class. None of the officials were born in Middlesbrough, which reflected the various geographical backgrounds of the town's population; in 1881 45 percent of the population were born outside of Yorkshire.[47]

Following the AGM, the *North-Eastern Weekly Gazette* advised the club's supporters,

> To work shoulder to shoulder in order that the club may be brought back to the honoured position it has occupied for years until the past disastrous season. Let no ill-feeling be harboured, but rather let the minority gracefully submit to the wishes of the majority, and assist them in making next season one of the most brilliant that we have experienced.

The newspaper was pleased that the club had retained its amateur status. Importations and payment, it argued, would have led to the replacement of gentlemanly play with brute force, and "the large body of ladies who weekly take up their position on the grand stand and round the ropes would . . . leave the field in disgust."[48] The *Northern Review* was also delighted with the outcome of the meeting, pleased that the "treacherous quicksands of professionalism" had been avoided, for it would have "crush[ed] our town players to the wall." The question remained however, "Will the professionalists [sic] form a new club on their lines, or continue to endeavour to filch the Linthorpe Road Ground?"[49]

At the start of the following season, the press was still undecided on professionalism, not helped by the statement of the Cleveland Association that "in view of the inchoate regulations of the English Association

Table 3.1. Middlesbrough Football Club officials, 1889–1891.[1]

	Role	Occupation	Employment Status	Address	Place of birth	Servants
Henry Cochrane	President	Engineer, iron founder, Justice of the Peace	Employer	The Longlands, Middlesbrough	Dudley, Worcestershire	5
John Vernon Cooper	President (1891)	Ironworks manager	Employed	West Brook Villa, Grove Hill, Middlesbrough	Kent	1
Thomas Bach	Deputy-captain	Publican	Employer	Masham Hotel, 49 Linthorpe Road, Middlesbrough	Pitchford, Shropshire	None
Samuel Bateman	Acting vice-president	Doctor		57 Grange Road West, Middlesbrough	Ireland	1
John Thomas Belk	Honorary vice-president	Recorder		2 Park Villas, Park Road North, Middlesbrough	Pontefract, Yorkshire	6
Albert Borrie	Financial secretary	Solicitor	Employed	99 Linthorpe Road, Middlesbrough	Gateshead, County Durham	None
David Caddick	Committee	Cashier	Employed	1 Borough Road West, Middlesbrough	Ebbw Vale, Wales	None
Jackson Ewbank	Honorary vice-president	Commercial traveler	Employed	Church Balk Lane, Pontefract	Pontefract, Yorkshire	None
Frederick Hardisty	Secretary	Clerk	Employed	22 Pembroke Street, Middlesbrough	Harrogate, Yorkshire	None
Alfred Mattison	Committee	Licensed victualler	Employer	Albert Park Hotel, Linthorpe Road, Middlesbrough	Richmond, Yorkshire	2
Samuel Sadler	Honorary vice-president	Chemical manufacturer	Employer	Preston Hall, Eaglescliffe	Oldbury, Worcestershire	3
Thomas Sanderson	Honorary vice-president	Living on his own means*		Cumberland Villas, Borough Road East, Middlesbrough	Carlisle	2
William H. Thomas	Honorary vice-president	Printer and publisher	Employer	10 West Terrace, North Ormesby, Middlesbrough	Pickhill, Yorkshire	None
Eugene Wethey	Treasurer	Bank manager	Employed	Hudworth House, Nelson Terrace, Coatham	Exeter	2

[1] 1891 census; *Northern Echo*, 15th May 1889, 28th May, 15th June 1891
*1881 census—slate merchant

on the subject of professionalism," they would defer any decision on professional football themselves for the following year.[50] The quotation from Wood at the AGM, and that from 'Rambler' early in 1889 (which suggested acquiring men who "in return for work at their own trade, will devote Saturday afternoons to football") would suggest that there had been a shift toward working-class players.[51] Alongside the middle-class composition of club officials, there was evidently a distinction between working-class players and their club superiors. Even though overt professionalism had been dismissed, it is apparent that there were no objections to importing players and finding them employment in the town. The *Northern Review* suggested that as "there is now plenty of work at Middlesbrough for steady and good workmen. . . . I shall not be the least surprised to find the Middlesbrough team strongly reinforced."[52] With talk of splits and divisions seemingly behind them, the season started well, leading "Rambler" to comment that the club was "still to the fore . . . despite the croaking and evil foreboding indulged in during the past few months" by those favoring professionalism.[53]

At the end of September 1889, middlesbrough were beaten at Newcastle East End. The Middlesbrough forwards were reportedly disorganized and had played "a wretchedly loose game."[54] A few days later, it became apparent why some of the team had played so badly when five of the forwards and one half-back[55] sent a petition to the committee requesting that they be paid for playing (10s for a win and 7s 6d for a draw or defeat). A meeting was held to discuss the matter, and after a "protracted discussion," it was agreed to carry on with the present arrangements. A hopeful application was to be made to the Football Association asking them to adopt a rule whereby players could be paid for loss of time but still retain their amateur status.[56] Reaction in the local press was mixed. The *Northern Echo's* 'Observer' suggested that the players' proposal "cannot be regarded with either surprise or indignation" as other important clubs in the area already paid their players. Professionalism was inevitable, and 'Observer' pointed out that the club's committee had no problem arranging games *against* professional teams.[57] The *Athletic News* (a vocal supporter of professionalism) pointed out that, "dissension has been rife amongst their supporters as to the advisability of strengthening their team with professional help."[58] In contrast, 'Rambler' in the *Northern Review* declared that "the whole town has been laughing at [the players] ever since" they had submitted their petition. He wondered whether the players had given enough thought to becoming professionals,

> How their private liberty, indulgences, luxuries, would be forbidden by the committee who paid them, who, naturally, would allow nothing to interfere with the getting of full value for their money. At one sweep, away would go

baccy, beer, etc, and strict training insisted upon. Life would not be worth living![59]

The *North-Eastern Weekly Gazette* thought that it would have been better if the players "who think they have risen to such a standard . . . as to deserve recompense," had left the club when professionalism had been rejected at the AGM. Instead, these "wilful schoolboys" had conspired to deliberately lose the game at Newcastle.[60]

Further poor results on the field changed the dispute from one between the players and the club to a larger one involving members and spectators. A requisition signed by eighty members of the club was presented to the committee, and another meeting requested. It was felt that those in favor of professionalism would now find a considerable number of members in agreement as a change in results was sought, though the *North-Eastern Weekly Gazette* thought that the committee would receive "every support from the footballers of the town."[61] Six resolutions were to be proposed at the meeting, the most significant of which were:

- That a vote of censure be passed upon the committee for mismanagement.
- That the following members of the committee be asked to resign office—Messrs R. Peel, Kedward, W. H. Thomas, and A. Mattison.
- That the resolution passed at the general meeting against the payment of players be rescinded.
- That the committee in future have power to pay players providing the players wish it.[62]

With 1,800 people reportedly present at the meeting, it was alleged that the committee "had failed to give them the best possible football procurable" and that the players had not been treated with "proper respect and consideration." The proposal of censure was put to the meeting by a show of hands, and the chairman, Henry Cochrane, declared that it had not been carried, resulting in uproar; both the *North-Eastern Daily Gazette* and the *South Durham & Cleveland Mercury* suggested that judging by the show of hands, the resolution should in fact have been passed. The two resolutions regarding the payment of players were dismissed out of hand by the chairman, "amid increasing excitement and disorder and an incessant storm of angry cries."[63]

The *Athletic News* thought that those present had "behaved more like lunatics at large than sober citizens." It was hoped that "the spirit of discord would be replaced by peace . . . and the club would start on a fresh basis."[64] The *Northern Echo's* 'Observer' reminded the committee members that although they were not paid, they were still "equally amenable to the club majority as if they were." They had "a certain inclination to be stiff-necked, to be very wrath that any single action of theirs should be so much questioned."[65] Once again 'Rambler' was pleased that the football club would not be selling its soul to professionalism,

> The Middlesbrough club is part of the town. Its duty as the town club is to encourage and help the athletic youths of the town in the fine pastime football. By knocking out local men and substituting foreigners could we feel the same pride as in a team of players bred and born amongst us? . . . By bringing professionals, would not the club be failing in one of its most important duties?[66]

The emphasis on "local men" is interesting to note given the absence of "local" men on the committee and in this instance refers to local amateurs rather than professional "outsiders." For a town such as Middlesbrough, with its large proportion of non-Middlesbrough-born residents, the definition of the term "local" may be more open to interpretation, particularly when it came to how people identified with the town in which they lived and worked.

The club was now irreconcilably divided and shortly after the meeting, an announcement was placed in the local press asking two thousand people to attend a public meeting to form a new football club.[67] The meeting was chaired by Malcolm MacDonald (a Scottish foreman plater) who stated that he simply wanted to "establish a club which should be carried on according to their own views which were not in accordance with the views of the committee of the existing club." There was only one resolution—"That in the opinion of this meeting of the football going public of Middlesbrough it is desirable that a new football club be formed as early as possible for the promotion of good football." This was seconded by one former Middlesbrough committee member who believed that the "the players had an equal right to share the money with anyone else." The new club would be run as a limited liability for which £2,000 was required and 113 shares were subscribed to by thirty-eight individuals at the meeting. MacDonald was asked "how the working men were to get on" (i.e., how they would afford to buy shares), to which he replied that the share capital would only be called for as it was required. He did not hide his preference for making money from the club, stating that he liked "the washers" (slang for coins; a term which quickly became the club's nickname).[68] Similarly, when Newcastle East End issued shares in 1890 it was hoped that the low price of shares would "make the scheme more popular and within the reach of the working classes."[69]

The large crowd that gathered for the meeting was felt to reflect the "perfect unanimity of feeling that existed with regard to the question of commencing a professional team to uphold the honour of the town." The

Athletic News' Teesside columnist noted that those behind the new club "had not misjudged the strength of public feeling or the amount of support upon which they could calculate." Not only did the new club have the backing of the people of the town, it was reported that "several of the Middlesbrough players have intimated to promoters their willingness to throw in their lot with them, as they are tired of playing for the love of the game."[70] The *Northern Echo*'s 'Observer' had little sympathy for the old club, who by ignoring the "palpable signs of the times," had made the formation of this new club inevitable. The leaders of the new club had recognized the public's desire for success, knowing that they "demanded higher class football, whether it emanated from Kirkcaldy, Timbuctoo or Cargo Fleet." This highlights the relative lack of importance given to the team being composed of 'local' players, in comparison to the repeated desire by the old Middlesbrough club for locals.[71] The *Northern Review* disagreed that the new professional team would inevitably play better football, as it would not be as "manly, straightforward, and honest as an amateur one." The reporter suggested that if football was no longer to be played for the love of the game, "let us shun the game as a pestilence."[72]

Three days after the formation of the new club it was reported that applications for shares already amounted to more than £500, and that the club was to be named Middlesbrough Ironopolis Football Company Limited (Ironopolis being a frequently used term for Middlesbrough).[73] The Memorandum of Association for the club states that premises and equipment were to be acquired for the playing of tennis, cricket, bicycle and tricycle riding, gymnastic and athletic exercises, matches, festivals and "assaults-at-arms," and that money would be distributed as prizes.[74] The Paradise Field on Linthorpe Road was leased (previously used by Middlesbrough Rovers Rugby Club), with invitations to tender for stands and ticket offices being submitted shortly afterward.[75] It was reported that Richard Bach, the brother of the Middlesbrough player Thomas Bach, was to be employed as the club trainer and groundsman, as his family connection made him "just the man for the job."[76]

The high costs entailed in running professional football clubs had led many clubs to be reorganized as limited liability companies. There was little chance that shareholders and directors would see a return on their investment. Most directors were middle class and were affluent enough to be undeterred by a lack of profits. Instead, as Holt suggests, investment offered "a sense of self-importance and pride at running an organisation around which so much local interest was centred."[77] Though most directors did not make money directly from their position, the "privileges of the directors' box" would have offered attractive business opportunities to those involved. Carter points out that the directors' main interest was the welfare of their club, and though they wanted to "enjoy the privileges of ownership" they regarded the selection of players as a perk of the job; directors were "not dissimilar to unpaid volunteers running a local social institution."[78] Mason states that the occupational composition of a club's directorate usually reflected the economic structure of the town and this is demonstrated in Ironopolis' directors.[79] Whereas Middlesbrough FC's officials represented the town's middle classes, Ironopolis' directors (see table 3.2) were more representative of the town's large working-class population, who made up a significant proportion of football spectators. The club's directors also included members of the increasingly important shopocracy and the lower-middle class, who, as will be demonstrated in the following chapters, became ever more visible in the administration of sports clubs. A number of directors had servants, which also indicates a degree of affluence.

Ironopolis had 221 shareholders holding 889 shares (see appendix 1), the vast majority of which were taken up between 1890 and 1891 (740 shares in 1890 and eighty-three shares in 1891). Their occupations are broadly skilled working class or lower-middle class, mirroring the class composition of the directorate. Eighty-eight shareholders can be categorized as having working-class occupations, and though this is a sizeable number many only bought single shares, while some more affluent individuals were able to purchase a greater number of shares. The occupational and socioeconomic backgrounds of the shareholders are broadly mirrored in the shareholders of the professional clubs of Newcastle West End and Sunderland Albion. Dixon et al. state that most of the shareholders of the three clubs were skilled working class, but the bulk of shares were owned by members of the middle classes. They suggest that for those who had neither "the social credibility nor the financial resources" to join gentleman's members clubs, share ownership and the "masculine camaraderie" of the football club may have offered "an alternative emotional support network."[80] It is possible to identify the place of birth of 163 of Ironopolis' shareholders. The geographical range of birthplaces reflects that of the population of the town in general, and as Dixon et al. point out, the financial backing of the three northeast clubs "came disproportionately from men without the tie of birth to the town which their company, and team, represented." Indeed, involvement with a football club gave such men "an entree to local society, or simply a measure of fellow feeling with their neighbours and workmates."[81] Only 21.4 percent of Ironopolis shareholders were born in Middlesbrough, and 35.6 percent of shareholders were born outside of County Durham, Northumberland, or Yorkshire. Thirteen shareholders were born in Scotland, three in Wales, and three overseas (Australia, Germany, and Russia).[82] Similarly, it is important to note where the shareholders lived. The home addresses of 194 shareholders can be identified. Of these, 93 percent lived in Middles-

Table 3.2. Ironopolis Football Club directors, 1889–1890.[1]

	Occupation	Employment Status	Address	Place of birth	Servants
John Armstrong	Blacksmith	Employed	9 Bottle Works Cottages, Dock Street, Middlesbrough	Carlisle	None
David Bookless	Athletic outfitter	Employer	73 Linthorpe Road, Middlesbrough	Berwick, Northumberland	None
James Henry Boolds (chairman)	Shipyard manager	Employed	Woodlands Road, Middlesbrough	London	2
Albert B. Crooks*	Engineer		West Hartlepool		
William Easton	Fruit merchant	Employer	68 Linthorpe Road, Middlesbrough	Whitby, Yorkshire	None
Joseph Elliott	Boilersmith	Employed	315 Newport Road, Middlesbrough	Middlesbrough	1
Thomas French	Fruit merchant	Employer	1 Queens Terrace, Coatham, Redcar	Durham	None
William Jackson*	Plater				
Malcolm Macdonald (vice-chairman)	Foreman plater	Employed	13 Pembroke Street, Middlesbrough	Scotland	None
George Marshall	Ship owner	Employed	Ayresome House, Newport Road, Middlesbrough	Boston, Lincolnshire	1
Arthur Camplin Richardson	Hatter and hosier	Employed	20 Sussex Street, Middlesbrough	Australia (British Subject)	1
Samuel Richardson	Tailor	Employer	193 Newport Road, Middlesbrough	Sheriff Hutton, Yorkshire	2
John Robinson	Boilersmith	Employed	191 Linthorpe Road, Middlesbrough	London	1
Thomas Sidgwick	Plater	Employed	Bright Street, Middlesbrough	Stockton, County Durham	None
Andrew Stonehouse	Fitter	Employed	2 Poplar Street, Middlesbrough	Marske, Yorkshire	None (lodger)
Edwin Thompson	Bank manager	Employed	42 Marton Road, Middlesbrough	Middlesbrough	None (lodger)
John Daniel Wood	Plater	Employed	11 Peacock Street, Middlesbrough	Middlesbrough	1

[1] 1891 census; Middlesbrough Ironopolis Football Company Limited, Memorandum of Association, BT 31/4608/30227, National Archives; North-Eastern Daily Gazette, 16th November 1889, 22nd February 1890; North-Eastern Weekly Gazette, 23rd November 1889
* Unable to locate on census, occupation taken from shareholders register

brough. Thirteen shareholders lived outside of the town; three lived in London and the remaining ten lived elsewhere in the Northeast.[83] Eight female shareholders can also be identified, all of whom were related to male shareholders, including the twelve-year-old daughter of the club's secretary, Edith Windross, who held one share.[84] In comparison, Newcastle East End and Sunderland Albion had one female shareholder each, and Newcastle West End had none.[85] It is interesting to note that William Wallace and his son James held twenty-five shares each, as did his wife and daughter, Ann and Mary, so that the Wallace family held 11.2 percent of Ironopolis' total shares. The number of shares held by directors during Ironopolis' existence varied, and it was not always the case that those with higher paid jobs owned more shares. The two directors with the most shares—Thompson, a bank manager, and Boolds, a shipyard manager—held twenty-nine and twenty-seven respectively, but the seven directors with ten to twelve shares, included two boilersmiths and a plater. Conversely, the nine directors who held only four or five shares included two doctors and an engineer.[86]

Middlesbrough's response to the formation of Ironopolis, despite their abhorrence for the payment of players, was to turn away from amateurism themselves. With two players (Hopewell and Taylor, who had petitioned the club for payment) already having left for Ironopolis, the committee were faced with the potential desertion of more players. The committee met to discuss whether "they ought not to yield to the recent emphatic demand of a large proportion of the members to introduce the professional element." Professionals were to be advertised for immediately, though preference would be given to players who were already with the club.[87] The club hoped that a forthcoming meeting of the Football Association would rule in favor of their proposal that players could keep their amateur status while being refunded for loss of wages. William H. Thomas argued that "they did not consider it fair to those amateurs in a lower sphere of life," while Mattison claimed that there were hundreds of professionals who would prefer to be reinstated as amateurs if they could be refunded their expenses.[88]

The *Northern Echo*'s 'Observer' suggested that if Middlesbrough's committee "had only bowed their stiff necks before a public feeling which was sweepingly in favor of professionalism, nobody would have dreamt of starting a new club." 'Rambler' in the *Northern Review*, on the other hand, blamed Ironopolis for the unfortunate situation the old club now found themselves in—"If the Ironopolis club had been wise, no interference would have been attempted with the members of the Middlesbrough team . . . the taking of the old club's players has forced it into the present position."[89] Within a few days of Middlesbrough turning professional, they had reportedly received one hundred applications from professional players, while Ironopolis had nearly two hundred applications. Five

Middlesbrough players turned professional, but supporters were "waiting for an introduction to that touch of brilliancy in the form of new blood that will make the whole complete."[90] The *North-Eastern Weekly Gazette* eagerly stated that,

> Already the spirit of rivalry is taking hold of the football community, and matters promise to be exceedingly lively during the remainder of the season. One thing is certain, the supporters of the game in the town will be treated to a much superior exhibition than has been the case for the past two seasons.[91]

Ironopolis played their first game against Gainsborough Trinity on 14th December.[92] "Substantial barricades" were erected at the Paradise Ground to prevent "the encroachment of the spectators," and special accommodation was provided for the press. With Middlesbrough playing at Darlington, the game attracted a large crowd,

> Arriv[ing] on the scene of action, there was such pushing and crushing and scrambling as would have delighted the heart of any theatrical proprietor— hundreds, nay thousands, were hustling and bustling before the pay-boxes to exchange their modest sixpence for the ticket of admission. Meanwhile the promoters of the club looked on with satisfied feelings. At last, however, the surging tide of humanity had passed the entrance gates, and crowded the capacious stand, and there could not have been fewer than 4,000 spectators on the field.[93]

The *North-Eastern Weekly Gazette* commented that "it was a treat to witness the various directors and committee men as they strutted about the ground, prouder by far than anyone else in the capital of Cleveland that afternoon."[94] The local press continued to reflect on the effects of paying players now that professional football had come to Teesside. Despite repeated calls throughout the year for improvements to the team, an editorial in the *North-Eastern Weekly Gazette* now argued instead that professionalism had turned football into,

> a mere medium of speculation . . . a rivalry between town and town, in which the one competes with the other, not in the prowess of its own sons, but in financial resources which enable it to hire paid champions from without. It is difficult, however, for an individual club to resist the widespread professional tendency . . . professionalism degrades every form of sport which it touches, and renders it a potent power for evil.[95]

In contrast, an editorial in the *South Durham & Cleveland Mercury* stated that the popularity of the game was evidence that for "the majority of people attendance at football matches is not a practice in need of defence." The public demand for professionalism could not be denied, as spectators "grow more and more connoisseurs in the niceties of the play, and more and more exacting in their expectations from the players." It followed that the game's "highest exponents must be provided for by the proceeds of the game itself."[96] The *Athletic News* suggested that the formation of Ironopolis had forced Middlesbrough to improve their own team, stopping their inexorable decline, and the *North-Eastern Weekly Gazette* had to concede that "the game is taking a deeper hold of the public than ever, and it will be many seasons before our popular winter game begins to show any signs of being on the wane."[97]

In February 1890 a meeting was held to discuss the prospect of the two clubs amalgamating. Albert Henry Sanderson of the Ironopolis committee stated that it was already apparent that the town did not have room for two successful clubs. The Middlesbrough committee proposed that only one club should exist in the town, and with this in mind they were "prepared to consider any proposal that may be made by the Ironopolis Club by which that club may cease to exist." Ironopolis informed Middlesbrough that they would join with them on the payment of £650 compensation, or would buy out the old club themselves, but this proposal was considered "an absurd one."[98] The prospect of amalgamation was over and it would now be "a struggle to the end, the club that can bear the strain the longest being sure to come out topmost."[99] 'Rambler' ridiculed the "farcical nature" of Ironopolis' proposition,

> Whoever outside the Ironopolis ever dreamed that the Middlesbrough club would willingly burden itself with a debt so great to please a body of men who have done their best to hurt it, and failed. Ironopolis have had their best chance . . . the old ground will attract the bulk of the spectators, in spite of cheap tickets sold at the shipyards.[100]

With any thoughts of amalgamation gone, it was announced at the first meeting of Ironopolis' shareholders that "the working of the club had been somewhat crippled for want of capital." A further £100 was subscribed, with an additional one hundred new shares being taken up. Accommodation at the Paradise Ground was felt to be the aspect where the club was second to Middlesbrough and tenders were invited for the erection of stands to hold two thousand spectators.[101] By March 1890 they had played eighteen matches, winning eleven, and club director William Easton announced that Ironopolis had "earned the approbation of the public by introducing a better exposition of the game."[102] Eager to attract supporters and increase gate receipts, the club arranged a match to take place by lamplight resulting in a crowd of three thousand and a 10–2 victory over Sheffield.[103] This was followed by a victory over Football League side Aston Villa in front of a crowd of three thousand, with £70 in shares being taken up immediately afterward.[104] Ironopolis sought to increase interest in football further by introducing a medals competition between local junior clubs. The aim of the competition was the production of an Ironopolis reserve team through the discovery of "unrecognised local talent." All matches in the contest were to be played on the Paradise Ground, ensuring that the club would also benefit monetarily.[105]

RIVALRY AND THE RISE OF IRONOPOLIS FC

Local enthusiasm for football was evidenced at the 1890 Cleveland Charity Cup Final, when Middlesbrough played Ironopolis for the first time. "Rambler" informed his readers that "you cannot move a yard along any thoroughfare without overhearing some prophetic utterance as to the result of the great fight."[106] The match was played in front of around twelve thousand spectators and ended 0–0.[107] The *Northern Echo* was pleased to report that there had been "an almost entire absence of ill-feeling or rough play . . . the game was one of the pleasantest that has been seen in the town." Having already commented that Ironopolis tickets were sold at the shipyards, 'Rambler' also remarked on the partisan nature of the crowd, noting that their supporters were easily identified,

> If emblems went for anything the Washers were strong favourites, and I should say that foremen and storekeepers must have noticed an extraordinary consumption of brass and iron washers during the past week. The nickname which I give them in jest has been adopted by the Ironopolis' supporters in earnest, and washers from the size of a sixpence to almost a cart wheel, and made of almost every known metal were worn on the caps or breasts of large numbers of spectators.[108]

The replay drew a crowd of six thousand, and Ironopolis won 2–0. That they had drawn the first game and won the second led the *North-Eastern Weekly Gazette* to conclude that Ironopolis were clearly the better of the two teams, particularly as they had played with "a dash that was irresistible."[109]

Middlesbrough's balance sheet no longer looked quite as healthy as in previous years. Despite an income of over £1,800 the club was left with a balance of only £22 15s 7d. £148 15s 9d had been spent on obtaining players, with a further £420 on wages for professionals and a trainer.[110] Ahead of their AGM in May it was proposed that members' annual subscriptions be increased as a means of raising money, and the increased cost would also "keep many precocious and impertinent youngsters out of the covered stand, where they have . . . been a source of annoyance . . . [and] have taken up valuable seating room."[111]

Ironopolis was admitted to the Northern League for the 1890–1891 season,[112] and also arranged other fixtures with a number of strong sides. Due to the number of games Middlesbrough had played away from

home, Ironopolis had previously attracted the greater number of spectators for their home matches, and the older club decided not to issue
a fixture list "owing to the advantages it would give the Ironopolis."[113]
Season tickets were available for Ironopolis at the same price as those for
their rivals, and the club's captain and a number of other players were
reported to have joined the athletics club, as they were "beginning to
see the necessity of thorough training."[114] It was becoming increasingly
evident that the two clubs had to try hard to secure the support of the
football-going public. It was not uncommon that both teams would have
home games on the same day. For example, an announcement in the
North-Eastern Daily Gazette advertised Ironopolis versus Chirk (the Welsh
champions), which kicked off at 3:45 p.m., and admittance would be half
price at half-time. Middlesbrough's game against South Bank kicked off
at 3 p.m. and therefore by the time it had finished spectators would also
have time to go to the second half of Ironopolis' match as their grounds
were so close together.[115]

The first Northern League match between the two sides attracted a
crowd of around ten thousand–twelve thousand to Middlesbrough's
ground. "No local event, not even royalty, has provoked so much absorbing interest," commented 'Rambler.' The crowd was a "strong but
good humoured one" and had used "less of that foul language too often
to be met with on our football fields."[116] The match epitomized both the
rivalry and the benefits that had arisen from having two teams in the
town. There was now "a general alertness and go-ahead spirit in catering for public patronage," as well as a "manifestly improved" standard
in play "for the delectation of the . . . public."[117] In early 1891 'Rambler'
welcomed Ironopolis as the opposition they posed to the Middlesbrough
team "helps to keep the players up to the mark." Moreover, the rivalry
between the two teams had "drawn into the football vortex thousands
who never previously saw a match, and converted them into eager enthusiasts." Football's popularity seemed in little doubt as on the same
Saturday afternoon Middlesbrough drew a crowd of four thousand,
while three thousand watched Ironopolis.[118] Both teams were capable
of attracting sizeable crowds, and it would appear that many spectators
simply wanted to watch good football and did not necessarily associate
themselves with one team or the other. For example, when Ironopolis
played Blackburn Rovers in the FA Cup in mid-January, the crowd was
between eight thousand and ten thousand. With Middlesbrough's game
that day against Stockton postponed, some spectators "rather than be
done out of a match, overcame their scruples" to watch the holders of the
FA Cup instead.[119]

Middlesbrough and Ironopolis met again in the Northern League in
late March 1891, where a crowd of ten thousand at the Paradise Ground
witnessed another win for Ironopolis. The *South Durham & Cleveland Mer-*

cury commented that it was "most creditable to the players that, in spite of the rivalry which exists between the clubs, there should have been so few manifestations of ill-will." This contrasted with some members of the Ironopolis committee who "loudly condemned certain discreet tactics of the town team."[120] Ironopolis won the Northern League shortly afterward, and rather than congratulate the club, 'Rambler' commented that with the two Middlesbrough clubs at the top of the League it could now be considered the home of northern football (despite the fact that Sunderland AFC had just completed their first season in the Football League). Though neither the FA Cup nor the Cleveland Cup rested in Middlesbrough, 'Rambler' was of the opinion that "the League results are more reliable" and the records of the two clubs placed the town "in a very high niche of football fame."[121]

Following Middlesbrough's comparatively unsuccessful season, a resolution was passed at their AGM that members "voluntarily subscribe" toward a fund for improving the team. This decision came after their accounts showed a loss, as more than £1,097 had been spent on obtaining and keeping players. William H. Thomas stated that during the course of the club's existence "an extraordinary claim had never been made on the members, and he thought that [this] was a fitting opportunity when some strong effort might be made" to secure new players. It was, in his opinion, "not the duty of the executive to go to any considerable amount above their means." There had been members who "had not been shy in finding fault with the committee," and with more money to spend on players, such accusations would be eliminated; more than £46 was subsequently promised.[122]

Details of Ironopolis' accounts were published ahead of their AGM. Perhaps to soften the blow for the shareholders, the figures supplied covered nearly two years, making their income appear much greater than their rivals; income totaled £3,244 5s 2d, but the club recorded a considerable loss of £513 12s 10d (compared to Middlesbrough's loss of just over £88).[123] At the subsequent meeting, one of the directors stated that the club had indeed made a loss in their first year, but had made a profit during their second season, "and in the season to come, being now an established and well-known club, they hoped that they would make a still bigger profit." Despite successes on the pitch, the secretary of the club argued that "the directors have been handicapped at every way" by, for example, their ground being "out of the way and people having to pass the other club's ground." Nevertheless, the Paradise Ground had been secured for another year and was to be extended, including the building of a cycle track. It was felt by 'Milo' in the *Northern Echo* that profit and loss would be of little concern to the committee as they had "the satisfaction of knowing that the support which the public have accorded them has been even greater than that secured by the old club."[124]

In January 1892 the issue of amalgamation was raised again. It was felt that this was the only way that a team from Middlesbrough would be able to compete with the best in the country. 'Observer,' in the *Northern Echo*, argued that,

> if there is a strong determination on both sides to sacrifice personal ideas and prejudices for the advancement of the game no doubt means will be found of surmounting all difficulties, banishing all bitterness, and joining again hand-in-hand those who for so many years were united in the one laudable object of promoting the success of the Middlesbrough club.[125]

The *Northern Review* attempted to gauge public reaction to amalgamation and featured two pages of interviews with "some of the shining lights in the football world." Responses suggested that some spectators did identify with one particular team and that a rivalry existed between the supporters of the two clubs. Angus Macpherson (secretary of Middlesbrough Amateur Swimming Club) favored amalgamation, stating that the present rivalry between the two sets of supporters was "more prejudicial to the interests of the game than anything . . . let us get rid of the squabbling and a healthful stimulus would follow." Edwin Thompson (an Ironopolis director) stated that there was a certain amount of "bad feeling" among the teams' followers, and claimed that "a system of boycotting exists in the town. Ironopolis people won't trade with Middlesbrough people and vice versa." Harry Walker (secretary of the Northern League) agreed, contending that there was "dissension in families, strained relations in business, and other unpleasant matters which have been the result of the existence of two clubs." Frederick Hardisty (acting president of the Middlesbrough Club) favored amalgamating but also felt that gates would decrease "for there would not be the interest that now exists." William Easton (Ironopolis director) thought that one combined club would be capable of joining the Football League, and Thomas Sidgwick (another director of Ironopolis) regarded amalgamation as necessary, suggesting that it would allow the club to build "one of the finest football, cricket and cycling grounds in the country." A number of female football followers were also interviewed, none of whom were in favor of amalgamation. One stated that she would "never subscribe one penny to get the Washers out of debt; they have made their bed and let them lie on it."[126]

The *Northern Review's* aversion to professionalism was further demonstrated by two essay competitions for the newspaper's 'Our Lads' Club' section. In October 1891 members were invited to give twelve reasons why amateurism was preferable to professionalism, and in January 1892 members were asked to suggest ways of encouraging amateur football. One of the winning essays for the second competition, by sixteen-year-old office boy Arthur Mennell, argued that the payment of footballers was "something scandalous, and sooner something is done to obviate this the better"; it was "one of the evils of our country." Before the importation of players, he suggested, a victory for the local team had given "some credit to the town." The other winning essay, by fourteen-year-old Humphrey Thompson, suggested that money was transforming amateur players into "regular working football machines who rise and fall in value like pig-iron or railway stocks." He proposed however, that there also ought to be "some substantial individual prizes for amateur players," or some "article that they might have about them" so that when they were older it would give them "sweet remembrance of their amateur football days."[127]

Two weeks before Middlesbrough and Ironopolis were due to play each other in the final of the Cleveland Cup in March 1892, they met for a friendly match which the old club won 5–1. "The decisive character of . . . victory," wrote the *South Durham & Cleveland Mercury*, "sent the partisans of the senior organisation into little short of hysterical raptures."[128] Should the Middlesbrough players beat their rivals in the cup they were to be "treated handsomely" by the club[129] but they were beaten 4–0. There was a crowd of twelve thousand of "the strongest-lunged individuals I have ever come across on a football ground" according to 'The Free Critic' in the *Athletic News*, and the game evidently caused fighting to break out in the crowd, as the *South Durham & Cleveland Mercury* stated that there had been "more than one pugilistic exhibition between the rival teams' supporters."[130] Having already won the Cleveland Amateur Cup, in April Ironopolis were confirmed as champions of the Northern League, beating Middlesbrough again to win the Charity Cup ten days later; Middlesbrough could "no longer hold any pretentions to rivalry with the younger organisation."[131]

The 1891–1892 season had proved successful for Ironopolis, and in order to have a share of their success, it was no surprise that Middlesbrough were willing to return to amalgamation. 'Rambler,' so often opposed to the new club but eager for success, stated that,

> The differences between the two parties were settled long ago, and what remains are simply sentimental and fanciful. . . . Why continue the struggle? Who can benefit? With one professional team of high class in the town, the football honors of the world can be bid for with every hope of success.[132]

Middlesbrough's minute book shows that the club decided to enter negotiations when the Football League was extended, though it is not clear whether they hoped to join the First or Second division.[133] Terms of amalgamation were agreed between the two clubs in May; the new club was to be called Middlesbrough & Ironopolis United Football & Athletic Company Limited, accompanied by the formation of a new limited liability company.[134] It was decided that a letter would be sent to the Football League asking that the amalgamated club be admitted for the coming season, but shortly after it was reported that the negotiations between the two clubs had stalled and Ironopolis now refused to sign the application to the League. Subsequently two applications were made, one from each club, both of which were unsuccessful.[135] Further meetings were held during the following week, with revisions being made to the conditions of amalgamation as both committees "were wishful for further enlightenment upon certain points," but by the end of May the amalgamation had once again fallen through.[136]

At Middlesbrough's AGM in May 1892, Albert Borrie (the club secretary) confirmed that terms had in fact been finalized, but it had proved impossible to agree on a name. Blame was placed squarely with Ironopolis for the collapse in negotiations, Middlesbrough now stating that they had only entertained the notion in order to give their rivals a "helping hand out of the position into which they had forced themselves."[137] The end of negotiations, according to 'Rambler,' "enraged the members of the Middlesbrough club, as to make them thoroughly determined to do everything it is possible to do to command success" and it was therefore resolved that Middlesbrough would be conducted on limited liability principles, thus providing the funds for the committee to strengthen the team. Three hundred and two £1 shares were taken up at the AGM which, the club's president stated, "spoke well for the interest that the members took in the welfare of the club."[138] Borrie was elected as secretary of the new Middlesbrough Football & Athletic Club Company Limited, and twelve directors were either appointed or elected, eight of whom can be identified—a doctor, a hatter, a cashier, a butcher, a butcher's manager, a clerk, a plasterer, and a printer and publisher. Only four had previous involvement in the club. In comparison to the club's officials detailed already, the majority of these directors were lower-middle class—only three of them had a servant and three were employers.[139]

In mid-October Middlesbrough's shareholders were informed that the officials were "dissatisfied with the performance exhibited by some of the players, and . . . it would be essential to obtain some new men." Indeed the club's minute book records that the chairman and secretary duly went to Scotland to procure three new players.[140] In November, the committee announced that only 550 shares had been taken up. A further one hundred were subscribed with the directors emphasizing that "one and all should do their utmost and put their shoulders to the wheel to enable the directors to be in no way hampered by financial troubles."[141] There was evidently still some uncertainty about the club's future as just over six months after forming the limited liability company, a meeting was held at which views were expressed "upon the present position of professional football and the advisability or otherwise of continuing a professional team," but it was decided that the club should continue.[142]

Middlesbrough ended the 1891–92 season with a loss of £310 10s 3d. In comparison, Ironopolis' loss totaled £952 12s 2d. The older club had spent £1,455 on players' wages, their rivals £1,451. £2,149 in gate receipts had been taken at the Linthorpe Road ground, whereas Ironopolis had only received £1,756.[143] The minute book for Middlesbrough gives an indication of players' wages during this period. Players were paid between 30s and £3 5s a week. Bonuses ranged from £7 10s to £40, and some players received an additional payment of between £5 and £10 on playing their first match.[144] The club helped new players to find work on their arrival in the town or paid them until a job could be found, which no doubt would have made the decision to join the club much easier, and would have secured players a greater income before the season commenced. It was stated that if Galbraith arrived at the club before 1st August 1892 he would be paid 25s a week until he was found work as a plater. Similarly it was recorded on 1st July that Mackay was to be paid 25s a week until he found work or until the season started, and when Blyth signed in November he was paid 20s a week until a job was found.[145] The minute book also shows that fees were paid out by the club to agents. When Galbraith was signed, his agent was paid £5; half when the player signed and half when he played his first game. Another agent was paid £7 10s per player, and the club's trainer was paid £3 a week.[146]

Middlesbrough's minute book also records the difficulties experienced by the club with footballers' behavior, and drinking in particular. Roberts had used foul language toward the directors, had been "addicting himself to drink" and asked to leave the club. He was duly released, because of drinking and his conduct, but also in part because he had not shown "such skill and ability in his play" as had been expected.[147] Galbraith had been drunk twice and had "stayed out [for] several nights," and was suspended for a month. Two weeks after his last offense, Galbraith was again "hopelessly drunk," and was suspended again for two months.[148] Stephenson was cautioned after staying out until 11.45 p.m. and questions were raised about his sobriety, and McCrone was reported to have disappeared.[149] McKnight was suspended for not playing to the best of his abilities, particularly in one match where "he did not endeavour to play in anything like the manner he can do and . . . did not try."[150]

Ironopolis was said to be hindered by the lack of shares taken up. Of the £2,000 available, in August 1892 only £844 had been subscribed, of which £192 10s remained unpaid.[151] A bazaar was held in September 1892 to raise funds for the club, and it was hoped that the proceeds would enable the club to move to the Ayresome Park Estate where they would be able to provide facilities for cycling and athletics as well as a new football ground. The bazaar raised £450, which after expenses left £275 available for the club to spend on the ground.[152] On opening the bazaar, Isaac Wilson (the former MP for Middlesbrough) commended the football club for giving "pleasure, health, and recreation to the inhabitants of the town." The Marquis of Londonderry attended to present the Northern League trophy to the Ironopolis chairman, and he sang the praises of football, noting that, "it required health and strength, fixity of purpose, swiftness of foot, and that bull-dog courage which was characteristic of the British nation."[153]

Another Ironopolis victory over Middlesbrough was recorded in December 1892, there being "little ground for doubting as to which is now the better team."[154] The victories continued for Ironopolis, and by 28th January 1893 they had won the Northern League for the third consecutive season.[155] Their status as the better of the two teams was further enhanced when they reached the quarter final of the FA Cup in February. Having attracted a crowd of ten thousand in the previous round, it was not surprising that the crowd at the next game against Preston North End was estimated to have been fourteen thousand–fifteen thousand (compared to 1,500 at Middlesbrough's home game on the same day), which would have included a number of spectators who might normally have watched Middlesbrough play instead. 'Rambler' suggested that the committee "must have thrilled and glowed when they viewed the mighty concourse of spectators," as the large crowd meant gate receipts of more than £470. The *Athletic News* commented that,

> It was a "red letter day" in every sense of the term, in the history of the Ironopolis club. Here, there and everywhere it was the one and only topic discussed. . . . I never remember witnessing so much excitement over a football match as prevailed on every side during Friday or Saturday. From the north, south, east and west did the people flock in Middlesbrough.[156]

THE END OF PROFESSIONALISM

The death knell first sounded for professionalism in February 1893 when it was announced that Middlesbrough's professional players had to take a pay cut or leave the club. Players had already had their pay reduced to £1 per match "owing to their indifferent performance." The players were now informed that,

> In consequence of the wretched performances of the team and the serious effect this had had on the gates and was likely to have and the consequent severe loses which would have to be met in order to carry out the season's programme, it was unanimously resolved that all players paid by the week

be informed that for the remaining part of the season they would only be paid 30s per week.[157]

This would have meant considerable pay cuts for many players. Five players did not agree to the reduction in wages and two subsequently joined West Bromwich Albion while another defected to Ironopolis. A number of local amateurs offered their services to the club, and it was "gratifying to the Middlesbrough executive to find that with six local lads among the team" they were able to win their next game against Royal Arsenal.[158] The cut to the players' wages effectively signaled the end of professionalism for the club, and on 23rd March it was confirmed that they would be reverting to amateurism. This was welcomed wholeheartedly by 'Rambler' who stated that the main problem with professionalism had been the "high rate of remuneration paid for very little work which has made so many players idle loafers on the street," as demonstrated by the incidents of drunken behavior above. If players had been paid less, alongside completing "an honest week's work," there would have been little of the "humbug and humiliations the manager and supporters of clubs have been compelled to bear." It was felt nevertheless that a couple of professionals should be retained by the club, to "keep our lads up in fast work" and to look after the ground.[159] At the end of the season, Middlesbrough's accounts showed that the club had made a loss of over £645, proof according to the *Athletic News*, that "the Iron Capital is not yet big enough to run two professional clubs." Middlesbrough's subscriptions had more than halved, and gate receipts totaled £400 less than the previous season despite an increase in admission prices, and the directors concluded that "interest in professional football in this district was very materially on the wane." It was proposed that the club ask Middlesbrough Vulcan to amalgamate with them (to which the smaller club's committee unanimously agreed), which would "prove of the greatest benefit in forwarding amateurism," and bring new (and free) players in to the club.[160]

The relatively small crowd of two thousand for the Cleveland Charity Cup final between Middlesbrough and Ironopolis led the *Athletic News* to claim that "the game is to all intents and purposes a dead letter." Despite the fact that Ironopolis had not yet announced whether they would continue with professionalism, they decided to proceed with their new ground and cycle track at Ayresome Park.[161] The club failed in an application to join the Second Division of the Football League in June 1893, and shortly afterward the Northern League announced that they would only allow amateur teams to compete.[162] Following Accrington's withdrawal from the Second Division, Ironopolis succeeded in a second application to join the League. 'Rambler' wondered whether the club's directors deserved "congratulation for great and wonderful boldness and foresight, or condemnation for extraordinary foolhardiness." The *Athletic News*, on the other hand, thought that their admission to the Football League had "roused the enterprise" of the club.[163]

In a circular to shareholders, Ironopolis' chairman promised that joining the Second Division would provide the supporters with a "better class [of] football." However, shareholders were also asked to take up a fully paid £1 share (which would include a season ticket), and to use their "best endeavours to induce one or two . . . friends to take up the same amount." The onus was placed on the club's supporters as it was stated that without "the necessary support they cannot carry on the club." It was confirmed at Ironopolis' AGM in August (at which there were only twenty-four people present) that the club had a debt of £246 13s 9d, though the committee were quick to point out that this was less than the previous season. It was proposed to pay players less—£1 a week and no bonus (considerably more than the reduction in wages to 30s that Middlesbrough had introduced), even though they were already being paid less than professionals elsewhere, a situation that meant that at the start of the 1893–1894 season the team only included one player from the previous season. The team had received a £35 bonus on winning the Northern League but it was pointed out that they had done "nothing after the money was given them"; it was agreed that it had been a mistake to award them a bonus before the season had actually finished. In contrast to Middlesbrough's statements, the chairman proclaimed that "it would be utterly impossible to run an amateur team in opposition to a professional team in the town."[164] On the opening day of the season in September 1893, Middlesbrough played Stockton at home with a crowd of only seven hundred. On the same day, Ironopolis were beaten by Liverpool in their first Second Division match at the Paradise Ground in front of a relatively modest two thousand spectators.[165]

The gates for both Middlesbrough clubs remained small. The *Northern Review* stated that this could be attributed to the trade depression[166] suggesting that if trade did not pick up, both clubs "will bear a big share of the paucity of funds." However, 'Rambler' also suggested that if Ironopolis were in trouble, "it is of its own seeking and the blows it may receive will be deserved."[167] In December a friendly game at the Paradise Ground against Darlington attracted a crowd of only two hundred spectators, leading the *South Durham & Cleveland Mercury* to wonder "how the "Nops" executive manage to keep the club going."[168] The answer to this was that they no longer could. The *North-Eastern Daily Gazette* reported on 15th December 1893 that a notice had been issued to the shareholders informing them that a resolution would be submitted suggesting the club enter voluntary liquidation and it was unanimously agreed to wind up the club. The directors blamed the "very dull state of trade and the small amount of support that was being extended to the club." This was coupled with the fact that more than £1,574 was owed to creditors, one of whom had already taken the club to court. Nevertheless the committee resolved to continue the team to the end of the season, after which it would be restructured and an "experienced working committee formed to manage the match department."[169] The *Athletic News* viewed the decline of the club as "a sample of what we may expect if the present ruinous wages are paid to players." For 'Rambler,' it merely confirmed that the club's decision to stick with professionalism had been a bad one. More importantly, it had had "a bad effect on the whole of the clubs in the district . . . if the Nops had followed the lead of the other clubs everyone would have benefitted."[170]

The slump in football's popularity continued into 1894. Ironopolis' first-round FA Cup tie at the Paradise Ground attracted only 1,500 spectators; a fraction of the crowd that had attended a year before. In contrast, for Middlesbrough's tie against the professional club Newton Heath in Manchester, the club felt it necessary to reserve two saloons on the train across the Pennines and provide cheap hotel accommodation for travelling supporters.[171] Indeed, the average attendance for Ironopolis' home League matches was 1,300, the lowest for both divisions, whereas that for Middlesbrough's first season in the League in 1899–1900 was 5,925.[172] The *Northern Review* felt that both of Middlesbrough's clubs could have done more to attract bigger crowds. 'Rambler' suggested that it was "bad business" that games had not been organized between the two. Apart from the money that would have been generated, "it might raise up the keen partisanship so frequently denounced, but which created thousands of spectators, and so help the clubs substantially."[173]

That professionalism could not survive in Middlesbrough was further evidenced when Ironopolis' directors informed their players that they could no longer afford to pay them at all, offering instead, "the privilege of playing until the end of the season." It was expected that only two or three players would immediately leave the club, with the rest staying at Ironopolis until the end of the 1893–1894 season—the *Athletic News* reported that employment had been found for almost all of the players meaning that they could afford to play for nothing.[174] The local press speculated as to whether the club would be in existence the following season. 'Rambler' hoped that the club would carry on "if only to do something to recoup those who have, in storm and sunshine, stuck to the club," while the *North-Eastern Daily Gazette* stated that those involved with the club were "more determined than ever that they will not allow themselves to be snuffed out."[175] Having received "numerous applications from players of good repute," in late April, the *Northern Echo* reported that Ironopolis had acquired eight new players from Scotland to play in a game against Newcastle attended by three thousand spectators.[176]

While Ironopolis continued their decline and drop in standards of play, Middlesbrough succeeded in winning the Northern League, the Charity Cup, and the Cleveland Cup. The latter drew a crowd of only two thousand, but thankfully the "rough and rowdy lot" were absent.[177] The decision to revert to amateurism was clearly justified. At Middlesbrough's annual dinner, the captain (Thomas Bach) remarked that the team and directors had never before been on such harmonious terms. William H. Thomas, in congratulating the team on their successes, was delighted to have justification for his belief that "the game should be played for the benefit of the players and not for the benefit of the spectators, for when it became the latter a noble game became degraded."[178] The club's accounts further vindicated the decision to abandon professionalism, as all loans had been paid off, the overdraft was reduced by £100 and a profit of more than £29 had been made—"a most satisfactory and welcome change after the depressing experience of the last few seasons" according to Borrie.[179]

A meeting of the Ironopolis committee was held on 30th April 1894 at which it was decided that the club would continue as a professional side. The *North-Eastern Daily Gazette* stated that if a good team was brought together there seemed "little fear but that the efforts of those in authority will be heartily supported by the public, for there are many hundreds of enthusiasts in the North who would willingly travel a few miles to see . . . a really good team on the Paradise ground."[180] However, just ten days after the committee's announcement, a resolution was passed declaring,

> That in consequence of the high rent asked for, and other demands made by the tenant of the Paradise Field, and their inability to secure another ground, the committee, with great regret, find it impossible to carry on the club for the present.[181]

By late May Ironopolis had given up their place in the Football League. The *Athletic News* reported that after a storm had damaged the stands at the Paradise Ground, "the landlord came round and relieved the club of the ground."[182] The last mention of Ironopolis in the local press is their inclusion in the preliminary round of the FA Cup, published in the *South Durham & Cleveland Mercury* in August 1894. This passes by without any further comment, their place being taken by another side when the tie was played.[183]

CONCLUSION

It is evident that the failure of professional football can be attributed in part to the strength of the amateur ethos, both among those running

Middlesbrough FC and within large sections of the very vocal press. For example, when Middlesbrough were presented with the Cleveland Charity Cup in 1893 by shipbuilder Waynman Dixon, he remarked that their return to amateurism was "a great satisfaction to many of the old supporters." He stated that when professionalism encroached on sport "it tended to lower it," and it was no longer "pursued for those health-giving and ennobling qualities which they desire to see."[184] At the beginning of the period examined here, professionalism was abhorred, the payment of players only being undertaken by Middlesbrough in order to avoid being swept away by Ironopolis. The *North-Eastern Daily Gazette* argued that the introduction of professional football had meant that "a vast demand has been created for the public amusement of looking on" at the game. Now, it was the "paymaster" who decided whether matches would be "cunningly lost" or "deliberately thrown away"; the "bubble of the sport's popularity" was about to burst.[185]

It was suggested on a number of occasions that professionalism would lead to a desertion of Middlesbrough's more respectable supporters, as a direct link was made between the professional game and a decline in the behavior of spectators. Shortly before the formation of Ironopolis, the *North-Eastern Weekly Gazette* reported on rumors that the importation of players would mean that "the better class of people" would stop attending football matches.[186] Likewise in 1893, the *Northern Review* suggested that the decline of professionalism would thankfully mean "the desertion of the rowdy crew" and the "hundreds of foul-mouthed blackguards" who had forced out the more respectable spectators.[187] The 'Our Lads' Club' essays in the *Northern Review* also stated that "the spectators at professional matches generally behave in a much worse manner than do those at amateur matches," and a few months later another member of the club noted the "rowdyism" displayed by professionals on their train journeys to matches.[188] Middlesbrough's secretary stated in May 1893 that the club was hopeful that "many old supporters of the game who had lost their interest in it would . . . renew their support in the future."[189] The *Northern Review* differentiated between Middlesbrough's supporters and those favoring professionalism claiming that the majority of those who had attended the meeting to form Ironopolis were "of the callow youth type, who are never admitted into the councils of the premier club."[190] The partisanship that accompanied professional football led the *Northern Review* to argue that there was a danger that the sport would "burn out owing to excess passion poured upon it." "Howling like madmen, the shoulder-high absurdity, and general rejoicing over a victory" had no place in football.[191] Nevertheless, it is also clear that the short-lived rivalry between Middlesbrough and Ironopolis did bring about an increased interest in football in the town, assisted by the amount of coverage given to football in the local press. When Ironopolis were disbanded, the *Athletic News* abandoned their Teesside column, remarking that,

> Teesside football does not make much of a figure in these columns, for the simple reason . . . that Teesside football has become such a minor quantity. Time was when Middlesbrough was the northern metropolis of the game.[192]

While it is not possible to compare the shareholders of Middlesbrough and Ironopolis, a comparison can be made between the directors and officials of the two clubs. It would certainly appear that the officials of the newer club were more diverse in background, some directors having working-class occupations. The reasons why individuals chose to involve themselves with either club are unclear. Ironopolis was formed because supporters wanted to watch a higher standard of football rather than because they thought that players should be paid for doing so. There is also little evidence to suggest that most ordinary supporters or shareholders felt any particular affinity with their club, it having been suggested that many people watched whichever team was able to offer the best football on a Saturday afternoon. However, that there was little to differentiate the two clubs might help to explain why this attempt to establish professional football failed. The clubs' grounds were close together and the price of admission was the same, and there was little to choose between the teams for much of the period. The town could not generate the large amounts of money necessary to maintain both clubs. Ironopolis made it as easy as possible for working people to buy shares, but this left the club constantly waiting for money. The large amounts of money involved, rather than the principles of amateurism and professionalism, made the downfall of one of the clubs inevitable.

NOTES

1. *Northern Echo*, 4th May 1894.
2. Portions of this chapter were originally published as "A Noble Game Became Degraded: The rise and fall of professional football in Middlesbrough, 1889–1894," *North East History* 45 (2014), pp. 63–80.
3. T. Mason, *Association Football and English Society 1863–1915* (Brighton, 1981), p. 31; M. Taylor, *The Association Game: A history of British football* (Harlow, 2008), p. 39.
4. Mason, *Association Football*, p. 33; Taylor, *The Association Game*, pp. 40–43.
5. M. Shearman, *Athletics and Football* (London, 1889), pp. 360–362.
6. A player was no longer an amateur if he received any remuneration above expenses; eligibility for cup games was dependent on residential or birth qualifications (players had to live within six miles of the club's headquarters); changing clubs during the season was banned without permission from the FA; and in-

volvement in the committees of clubs or associations by professionals was prohibited, A. Harvey, *Football: The first hundred years, the untold story* (Abingdon, 2005), pp. 216–217; Mason, *Association Football*, p. 74; Taylor, *The Association Game*, p. 50.

7. N. Carter, *The Football Manager: A history* (Abingdon, 2006), p. 11, p. 23.

8. Carter, *The Football Manager*, pp. 18–19; M. Taylor, *The Leaguers: The making of professional football in England, 1900–1939* (Liverpool, 2005), chapter 1 passim; Taylor, *The Association Game*, p. 65.

9. Quoted in Taylor, *The Association Game*, p. 67; W. Vamplew, *Pay Up and Play the Game: Professional sport in Britain, 1875–1914* (Cambridge, 1988), p. 63.

10. *North-Eastern Daily Gazette*, 1st May 1885.

11. *Cleveland News, Ayton, Broughton, Bilsdale, Hutton and Swainby Record, Yarm and Stokesley Advertiser* (hereafter *Cleveland News*), 17th January 1885; *North-Eastern Daily Gazette*, 1st May 1885.

12. *Cleveland News*, 31st January 1885.

13. *Cleveland News*, 22nd August 1885; *North-Eastern Daily Gazette*, 15th May 1885.

14. *Northern Review*, 4th December 1886; *South Durham & Cleveland Mercury*, 25th September 1886.

15. *Weekly Exchange*, 15th May 1886.

16. *Northern Echo*, 22nd November 1886; *Weekly Exchange*, 6th November 1886.

17. *Northern Review*, 2nd April, 14th May 1887.

18. *Northern Echo*, 14th May 1887.

19. In comparison, Aston Villa FC had 382 members in 1889 and Blackburn Rovers FC already had seven hundred members in 1881–1882—Mason, *Association Football*, p. 35, p. 213.

20. *Northern Echo*, 14th May 1887; *Weekly Exchange*, 21st May 1887.

21. The 1891 census records that he was a marine engineer.

22. 1891 census; *Northern Review*, 3rd, 10th September, 22nd October 1887.

23. *Northern Review*, 5th November 1887.

24. *Northern Echo*, 28th November 1887; *Northern Review*, 26th November 1887.

25. *Northern Echo*, 5th December 1887; *Northern Review*, 3rd December 1887.

26. *Northern Review*, 14th January 1888; *South Durham & Cleveland Mercury*, 14th January 1888. Old Foresters complained about the pitch, and a replay was ordered though Old Foresters refused to travel north again to play the tie—*Northern Echo*, 14th, 16th, 21st January 1888.

27. *Northern Echo*, 4th February 1888; *South Durham & Cleveland Mercury*, 4th February 1888.

28. *Northern Echo*, 28th April 1888.

29. *Northern Review*, 14th April, 18th August 1888.

30. Quoted in Harvey, *Football: The first hundred years*, p. 218.

31. A. Budd, "Past Development in Rugby Football, and the Future of the Game," in Rev F. Marshall (ed.), *Football — The Rugby Union Game* (London, 1892), pp. 131–134.

32. Quoted in Carter, *The Football Manager*, p. 18.

33. R. Holt, *Sport and the British: A modern history* (Oxford, 1989), pp. 106–107; M. Huggins, *The Victorians and Sport* (London, 2004), p. 65.

34. 'Rambler' openly stated that he was a member of the club on 5th February 1890.

35. *Northern Review*, 8th September 1888; Sunderland AFC had split over issues of professionalism early in 1888, resulting in the formation of Sunderland Albion, and Newcastle West End (January) and Newcastle East End (June) both turned professional in 1889—see P. Joannou and A. Candlish, *Pioneers of the North: The origins and development of football in north-east England & Tyneside, 1870–93* (Derby, 1993).

36. *Northern Review*, 20th October 1888.

37. In 1903, among the members of the FA Council there were seven schoolmasters, five accountants, and five journalists. Likewise, those that ran the Cleveland Association were also middle class. In 1889 the president and one of the vice-presidents were solicitors (William L. Carrick and Albert Borrie), and in 1887 the Earl of Zetland was chosen as honorary president—1891 census; *North-Eastern Daily Gazette*, 6th May 1887; *Northern Echo*, 29th May 1889.

38. *Northern Review*, 8th December 1888.

39. *Northern Review*, 2nd, 9th February 1889.

40. *North-Eastern Daily Gazette*, 31st January 1889.

41. *North-Eastern Daily Gazette*, 2nd February 1889.

42. *North-Eastern Daily Gazette*, 7th February 1889.

43. *North-Eastern Daily Gazette*, 13th February 1889.

44. *Northern Echo*, 25th March 1889.

45. *North-Eastern Weekly Gazette*, 27th April, 18th May 1889.

46. *North-Eastern Weekly Gazette*, 18th May 1889; *Northern Echo*, 15th May 1889; *Northern Review*, 18th May 1889.

47. E. G. Ravenstein, 'The Laws of Migration," *Journal of Royal Statistical Society* XLVIII (1885), p. 216.

48. *North-Eastern Weekly Gazette*, 18th May 1889.

49. *Northern Review*, 18th May 1889.

50. *Northern Echo*, 29th May 1889; The "inchoate regulations" refers to the relaxation of the birth and residency rules for professional footballers, which lead to an influx of players from Scotland—Harvey, *Football: The first hundred years*, p. 222; W. Vamplew, 'Playing for Pay: The earnings of professional sportsmen in England 1870–1914," in R. Cashman, and M. McKernan, (eds.), *Sport, Money, Morality and the Media* (Queensland, 1980), p. 118.

51. However, it is difficult to identify many of the players at this time, other than Thomas Bach and Thomas Cronshaw (teacher)—1891 census; *Northern Review*, 2nd February 1889.

52. *Northern Review*, 31st August 1889; The committee was evidently not afraid of spending more money, as further general improvements were made at the club. The *Northern Review* reported that the players were to be lent their own "football costumes, including shirts, knickers and kickers." The ground had been fitted with washbasins and toilets, with "gas fires, easy chairs, spittoons etc to follow"—*Northern Review*, 14th September 1889.

53. *Northern Review*, 21st September 1889.

54. *North-Eastern Weekly Gazette*, 5th October 1889; *Northern Echo*, 3rd October 1889; *Northern Review*, 30th September 1889.

55. Copeland, Cronshaw, Dennis, Hopewell, Taylor and Wilson.

56. *North-Eastern Daily Gazette*, 3rd October 1889; *Northern Echo*, 3rd October 1889.

57. *Northern Echo*, 5th October 1889.

58. *Athletic News*, 7th, 14th October 1889.

59. *Northern Review*, 5th October 1889.

60. *North-Eastern Weekly Gazette*, 5th October 1889.

61. *North-Eastern Weekly Gazette*, 19th October 1889; *Northern Echo*, 19th October 1889.

62. *North-Eastern Weekly Gazette*, 19th October 1889.

63. *North-Eastern Daily Gazette*, 24th October 1889; *North-Eastern Weekly Gazette*, 26th October 1889; *Northern Echo*, 26th October 1889; *South Durham & Cleveland Mercury*, 26th October 1889.

64. *Athletic News*, 28th October 1889.

65. *Northern Echo*, 26th October 1889.

66. *Northern Review*, 26th October 1889.

67. *North-Eastern Daily Gazette*, 25th October; *Northern Echo*, 26th, 28th October 1889.

68. *North-Eastern Daily Gazette*, 30th October 1889; *Northern Echo*, 30th October 1889; *South Durham & Cleveland Mercury*, 2nd November 1889; All those who became shareholders were to be admitted to the ground for free, with season tickets issued to nonshareholders for 5s; The *Northern Review* stated two years later that MacDonald had "promised to put 'washers' into the pockets of all who became shareholders of Ironopolis Limited." He was "so tickled by the expression, and the improbability of the promise being fulfilled, that he applied the term 'Washers' to the new club, and it stuck"—*Northern Review*, 17th October 1891.

69. Nevertheless the cost of a share represented at least two days' wages even for a skilled worker—N. Garnham and A. Jackson, "Who Invested in Victorian Football Clubs? The case of Newcastle-upon-Tyne," *Soccer and Society* 4, 1 (2003), p. 59.

70. *Athletic News*, 4th November 1889; *North-Eastern Weekly Gazette*, 2nd November 1889.

71. *Northern Echo*, 2nd November 1889.

72. *Northern Review*, 2nd November 1889.

73. The first choice of name for the club was "Middlesbrough Football Company Limited." Unsurprisingly this was objected to by the old club, and the name was changed. *North-Eastern Daily Gazette*, 1st November 1889; *Northern Review*, 16th November 1889.

74. Middlesbrough Ironopolis Football Company Limited, Memorandum of Association, BT 31/4608/30227, National Archives.

75. *North-Eastern Daily Gazette*, 5th, 9th, 16th November 1889; *South Durham & Cleveland Mercury*, 23rd November 1889.

76. Thomas and Richard Bach's brother Phil also went on to play for Middlesbrough, and their brother Frank became a director of Middlesbrough in 1892; *Athletic News*, 7th December 1889; *North-Eastern Weekly Gazette*, 7th December 1889.

77. Holt, *Sport and the British*, pp. 282–285.

78. Carter, *The Football Manager*, pp. 26–29; Mason, *Association Football*, p. 48.

79. Mason, _Association Football_, p. 49.

80. P. Dixon, N. Garnham and A. Jackson, "Shareholders and Shareholding: The case of the football company in late Victorian England," _Business History_ 46, 4 (2004), p. 513, p. 520; Dixon et al. only identified seventy of Ironopolis' shareholders, but this analysis has also used the club's Register of Members, which has enabled the identification of a far greater number of shareholders (221).

81. Dixon, Garnham and Jackson, "Shareholders and Shareholding," p. 514, p. 519.

82. 1891 census; Middlesbrough Ironopolis Football Company Limited, Memorandum of Association, BT 31/4608/30227, National Archives; Ironopolis Register of Members, U/S/1489, Teesside Archives.

83. 1891 census; Middlesbrough Ironopolis Football Company Limited, Memorandum of Association, BT 31/4608/30227, National Archives; Ironopolis Register of Members, U/S/1489, Teesside Archives.

84. 1891 census; Middlesbrough Ironopolis Football Company Limited, Memorandum of Association, BT 31/4608/30227, National Archives; Ironopolis Register of Members, U/S/1489, Teesside Archives.

85. Dixon, Garnham and Jackson, "Shareholders and Shareholding," p. 507; Garnham and Jackson," "Who Invested in Victorian Football Clubs?," p. 61.

86. Middlesbrough Ironopolis Football Company Limited, Memorandum of Association, BT 31/4608/30227, National Archives; Ironopolis Register of Members, U/S/1489, Teesside Archives. In addition to this list there are a further three directors mentioned at the club's meetings who cannot be identified on the shareholders register—Allan, G. Robinson and Parry.

87. _North-Eastern Daily Gazette_, 26th November 1889.

88. _Athletic News_, 25th November 1889; Middlesbrough's proposal to the Football Association for 5s for loss of wages was defeated by an overwhelming majority despite the "eloquence of Mr W. H. Thomas" at the meeting. The defeat of the proposal was felt to be inevitable, despite the fact that "the majority of [FA] members believe in it, and acknowledge it must become law eventually." It was felt though that Middlesbrough's resolution was "immature," perhaps because they had only recently begun to favor the payment of players themselves— _Athletic News_, 16th December 1889; _North-Eastern Weekly Gazette_, 14th December 1889; _Northern Review_, 14th December 1889.

89. _Northern Echo_, 30th November 1889; _Northern Review_, 30th November 1889.

90. _Athletic News_, 2nd, 9th December 1889; _Northern Review_, 7th December 1889; Members of the Ironopolis committee had reportedly been to Scotland "on a mission to secure professionals," as well as having made approaches to many Sunderland Albion players and to one from St Augustine's. Middlesbrough's committee also visited Scotland, "leaving no stone unturned in order to get the best talent that it is possible to obtain"—_North-Eastern Weekly Gazette_, 7th December 1889.

91. _North-Eastern Weekly Gazette_, 30th November 1889.

92. _Northern Echo_, 14th December 1889; The team was as follows (their previous club in parentheses)—G. Smart (Birtley), T. Anderson (Arthurlie), J. Mathew (Strathmore), J. A. Elliott (Arthurlie), R. F. Thompson (Arthurlie), W. Hopewell—captain (Middlesbrough), T. Cronshaw (Middlesbrough), J. McGregor (Strath-

more), T. J. Morrisey (Dundee Harp), J. Taylor (Middlesbrough), T. Seymour (Arthurlie).

93. *Northern Echo*, 16th December 1889.

94. *North-Eastern Weekly Gazette*, 21st December 1889.

95. *North-Eastern Weekly Gazette*, 14th December 1889.

96. *South Durham & Cleveland Mercury*, 30th November 1889.

97. *Athletic News*, 20th January 1889; *North-Eastern Weekly Gazette*, 4th January 1889.

98. *North-Eastern Weekly Gazette*, 15th February 1890; *South Durham & Cleveland Mercury*, 15th, 22nd February 1890.

99. *North-Eastern Weekly Gazette*, 22nd February 1890.

100. *Northern Review*, 15th February 1890.

101. *North-Eastern Daily Gazette*, 22nd February 1890; *North-Eastern Weekly Gazette*, 1st March 1890.

102. *North-Eastern Daily Gazette*, 8th March 1890; *Northern Echo*, 8th, 10th March 1890.

103. *Athletic News*, 10th February 1890; *Northern Echo*, 7th, 8th February 1890.

104. *Athletic News*, 17th March 1890; Matches were also arranged against Glasgow Celtic, Preston North End, Sheffield Wednesday and West Bromwich Albion—*North-Eastern Weekly Gazette*, 15th March 1890.

105. *Athletic News*, 31st March 1890; *Northern Echo*, 12th April 1890.

106. *Northern Review*, 26th April 1890. The charities to benefit from the game were the North Riding Infirmary and the North Ormesby Cottage Hospital.

107. *Athletic News*, 12th May 1890; *Northern Echo*, 7th May 1890; *Northern Review*, 17th May 1890.

108. *Northern Echo*, 28th April 1890; *Northern Review*, 15th February, 3rd May 1890.

109. *North-Eastern Weekly Gazette*, 17th May 1890.

110. *North-Eastern Daily Gazette*, 10th May 1890.

111. *North-Eastern Weekly Gazette*, 26th April, 24th May 1890; Fees were increased from 5s to 7s 6d for seniors, and for juniors and ladies the cost would be 5s for entrance to the field and stands, and 2s 6d to the field.

112. Middlesbrough FC had been in the Northern League since its inception in 1889.

113. *Athletic News*, 1st September 1890; *Northern Echo*, 12th August 1890; *Northern Review*, 30th August 1890.

114. *Athletic News*, 29th September 1890; *North-Eastern Daily Gazette*, 15th, 24th September 1890; *Northern Review*, 20th September 1890.

115. *North-Eastern Daily Gazette*, 26th September 1890; The grounds of the two clubs were around 10 minutes' walk apart.

116. *North-Eastern Weekly Gazette*, 8th November 1890; *Northern Echo*, 3rd, 8th November 1890; *Northern Review*, 1st, 8th November 1890.

117. *Athletic News*, 10th November 1890.

118. *Northern Echo*, 5th January 1891; *Northern Review*, 22nd November 1890, 24th January 1891.

119. *Northern Echo*, 19th January 1891; *Northern Review*, 24th January 1891.

120. *South Durham & Cleveland Mercury*, 4th April 1891.

121. *Northern Review*, 25th April, 9th May 1891.

122. *Athletic News*, 25th May 1891; *North-Eastern Daily Gazette*, 28th May 1891; *North-Eastern Weekly Gazette*, 30th May 1891; *Northern Echo*, 28th May 1891; It was also decided that a section of the covered stand would be reserved for which tickets would be £1 1s a year, or 10s 6d for ladies.

123. *Athletic News*, 22nd June 1891.

124. *North-Eastern Daily Gazette*, 23rd June 1891; *Northern Echo*, 16th, 24th June 189.

125. *Northern Echo*, 26th January 1892.

126. *Northern Review*, 6th, 13th February 1892.

127. 1891 census; *Northern Review*, 30th January 1892.

128. *South Durham & Cleveland Mercury*, 19th March 1892.

129. Minute Book of Middlesbrough Football & Athletic Company Limited (hereafter Minute Book of MFC), 14th March 1892.

130. *Athletic News*, 28th March 1892; *Northern Review*, 2nd April 1892; *South Durham & Cleveland Mercury*, 2nd April 1892.

131. *Northern Echo*, 19th April 1892.

132. *Northern Review*, 7th May 1892.

133. Minute Book of MFC, 25th, 25th April 1892.

134. Minute Book of MFC, 6th, 17th May.

135. *Athletic News*, 16th May 1892; *North-Eastern Daily Gazette*, 9th, 11th May 1892; *Northern Echo*, 14th May 1892; Applications were not made to join the new Second Division, Middlesbrough stating that "the class of clubs and the distance . . . [were] prohibitive"—*Northern Echo*, 21st May 1892; Taylor, *The Leaguers*, p. 7.

136. *North-Eastern Daily Gazette*, 18th May 1892; *Northern Echo*, 21st May 1892.

137. *Athletic News*, 13th June 1892; *Northern Echo*, 31st May 1892.

138. *North-Eastern Daily Gazette*, 31st May 1892; *Northern Echo*, 31st May 1892; *Northern Review*, 18th June 1892; Payment for the shares would be spread over the year with only 5s needed initially, and season tickets for shareholders would be priced at 2s 6d, "terms remarkable for ease and are such as every member can tackle."

139. 1891 census; *North-Eastern Daily Gazette*, 14th June 1892.

140. Minute Book of MFC, 24th October 1892; *Athletic News*, 17th October 1892.

141. *North-Eastern Daily Gazette*, 23rd November 1892.

142. Minute Book of MFC, 8th December 1892.

143. *Athletic News*, 23rd May 1892; *North-Eastern Daily Gazette*, 20th May 1892.

144. Minute Book of MFC, 7th March, 4th April, 13th June, 7th November 1892; Wages would appear to have been relatively high. In 1893 the average professional's wage was estimated at £3 a week and £2 a week in the close season, but it is also suggested that those playing in the Football League received 30s-40s a week—M. Taylor, "Beyond the Maximum Wage: The earnings of football professionals in England, 1900–39," *Soccer and Society* 2, 3 (2001), p. 103. Though we do not have directly comparable wages for workers in Middlesbrough, coal hewers and laborers in Durham were paid 30s and 22s 6d per week respectively in 1888—Mason, *Association Football*, p. 103.

145. Minute Book of MFC, 13th June, 1st July, 7th November 1892.

146. Minute Book of MFC, 13th June, 8th August 1892; The club's trainer, E. Stephenson, replaced Joseph Grierson, who, according to the minute book, had "failed to report back," and would be staying with Ironopolis (8th August 1892). The *North-Eastern Daily Gazette* had noted in 1890 that the standard of Ironopolis' play was "due to the indefatigable attention paid to the men's bodily welfare" by Grierson—24th September 1890. The 1891 census lists Grierson as a brass finisher.

147. Minute Book of MFC, 10th October 1892.

148. Minute Book of MFC, 4th, 16th November 1892.

149. Minute Book of MFC, 30th November 1892.

150. Minute Book of MFC, 28th February 1893.

151. *Northern Echo*, 20th, 26th August 1892; At their AGM, the shareholders were informed that their debt was due to "a most unfortunate and unforeseen combination of circumstances." For example in the Cleveland Cup they had played St Augustine's in a snowstorm resulting in a small gate with their half amounting to only 11s 8d. At the replay of this tie at the Paradise Ground, "their half of the gate barely covered the cost of cleaning the snow from the ground." More significantly the miners' strikes in Durham had coincided with a point in the season when the club had hoped to get good gates, and instead "had to admit hundreds of spectators free who under ordinary circumstances would have paid for admission." The strikes are not mentioned by Middlesbrough as having affected their attendances.

152. *Northern Review*, 8th October 1892.

153. *North-Eastern Daily Gazette*, 27th, 30th September 1892; *Northern Echo*, 28th, 30th September 1892.

154. *South Durham & Cleveland Mercury*, 10th December 1892.

155. Only six clubs competed in the Northern League in 1892–1893, therefore the title was won relatively early in the season when Ironopolis won nine of their ten League fixtures.

156. *Athletic News*, 20th February 1893; *Northern Echo*, 20th February 1893; *Northern Review*, 26th February 1893.

157. Minute Book of MFC, 27th, 28th February 1893.

158. Minute Book of MFC, 1st, 3rd, 13th March 1893; *Athletic News*, 6th, 13th March 1893; *North-Eastern Daily Gazette*, 3rd March 1893; *Northern Echo*, 4th, 7th March 1893.

159. Minute Book of MFC, 23rd March 1893; *North-Eastern Daily Gazette*, 24th March 1893; *Northern Review*, 11th, 25th March, 1st April 1893.

160. Minute Book of MFC, 4th August 1893; *Athletic News*, 29th May 1893; *North-Eastern Daily Gazette*, 26th May, 1st June 1893; *Northern Review*, 22nd July 1893.

161. *Athletic News*, 24th April, 8th, 22nd May 1893.

162. *Northern Review*, 3rd, 10th June 1893.

163. *Athletic News*, 21st August 1893; *North-Eastern Daily Gazette*, 14th August 1893; *Northern Review*, 5th, 19th August 1893; M. Taylor and J. Coyle, "The Election of Clubs to the Football League 1888–1939," *Sports Historian* 19, 2 (1999), p. 11.

164. *North-Eastern Daily Gazette*, 21st, 25th August 1893; *South Durham & Cleveland Mercury*, 16th September 1893.

165. *Northern Review*, 9th September 1893; *South Durham & Cleveland Mercury*, 9th September 1893.

166. On the local depression in shipbuilding, see *North-Eastern Daily Gazette*, 18th, 28th October 1893 where it was stated that three thousand people were in receipt of outdoor relief and that there had been an increase in inmates in the workhouse.

167. *Athletic News*, 4th, 11th December 1893; *Northern Review*, 4th, 25th November 9th, December 1893.

168. *South Durham & Cleveland Mercury*, 2nd, 9th December 1893.

169. *Athletic News*, 26th December 1893; *North-Eastern Daily Gazette*, 15th, 22nd December 1893.

170. *Athletic News*, 26th December 1893; *Northern Review*, 23rd December 1893.

171. *Athletic News*, 29th January 1894; *Northern Review*, 20th January 1894; *South Durham & Cleveland Mercury*, 27th January, 3rd February 1894.

172. B. Tabner, *Football Through the Turnstiles Again* (Harefield, 2002), pp. 93–96

173. *Northern Review*, 13th, 27th January 1894.

174. *Athletic News*, 26th February 1894; *North-Eastern Daily Gazette*, 17th February 1894; *South Durham & Cleveland Mercury*, 23rd February 1894.

175. *North-Eastern Daily Gazette*, 20th February 1894; *Northern Review*, 24th February, 10th March 1894.

176. *Athletic News*, 16th April 1894; *Northern Echo*, 28th, 30th April 1894.

177. *Northern Echo*, 2nd April 1894; *Northern Review*, 7th April 1894.

178. *Northern Echo*, 4th May 1894.

179. *North-Eastern Daily Gazette*, 31st May 1894; *Northern Review*, 26th May 1894.

180. *North-Eastern Daily Gazette*, 3rd May 1894; *Northern Echo*, 1st May 1894.

181. *North-Eastern Daily Gazette*, 11th May 1894.

182. *Athletic News*, 11th June 1894; *Northern Echo*, 30th May 1894; *Northern Review*, 19th May, 9th June 1894; The Football League told Ironopolis that "if at any time they should be in a strong position and apply for a place in the League, such application should be treated as favourably as possible"—S. Inglis, *League Football and the Men Who Made It* (London, 1988), p. 41.

183. *South Durham & Cleveland Mercury*, 17th August 1894.

184. *North-Eastern Daily Gazette*, 23rd April 1894.

185. *North-Eastern Daily Gazette*, 4th January 1894.

186. *North-Eastern Weekly Gazette*, 19th October 1889.

187. *Northern Review*, 9th December 1893.

188. *Northern Review*, 17th October 1891, 30th January 1892.

189. *North-Eastern Daily Gazette*, 31st May 1893.

190. *Northern Review*, 2nd November 1889.

191. *Northern Review*, 21st November 1891.

192. *Athletic News*, 5th November 1894.

FOUR

Amusement and Recreation

An Expanding Sporting Culture, 1885–1900

Despite the growth of both amateur and professional football as *the* spectator sport from the middle of the 1880s, other aspects of Middlesbrough's sporting culture continued to develop, embracing a wide variety of competitive and recreational sports.[1] Though none attracted the same sustained level of attention from either the public or the press as football, the number of sports clubs grew throughout this period, allowing for an increase in participation. Participants were largely drawn from the town's lower-middle and middle classes, and for those with free time and a disposable income, it was possible to be involved in a number of sports and clubs. For most working-class men and women, their only contact with sport was spectating at large events or attending sports days. This chapter examines the growth of a number of sports, outlining why some thrived, others declined, and some, such as baseball, proved to be passing trends. A number of clubs retained their exclusivity, and this chapter looks at how and why this was achieved. Moreover, by outlining the sheer number of clubs that were formed before the end of the nineteenth century, this chapter demonstrates the growing popularity of sport despite the difficulties faced by some clubs.

The development of sport in Middlesbrough was defined by the growth of clubs among the town's middle-class groups. As well as the precarious existence of those clubs that struggled to increase membership, other clubs, new and old, flourished. In outlining the reasons behind the proliferation of clubs, Clark points out that such organizations catered to "a growing plurality of interests," often driven by commercialism, competition, fashion, and specialization. Clark notes that religious and philanthropic organizations struggled to increase membership, while commercial, municipal, and voluntary clubs gathered support, and it was the latter that were the most successful in Middlesbrough. Furthermore, Gunn has suggested that the purpose of clubs was "to provide an arena for eating, drinking and socializing for middle class men," and Middlesbrough's clubs offered the chance for the migrant middle class to socialize together.[2] As Lowerson states, within urban and suburban settings, sports clubs assisted greatly in "delineating status and social achievement."[3]

THE EFFECT OF THE TOWN'S EXPANSION AND URBANIZATION

While many sports grew during this period, two factors affected the development of some clubs—the continued expansion of Middlesbrough and its industries, and the popularity of football. It was reported on a number of occasions that land occupied by sports clubs was required for building purposes. Despite the inevitable damaging effect this had on clubs (particularly financially), little opposition or complaint was reported in the local press; building and the expansion of business was unavoidable, being necessary to continue the town's progress. Yet as the town continued to grow, it became increasingly difficult for sports clubs to find available and affordable land on which to play. Middlesbrough Cricket Club was greatly affected by building plans. In August 1891 it was reported that the club would soon be required to leave their ground as the land was required for building. The *Northern Review*'s 'Rambler' wondered,

> Is it in vain to look to the Middlesbrough Owners for relief from dread that the thousands of pounds sunk, money spent, voluntary and paid labor, should be as nothing some day when the postman drops at the Secretary's door the six months notice to quit [the land].[4]

In November 1892 the club confirmed that they would have to leave their ground and the secretary (Albert Borrie) reported that "they had every reason to hope that the Middlesbrough Owners were prepared to render assistance in the matter," while the club's president assured members that the Owners would bear the cost of moving and had earmarked land for the club in the Grove Hill area.[5] The assumption that the Owners would assist suggests that they were relied upon to help the town in difficult times. The monetary assistance that was forthcoming from local elites may also indicate the importance accorded to the sport, and indicates a desire to see the sport flourish. 'Rambler' called on "every member, the gentry and tradesmen of the town" to offer their assistance in the face of the indifference of the committee,

> The average individual expects to get his amusement and recreation, not only free but without any bother on his part, and who takes on the burden doesn't trouble him in the least. He overlooks the fact that the word 'free' is

now an absurdity, somebody pays and generally not the people who gain the advantages. . . . It is time the apathy which exists was smashed, and the fur made to fly.[6]

The new ground was erected at Breckon Hill Road, a location that was thought to be "as good as can be expected" as it was fifteen minute's walk from the train station and the same distance from the arterial Linthorpe Road. The Middlesbrough Owners contributed £100 to the £400 costs. When this was announced to the club's members, Councillor John Mardon said he was sorry that "the employers of labor in Middlesbrough did not give that encouragement to sport that they might well do, but it was as little as the Middlesbrough Owners could do for a town out of which they had made so much money."[7] The *Northern Review* thought there would be little problem in raising the rest of the money as there were not only many who "derive much pleasure from reading the newspaper accounts" of cricket matches, but a much larger number who "in their youthful days, when the cares and ties of business were nonexistent [sic] . . . took part in many an exciting match, and who . . . still take a lively interest in the game."[8] This suggestion was borne out as within a few weeks, £123 6s had been promised in subscriptions. The *Northern Echo* listed some of the contributors to this fund, which included a number of industrialists and employers, including the ironmasters John Mills and Bernhard Samuelson. That the largest donation of £20 came from a Swedish ironmaster, John Gjers, suggests that concern for the club was not just centered on preventing the demise of a quintessentially English game, and that the club may have been ascribed a more important role in the community.[9]

As Middlesbrough Bowling Club also played at the cricket ground they were left without a green when the cricket club moved. Its secretary had asked the Middlesbrough Owners whether "they would be prepared to let the same or any portion" of the old cricket ground, or alternatively whether "they could offer us any other piece of land which would be suitable for making a bowling green." The secretary also made enquiries about two other pieces of land, but in the summer of 1895 the club played their games in Albert Park.[10] In October a subcommittee of the club visited a tennis ground in Linthorpe and the ground of Ironopolis FC to assess their suitability,[11] and in early 1896 it was agreed that the club would purchase land in Linthorpe. Subscriptions were increased from 5s to 10s to cover the costs, and a circular was sent to members to ask how many shares they were willing to purchase.[12] A ten-year lease was subsequently secured and the committee was authorized "to borrow all money necessary from the members of the club."[13]

When the formation of a sailing club was proposed in 1888, it was pointed out that there was an "entire lack of a suitable place to keep, or moor, small craft" on the river, and at the first dinner of the Tees Sailing Club in 1891 it was stated that "the great drawback which the club had to contend with was the want of a proper mooring place for their boats."[14] The lack of space on the river and the associated costs of building new premises was epitomized by the problems encountered by the Middlesbrough Amateur Boating Club. In 1897 the club was informed that Samuelson & Co ironworks (whose owner, Sir Bernhard Samuelson, was a vice-president of the club) required the land occupied by their boathouse in order to extend. That the club's boathouse was located among the town's industry was demonstrated by the *Cleveland News'* description of the location "with its clouds of smoke, mountains of slag, and bad access to the river."[15] In February 1898 a circular was issued informing the public of Samuleson's plans, stating that,

> The committee confidently hope that all the members, past and present, will realize the need of a combined effort to carry the club through this crisis in its history. . . . The club is free from debt, and it is therefore hoped that the extraordinary difficulty now presenting itself will be overcome. It is very desirable that such a healthy pastime as rowing should not be allowed to fall through in Middlesbrough.[16]

At a subsequent meeting of the club, it was reported that a new boathouse would cost £250. Raylton Dixon (the club's president) donated £20, John Livingstone & Sons £7 2s, £50 was promised to the club at the meeting and a further £65 subscribed at the AGM a month later. Dixon informed the club that he had met with Sir Joseph Pease (one of the Middlesbrough Owners) who was "very anxious in any way to help so good an institution."[17] The club decided to proceed with a site offered by Samuelsons further down the river, stating that they "either have to accept the site offered to them or wind up the club." However, they were informed a few months later that Samuelson's would not in fact require them to move for one or two years.[18] In July 1900, the club was given two month's notice to move, but they were still without a suitable site four months later. Their boats were initially moved to Craggs & Sons at Stockton and were then sold for £19, with the premises and fittings also sold for only £15 10s.[19]

Middlesbrough Rovers Rugby Club also struggled to find a permanent home. Some reports at the start of this period state that they played at the football club's Linthorpe Road ground, while it was also reported that they played at the Paradise Field, which, suffering from "dirty approaches and the unhealthy smells from the manure heaps," had deterred many from visiting the ground.[20] In late 1888 the *Northern Review*'s 'Rambler' announced that the club had died "of sheer inanition, after a lingering existence," and published a somewhat mocking notice on behalf of the club:

Wanted: By the members of the lately defunct Middlesbrough Rovers (Rugby) Club, something to do on Saturday afternoons. No honorable occupation refused, not even places in the best Association teams.[21]

There was no further mention of the club in the local press until November 1892, when it was reported that an "influential meeting of gentlemen" had been held for the purpose of forming Middlesbrough Rugby Club. Their new field on Marton Road was further out of Middlesbrough than they would have preferred (two miles from the center of the town) and was not served by public transport.[22] Though the club's second game was watched by "quite a fashionable party of spectators" and was kicked off by the mayor, a year later the club were required to find another field as the land was required for the new asylum. The role of the Owners is demonstrated again when the club's president (Dr. John Ellerton) reported in 1893 that the committee would "wait upon the Middlesbrough Owners and the Cricket Club with a view to obtain permission to play on the old cricket club ground."[23] In early 1894, the club was using a field in Linthorpe Village, and the *North-Eastern Daily Gazette* proclaimed that "interest in the rugby code at Middlesbrough has seen wonderful developments"; the number of spectators at one match being "a revelation to many of the older supporters of the game."[24] There was no further mention of the club until August 1900, when the *North-Eastern Daily Gazette* published a circular from Mr. A. Backhouse Fossick suggesting "the formation of a football club under Rugby Union Rules," which "would be welcomed by a number of old public school men and others who reside in the district."[25] Another effort was made to resurrect the game in 1912, when a game was arranged between a team from Middlesbrough and district and Hartlepool Rovers.[26] A further attempt was made a year later. A letter was published in the *Sports Gazette* which as in 1900, linked the game to public schools. It suggested that, "there must be sufficient 'Varsity, public school men, and other interested people in Middlesbrough" to warrant the formation of a new club. Despite this assertion, a club was not formed until 1920.[27]

The shortage of land and open spaces was demonstrated again on a number of other occasions. For example when discussions took place in 1890 about the possibility of building a cycle track, the North Ormesby & Middlesbrough Cycling Club stated that not only was such a venture too costly, but that there was no suitable land on which to build.[28] Six years later when Erimus Baseball Club was formed, they were forced to play their home matches in Haverton Hill (on the north side of the Tees in County Durham) "owing to the scarcity of suitable grounds in Middlesbrough."[29] Furthermore in the same year, Middlesbrough Baseball Club had no choice but to accept the "onerous, arbitrary and unfair" rental agreement with Middlesbrough FC to play their matches at the Linthorpe Road ground as there were so few suitable fields on which to play.[30]

THE EFFECT OF FOOTBALL

As well as having to contend with the difficulties of finding somewhere to play, both Middlesbrough Cricket Club and Middlesbrough Rovers Rugby Club partly attributed their demise to the popularity of football. By the mid-1890s rugby in the Northeast had been marginalized by the success of the region's football clubs.[31] Collins suggests that it was hoped that the increasing popularity of football among the working classes would "help reassert the social exclusivity of rugby," and the sport's exclusivity contributed to its lack of progress in Middlesbrough as the town's upper-middle class was not big enough to sustain a club.[32] It is indicative of Rover's problems and the popularity of football that their ground was taken over by Ironopolis Football Club. With games being played at the same time of year, it was difficult for rugby to compete with football given the growing number of football teams and leagues in Middlesbrough. Without a local rivalry to inject some excitement (as had proved important in the case of football with Middlesbrough's cup matches against Redcar), interest in Rovers continued the decline that had begun at the start of the decade. In April 1885, the *Northern Echo* reported on Rovers' game against Halifax Free Wanderers on the Linthorpe Road football ground, and pointed out that the attendance was "far short" of the two thousand spectators who had watched Middlesbrough FC play there the day before.[33] Though the club had once been "the embodiment of rugby greatness" in the area, they only had sixty-seven members, in comparison to Middlesbrough FC's 550, and despite "the gallant efforts of enthusiasts of the rugby game" rugby was "slowly dying out in Middlesbro.'"[34] Coupled with the difficulties in finding a field on which to play and the costs of moving grounds, it is hardly surprising that the club had disappeared by 1897.

Although cricket and football were played at different times of year, and were therefore not competing for the same spectators, it was becoming increasingly apparent that cricket could not compete with football in terms of enthusiasm among the sport's enthusiasts. Moreover, it was felt that cricket lacked the excitement of football (particularly the rivalry played out in the press between Middlesbrough and Ironopolis), to which spectators had become accustomed, and when the cricket season began in the summer, the sport on display did not hold their attention. It is this aspect, more than interest in football per se, that affected cricket's popularity. As Sandiford states, cricket's officials felt that the sport needed to be "buttressed and preserved in the face of rapid cultural and technological growth." Thus while football was blamed, cricket itself also needed to innovate. In 1885 the Cleveland & Teesside Cricket Association was formed as a means of rejuvenating local cricket. It was felt that the game "was at a very low ebb," and a cup competition was introduced in an attempt to emulate similar successes in football. It was hoped this would be the "means of causing a little excitement and infusing more interest into the game."[35] Neither the local Association nor the cup did much to help the fortunes of Middlesbrough's clubs. Although the *Northern Review* suggested that the Ironopolis Cricket Club in South Bank was notable for an "absence of backbone and stability in the club management,"[36] the *Daily Exchange* blamed the committee of Middlesbrough Cricket Club for their own misfortunes, and pointed out the necessity of "a revival of interest and revival of life" in the club. After all, cricket "should not be allowed to drop into the second place" behind football.[37] Football had "swallowed up all interest in other athletic games," but cricket was the "older, more scientific, the more national game." It was thought that if the members and committee "put their shoulders to the wheel, the slough of despond will soon be past."[38] The popularity of football was demonstrated in January 1889 when the cricket club arranged a football match on their field to take advantage of the influx of people in the town for the visit of the Prince and Princess of Wales. It attracted a crowd of seven thousand and gate receipts of £100.[39] The *Northern Review* commented that, "those of us who remember Middlesbrough cricket more than twenty years ago, can only sigh when we look at it now. In those days we had at Middlesbro' one of the best town elevens . . . the equal of most county teams."[40]

The cricket club could not compete with the football club when it came to attracting spectators. Nevertheless a gate of 900–1,000 for a cup tie in July 1890 was regarded as evidence that there was "a large number of people who take an interest in cricket, and who, if properly catered for, would follow the game in the same faithful manner as they do football." The spectators were described as "all vivacity and life, in marked contrast to the apathy and listlessness generally pervading the cricket fields of the district." The popularity of football in the town is further demonstrated by the comment made in the *North-Eastern Weekly Gazette* that the Middlesbrough cricket professional (George Millar) would become even more popular after he expressed a willingness to play for the football club.[41] At the end of 1890, a piece appeared in the *North-Eastern Weekly Gazette* asking whether innovations could be made to cricket to make it more exciting,

> Can the conditions under which the game is played be so varied as to render it more attractive and, therefore, more profitable to all concerned? Some

may say we don't want to see cricket played for profit . . . but still there is no reason why something should not be done to make the game more attractive. My impression is that the larger the number of spectators the more interest do the players take in the game.[42]

This demonstrated the recognition by some, that cricket was to be increasingly regarded as a business, and one which should pay more attention to its finances. Though Sandiford has stated that cricket's administrators resolutely refused to sell the game as a spectator sport in the way that those administering football had, there was a recognition of the possibility that cricket was in danger of being overtaken by football. The comparative lack of excitement at cricket matches was demonstrated by one contemporary writer who pointed out that spectators at matches often came to the ground "to pass away the time . . . solaced by tobacco and occasional 'half-pints,'" in a "drowsy and apathetic state."[43] Further efforts were made to encourage cricket in Middlesbrough with the formation of the Middlesbrough Park Cricket League in 1891, and the securing of a visit by the touring professional team the United All England Eleven in May 1891, led the *Northern Echo* to praise the cricket club in its "endeavors to resuscitate the interest of the Middlesbrough public in the noble game."[44] The novelty of a visit by a team of "lady cricketers" drew a crowd of 1,500 to Middlesbrough's cricket ground, the largest at the ground for some time, and it was suggested that "no doubt our local players would feel a twinge of envy at the greater attractive powers of the fair sex."[45]

SUCCESSFUL CLUBS AND FADS

Though Middlesbrough Cricket Club struggled, cricket was still favored by many "as the game least tainted by human foibles"; indeed the *Daily Exchange* described it as "the English national game *par excellence*."[46] There was no other game "so suitable to every rank and station in society, or in which representatives of every class can join."[47] This idea was reiterated by 'Rambler' in the *Northern Review*,

> Could anything be more restful for the toiler in our ironworks than a quiet afternoon at a cricket match. Would not the nerves and health of anxious iron-broker and harried masters be more readily soothed by an hour on the green field, chatting with friends over the incidents of the afternoon and the reminiscences of days when hits for six among themselves were not uncommon. What a delightful change it would be to driving along the unwilling spirit and flesh in the office or, among the more luxuriant, dawdling about the palatial club rooms of the town.[48]

Therefore the problems encountered by Middlesbrough Cricket Club need to be compared to the development of other cricket clubs, and should also be viewed alongside the failure of baseball to replace it as *the* summer sport (see below). In 1894 Newport Cricket Club reported an increase in membership and stated that on some Saturdays they had been able to field three separate teams, such was their popularity.[49] Furthermore, in 1896 the Teesside Cricket League claimed that "in no way has the interest in its doings diminished . . . for players and club have vied with each other in a friendly and amicable spirit to reach the goal of their ambition."[50]

Little information is given on most of the smaller clubs, and it is often difficult to identify the individuals involved. However, the available information suggests that many of these clubs, against whom Middlesbrough Cricket Club had to compete for cricket enthusiasts, benefited from the patronage of members of Middlesbrough's small establishment. This may explain why the town club could not manage to get the support they desired from the gentlemen and professionals of the district. In 1899 Middlesbrough's president (John Vernon Cooper) had suggested that "greater effort should be made to get people to join the club." It is evident that Cooper envisaged recruiting affluent members, as he suggested that if one or both of the secretaries joined him at the Royal Exchange "they might be able to get some 30 or 40 members to join the club."[51] A year later it was suggested again that a club official be appointed to "call upon gentleman and tradesman locally who should take an interest in the game, and in the club as an institution."[52] However, some of these gentlemen were already involved with other clubs. North Ormesby Cricket Club's president until 1896 was a Justice of the Peace and Lord of Ormesby Hall (James Stovin Pennyman), succeeded by his son, a barrister (James Worsley Pennyman).[53] Newport Cricket Club's president in 1898 was William Hanson, the managing director and partner of Newport Ironworks and president of the elite Cleveland Club.[54] Bolckow Vaughan & Co's Iron and Steel Works Cricket Club was formed in July 1898, with the works' general manager appointed president.[55] Tees Oil Works Cricket Club had the firm support of the works' owner, the councillor and former mayor Theophilius Phillips, who had purchased a field for his employees and their families in 1898 and "placed it at the disposal of the club free of rent or any other expense."[56]

The popularity of cycling also increased throughout the period; as Rubinstein has argued, it was "an ideal form of middle class self-expression" particularly for those who wanted to be at "the forefront of social behavior at a time when values were fast changing and active forms of recreation were becoming increasingly popular."[57] Beaven's assertion that the bicycle was a "symbol of a widespread sense of modernity"[58] can be applied in particular to Middlesbrough, a place that its leading citizens viewed as the epitome of modern Britain. The number of cycling clubs in existence meant that there were organizations to suit all aspects of the sport, from racing to recreational and social cycling, helping to sustain the sport's popularity. As 'Rambler' in the *Northern Review* remarked, "Who would not be [a] cyclist? To possess a steed that is swift but not hungary [sic]; to ride wherever roads lead and fancy listeth."[59] However, the price of bicycles still precluded many people from taking part. Advertisements in the *North-Eastern Daily Gazette* in 1889 listed bicycles for sale at Carlings from £2 to £4 10s, and a year later the same company's prices ranged from £1 to £17 10s. In 1896 the Teesside Cycle Corporation's prices ranged from £3 17s 6d to £8 10s for ladies' bicycles, and £4 15s to £10 for men's, and C. Duncan & Co's prices ranged from £6 10s to £30. Indeed Rubinstein stated that between 1895 and 1897 the best bicycles cost £30 or more. In contrast an advertisement in 1889 advertised the sale of bicycles for 2s 6d a week, suggesting that some of the town's less well-off individuals could purchase bicycles.[60]

A wide variety of cycling events and clubs were reported in the local press. In 1885 the North Ormesby Cycling Club held fifty-one outings, many of which were road races, and a year later the club held an up hill race of seven hundred yards, and a "very fast" five-miles road race for sixteen participants.[61] In 1887 three hundred spectators gathered to watch the finish of a race of the North Ormesby club, while in 1890 the *Northern Echo* reported on a race from Middlesbrough to Redcar to decide "the heavy-weight champion of Middlesbrough" (as the joint weight of the two cyclists was more than thirty stones).[62] By 1891 the North Ormesby & Middlesbrough Cycling Club had 110 members, but a year later the club reported that team racing had been a failure "owing to petty jealousy among the members," and that there had been a drop in membership due to the increased cost of subscriptions.[63] The Cleveland Temperance Cycling Corps was formed in March 1893 for "none but pledged abstainers" in Middlesbrough, Thornaby, and Redcar, with branches formed across the district.[64] The sheer number of cycling clubs in existence was demonstrated in 1892 when the *Northern Review* published the details of secretaries of twenty-six Teesside clubs (including eight in Middlesbrough and two in South Bank),[65] and the *South Durham & Cleveland Mercury* listed eleven Middlesbrough clubs taking part in that year's cycling parade.[66] The formation of new clubs was also reported, for example Middlesbrough Centenary Cycling Club in connection with the Wesleyan Centenary Chapel, and Middlesbrough Rovers Cycling Club, which was "to be composed of first-class artisans" (the club's first sub-captain was a machine printer, and the secretary was a plumber).[67] Many members of the Middlesbrough Wednesday Half-Holiday Cycling Club were shop assistants, and prizes were distributed to those who had attended the most club runs. As Rubinstein suggests, to the lower-middle classes, cycling offered "a blessed release from the tyranny and drudgery of daily life."[68]

Such was the increase in the number of cyclists in the town that an association was formed to "regulate all matters pertaining to cycling exclusive of sports and cycling club private business," and the National Cyclists' Union (NCU, established in 1878) formed the North Riding & South Durham Centre. Indeed *Cycling* commented that, "I cannot but think that for a town of its size Middlesbro' has the most cyclists. I never saw so many machines anywhere."[69] It had been the intention of Ironopolis FC to build a cycling track at their proposed new ground which would have added greatly to the club's income.[70] The *Northern Review* felt it was "a great joke" that a track would in fact be laid out by the Grangetown Athletic Club on the edge of Middlesbrough first, even if it was set to be "one of the finest in England."[71] Indeed, a year later the amateur sports day held at Grangetown attracted three thousand spectators and included the one-mile race of the local NCU and the team race for the North of England Centre Championship.[72]

Despite the large number of local races that were reported in the press, the *Northern Review*'s 'Rambler' suggested that "the racing world is so exceedingly shady that I cannot help feeling glad that racing, pot-hunting etc . . . are not the pursuits of our local cyclists." In the same publication 'Cyclist' disagreed, stating that the fifty miles competition of the North Ormesby & Middlesbrough Cycling Club was "a distinct feature of the year."[73] Furthermore, Bury and Hillier suggested that racing was "both amusing in itself and productive of great good to the general body of cyclists who care nothing about racing."[74] Further evidence of an interest in racing was demonstrated by the formation of the Cleveland Roads Club in January 1894 whose purpose was to develop long-distance riding—the qualification for membership was the ability to cycle one hundred miles in twelve hours. The club's captain, J. W. Pearson, broke the record for cycling from Middlesbrough to York and back in September of the same year. "Cyclist," writing in the *Falcon*, noted that other cyclists quickly tried to emulate Pearson's feat and hoped that it would "continue with that true spirit of sportsmanship which characterises the fin de ciecle [sic] cyclist."[75]

Cycling's ability to express notions of local identity was demonstrated by two races in 1895. A mile race between two cyclists from Middlesbrough and Ferryhill, County Durham, in July attracted "tremendous interest," the local winner being "carried shoulder high to the dressing tent" after his victory.[76] Three months later, a "vast amount of excitement and indignation" was said to be felt by local cyclists when it was discovered that a rider from Sunderland, Lee Huntley, was to be invited to Middlesbrough to beat the fifty miles record. It was reported that "with a view to the honour and prestige [of the town] being upheld" Jack Newton of the North Ormesby & Middlesbrough club was sought out. Even though he had apparently "been working all night, and was in bed . . . on the circumstances being explained he at once expressed his willingness to try his luck." Though Huntley had retired part way through the race, the *North-Eastern Daily Gazette* wrote that, "the greatest jubilation is evinced by local wheelmen at the way in which the Wearsider was vanquished."[77] The importance placed on this race is a further indication of the existence of northeast rivalries, and demonstrates that such rivalries could be played out in a variety of contexts.

In 1896 the Cleveland Roads Club ensured that their less energetic and nonracing members were still able to take part by introducing a road race of a limited distance. Though the club had claimed to be "second to none in the North of England, not only in catering for its members, but also for possessing several of the best riders in the district," by May the club had given up road racing with races to be held on the track instead.[78] The Cygnus Club was formed in 1900 for the purpose of "fostering racing and looking after the interests of wheelmen who are to be found on the track,"[79] but the increase in membership of Middlesbrough Cycling Club (formerly Rovers) in 1894 was attributed not to exciting races but to their premises now possessing billiard tables, a games room and refreshments.[80]

The appeal of cycling showed no signs of decreasing. 'Velo' in the *South Durham & Cleveland Mercury* argued that cycling was far from "a phase of fickle fashion" due to the freedom it gave to the cyclist; "as soon as one has learnt to ride one is entirely free and independent, and cycling can be enjoyed either with or without companions."[81] Such was the popularity of cycling in the town, that the *North-Eastern Weekly Gazette* proclaimed that, Middlesbrough could "boast of having . . . [a] vast army of devotees of the wheel who take an interest in racing."[82] By 1898 there were at least twenty-two cycling clubs in the town. A Cycle Agents' Association was formed and a cycle exhibition (including cycle polo and trick riding) was included at the Middlesbrough Trades Exhibition (an event which subsequently attracted around 20,000 visitors).[83] A demonstration of bicycle polo by an Anglo-American team at the Town Hall also proved popular. "To the most accomplished cyclist it is a revelation," wrote the *Middlesbrough & Stockton Evening Telegraph*, "and to the non-cycling fraternity it is little short of miraculous."[84]

That tennis was also very much in fashion in the mid-1880s was demonstrated by the decision of Middlesbrough Cricket Club in 1886 to introduce a tennis section as a means of raising money and increasing interest in the club. The *Northern Review* agreed with this move, stating that "if the club is to make ends meet, it must look out for other attractions to supplement cricket," and it was reported a year later that the club's two tennis courts were in use every evening.[85] Advertisements began to appear in the local press for tennis equipment, such as that for H. Pilcher, a hatter and hosier,[86] selling tennis shirts, trousers, and racquet cases, and Tom Imeson who sold boots and shoes was "ever ready to promote a popular game," and offered to give each member of Middlesbrough Tennis Club a racquet in order to be associated with the newly popular sport.[87] Matches were played every Saturday by most of the town's tennis clubs, and the Linthorpe Club held their own tournament in 1888, though it was described as "a social picnic with tennis thrown in." The game proved popular with those who had moved to the suburbs, away from the working-class center. As Lake suggests, clubs were often designed to foster a sense of rural life within an urban environment.[88] 'Milo' in the *Northern Echo* remarked that tennis was "flourishing" in Middlesbrough, there being a large number of new players, and 'Rambler' in the *Northern Review* suggested that,

> The game of tennis is rapidly enfolding the whole district in its manifold charms. Not only the young, but middle-aged and elderly folk are becoming its enthusiastic votaries. There are many unbelievers yet who deride and call tennis a ladies' game. I can only say to them: "Take a turn with the racquet," and if they don't feel foolish in five minutes, their case is hopeless. . . . It is one of the most healthy and social games ever invented.[89]

However, 'Rambler' doubted whether "the people who have leisure to devote to playing or watching throughout a three day's tournament, are sufficiently numerous in this district."[90] Indeed that the numbers of participants soon decreased would suggest that the town's small middle class did not have sufficient time, or the space in private gardens to sustain the sport. The cricket club decided to abandon its tennis section in 1890, and 'Rambler' stated that he had received no news of club fixtures, instead only hearing of "great jinks and high tea on the lawn every Saturday."[91] Very few reports of tennis matches in Middlesbrough appeared in the local press during the following decade, leading 'Rambler' to conclude that the "once-popular game is rapidly declining."[92]

Though in contrast baseball was aimed at the town's large working-class population, its popularity was also only short-lived. It was unable to find a place in the town's sporting landscape, despite the gap in the calendar left by cricket's wavering popularity. The sport had to win over a number of skeptics as well as those who disapproved of the American sport's attempt to take the place of the English game of cricket. In 1889 the prominent Middlesbrough industrialist Samuel Sadler spent three months in America and returned with "a profound admiration" for the sport.[93] A few months later, a meeting was called to discuss "the desirability of promoting the American game" in Middlesbrough. Sadler, "an ardent lover of outdoor sports," thought the game included "all the merits of cricket, and all the excitement, earnestness and energy and the go which had made football so popular in England." Newton Crane, the president of the English National Baseball League, stated that baseball was a "plucky, manly sport," and one that was ideally suited to Middlesbrough.[94] A circular was sent out to the secretaries of sports clubs to ascertain their interest, and following training from two visiting Edinburgh University students (from North America), baseball sides were formed in connection with football or cricket clubs in Bishop Auckland, Darlington, Eston, Middlesbrough, and South Stockton.[95]

'Rover' in the *North-Eastern Weekly Gazette* suggested that the sport would "take a fast hold upon the public" and that the "'leisure class' may have the game of cricket to themselves." The game would be attractive to the "Cleveland toilers," who, according to 'Rover,' "will welcome any legitimate excuse for tearing themselves away from the attraction of the public-house."[96] However, the first practice game only attracted around forty spectators, and the first exhibition match had a crowd of either two hundred or 1,500 depending on the newspaper report. Undeterred, 'Rover' stated that the game could be "fast and exciting, and there is every evidence of a thirst for a proper knowledge of the game amongst the masses."[97] Indicating the strength of local cricket, 'Forward' in the *Athletic News* suggested that cricketers were "so enamoured with their old love, the best of all games, that they will have none of it,"[98] but the *Northern Review*'s 'Rambler' thought that baseball was "more interesting than cricket," and all the game needed was the right men to organize it. When the team connected with Middlesbrough FC played their second match against St Augustine's of Darlington, it drew a crowd of only two hundred, but it was pointed out that this was still "ten times the muster at a good cricket match."[99] The Cleveland & South Durham Baseball Association was formed in June 1890 (a year before the formation of the National Baseball Association), and a cup and medals were offered for the following season.[100] A year later, a challenge cup was also given to the Association by the American sports goods manufacturer Albert Spalding, and Samuel Sadler promised medals to the winners.[101]

Attempts to popularize the sport were no doubt hampered by there being only three clubs in the local Association's competition (St Augustine's of Darlington, Eston, and Middlesbrough), and the Association's secretary said that "all they asked was that the game might be given a fair and unprejudiced trial by the public," rather than being dismissed immediately because it was an American game or rounder's with another name.[102] At the start of the 1892 season it was reported that Middlesbrough Baseball Club had hired a professional trainer, and it was proposed that matches would be played against professional teams from the Midlands would result in some "rattling games." The team was also requested to play exhibition games across the north of England to popularize the sport.[103] In August 1892 Middlesbrough beat Derby St Thomas's to win the English Baseball Cup in front of three thousand spectators at the Linthorpe Road ground. "There can scarcely now be any doubt," stated the *South Durham & Cleveland Mercury*, "as to the place which baseball is destined to occupy ere long in the race for popularity as a summer field sport in Middlesbrough."[104] Despite Middlesbrough's success, the local Association reported that fewer clubs had been formed than they had hoped for, but the "increasing enthusiasm of players and spectators, the increased gates and the . . . number of games played augured well for future success."[105]

However, baseball was in direct competition with cricket, a well-established sport, notwithstanding the assertion by the *Athletic News* that baseball suited the "Yankee-like enterprise and energy of Ironopolis."[106] A circular was issued in January 1894 reminding sports clubs that baseball "is calculated to materially improve all those who take part in athletics, but especially football players"; it was a "splendid means of keeping players together during the summer months," marking the game out as a rival to cricket.[107] *English Sports* stated that much baseball went unreported. A game that attracted more spectators "than all the cricket matches put together over a wide district," received little or no coverage.[108] New clubs were formed in Linthorpe and Grangetown, and in 1894 the Afco club was formed by the Anderston Foundry Company. A baseball team was also formed in connection with Ironopolis FC by Nathaniel Harrison[109] and Albert Easton,[110] with Dr. John Ellerton elected president. However, when the Middlesbrough and Ironopolis clubs met there was an "unexpectedly sparse attendance," given the rivalry that had existed between their namesake football clubs.[111] Middlesbrough failed to win either the local or national cup competition, and the *North-Eastern Daily Gazette* argued that, "considering the talented players at their disposal, the pioneer club can hardly be congratulated on the record for the season."[112]

Middlesbrough Football Club placed conditions on which the baseball club were able to rent the Linthorpe Road ground, and it is clear that baseball would have boosted the football club's income. Rent was £10 plus 10 percent of match receipts, and 5d a week was required for the services of the club's groundsman. In addition, the football club's directors were to be given free admission on all occasions. The baseball club were responsible for damages, and proper precautions had to be taken to preserve the condition of the turf. In November 1896, the baseball club requested a reduction in rent, but the football club would not accommodate them.[113]

The popularity of baseball rose gradually. In 1895 there were two divisions to the Cleveland & South Durham League,[114] and a game at

Stockton against Middlesbrough attracted a crowd of four thousand.[115] A match between Middlesbrough and the newly formed Erimus club was described as drawing "a most aristocratic assemblage," including the mayor, Sadler, and Doctors Ellerton, Longbotham, and Young.[116] Sadler's enthusiasm for the sport was in evidence again when he covered the costs of the medals for the winners of the Cleveland & South Durham league, donated two guineas to the Middlesbrough club, and provided medals to the best baseball teams in the country.[117] Middlesbrough reached the final of the national competition again in August 1897 but were beaten by Derby in front of four thousand spectators at the Baseball Ground.[118] A year later the club recorded a debt and due to the football club's stipulations, decided to look for another field. Joseph Wright (a member of the baseball club's committee) said, "I doubt whether we can go on this year," and suggested that the reason for baseball's apparent failure was that in Cleveland, they had "failed to attract a gentlemanly enough type of player." The available players, who were mostly footballers, were "unpunctual and unreliable" and therefore many patrons had withdrawn their support.[119] Bloyce suggests that there was a belief that there were already many sports to choose from in England, whilst some contemporaries regarded baseball as inferior simply because it was not English. Importantly, some journalists and cricket supporters regarded baseball as a threat to the ultimate English summer sport, while others thought that baseball did not adhere to the amateur ideal.[120] Despite the assertion of the *Middlesbrough & Stockton Evening Telegraph* in 1897 that "baseball is not dying but looking quite alive," there was no further mention of the game until an attempted revival in 1906.[121]

EXCLUSIVITY AND CLASS

A number of sports or clubs remained socially exclusive throughout this period, with members of the town's middle class dominating as officials and participants. Morris's description of officials of voluntary organizations is mirrored by those running Middlesbrough's sports clubs. Morris states that club presidents were usually high-status local leaders, secretaries were often solicitors, and the treasurer was invariably a local banker or merchant. Such a structure was "the perfect compromise between middle class people striving for self-respect and independence, and the reality of hierarchical society." Gunn's assertion that social clubs could act as refuges from city life, "sealed off from private cares and duties," is also reflected in Middlesbrough's middle-class club culture, which allowed for distance between employers and employees.[122] Huggins has noted that sport played an important role in the formation of social relationships in increasingly urbanized environments, providing "a key source of friendship, fellowship and fraternal identity," particularly relevant to those Middlesbrough residents who were new to the town. That Middlesbrough's sports club provided a means by which the town's elite could play and watch together away from the working populace is supported by Huggins's suggestion that such clubs could actively avoid "any undignified opportunity of defeat by social inferiors."[123] Details of the following clubs demonstrate the dominance of Middlesbrough's small middle class in the town's sporting culture.

One of the best examples of the exclusivity of many of the town's clubs is the Middlesbrough Amateur Boating Club. The officials of the club in the late 1880s were upper-middle and middle class, including a shipbuilder and two ironmasters. A decade later, twelve members of the club's crew can be identified, and lower-middle- and middle-class occupations dominate. The inclusion of two individuals from Germany demonstrates the role of clubs in socializing newcomers into the community (see table 4.1).

The social events of this club often took precedence over rowing, and the cost of their annual ball demonstrates the money needed by members to participate. In 1895 tickets were priced at 12s 6d for a couple, 7s 6d for a single gentleman and 6s for a single lady.[124] In contrast, the boatman engaged by the club on a month's trial in 1896 was paid 6s a week, and his successor three months later was paid 8s a week.[125]

In contrast to the Boating Club and its events, Middlesbrough's first sailing regatta in 1888 was open to "yachts, cobles, pilot boats, foy boats and even sand wherries." It was attended by thousands of spectators and the *Northern Review* noted "the enthusiasm displayed, both amongst the owners of sailing craft and the general public." Unusually, the participants were from a variety of backgrounds. For example, the competitors in the trimmers' race (using shovels rather than oars) "came straight from their work, with faces begrimed with coal dust," and the event also allowed those to take part who would otherwise be banned from amateur rowing events as they made their living on the river. Seven of the competitors can be identified as working on the Tees—three pilots, a boatman, a toy boatman, a mariner, and a sailorman.[126] Entrance fees were also relatively low, 2s 6d, for the coble, toy, pilot, and pleasure boat races, with prizes of £3, £2 and £1.[127]

The players of the town's only rugby club were similar in background to the Boating Club's members. Indeed the vice-captain was also a rower. In the mid-1890s the playing membership of the re-formed club was firmly middle class, including a mechanical engineer, a stock and share broker, a member of the clergy, a doctor, an iron and ship broker, and the stepson of a steamship owner.[128]

Table 4.1. Middlesbrough Amateur Boating Club crew members, 1896[1]

	Occupation	Employment Status	Address (1901 census)	Place of birth	Servants
Alfred Burtt	Railway bridge engineer		4 Clarendon Terrace, Middlesbrough	Middlesbrough	1
Arthur Busby	Clerk	Worker	89 Church Street, Middlesbrough	Middlesbrough	None
James S. Crone	Stock and share broker	Employer	49 Newcomen Terrace, Coatham	North Ormesby, Middlesbrough	1
Frederick Drück	Foreign correspondent		62 Grange Road East, Middlesbrough	Germany	None (boarder)
Sidney Edward Geary	Clerk	Worker	2 Park Terrace, Linthorpe Road, Middlesbrough	Redcar, Yorkshire	None
Robert Hutton	Clerk	Worker	48 Oswald Terrace, Middlesbrough	Newbiggen, Northumberland	None
James Lithgow	Auctioneer	Worker	Knoll Villa, Thornfield Road, Middlesbrough	Middlesbrough	None
William J. McDonald	Cashier	Worker	Summerlee, Longlands Road, Middlesbrough	Middlesbrough	1
Otto R. Muller	Iron merchant	Employer	Strathellen, Saltburn	Germany	2
Arthur Newhouse	Draper's manager	Worker	45 Kensington Road, Middlesbrough	Middlesbrough	None
Ernest Newhouse[a]	Civil engineer			Middlesbrough	
Henry Winterschladen	Wine merchant	Worker	Rhine Lodge, Grove Hill, Middlesbrough[b]	Middlesbrough	

a 1901 census shows Ernest Newhouse as a visitor at 7 Addington Square, Margate

b 1891 census

1 1901 census; Northern Echo, 11th May 1896; for details of the club's officials (two of whom were also born in Germany) see Weekly Exchange, 2nd April 1887

The middle-class roots of tennis in Middlesbrough were demonstrated in one of the first descriptions of the game in the *Northern Review* in 1886, which reported on a tournament at the residence of "a wealthy legal gentleman," where the competitors in the final match were "a lawyer and a doctor versus a doctor and a genial friend."[129] Lake states that tennis became a popular game among the elite through exclusive clubs or the necessity of owning land if playing at home, as well as the growing popularity of Wimbledon in the social calendar; the sport became "an important vehicle for enhancing status." Indeed the place of tennis within the sporting culture of Middlesbrough's middle class was solidified as, as Lake points out, clubs enforced ever more rigid membership restrictions in order to retain their social exclusivity.[130] Competitors at a 1888 three-day tournament of the Middlesbrough Tennis Club included three doctors, two members of the clergy, a grease and oil manufacturer, an iron merchant, a solicitor, and the daughter of a shipbuilder, and involvement in an exclusive sport would indeed have enhanced their status.[131] Five of the six officials of the club can also be identified, all of whom were upper-middle and middle class—an ironmaster (Lawrence Farrar Gjers), a shipbuilder, a managing engineer, an under manager of a shipyard, and an iron merchant.[132]

The founders of the Middlesbrough Amateur Athletic Club included a merchant and three clerks, and the first vice-presidents included an ironmaster, a doctor, a chemical manufacturer and an MP.[133] The first officials of the Middlesbrough Amateur Cycling Club included more members of the lower-middle class, as well as professionals—two clerks, a solicitor, a chemist, a doctor, a fruiterer, a jeweler, and a steam-ship broker; in contrast, the sub-captain was a laborer.[134] In comparison, the North Ormesby & Middlesbrough Cycling Club had more of a cross-class composition. In 1896 the president was a cement merchant and vice-presidents included a doctor and a baker. A blast furnaceman was chosen as treasurer, the captain was a blacksmith, and his deputy was a steelworker.[135]

Few clubs were explicit in their desire to remain exclusive, but the president of North Ormesby Cricket Club, James Worsley Pennyman, stated that he wanted "to keep the club a high class concern." He claimed that, "In a place like N. O. [North Ormesby] clubs at times get into the hands of a second or third rate set of people, so that the whole thing might become low class and disreputable." The club was prohibited from providing alcohol or allowing gambling to take place on the field, which suggests that drink and betting were sometimes a part of Middlesbrough's sporting culture and that action needed to be taken against it. He made it clear that cricket was the only game the club was allowed to play on the ground, as football and running were "games that might become low class." He

Table 4.2. North Ormesby Cricket Club officials, 1897[1]

	Role	Occupation	Employment Status	Address (1901 census)	Place of birth	Servants
James Worsley Pennyman	President	Barrister and Lord of Ormesby Hall				
Alfred O. Cochrane	Vice-president	Ironmaster	Employer	Norton House, Coatham	Stourbridge, Worcestershire	7
Charles Essert	Secretary	Pipe molder	Worker	92 South Street, Whittington, Derbyshire	Normanby, Middlesbrough	None
William Knott	Vice-president	Doctor	Own account	Lodge, Southfield Grove, Middlesbrough	Wolverhampton, Staffordshire	3
William T. Lawson	Vice-president	Clerk in Holy Orders		Vicarage, Kings Road, North Ormesby, Middlesbrough	Isle of Man	2
William G. Pennyman	Vice-president	Clerk in Holy Orders		13 Cadogan Gardens, Chelsea, London	Ormesby, Middlesbrough	7
Lieut Col Samuel Sadler	Vice-president	Chemical manufacturer		Southlands, Preston-upon-Tees	Oldbury, Worcestershire	4
Thomas S. Stainthorpe	Vice-president	Nurseryman	Employer	Nursery Gardens, Ormesby, Middlesbrough	Carlton, Yorkshire	2
Matthew Thompson	Vice-president, captain, treasurer	Innkeeper	Own account	27 Smeaton Street, Middlesbrough	Sadberge, County Durham	1
Gabriel Vertigan	Committee	Laborer	Worker	10 Jubilee Street, North Ormesby, Middlesbrough	Sculthorpe, Norfolk	None
James Windross	Vice-president	Assistant overseer		Alnwick Holme, The Avenue, Middlesbrough	Middlesbrough	1

[1] Stephenson, Ormesby Urban District, p. 23; 1891 and 1901 census; North-Eastern Daily Gazette, 28th November 1895, 12th November 1897

Table 4.3. Middlesbrough Amateur Swimming Club officials, 1898[1]

	Role	Occupation	Employment Status	Address (1901 census)	Place of birth	Servants
Thomas Baker	Vice-president	Oil merchant	Employer	8 Glenholme Terrace	Hexham, Northumberland	None
John Vernon Cooper	Vice-president	Ironworks manager	Worker	Westbrook, Marton Road	Kent	1
Charles Ephgrave	Vice-president	Grocer	Out of employment	Ravenscroft, Roman Road	London	2
John Forbes	Vice-president	Baker and confectioner	Employer	20 Park Road North	Scotland	1
Richard Hawman[a]	Vice-president	Blast furnace engineer	Employed	94 Marton Road	Middlesbrough	None
James Keating	Committee	Engraver	Own account	131 Albert Road	Thirsk, Yorkshire	None
Alexander Main	Vice-president	Retired stationer		2 Pretoria Terrace	Whitby, Yorkshire	None (boarder)
John Mardon	Vice-president	Provision merchant's assistant	Worker	25 South Street	Ashburton, Devon	1
Alfred Mascall[b]	Vice-president	Watchmaker and jeweler		23 Linthorpe Road		
Charles Henry Newhouse	Treasurer	Draper's manager	Worker	Windsor House, Normanby	Middlesbrough	2
Theophilius Phillips	Vice-president	Oil manufacturer	Employer	Eglantine, The Crescent	Monmouthshire, Wales	3
Charles W. Sheppard	Vice-president	Bank manager		Hudworth House, Coatham	Salford, Lancashire	2

[a] 1891 census

[b] Details taken from *Kelly's Directory of North and East Ridings of Yorkshire, 1897* (London, 1897)

[1] 1901 census; *Middlesbrough & Stockton Evening Telegraph*, 25th January 1898; see also the officials of Middlesbrough Bowling Club, who included shopkeepers and members of the lower-middle and middle classes—Minute Book of Middlesbrough Bowling Club, 20th December 1897.

was insistent that the club maintain its reputation and that a clause be included in the lease stating that cricket was to be the only game played on the field—"As a great part of my object in letting the ground is to be able to exercise some pressure to keep things select, and as the omission of the provision I want might let in the very evil I am trying to guard against, I must have the clause in somehow."[136] Pennyman had become president of the club in 1896, and despite his statements the club's officials a year later were diverse in background, including an ironmaster and members of the lower-middle class as well as two working men (see table 4.2). In contrast, Middlesbrough Cricket Club's officials in 1889 included an ironmaster, an ironworks manager, a solicitor, an engineer and a bank manager.[137]

Many of those involved in the running of the Middlesbrough Amateur Swimming Club in 1898 can be identified. Their occupations were more varied than was the case for some clubs, though still lower-middle and middle class, and reflects the increasing visibility of the shopocracy in the town's sporting and civic culture (see table 4.3).

In contrast to many of Middlesbrough's clubs, in the early 1880s it would appear that quoits was played by men from a cross section of society. There was certainly involvement by the middle classes in the sport, as demonstrated by the presence of the mayor when Erimus played a match at Whitby in 1881. He traveled to the game "by his Worship's yacht" with some of the players and "a few friends."[138] Furthermore the president of the same club stated in 1895 that the club was one of "gentlemen" and "a happy family because there were no variances or differences between the members."[139] A number of players can be identified from the Eston and Erimus clubs, and there is a noticeable difference in the occupations of the participants, Eston having two innkeepers, five miners, and a laborer among their players,[140] while those of Erimus were lower-middle class, including two clerks, a marine inspector, a shoemaker, an earthenware manager, and a relieving officer.[141]

NONCOMPETITIVE AND RECREATIONAL SPORT

A number of clubs and sports existed that did not involve competitions or participation in leagues. Some were also often bound up with ideas of rational recreation, emphasizing the qualities that sport could instill in participants. Such clubs often had smaller memberships and were less popular, despite also holding public events. Though some members of the boating club took part in regattas, it is apparent that many members were not active rowers. At the club's AGM in March 1885 it was reported that very few members had participated at the Tees regatta the previous summer. Despite the notion that a regatta ought to be "a picnic with boating as a leading feature," members were informed that unless they took "a more active part in these annual races, the club cannot be expected to gain financially from them."[142] In 1885 the club had fifty-four members, but two years later this had dropped to fourteen, and the *Northern Review*'s 'Rambler' chastised the club for lack of activity. He sarcastically remarked that the club should be "proud, very, you ought to be, for mighty deeds have been done! What trophies of might and skill ye hold!"[143] However, a year later the same newspaper reported that the club had undertaken such a strict training regime that "the regulation pint of beer is the maximum any individual will allow himself to indulge in."[144] The 1891 joint regatta with the Stockton Amateur Boating Club (at which the two clubs intended to compete for the Ironmasters' and Tees Challenge Cups) was regarded as a failure. Stockton withdrew, the committee had failed to advertise the event, neither music nor a refreshment tent were provided, and subsequently "the attendance was not extensive."[145] In contrast, the committee paid a great deal of attention to the organization of its first ball, for which a number of meetings were called to discuss the "music, catering and style of invitation card."[146]

Many cyclists did not cycle competitively, participating instead as a means of recreation, as it offered "an agreeable amount of physical labor by those who otherwise led a sedentary life."[147] There was a distinct line drawn between those who raced and those who did not. The mass popularity of cycling meant that it no longer attracted gentlemen, and the racing element had a rather "unsavoury reputation" as new bicycles were faster and resulted in more competition.[148] In 1885 the *Cleveland News* suggested that the chief aim of the Middlesbrough Cycling Club ought to be to "get the members together for social rides into the country as frequently as possible"; track-riding and "pot-hunting" on the other hand, were to be avoided at all costs.[149] By 1891, Middlesbrough Rovers Cycling Club was the largest club in the town with 175 members. With their own premises (which unusually, were independent of a public house) they were regarded as "a proper social, as well as a cycling club."[150] Though there was a great deal of interest in cycle races, the *Falcon*'s 'Cyclist' stated that there were many who longed for the cycling club to return to their traditional ways of "the club ramble, the club tea, the club photo, the club ladies' day, or the other numerous club fixtures which, before the advent of the scorcher, were so popular." There was a "very large number of the wheel community . . . who care nothing for mere matters of speed."[151] The "scorcher," increasingly associated with young male riders, conflicted with the notion that cycling could act as a diversion from the perils of city life, gambling, and drink.[152] An advertisement for bicycles in the *North-Eastern Daily Gazette* informed readers that "health and cycling go hand in hand . . . the quickest and most economical and invigorating way of taking exercise is by cycling,"[153] and the secretary of the Middlesbrough YMCA Cycling Club stated that the club "was not organized for scorching, but to provide healthy recreation and instruction for the members." Similarly in 1893, a Fellowship of Cyclists was formed and among its aims were "to keep clear of scorchers and the rowdy element." The steep subscriptions of this club of £1 1s for the first year and £2 2s thereafter, meant that there was little chance that "rowdy," working-class cyclists could join.[154]

The Middlesbrough Amateur Athletic Club was formed in 1885 and two years later the club had their own premises including expensive gymnasium equipment for its eighty members. In 1888 a boys' class (twenty-five members) was formed, and a paid instructor appointed.[155] A harriers section was also formed, and sixteen members took part in the first run, who "presented a very smart appearance dressed in white knickerbockers and jackets," though the club had to concede a year later that the harriers "very seldom took runs."[156] In 1889 the secretary remarked that the club had "gone on steadily increasing year by year, but he was not yet satisfied with the position attained." He proposed that they should not only practice athletics "pure and simple," but also "proceed to that which would give free play to that hardness and muscular development that had been attained in the practice room."[157] A year later, the club had 155 senior members and 72 juniors, and classes were added for ladies and girls.[158] Classes comprised aspects of physical culture as well as aesthetically pleasing displays, as demonstrated by this description of an exhibition,

> The lady members took a prominent part in the programme, which opened with a "lantern maze" executed by members of all three sections, ladies, seniors and boys. The effect of the long sinuous lines of colored lights, whirling about apparently in inextricable confusion, but really forming geometric patterns, was very pretty, and evoked hearty applause. Dumb bell exercises by all three sections, fencing, sabre practice, boxing . . . quarterstaff, single stick, the flying rings and vaulting horse combine to make up a unique athletic performance.[159]

By 1896 the Athletics Club (now often known as Middlesbrough Gymnasium) was able to proclaim that "the keen interest and vigorous energy at present displayed by the members augured well for unprecedented success."[160]

By the 1880s, swimming was not only popular with the middle classes, but was also regarded as "an important element in the development of the masses' physical condition."[161] Indeed the *Daily Exchange* thought that the Middlesbrough Amateur Swimming Club offered "a most meritorious movement for the instruction of those who are unable and desirous of learning to swim."[162] Furthermore, a great number of public events meant that it also became popular for spectators. The *Weekly Exchange* reported on the opening night of the swimming club in March 1886 when the thirty club members demonstrated "ornamental and plain swimming," as well as a water polo match. The newspaper suggested that the club's instructor "will soon have as many pupils as he may reasonably be expected to wish for."[163] The club held its first gala in July at which "all available space was occupied," including a "fashionable company of spectators" in the higher priced seats (in an elevated gallery so as to be "out of reach of the splashing").[164] At the club's first dinner, the captain urged the members to make the club more successful and stated that,

> Middlesbrough was at one time a bright and shining luminary in the cricket world, while in the football field of today she stood in the fore front par excellence. With ordinary individual interest and effort, therefore, on the part of each member, there was nothing to stop their[s] becoming one of the best clubs in the country.[165]

The popularity of swimming events can be attributed to the location of baths in highly populated areas and to the attraction of the baths as a warm and comfortable setting. Furthermore, success was assured by holding events on weekday evenings, when swimming did not have to compete with weekend sports such as football.[166] A variety of events were held by the Amateur Club, some with an element of competition, and offered another form of entertainment for the paying public. In 1886 the manager of the baths, Joseph Weddell, gave "a most edifying and masterly exposition of swimming" including sleeping, walking, eating, and writing underwater. A year later a number of swimming events were held, including a contest between two amateurs (for £6 6s) of one mile, a half mile, and one hour "for the championship of Middlesbrough," and a gala of seven swimming and diving events.[167] The club held their first water polo match in 1886, and a separate committee was appointed two years later. A number of water polo matches were held in 1888, which were said to cause a great deal of excitement, there being "quite as much keenness exhibited over these events as is weekly the case over the football matches."[168] A contest for walking the greasy pole in fancy dress was included at the Amateur club's gala in 1889, the event being won by George Snow, who was dressed as "a fearsome crocodile." There were complaints, however, that another competitor was "dressed up in female attire" and "imparted an amount of vulgarity in his display which cannot be too severely condemned." In April 1892 the gala included a team race between Middlesbrough and Darlington, and an event in November included a replica shipwreck and a lifesaving demonstration.[169] In 1894 the club's gala, "in order to create a greater interest in swimming," included the amateur champion of England, J. H. Tyers.[170] The Middlesbrough

Police Swimming Club held their first gala in June 1896, and prizes were presented by Mayor Theophilius Phillips, who remarked that he was "glad to find that the members of the force, in addition to protecting life and property ashore, were qualifying themselves for similar noble services on the deep."[171] In 1899 the Seaman's Institute also held their first gala, including an exhibition of "fancy swimming" by 'Professor' Thomas Hatfield and his seven- and five-year-old sons.[172]

By 1890, membership of the Amateur club had increased to 120, plus twenty-six junior members, but the *Northern Review*'s 'Rambler' argued that the club "does not meet with the support it deserves" given that the population of the town was now almost eighty thousand.[173] In 1894 the members of the club were called upon to "place the many advantages of swimming before their friends in order that the membership might be increased," but two years later the club reported a decline in membership.[174] While in 1897 the secretary commented that some of the galas had "not been so satisfactory financially as could be wished," it was also reported that one thousand spectators had watched a swimming exhibition by Thomas Hatfield in "rough seas" at nearby Coatham.[175]

PROFESSIONALISM AND COMMERCIALISM

Apart from football, there was little professional sport in Middlesbrough during this period. Those professional contests that did take place were invariably accompanied by crowds of spectators, and the money at stake would have also have attracted gambling. Prizes were offered at a small number of footraces. On New Year's Day in 1885 a race of 120 yards for £5 contests, attracted "a capital entry and a good gate." The race's same promoters organized races over two weekends a month later for which the winner of the 120 yards received £5.[176] A race a year later drew a crowd of three hundred spectators and sixty-seven entrants, and another race for £15 a side between two local competitors was held in 1888. The prize money had increased to £30 the following year for a race watched by four hundred spectators.[177] Pedestrian races for prizes had not been reported in the local press for some time when the Butchers' Handicap was held in 1896, attracting a much larger crowd of two thousand and 125 entrants for a prize of £10 for first place.[178]

After the race involving Robert Boyd in 1882, professional rowing did not make any further inroads in to Middlesbrough's sporting culture. In 1886 a former world champion professional rower, the Canadian Edward Hanlan, came to Middlesbrough to visit Boyd (one of his former opponents). The *Daily Exchange* reported that thousands of people awaited his arrival and hoped that his visit would increase interest in rowing,

> It will not come amiss if his visit should revive an interest in local aquatics. It seems now that football is the sport that absorbs all interest. . . . North coun-trymen in the last generation were noted for their interest in aquatics. . . . It is a pleasant and agreeable pastime, and one which quite as much as any other affords excellent muscular training to its devotees.[179]

In the summer of 1897 it was reported that the rowing champion of New Zealand Charles Stephenson, had moved to the Shakespeare Inn in Middlesbrough (previously run by Boyd, who had died aged thirty-three in 1887). In an interview with the *Middlesbrough & Stockton Evening Telegraph* he said that he thought there was "a capital chance to start a professional club" in the town. He pointed out that there was "a lot of able-bodied, healthy lads about, a good river, and, with the support from the leading men, I do not see why we should not turn out a champion." He quickly organized a race between two local "crack oarsmen" and a keelboat handicap which produced a "capital entry."[180] A contest was arranged between Stephenson and William Albert Barry of London for £100 a side. There was reportedly a large gathering of people each time deposits were placed down at the Shakespeare Inn, and the race itself would no doubt have drawn a huge crowd. However, due to the small-pox epidemic, the race never took place as Barry refused to start his train-ing on Teesside.[181]

In marked contrast to much of the amateur sport in Middlesbrough, in October 1890 it was proposed that a horse race be established. The mile-long course was to be constructed at the Ayresome Grange Farm, to accommodate flat and hurdle races twice a year. The *South Durham & Cleveland Mercury* applauded the proposal, arguing that "no place would better support 'the sport of kings' than the busy capital of Cleveland."[182] Within a week of the suggestion, £200 had been guaranteed and it was proposed to form a limited liability company as all of the £5 shares had been immediately taken up. 'Rambler' suggested that a race meeting for Middlesbrough would put the town "on a level with our elder and more dignified neighbours," but in mid-November it was reported that the scheme had fallen through, as terms could not be agreed.[183]

THE CLEVELAND AND MIDDLESBROUGH ATHLETIC INSTITUTE—RATIONAL RECREATION IN ACTION?

Although the horse race would have involved money, professionalism, and a great deal of gambling, a few months later, an organization was formed that stood for quite the opposite. The short-lived Cleveland and Middlesbrough Athletic Institute endeavored to "raise the moral tone of football players and supporters." Its members would be able to "attain a higher social and moral position in life."[184] Proponents of rational recreation endeavored to create model citizens by reforming the leisure habits of the working class, using sport as "an instrument of social discipline." However, expanding towns and cities were perceived as obstacles for the middle-class initiatives that were designed to "improve popular leisure patterns." Beaven points out that the provision of rational alternatives was not enough; intervention in working-class leisure was necessary.[185] John Reed Jr. (secretary of the Cleveland Football Association and the Cleveland & Teesside Cricket Association) proposed the formation of the Institute. Making explicit reference to the behavior of the town's working classes and the desires of the town's leaders for a more decorous society, he suggested that individuals be elected to "control the conduct of the house . . . on the lines adopted at the large public schools of Rugby and Eton."[186] Furthermore, the Institute was to provide facilities to sports clubs that at present were only available at a public house, and bad language, gambling and intemperance would not be tolerated. The Cleveland FA and both of the town's football clubs would be able to hold their meetings there for a fee.[187] The proposal met with huge support in the local press. An editorial in the *North-Eastern Daily Gazette* stated that it would be "a great step in advance of the direction of moral reform" and would prevent cricket and football from being tainted by gambling. The *Northern Review* also hoped that such an establishment would "grapple with a pressing social question, how to clear the streets thronged nightly by football enthusiasts," and the *North-Eastern Weekly Gazette* thought the Institute would "do away with a great amount of the evil existing" in connection with football.[188]

The Institute was to provide dressing and recreation rooms for football, cricket, cycling, harriers, and other sports clubs, and would "divorce the connection that has grown up with hotels." Subscriptions would be low "so as to be within the means of those we wish to benefit." Donations were quickly promised by the mayor, the borough accountant, and Jordison's publishers among others. Reed informed the Cleveland FA that they could not "ignore their moral obligations to those placed in their charge," and they agreed to subscribe £15 a year; Middlesbrough FC also promised £10 a year.[189] 'Cyclist' in the *Northern Review* outlined the benefits of the Institute to cyclists, stating that it would have "a great many more advantages, which cannot be expected from the hotel or inn, and will conduce to the healthy recreation of the mind and body any time when cycling is impracticable." By early May 1891 more than £100 had been raised.[190] At the opening of the Institute in August the mayor stated that he thought, "it was well to free such institutions as football clubs from the influences of public houses because most of the members were young men, and were [easily] led astray."[191] Within two months the Institute had four hundred members. According to the *Northern Review*, it was a place where "you can combine amusement with instruction, and whilst passing a pleasant hour or two, make yourselves masters of an art which will be of value to you through life." That the Institute was more than somewhere for sports clubs to meet is evidenced by the educational, singing, and dramatic classes that were held and the inclusion of a library.[192] A "lads' club" was also established, teaching fretwork, joinery and athletic exercises for a subscription of 1s 6d. It was to take boys "away from that 'education of the streets' which in a town like Middlesbrough is always a most undesirable factor in a lad's life."[193]

However, the Institute did not receive as much support as had been hoped for from the town's smaller sports clubs. The committee decided to ask such clubs to hold their meetings in the Institute, while leaving the question of their subscription open. Efforts were also made to get individual cyclists who were not attached to a club to join.[194] In October 1892 the Institute's committee stated that it was with "deep reluctance [that] they feel compelled to ask their patrons to give help for another year." The *Northern Echo* suggested that, "the work done by the Institute is so worthily commendable that no doubt football patrons will give a ready response." However, with no further news on the progress of the Institute, the *Northern Review* reported in July 1893 that after less than two years in existence, it would be closing.[195] Given the difficulties already encountered by many clubs in raising money, the additional costs of holding meetings in the Institute no doubt proved too great.[196] It might also be assumed that it proved difficult to "divorce the connection that has grown up with hotels" as the Institute had hoped to do. Perhaps the idea that the relationship between pubs and sport was an unhealthy one was not a notion to which all local sportsmen subscribed.

SPORTS DAYS

Sports days flourished during this period, frequently attracting larger crowds and more members of Middlesbrough's elite than any other sporting events, demonstrating both an appetite for sport as well as for affordable entertainment. Such events also offered opportunities for people to take part in sporting activities who would not normally have had the opportunity to do so. Sports days offered an opportunity for a cross section of the community to enjoy sport together, and they were also "necessary to raise funds to carry on the proper functions of the club."[197] Financial returns varied. In 1889, Middlesbrough Cricket Club made £60 profit, and £87 profit in 1896, but only £32 a year later.[198] In comparison, North-Ormesby & Middlesbrough Cycling Club made a loss of £3 on their sports day in 1892 as the fifty-mile road race had "proved expensive," but in 1899 a profit of over £76 was recorded.[199] Sports days were held by a range of clubs and other organizations, and most events included the same foot and cycle races, as well as some more unusual contests. In 1885 the prizes at the sports of Middlesbrough High School were presented by the wife of Middlesbrough's MP Isaac Wilson, and as well as flat races included a pole-eaping handicap, a football dribbling race, and a sack race.[200] In 1888 the first sports day of Britannia Rovers Football Club included a stone-gathering race for children and a bicycle race for employees of Dorman Long & Co iron and steel works. The Tees Submarine Miners' sports day the following year included entirely different events such as a duck catching contest and connecting an electro-contact mine, and the sports of Middlesbrough FC included a tug day-of-war contest between seven works' teams and a horse leaping competition. The Middlesbrough Police Cricket Club's sports day in 1900 included a flat race for the sons of policemen and a skipping race for their daughters.[201] The joint athletic sports day of the North Ormesby & Middlesbrough Cycling Club and the Grangetown Athletic Club in 1898 included professional cyclists. The number of spectators was estimated at between 7,500 and nine thousand, and it was suggested that the profit be put towards either a "palatial club-house" or a "fund for ruining [the] Grangetown track by providing one at Middlesbrough."[202]

Attendances fluctuated at these events. Despite an attendance of three thousand spectators for the Grangetown sports day in June 1893, that of Ironopolis Cricket Club in August was small, as "the public are getting tired of sports week after week."[203] In comparison 1,032 passengers arrived by train alone for the sports day of North Ormesby & Middlesbrough Cycling Club in 1896, an event with two hundred entrants, and two years later the Grangetown sports day attracted 7,500 spectators, due to the increased popularity of cycling.[204] The joint event of the North Ormesby club and the Grangetown Athletic Club in 1899 had eight thousand to ten thousand spectators, with crowds of people unable to get into the grounds.[205] In 1900 the biggest cycling event to have been held in Middlesbrough took place, with the championship races of the NCU. The Grangetown track saw a record crowd of nine thousand–ten thousand for the eight races, both professional and amateur, though the *Northern Echo* was eager to point out that the amateur races were "intrinsically more popular."[206]

The success of such events led to a proliferation of betting and an increase in the number of professional competitors; according to the *Northern Review*'s "Rambler," "the genuine athletes who compete in a spirit of honourable emulation . . . [are] few and far between." Amateur sports days were now "a matter of business" where "the betting ring determines results."[207] Ironopolis FC's Highland Sports in 1890 were condemned by the *North-Eastern Weekly Gazette* for the presence of many "knights of the pencil," despite it having been stated beforehand that betting was prohibited. "Bets were made in tones loud enough to be heard anywhere on the ground," and as police were not present "the scum of race followers plied their nefarious practices . . . with impunity."[208] Sports days often involved a number of valuable prizes for both professional and amateur athletes, adding to the interest in the races. In 1890 the sports day of North Ormesby & Middlesbrough Cycling Club had prizes of £75, £50 worth of prizes were handed out at Middlesbrough Cricket Club's sports day, and the smaller Ironopolis Cricket Club sports day also had prizes totaling £10 for professional sprint races.[209] Six years later, the prizes of the North Ormesby & Middlesbrough Cycling Club ranged from a trophy worth fifteen guineas, to a kettle and a case of fruit spoons.[210] 'Rambler' argued that "but for amateur sports a large number who take part now would join the professional ranks, but not so long as *amateur* sports pay them better." The "true amateur who would be content to strive for honour alone," was becoming increasingly rare.[211]

WOMEN AND SPORT

Athleticism and femininity were deemed incompatible in the late Victorian period. As Parratt states, women's sport had to show the acceptance of "conservative notions of appropriately ladylike behaviour," and sport in general only served to reinforce the different roles of men and women. Women had to "project an image of moderation and becoming femininity, and her sporting experience was consequently . . . a liberating and constraining one."[212] Furthermore, competitive sport was incompatible with the "ideal" Victorian woman, with recreational sport being favored, though a *small* amount of physical fitness could also enhance femininity.[213] In addition, Holt has pointed out that some sports underlined the traditional view of women—outside of school, women's sports were "rooted in a new kind of suburban culture, centred around the family garden and the private club," and it was only in the affluent suburbs of larger cities that women's post-school sport flourished.[214]

There were very limited opportunities for women in Middlesbrough to partake in sport during this period, and those options that were available were not open to working-class women due to inevitable constraints of time, money, and space. One of the few sports that had female participants and in which men and women could play together was tennis. For female tennis players, the game was "a social asset providing training in graceful and charming movements."[215] While middle-class gentlemen could demonstrate their physical prowess and dexterity, women were able to emphasize their grace and carefree attitude toward competitive sport.[216] In May 1887 the tennis section of Middlesbrough Cricket Club had to provide an extra net to allow ladies to practice among themselves "until they get more adept at the game, when they will no doubt unblushingly join the males." The suburban Linthorpe Tennis Club also had a number of female members, though the *Northern Review* suggested that many of them only joined as a means of meeting "vivacious bachelors."[217] Female competitors at two tennis tournaments in 1887 and 1888 included two elementary school teachers, a university student, the daughter of an ironmaster, the daughter of a wine merchant, and two daughters of a shipbuilder.[218]

By the 1880s female swimming had become a physical activity that men not only tolerated, but one which they sometimes actively and publicly promoted, and many women felt that they could participate without fear of social stigma. Members of the medical profession were key supporters of female swimming; in fact swimming epitomized the "medically appropriate sportive exercise for the modern woman."[219] In September 1888 the *Northern Review* reported that with the approval of the town's doctors, thirty or forty ladies had applied to join the ladies' branch of the town's swimming club. At the club's gala a year later, two women competed in the ladies' race, the winner possessing "a powerful but graceful stroke."[220] There was evidently interest in swimming among a number of women, as the council's Sanitary Committee were required to extend the hours set aside for the club's private use of the baths to "give facilities to the gentler sex for acquiring the natatory art." Indeed by February 1891 the club had thirty-four female members, of whom eleven were juniors, increasing to forty-five members in 1894. One member proposed at a meeting of the club that they be given power to elect their own committee "to have full control of the ladies' section during the time set apart for their practice," including setting rules and organizing competitions.[221] The *Northern Review*'s 'Rambler' described it as "the old question of women's rights," suggesting that the ladies "came bravely (though perhaps with inward trembling and with a readiness to run away at the slightest provocation) to the meeting." Their involvement in the selection of the male members of the club reportedly led to the election of Henry Horseman as captain as he was "a young man and a bachelor," and of Thomas Brown, "a gay young bachelor," as deputy-captain.[222] The ladies gala in October 1891 drew a great deal of interest, the swimming baths being "crowded with ladies." The participants "betrayed none of that fear of the water usually shown by ladies." Some of the participants can be identified as the daughter of a shipyard manager, the daughter of a police officer, and the daughters of a butcher.[223] In contrast to the relatively sedate surroundings of the swimming baths, in 1890 the sailing regatta was brought to a close when Lilly Weddell, the six-year-old daughter of the swimming baths manager, swam across the Tees, being "heartily applauded for her plucky effort."[224]

In 1888 the Middlesbrough Amateur Athletic Club began a ladies' class, and three years later the Ladies' Athletic Club was formed "for the purpose of physical training." The *Northern Review* remarked that "the spirit in which they have taken up physical training will eventually tell very seriously." Within a few months there were fifty-eight members in the ladies' section and twenty-three in the girls' section, increasing to forty in 1894.[225] It is not possible to identify any of the female members of the ladies' section of the club, though the female officials were certainly middle class. The first president was Mercy Sadler (the wife of Samuel Sadler), Fanny Caddick (the wife of the Athletic Club's secretary, a cashier) was elected as secretary, and the wife of the ironmaster Lawrence Farrar Gjers was elected treasurer. In 1897, the vice presidents were the wives of a doctor and an ironmaster, though in contrast the captain of the girls' club can be identified as a dressmaker.[226]

Opinions were often expressed about the unsuitability of cycling for women. Of all sports, cycling attracting the most attention from doctors, it being described alternately as both producing and curing an array of disorders, and as having a deleterious effect on reproduction and childbirth.[227] In 1892 it was reported that the Middlesbrough Amateur Athletic Cycling Club had a number of female members, and the Middlesbrough Wednesday Half-Holiday Cycling Club enrolled its first female member in May 1896. A year later two female members were also elected to North Ormesby & Middlesbrough Cycling Club, and in 1899 the Middlesbrough Ladies Wednesday Club was formed.[228] In the same year, the secretary of Middlesbrough Rovers stated that the introduction of ladies to the club had been "one of the secrets of its success," and by 1900 the club was said to have the largest number of mixed members.[229] Advertisements appeared in the *North-Eastern Daily Gazette* for a "cycle riding school" where ladies would be "properly taught by experienced teachers."[230] McCrone argues that more than any other sport, cycling gave women "their most significant experience of physical exercise," and played a crucial role in breaking down conventions.[231] However, the number of female cyclists in Middlesbrough was small despite the assertion of the *South Durham & Cleveland Mercury* that cycling gave women "a freedom which they have never previously enjoyed. . . . It will make them freer and healthier, happier and less trammelled by the foolishness and restraints of fashion."[232]

CONCLUSION

Overall, Middlesbrough's sport continued to grow at the end of the nine-teenth century. Samuel Sadler stated in 1890 that "the happiness of the people was perhaps just as well encompassed by exercising their muscle and adding to their health," and this idea was adhered to by many members of the town's middle classes, as evidenced by the number of clubs in existence.[233] The diverse range of sports that were played meant that a variety of tastes could be catered for. Bowling, for example, was said to be ideal "for those who are a bit too heavy and stiff for football and cricket and it at the same time affords a trial of skill and patience," and there was no game like tennis "for exercising every muscle of the body."[234] New sports and those that were temporarily in vogue were eagerly taken up, some with more success than others. The popularity of tennis was short-lived, for example, but cycling rarely went out of fashion, there being a great number of clubs with varying levels of activity. The growing popularity of football, coupled with a lack of available outdoor space, meant that some clubs were prevented from expanding. Moving grounds necessitated an outlay of money that most clubs could not afford, and some clubs were perpetually raising funds to rebuild facilities. That such circumstances should have hindered the development of some sports at a time when sport in general was growing is an unfortunate consequence of Middlesbrough's growth. Some sports were not capable of attracting large memberships, and it is perhaps no coincidence that many of the less popular clubs were those of less competitive or recreational sports. The most successful cycling clubs in terms of membership, for example, were those that took part in racing. Furthermore, sports such as rowing and rugby only had one club, meaning a lack of competition and thus less excitement for spectators.

Middlesbrough's club culture offered opportunities for the town's elite to socialize with like-minded people, away from the lower classes, and allowed newcomers a chance to integrate in new surroundings. The most elite sports clubs acted as replacements for the long-standing traditional institutions that the town lacked. The middle-class makeup of the vast majority of sports clubs limited membership numbers, making it difficult for some to continue. Amateurism still dominated the sporting scene. Raylton Dixon, one of the founding members of the Boating Club, favored the sport as there was "less money making" in rowing.[235] The amateur ethos was further demonstrated, for example, by the Cleveland Roads Cycling Club when they handed out small prizes that would not lead to "training and undue preparation."[236] There were very few opportunities for workers to play sport, being excluded by subscription costs, a lack of free time, and the exclusive nature of many clubs. Spectator sports such as football, baseball, and the increasingly popular sports days were, for many, the only opportunities available.

NOTES

1. Portions of this chapter were originally published as "A sport for the 'Yankee-like enterprise and energy of Ironopolis': Baseball in late nineteenth century Middlesbrough," *Cleveland History*, 104 (2013), pp. 23–30.

2. P. Clark, *British Clubs and Societies 1580–1800* (Oxford, 2000), p. 470, p. 474; S. Gunn, *The Public Culture of the Victorian Middle Class: Ritual and authority and the English industrial city, 1840–1914* (Manchester, 2000), p. 84.

3. J. Lowerson, *Sport and the English Middle Classes 1870–1914* (Manchester, 1995), p. 96.

4. *Northern Review*, 1st August 1891, 16th April 1892.

5. *North-Eastern Daily Gazette*, 3rd November 1892; *Northern Echo*, 3rd November 1892; Polley argues that as the Owners were able to sell land as and when it suited them, they were able to control the extension of the town from the beginning—L. Polley, "Housing the Community, 1830–1914," in A. J. Pollard (ed.), *Middlesbrough: Town and Community 1830–1950* (Stroud, 1996), p. 161.

6. *Northern Review*, 29th April 1893.

7. *North-Eastern Daily Gazette*, 3rd October 1893; *Northern Review*, 5th August 1893.

8. *Northern Review*, 30th September 1893.

9. Other contributors included the owner of Normanby Hall (Charles Lionel Atkins Ward-Jackson), an iron merchant and steamship owner (Joseph Torbock), an ironworks manager (John Vernon Cooper) and a bank (J. Backhouse & Co) 1891 census; *Northern Echo*, 8th November 1893; By the time the new cricket ground was opened in June 1894, £300 had been subscribed to the club, *Northern Echo*, 4th June 1894; *Northern Review* 23rd June 1894.

10. Minute Book of Middlesbrough Bowling Club (hereafter Minute Book of MBC), undated entries for 1893; A green attendant was paid 1s per night for his services, and a subcommittee was formed to take charge of ground improvements—Minute Book of MBC, 19th, 30th June 1895.

11. Minute Book of MBC, 15th, 30th October 1895.

12. Minute Book of MBC, 10th February, 18th, 25th March 1896.

13. Minute Book of MBC, 31st August 1896; A tender was accepted for laying out the new green of £21 15s, and the total cost of the six rinks, pavilion and committee rooms was £160. In order to increase club funds it was decided to make a number of life members for £5 whilst a £50 overdraft was also arranged—*North-Eastern Daily Gazette*, 3rd August 1897; Minute Book of MBC, 30th November 1896, 8th September, 5th October 1897.

14. *Northern Echo*, 26th September 1891; *Northern Review*, 10th March 1888.

15. Minute Book of Middlesbrough Amateur Boating Club (hereafter Minute Book of MABC), 10th June 1897; *Cleveland News*, 28th March 1885; That the club would have to move so that Samuelson's could expand had first been reported

in 1876. The club raised £25 for a new boathouse but the depression in trade prevented the club from raising a larger amount, and Samuelson's allowed them to stay—*Daily Gazette*, 14th March 1876.

16. *Middlesbrough & Stockton Evening Telegraph*, 12th February 1898.

17. Minute Book of MABC, 21st February 1898; *Middlesbrough & Stockton Evening Telegraph*, 22nd February 1898; *North-Eastern Daily Gazette*, 22nd February, 31st March 1898.

18. Minute Book of MABC, 22nd September 1898 and an un-dated entry; Money was still put toward the building of a new boathouse, £25 of the £36 16s profit made from the club ball in December 1898 was donated, with a further £14 8s 5d handed over the following year, Minute Book of MABC, February 1899, 13th February 1900.

19. Minute Book of MABC, 2nd July, 2nd October, 1st November, 11th December 1900.

20. *Cleveland News*, 3rd October 1885; *Northern Echo*, 12th October 1885.

21. *Northern Review*, 10th, 24th November, 8th December 1888.

22. *North-Eastern Daily Gazette*, 5th November 1892.

23. *North-Eastern Daily Gazette*, 12th September 1893; *Northern Echo*, 7th, 28th November 1892; *South Durham & Cleveland Mercury*, 3rd December 1892.

24. *North-Eastern Daily Gazette*, 16th January 1894; Though the associated costs of moving again had left the club with a debt of £7, the club joined the newly formed Cleveland Rugby League which was due to begin the following season—*Northern Echo*, 23rd April 1894; *Northern Review*, 28th April 1894; *Middlesbrough Rugby Union Football Club Eightieth Anniversary 1872–1952* (Middlesbrough, 1952) p. 11.

25. *North-Eastern Daily Gazette*, 15th August 1900.

26. *Football Mail*, 20th April 1912; *North-Eastern Daily Gazette*, 17th April 1912.

27. *Sports Gazette*, 7th June 1913.

28. *Northern Review*, 8th November 1890.

29. *Northern Weekly Gazette*, 7th March 1896.

30. *North-Eastern Daily Gazette*, 10th April 1896.

31. T. Collins, *A Social History of English Rugby Union* (Abingdon, 2009), p. 44.

32. T. Collins, *Rugby's Great Split: Class, culture and the origins of rugby league football* (Abingdon, 2006), p. 32.

33. *Northern Echo*, 7th, 8th April 1885.

34. *Daily Exchange*, 5th March, 28th September 1886; *Northern Echo*, 18th August 1888; *Northern Review*, 12th November 1887; An application was made to join the Durham County Association, and having been turned down due to the club not being in Durham, it was suggested that they move to Port Clarence in order to be in the county, a move that the members voted against—*Northern Echo*, 18th August 1888.

35. *North-Eastern Daily Gazette*, 23rd April 1885; K. A. P. Sandiford, "Cricket and the Victorian Society," *Journal of Social History* 17, 2 (1983), p. 310.

36. *Daily Exchange*, 22nd January 1886; *Northern Review*, 2nd October 1886.

37. *Daily Exchange*, 29th October 1886.

38. *Daily Exchange*, 8th November 1886.

39. *Northern Echo*, 24th January 1889; *Northern Review*, 26th January 1889.

40. *Northern Review*, 1st September 1888.

41. *North-Eastern Daily Gazette*, 1st November 1890; *North-Eastern Weekly Gazette*, 9th August 1890; *Northern Review*, 12th July 1890.

42. *North-Eastern Weekly Gazette*, 22nd November 1890.

43. Anonymous, "Cricket and Cricketers," *Blackwood's Edinburgh Magazine* 151 (January 1892), pp. 105–105; Sandiford, "Cricket and the Victorian Society," p. 309.

44. *North-Eastern Daily Gazette*, 1st May 1891; *Northern Echo*, 21st April, 2nd June 1891.

45. *Northern Echo*, 11th August 1891.

46. *Daily Exchange*, 29th October 1886; Sandiford, "Cricket and the Victorian Society," pp. 304–306.

47. Anon, "The Popular Pastime—Cricket," *Blackwood's Edinburgh Magazine* 140 (December 1886), p. 763.

48. *Northern Review*, 29th June 1889.

49. *North-Eastern Daily Gazette*, 21st April 1894.

50. *North-Eastern Daily Gazette*, 14th November 1896; A few months later, the Middlesbrough Cricket League was also formed, initially only consisting of four teams: Tees Oil Works, Gilkes Street Primitive, Cambridge House, and Melbourne—*North-Eastern Daily Gazette*, 26th March 1897.

51. *Kelly's Directory of North and East Ridings of Yorkshire 1897* (London, 1897), p. 179; *Middlesbrough & Stockton Evening Telegraph*, 8th November 1899; *Northern Echo*, 8th November 1899.

52. *Middlesbrough & Stockton Morning Mail*, 8th November 1900.

53. P. Stephenson, *Ormesby Urban District* (Middlesbrough, 2003), pp. 22–23 .

54. *Kelly's Directory of North and East Ridings of Yorkshire, 1897*, p. 179; W. Lillie, *The History of Middlesbrough* (Middlesbrough, 1968), p. 99; *Middlesbrough & Stockton Evening Telegraph*, 3rd March 1898.

55. *Middlesbrough & Stockton Evening Telegraph*, 11th July 1898; The Bolckow Vaughan club replaced the now dissolved South Bank Ironopolis Cricket Club.

56. *Northern Echo*, 4th July 1899; *Northern Weekly Gazette*, 14th May 1898.

57. D. Rubinstein, "Cycling in the 1890s," *Victorian Studies* 21, 1 (1977), p. 59.

58. B. Beaven, *Leisure, Citizenship and Working-class Men in Britain, 1850–1945* (Manchester, 2005), p. 109.

59. *Northern Review*, 10th March 1888.

60. Rubinstein, "Cycling in the 1890s," p. 57; *North-Eastern Daily Gazette*, 26th April 1889, 17th May 1890, 6th July, 21st November 1896, 13th February 1897.

61. *Daily Exchange*, 6th January 1886; *Northern Echo*, 13th, 21st September 1886.

62. *Northern Echo*, 11th July 1887, 10th, 24th June 1890; The cyclists were the landlords of the County Hotel (Samuel Hargreaves) and the Black Lion (Anthony Angerer). 'Milo' suggested that Angerer "cannot lay claims to British origin" (the 1891 census shows that he was a British subject born in Salzburg, Austria), and that he was beaten proved that "Englishmen, in whatever pursuit they are engaged . . . are always a match for their friends across the Channel"—1891 census; *Northern Echo*, 24th June 1890.

63. R. Goodall, "Cycling in North Yorkshire and South Durham, 1869–1914," unpublished MA thesis, Teesside Polytechnic, 1988, pp. 128–130; R. Goodall, "Cycling Clubs of North Yorkshire and South Durham, 1876–1914," *Bulletin of the*

Cleveland and Teesside Local History Society 57 (Autumn 1989), p. 23; *North-Eastern Daily Gazette*, 3rd, 11th, 16th July 1891, 1st December 1892; *Northern Review*, 16th April 1892, 28th January 1893.

64. *North-Eastern Daily Gazette*, 29th March 1893.

65. *Northern Review*, 2nd April 1892.

66. North Ormesby & Middlesbrough, Middlesbrough Fire Brigade Cycling Corps, Middlesbrough Athletic, Middlesbrough Rovers, Middlesbrough Ironopolis, Middlesbrough Wanderers, Middlesbrough North-Eastern Steel Works, South Bank Cycling Club, Middlesbrough Britannia, Eastmans' Cleveland Cycling Club, Middlesbrough Shop Assistants, *South Durham & Cleveland Mercury*, 23rd July 1892.

67. 1891 census; *Northern Review*, 27th April, 18th May 1889, 12th, 19th July 1890.

68. Rubinstein, "Cycling in the 1890s" p. 60; *North-Eastern Daily Gazette*, 21st November 1895.

69. *Cycling* quoted in Goodall, "Cycling in North Yorkshire and South Durham," p. 40; *North-Eastern Daily Gazette*, 24th July, 17th October 1891.

70. *Northern Echo*, 4th September 1891; *Northern Review*, 1st August 1891; see chapter 2.

71. *North-Eastern Daily Gazette*, 3rd September 1892; *Northern Review*, 12th March, 3rd September 1892; the facilities at Grangetown comprised an eight-acre field, a running track, cricket field, and football pitch.

72. *Northern Echo*, 19th June 1893; The team race included cyclists from Liverpool, Manchester, Newcastle and the West Riding.

73. Goodall, "Cycling in North Yorkshire and South Durham," pp. 128–130; *Northern Review*, 27th May 1893; After 1881, a professional cyclist was defined as one who rode or taught for money, but there were also a number of competitors who were semi-sponsored by cycle manufacturers around whom there were rumors of results-fixing—Viscount Bury and G. Lacy Hillier, *Cycling* (London, 1891), p. 43; Lowerson, *Sport and the English Middle Classes*, pp. 166–167 .

74. Bury and Lacy Hillier, *Cycling*, p. 40.

75. *Athletic News*, 17th September 1894; *Falcon*, 21st September 1894; *North-Eastern Daily Gazette*, 18th January, 15th September 1894; Ten days later Pearson's record was broken by Samuel Wood, only to be bettered again in early October by Jim Ackroyd (of Middlesbrough Cycling Club)—*Falcon*, 5th October 1894; *North-Eastern Daily Gazette*, 26th September, 3rd October 1894.

76. *South Durham & Cleveland Mercury*, 5th July 1895.

77. *North Eastern Daily Gazette*, 7th October 1895.

78. *Middlesbrough & Stockton Evening Telegraph*, 18th January, 3rd May 1900; *North-Eastern Weekly Gazette*, 9th May 1896; The National Cyclists' Union had banned racing on public roads in 1895.

79. *Middlesbrough & Stockton Evening Telegraph*, 22nd March 1900.

80. *North-Eastern Daily Gazette*, 18th October 1894, 16th January 1896.

81. *South Durham & Cleveland Mercury*, 19th June 1896.

82. *North-Eastern Weekly Gazette*, 10th October 1896.

83. Middlesbrough Cycle, Motor Car and Accessories Exhibition, U/ML(3)8/18, Teesside Archives; Goodall, "Cycling Clubs of North Yorkshire and South Durham," p. 27; *Middlesbrough & Stockton Evening Telegraph*, 4th February 1898, 6th March 1899; *North-Eastern Daily Gazette*, 14th January, 8th November 1898.

84. *Middlesbrough & Stockton Evening Telegraph*, 27th, 29th April 1899; *South Durham & Cleveland Mercury*, 5th May 1899.

85. *Daily Exchange*, 5th November 1886; *Northern Review*, 13th November 1886, 21st May 1887.

86. *Bulmer's History, Topography and Directory of North Yorkshire 1890* (Ashton-on-Ribble, 1890).

87. *Northern Review*, 21st April, 16th June 1888.

88. *Northern Review*, 11th August 1888; R. J. Lake, *A Social History of Tennis in Britain* (Abingdon, 2015), p. 42.

89. *Northern Echo*, 28th May 1889; *Northern Review*, 8th, 22nd June 1889.

90. *Northern Review*, 27th July 1889.

91. *Northern Review*, 3rd May, 14th June 1890.

92. *Northern Review*, 19th August 1893.

93. *Northern Echo*, 3rd September 1889, 15th March 1890.

94. *North-Eastern Daily Gazette*, 26th March 1890; *Northern Echo*, 26th March 1890.

95. *North-Eastern Weekly Gazette*, 19th April 1890; *Northern Echo*, 17th April 1890; *South Durham & Cleveland Mercury*, 5th April 1890; Crane also intended to place professional American players in eight English towns (including Middlesbrough) who would select and train local players. A guide was distributed containing the rules of the game, a diagram of the field and a list of clubs in Yorkshire, Durham and Northumberland.

96. *North-Eastern Weekly Gazette*, 29th March, 19th April 1890.

97. *North-Eastern Weekly Gazette*, 26th April, 10th May 1890; *Northern Review*, 26th April 1890.

98. *Athletic News*, 26th May 1890.

99. *Northern Review*, 7th, 14th June 1890; *South Durham & Cleveland Mercury*, 28th June 1890.

100. *Northern Echo*, 20th June 1890; Sadler was elected president, and the mayor of Middlesbrough (Richard Scupham), mayor of Darlington (Joseph Albert Pease), and Dr. Francis Townsend from Eston were elected vice-presidents. Walter G. Roberts, architect and surveyor, was also elected honorary secretary and treasurer.

101. *North-Eastern Daily Gazette*, 11th April, 30th May 1891.

102. *Northern Echo*, 17th, 18th August, 5th November 1891.

103. *Northern Echo*, 16th July 1892; *Northern Review*, 28th May, 4th June 1892.

104. *Northern Echo*, 29th August 1892; *Northern Review*, 1st October 1892; *South Durham & Cleveland Mercury*, 3rd September 1892; *Sportsman*, 29th August 1892.

105. *Northern Review*, 5th November 1892.

106. *Athletic News*, 15th May 1893.

107. *Northern Echo*, 23rd January 1894; *Northern Review*, 27th January 1894.

108. Quoted in D. Bloyce, "'Just Not Cricket': Baseball in England, 1874–1900," *International Journal of the History of Sport* 14, 2 (1997), p. 213.

109. From the United States of America, brother of Richard C. Harrison, the captain of Middlesbrough Baseball Club.

110. Son of Ironopolis FC director, William Easton.

111. *North-Eastern Daily Gazette*, 31st March 1894; *Northern Echo*, 2nd, 29th May 1894.

112. *North-Eastern Daily Gazette*, 1st, 28th September 1894; The club was awarded the Dewar Trophy by the National Convention of Baseball Clubs in Great Britain however, for the best fielding averages, which it was suggested was "the most costly ever offered for competition in this country in connection with inter-club sport." The trophy was reportedly so large that it would not fit through any of the doors or windows of the club's headquarters—*North-Eastern Daily Gazette*, 26th, 27th February 1895.

113. Minute Book of Middlesbrough Football & Athletic Company Limited (hereafter Minute Book of MFC), 30th March, 9th November 1896; *North-Eastern Daily Gazette*, 10th April 1896.

114. The teams were—Division 1: Darlington, Middlesbrough, Stockton, Thornaby; Division 2: Cleveland Amateurs, Middlesbrough Victoria, Middlesbrough 2nd, Stockton Blythwood, Stockton Social, Stockton Vulcan, Stockton 2nd, Thornaby 2nd. In early 1896 a Northern Baseball League was formed comprised of the clubs in the Cleveland & South Durham Association and the Northumberland & North Durham Association. The teams chosen to participate were Clara Vale, Middlesbrough, Stockton, Thornaby, Walker and Wallsend, *North-Eastern Daily Gazette*, 27th March 1896; *Northern Echo*, 25th February, 9th March 1896.

115. *Northern Echo*, 15th July 1895.

116. *Northern Weekly Gazette*, 30th May 1896.

117. *North-Eastern Daily Gazette*, 12th October 1896, 8th April 1897; *Northern Echo*, 13th October 1896.

118. *Sportsman*, 30th August 1897.

119. *North-Eastern Daily Gazette*, 27th April 1897; *Sporting Life*, 9th April 1898.

120. Bloyce, "Just Not Cricket," pp. 214–215; *English Sport* stated in 1894 that "baseball had shrugged off its professional and somewhat overtly commercial status . . . and for the present, and it must be hoped for always, baseball must be kept on purely amateur lines"—quoted in D. Benning and D. Bloyce, "Baseball in Britain 1874–1914," in B. Svoboda and A. Rychtecky (eds.), *Physical Activity for Life: East and West, South and North: The Proceedings of 9th Biennial Conference of International Society for Comparative Physical Education and Sport at the Charles University, Faculty of Physical Education and Sport, Prague, Czech Republic* (Prague, 1995), p. 399.

121. *Middlesbrough & Stockton Evening Telegraph*, 18th May 1897.

122. Gunn, *The Public Culture of the Victorian Middle Class*, p. 92; R. J. Morris, "Clubs, Societies and Associations," in F. M. L. Thompson (ed.), *The Cambridge Social History of Britain 1750–1950* (Cambridge, 1990), p. 414.

123. M. Huggins, *The Victorians and Sport* (London, 20004), pp. 100–102.

124. Minute Book of MABC, 30th October 1895.

125. Minute Book of MABC, 27th March, 29th June 1896.

126. 1891 census; *Northern Echo*, 25th September 1888; *Northern Review*, 1st, 29th September 1888; *Northern Echo*, 25th September 1888; *North-Eastern Daily Gazette*, 25th September 1888.

127. *North-Eastern Daily Gazette*, 19th September 1888.

128. 1891 and 1901 census; *North-Eastern Daily Gazette*, 25th January 1895, 10th July 1896; For players in 1885, see *Cleveland News*, 3rd October 1885.

129. *Northern Review*, 2nd October 1886.

130. Lake, *A Social History of Tennis*, p. 51; R. J. Lake, "Social Class, Etiquette and Behavioural Restraint in British Lawn Tennis, 1870–1939," *International Journal of the History of Sport* 28, 6 (2011), pp. 880–881.

131. 1891 census; *Northern Echo*, 13th, 14th, 16th July 1888; *Northern Review*, 9th June, 21st, 28th July 1888.

132. *Northern Review*, 5th May 1888; See also Linthorpe Tennis Club, *South Durham & Cleveland Mercury*, 19th May 1888.

133. 1881 census; *Daily Exchange*, 16th November 1886; *Teesside Weekly Herald*, 17th November 1906; see also the professional and middle-class officials of the Middlesbrough Baseball Club—*North-Eastern Daily Gazette*, 8th April 1897, and the players of Middlesbrough Caledonian Curling Club which included an iron-master—*Northern Echo*, 9th, 10th, 12th January 1891.

134. 1891 census; *North-Eastern Daily Gazette*, 8th March 1889; *Northern Review*, 27th April 1889; See also the officials of Middlesbrough Cycling Club, which was dominated by doctors, *North-Eastern Daily Gazette*, 16th January 1896, and Middlesbrough Magpies Cycling Club, *North-Eastern Daily Gazette*, 28th February 1896.

135. 1901 census; *Kelly's Directory of North and East Ridings of Yorkshire, 1897*; *North-Eastern Daily Gazette*, 23rd December 1896.

136. Letters from J. W. Pennyman to W. Lawson and William Trevor, 29th August, 10th November 1899, 19th, 22nd January 1900, U/PEN 5/332 Teesside Archives; Pennyman did change his mind about the provision of alcohol as the club "might build a good pavilion and want perfectly proper lunches or dinner there." Similarly, a quoits club played their games on Middlesbrough FC's ground and their lease stated that no drink was to be sold on the premises, the club being reminded by Middlesbrough that they should be "conducted properly in the future"—Minute Book of MFC, 29th August 1892.

137. 1891 census; *Northern Review*, 9th November 1889, 8th November 1890; *South Durham & Cleveland Mercury*, 9th November 1889.

138. *North-Eastern Daily Gazette*, 23rd August 1881.

139. *South Durham & Cleveland Mercury*, 29th November 1895.

140. 1881 census; *North-Eastern Daily Gazette*, 13th July 1883.

141. 1881 census; *Daily Gazette*, 20th April 1881; *North-Eastern Daily Gazette*, 23rd August 1881, 13th July 1883.

142. *Cleveland News*, 28th March 1885; *Daily Exchange*, 24th March 1885.

143. *Northern Review*, 2nd July, 27th August, 17th September 1887; *Weekly Exchange*, 2nd April 1887.

144. *Northern Review*, 30th June, 28th July 1888.

145. *North-Eastern Weekly Gazette*, 13th April, 8th June 1889; *Northern Review*, 3rd August 1889.

146. Minute Book of MABC, 17th, 30th October 1895, 27th January 1896; *North-Eastern Daily Gazette*, 19th December 1895; twenty-eight guests attended the ball, which resulted in a profit of £10 for the club.

147. Rubinstein, "Cycling in the 1890s," p. 59.

148. D. Birley, *Land of Sport and Glory: Sport and British Society, 1887–1910* (Manchester, 1995), p. 78.

149. *Cleveland News*, 28th March 1885; Similarly, the Middlesbrough Amateur Cycling Club was formed in 1889 and their first week of six "journeys out" ranged from visits to Darlington and Croft (sixteen miles from Middlesbrough) to Stainton (five miles away)—*North-Eastern Daily Gazette*, 18th April 1889; *Northern Review*, 11th May 1889.

150. *Northern Review*, 25th July 1891.

151. *Falcon*, 2nd November 1894.

152. Beaven, *Leisure, Citizenship and Working-class Men*, p. 111.

153. *North-Eastern Daily Gazette*, 22nd March 1897.

154. *North-Eastern Daily Gazette*, 23rd February 1893, 7th March 1895.

155. *North-Eastern Daily Gazette*, 1st February 1888; *Northern Review*, 8th October 1887.

156. *North-Eastern Weekly Gazette*, 16th February 1889; *Northern Review*, 19th May, 2nd June 1888.

157. *North-Eastern Weekly Gazette*, 16th February 1889; *Northern Review*, 23rd February 1889.

158. *North-Eastern Daily Gazette*, 5th March 1891; *North-Eastern Weekly Gazette*, 25th July 1891; *Northern Review*, 21st March 1891.

159. *North-Eastern Daily Gazette*, 19th April 1892.

160. *North-Eastern Daily Gazette*, 11th February 1896.

161. C. Love, "Local Aquatic Empires: The municipal provision of swimming pools in England, 1828–1918" *International Journal of the History of Sport* 24, 5 (2007), p. 625.

162. *Daily Exchange*, 2nd February 1885.

163. *Weekly Exchange*, 6th March 1886.

164. *Daily Exchange*, 29th June 1886; *Weekly Exchange*, 17th July 1886.

165. *Northern Review*, 5th March 1887.

166. W. Hayes, "Sport as Spectacle: Swimming in Victorian and Edwardian Britain," *Cahiers Victoriens et Édouardiens* 59 (2004), p. 110.

167. *Daily Exchange*, 1st June 1887; *Northern Echo*, 7th June 1887; *Weekly Exchange*, 17th July 1886, 28th May 1887.

168. *North-Eastern Daily Gazette*, 24th February 1888; *North-Eastern Weekly Gazette*, 28th March 1891; *Northern Review*, 3rd, 10th March, 2nd June 1888; Water polo matches were reported between Middlesbrough Amateur Swimming Club and Stockton and North Ormesby, and a further contest was reported between Middlesbrough Football Club and Stockton Water Polo Club—*North-Eastern Daily Gazette*, 29th June, 10th June 1888; *Northern Review*, 4th August, 1st December 1888; A year later the North-Eastern Water Polo Association was formed, and a challenge cup was donated by its president Albert de Lande Long (of Dorman Long iron and steel manufacturers)—*North-Eastern Weekly Gazette*, 7th September 1889; *Northern Echo*, 28th February 1889.

169. *North-Eastern Daily Gazette*, 5th June 1889, 9th November 1892; *Northern Echo*, 6th April 1892; *Northern Review*, 8th June 1889.

170. *North-Eastern Daily Gazette*, 27th February 1894.

171. *North-Eastern Daily Gazette*, 2nd June 1896; *Northern Echo*, 2nd June 1896; After making his speech Phillips competed in a race of two lengths of the pool against the Borough Surveyor, in which "he scored a very easy victory."

172. *North-Eastern Daily Gazette*, 5th October 1899; Hatfield, the baths superintendent, was credited for "the manifestly increased interest" in swimming, and with reference to coaching his son Jack, was described as "the finest and most encouraging of all trainers"—*Northern Athlete*, 29th October 1906; *Sports Gazette*, 26th July 1913.

173. *North-Eastern Daily Gazette*, 28th February, 21st March 1890; *Northern Review*, 8th March 1890.

174. *North-Eastern Daily Gazette*, 27th February 1894; *Northern Echo*, 5th February 1896.

175. *Middlesbrough & Stockton Evening Telegraph*, 13th August 1897; *North-Eastern Daily Gazette*, 2nd February 1897; *Northern Echo*, 3rd February 1897.

176. *Daily Exchange*, 2nd January 1885; *Northern Echo*, 2nd, 9th February 1885.

177. *Daily Exchange*, 10th August 1886; *South Durham & Cleveland Mercury*, 11th February 1888, 31st August 1889.

178. The Butchers' Handicap had first been held in 1874—*North-Eastern Daily Gazette*, 4th April 1896; Similarly a race over a quarter of a mile was held in Grangetown in 1898 for £15 a side, between a local man and a Scottish employee of Cleveland Steelworks—*Middlesbrough & Stockton Evening Telegraph*, 28th May 1898.

179. *Daily Exchange*, 22nd November 1886; The interest this visit generated and the subsequent races Stephenson attempted to organize reflects Wigglesworth's assertion that popular professional rowers in the Northeast fostered a "cult of personality," and being regarded as local heroes, they often found "doors open to them at many levels in society"—N. Wigglesworth, *A Social History of English Rowing* (London, 1992), p. 81.

180. *Middlesbrough & Stockton Evening Telegraph*, 31st July 1897; *Middlesbrough & Stockton Sporting Telegraph*, 9th July 1897; *North-Eastern Daily Gazette*, 13th July, 3rd August 1897.

181. *Middlesbrough & Stockton Evening Telegraph*, 16th February, 18th April 1898; *North-Eastern Daily Gazette*, 29th January 1898; Stephenson had earlier challenged Hanlan to a race on the Tees for £100–£200 a side but this did not materialize—*Middlesbrough & Stockton Sporting Telegraph*, 30th November 1897.

182. *Northern Echo*, 29th October 1890; *South Durham & Cleveland Mercury*, 1st November 1890; The suggestion originated with W. Robinson ("a gentlemen well known in the district in connection with coursing"), Robert Robinson (a farmer at Ayresome), John A. Dent (a brewer's traveler) and William Lambert (landlord of the King's Head Hotel)—1891 census; *Northern Echo*, 29th October 1890.

183. *Northern Echo*, 5th November 1890; *Northern Review*, 8th November 1890; *South Durham & Cleveland Mercury*, 15th November 1890; The reference to Middlesbrough's elder neighbors, refers to Stockton where races had been held since 1855. One newspaper referred to the mid-August races as "unquestionably the most popular meeting with the masses that we have in the north"—*North Star* quoted in M. Huggins, "'Mingled Pleasure and Speculation': The survival of the enclosed racecourses on Teesside, 1855–1902," *British Journal of Sports History* 3, 2 (1986), p. 163.

184. *North-Eastern Daily Gazette*, 28th February 1891.

185. Beaven, *Leisure, Citizenship and Working-class Men*, p. 17, pp. 27–28.

186. *North-Eastern Daily Gazette*, 28th February 1891.

187. *North-Eastern Daily Gazette*, 28th February 1891; *Northern Review*, 28th February 1891.

188. *North-Eastern Daily Gazette*, 28th February 1891; *North-Eastern Weekly Gazette*, 7th March 1891; *Northern Review*, 7th March 1891.

189. Cleveland and Middlesbrough Athletic Institute Minute Book, undated entry, U/S/384 Teesside Archives (hereafter Minute Book of CMAI); *North-Eastern Daily Gazette*, 20th, 28th March 1891; *Northern Echo*, 7th March 1891; Ironopolis stated that they "did not at present see their way to joining the institute"—*North-Eastern Daily Gazette*, 20th March 1891; Clubs subscribing £10 or more would have the use of a committee room and a dressing room, and thirty of their members would be able to join at no further charge. Cycling clubs with fewer than fifty members would pay £3, while those with more than fifty members would pay £5. Clubs with membership of fewer than twenty would be charged 5s, under 50 members 10s, and more than fifty members 21s. All such clubs would have the use of committee and dressing rooms, *Northern Review*, 30th May 1891.

190. Minute Book of CMAI, undated entry; *North-Eastern Weekly Gazette*, 25th April 1891; *Northern Review*, 25th April, 9th May 1891.

191. *Northern Echo*, 1st September 1891.

192. Minute Book of CMAI, 27th August, 5th October, 26th November 1891; *Northern Review*, 5th September, 17th October 1891.

193. *Northern Echo*, 1st September 1891; *Northern Review*, 11th July 1891.

194. Minute Book of CMAI, 26th November, 18th December 1891; *Northern Review*, 27th February 1892.

195. *North-Eastern Daily Gazette*, 28th October 1892; *Northern Echo*, 29th October 1892; *Northern Review*, 22nd July 1893; Despite the failure of the Institute, in May 1892 a meeting was held to consider the possibility of purchasing either the cricket or football field and forming a united sports club. The meeting was attended by cricket, football, athletic, cycling, and baseball clubs, and it was decided that the Middlesbrough Owners should be asked to reserve sections of the cricket and football fields in order that an athletics association could be formed—*North-Eastern Daily Gazette*, 11th, 12th May 1892.

196. For example, Ironopolis FC, whose finances were rarely healthy, had already erected their own rooms for meetings which also provided a place for the players "wherein he may pass the long evenings free from tap-room dangers"—*Athletic News*, 29th September 1890; *North-Eastern Daily Gazette*, 24th September 1890.

197. *Northern Review*, 4th July 1891.

198. *North-Eastern Weekly Gazette*, 24th June 1889; *Northern Echo*, 4th November 1897.

199. *Middlesbrough & Stockton Evening Telegraph*, 21st January 1899; *North-Eastern Daily Gazette*, 1st December 1892.

200. Programme for the Athletic Sports (boys) 1885, S/M/H/3/32, Teesside Archives.

201. *Middlesbrough Morning Mail*, 5th September 1900; *North-Eastern Daily Gazette*, 15th October 1888; *North-Eastern Weekly Gazette*, 31st August 1889; *South*

Durham & Cleveland Mercury, 23rd August 1890; See also the sports of the friendly society of the Loyal Order of Ancient Shepherds in 1889, and the 1899 annual picnic of the employees of the Tees Oil Works—*North-Eastern Daily Gazette*, 8th July 1889; *Northern Echo*, 4th July 1899.

202. *Middlesbrough & Stockton Evening Telegraph*, 2nd, 5th July 1898; *Northern Weekly Gazette*, 9th July 1898.

203. *Northern Echo*, 19th June 1893.

204. *Northern Weekly Gazette*, 16th May 1896; *South Durham & Cleveland Mercury*, 22nd May 1896, 8th July 1898.

205. *Middlesbrough & Stockton Sporting Telegraph*, 26th June 1899; *South Durham & Cleveland Mercury*, 30th June 1899.

206. *Northern Echo*, 25th June 1900.

207. *Northern Review*, 29th June 1889.

208. *North-Eastern Daily Gazette*, 9th August 1890; *North-Eastern Weekly Gazette*, 23rd August 1890.

209. *North-Eastern Weekly Gazette*, 5th July 1890; *Northern Review*, 10th May 1890; *South Durham & Cleveland Mercury*, 23rd August 1890.

210. *North-Eastern Daily Gazette*, 15th May 1896.

211. *Northern Review*, 4th July 1891; A rather different complaint was made in the *Middlesbrough Morning Mail* in 1900 which stated that the prizes at amateur sports days were always the same, and therefore once a competitor had won a prize there was no motivation to try to win again, *Middlesbrough Morning Mail*, 25th October 1900.

212. C. M. Parratt, "Athletic 'Womanhood': Exploring sources for female sport in Victorian and Edwardian England," *Journal of Sport History* 16, 2 (1989), p. 143; Some sports were also thought to be physically damaging to women, inducing "womb irritation," "pelvic disturbances," and muscular or skeletal damage—K. E. McCrone, *Sport and the Physical Emancipation of English Women, 1870–1914* (London, 1988), p. 199.

213. C. Parker, "Swimming: The 'ideal' sport for nineteenth-century British women," *International Journal of the History of Sport* 27, 4 (2010), p. 679.

214. R. Holt, *Sport and the British: A Modern HIstory* (Oxford, 1989), p. 118, p. 130.

215. Holt, *Sport and the British*, p. 126.

216. Lake, *A Social History of Tennis*, p. 29.

217. *Northern Echo*, 9th May, 28th June 1887; *Northern Review*, 21st, 28th May, 2nd July, 3rd December 1887; Indeed in 1890, Wilberforce suggested that such doubles matches were "an excuse for garden-parties and a vehicle for conversation"—H. W. W. Wilberforce, "The Four-Handed or Double Game," in J. M. Heathcote and C. G. Heathcote, *Tennis* (London, 1890), p. 291.

218. 1891 census; *Northern Echo*, 17th September 1887, 14th July 1888.

219. P. Vertinsky, *The Eternally Wounded Woman: Women, doctors and exercise in the late nineteenth century* (Manchester, 1990), p. 82; Parker points out that the health benefits of swimming were often "spurious and wide-ranging," but they were firmly believed, despite a lack of medical evidence—Parker, "Swimming," p. 680.

220. *North-Eastern Weekly Gazette*, 1st June 1889; *Northern Echo*, 5th June 1889; *Northern Review*, 22nd September 1888.

221. *North-Eastern Daily Gazette*, 21st February 1893; *Northern Echo*, 28th June 1890, 18th February 1891.

222. *North-Eastern Weekly Gazette*, 14th March 1891; *Northern Review*, 21st February 1891.

223. 1891 census; *North-Eastern Daily Gazette*, 13th October 1891; *Northern Echo*, 14th October 1891; *Northern Review*, 17th October 1891.

224. *Northern Echo*, 4th August 1890.

225. *North-Eastern Daily Gazette*, 20th October 1891, 7th June 1894.

226. 1891 and 1901 census; *North-Eastern Daily Gazette*, 20th October 1891, 7th June 1894, 20th January 1897.

227. Birley, *Land of Sport and Glory*, p. 80; Holt, *Sport and the British*, p. 124; McCrone, *Sport and the Physical Emancipation of English Women*, p. 201; Vertinsky, *The Eternally Wounded Woman*, pp. 76–80.

228. *North-Eastern Daily Gazette*, 24th March 1897; *North-Eastern Weekly Gazette*, 2nd May 1896; *Northern Review*, 16th April 1892; *Northern Echo*, 28th April 1899.

229. *Northern Echo*, 2nd October 1899; 17th December 1900.

230. *North-Eastern Daily Gazette*, 21st November 1896.

231. McCrone, *Sport and the Physical Emancipation of English Women*, p. 177.

232. *South Durham & Cleveland Mercury*, 19th June 1896.

233. *North-Eastern Daily Gazette*, 26th March 1890; *Northern Echo*, 26th March 1890.

234. *Northern Review*, 22nd June 1889, 13th May 1893.

235. *North-Eastern Daily Gazette*, 20th April 1891; *Northern Echo*, 20th April 1891.

236. *North-Eastern Weekly Gazette*, 9th May 1896.

FIVE

"An Increasing and Often Unreasonable Demand for Pleasure"[1]

The Diversification of an Urban Sporting Culture, 1901–1914

By 1901 Middlesbrough's population had reached 91,302 and following the extension of the Borough, had increased to 126,452 by 1914.[2] In 1911, 45.4 percent of the population was still employed in manufacturing, and the working population continued to be affected by patterns of boom and slump in the town's heavy industry.[3] Furthermore, in the years before the First World War, Middlesbrough experienced three periods of acute depression—following the Boer War, 1908–1909 and 1911–1912, the latter proving particularly damaging. However, even though the town's economy did not return to the affluent days of the 1870s, in 1914 Middlesbrough was still manufacturing a quarter of Britain's iron and steel output. While in broad terms, working-class living standards in the town had continued to increase since 1870, the gap between the best and worst paid also increased, and living conditions barely improved; almost 13 percent of the population lived in overcrowded housing in 1911.[4] Nevertheless Middlesbrough's sporting culture continued to grow. For some sports, the patterns of development remained the same as in the last decades of the nineteenth century, and the middle, in particular the lower-middle classes, continued to be central in both administration and participation. While no other sport could compete with football in terms of popularity or crowds, it was also pointed out that "there is nothing for the working man to do on a Saturday afternoon in summer."[5] New games entered the sporting landscape, and older sports continued, sometimes with decreasing numbers of participants. Opportunities for participation increased through the growth of work-based clubs; employers became the most important providers of sporting facilities for the workingman.

THE RELATIONSHIP BETWEEN CLASS AND SPORT

Class was still the most important factor in determining an individual's access to sport. As in the nineteenth century, Middlesbrough's middle classes played a crucial role in the development of sport. A large proportion of clubs had little working-class involvement, and this section will examine the backgrounds of the members of some of Middlesbrough's clubs. Which clubs retained their exclusivity? Were some sports more accessible than others? Huggins's description of the motivations of various middle-class groups applies to the section of Middlesbrough's population that participated most in sport. Parts of the middle class emulated upper-class sports, others saw sport as an opportunity to promote muscular Christianity, while another section, perhaps most prevalent in Middlesbrough, were simply more "prone to the pursuit of pleasure and personal gratification in their sports."[6] The role of Middlesbrough's lower-middle class continued to grow during this period, and their involvement in clubs reflects a desire to achieve higher status and a more respectable place in society. It is increasingly evident that for the lower-middle classes in Middlesbrough, sport offered an opportunity for "social bonding," providing a means of addressing their "social ambiguity," allowing them to build relationships with clients and with each other. As is clearly shown to be the case in Middlesbrough, sport enabled local hierarchies to be "cemented, demonstrated and exploited."[7]

The Middlesbrough Amateur Boating Club retained its exclusivity and middle-class makeup after the turn of the century. The occupational backgrounds of the club officials in 1901 demonstrates that the club remained one of the more upper-middle and middle-class clubs in the town, as it had been since its formation in 1866 (see table 5.1). The occupations of forty-nine of the club's sixty-nine members for 1899–1901 can be identified and their backgrounds were similar to the club's officials (see appendix 2).[8] Twenty-nine of the members had domestic servants, and twelve were employers. Three of the members were councilors, two were MPs, one was a former MP, two were alderman, and five had been mayor of Middlesbrough.[9]

As had been the case at the end of the nineteenth century, the continued expansion of industry along the Tees meant that the club struggled to find land for their boathouse. Having been forced to leave Newport and sell their boats in November 1900, in June 1901 the club were notified that Samuelson's no longer required the land and would consider plans for a new boathouse.[10] There is no indication in the minute book of the club that members felt aggrieved at having to pay to build another boathouse on the site they had just left. Instead, they were encouraged to "devote the whole of their time to the coaching, instruction and encouragement of the new members."[11]

At the club's dinner in 1905 the mayor "expressed admiration for the true spirit of sport that inspired the members of a purely amateur organisation." The presence of the mayor, Sir Samuel Sadler, and "leading lights of finance, commerce, industry and education" at the dinner, demonstrates the standing of the club among Middlesbrough's elite.[12] The sport's exclusivity was evidenced by the remark by 'Old Bird' in the *Sports Gazette* that "outside the Universities, rowing is only known as a sport among a limited number of enthusiasts."[13] Few actual races took place, so those against Middlesbrough's only local rivals, the Tees Amateur Boating Club from Stockton, did provoke some interest. The contest for the Ironmasters' Challenge Cup in 1907 drew a large crowd, despite the "rather colourless and dull locality in which the boathouse is situated."[14] Three years later, the *Teesside Weekly Herald* remarked that the annual joint regatta of the two Teesside clubs had grown in popularity, as was reflected in the large number of entries for the races which "would have done credit to Durham or any of the more notable regattas."[15] In 1914 the club was still dominated by the town's middle class; members of the crew included an apprentice ship draftsman, an assistant manager of a steelworks, an engineer, a clerk, an assistant schoolmaster and a Presbyterian minister.[16]

With entrance fees and subscriptions of £1 1s for gentlemen and 10s 6d for ladies and men under the age of twenty-one,[17] from its inception in 1908 the Middlesbrough Golf Club also belonged to the middle classes. As *Golf Illustrated* stated, it was "not a poor man's game"; it was "an expensive game suitable only for the moneyed and leisured classes."[18] Indeed Hill states that there can be little doubt that golf was "a game in which class and status was a major consideration in every aspect of its organisation."[19] Lowerson also suggests that clubs were devices for "encouraging emulation" among those who were unable to join.[20] Such descriptions undoubtedly apply to Middlesbrough Golf Club. The first president was the ironmaster Arthur John Dorman, replaced a few weeks later by a barrister, John James Emerson, and the other officials were undoubtedly middle class, demonstrated by the mandatory subscription by the vice-presidents of £3 3s (see table 5.2).

Vamplew characterizes the relationship between golf clubs and professionals as "one of master and servant." He points out that for some professionals the sport "brought economic prosperity; for none of them did it bring social equality." As one contemporary stated, "the professional is so truly the servant of the game, and the distinction between him and his employer so clearly accepted, that he never forgets his position."[21] Claude

Table 5.1. Middlesbrough Amateur Boating Club officials, 1901[1]

	Role	Occupation	Employment Status	Address (1901 census)	Place of birth	Servants
Sir Raylton Dixon	President	Shipbuilder	Employer	Gunnergate Hall, Marton	Newcastle	13
Henry H. Allison	Secretary	Ship draftsman	Worker	8 Woodlands Terrace, Middlesbrough	Stockton, County Durham	None (boarder)
John Amos	Vice-president	Manager of Tees Conservancy	Worker	Witham Lodge, Yarm Road, Preston-on-Tees	Newcastle	2
Edward P. Brett	Captain	Bank clerk	Worker	15 St John's Terrace, Middlesbrough	York	None (boarder)
Robert Craggs	Deputy-lieutenant	Mechanical engineer	Worker	43 Newcomen Terrace, Coatham	Middlesbrough	1
James S. Crone	Committee	Stock and share broker	Employer	49 Newcomen Terrace, Coatham	North Ormesby, Middlesbrough	1
Albert de Lande Long	Vice-president	Ironmaster		Hyde Park Court Residential Hotel, London	Ipswich	2
Arthur J. Dorman[a]	Vice-president	Ironmaster				
Frederick Drück	Committee	Foreign correspondent		62 Grange Road East, Middlesbrough	Germany	None (boarder)
Lawrence Farrar Gjers[b]	Vice-president	Ironmaster		Woodlands Road, Middlesbrough		
Charles Leljevahl	Committee	Iron merchant's clerk	Worker	Westbourne Grove, North Ormesby, Middlesbrough	Sweden	None (lodger)

Name	Role	Occupation	Status	Address	Birthplace	
Robert Mascall	Vice-president	Mayor, retired slate merchant		Fernwood, Marton Road, Middlesbrough	Westmoreland	1
Charles Mildred	Committee	Iron and steel merchant's agent	Own account	135 Grange Road East, Middlesbrough	Middlesbrough	None
Arthur Newhouse	Committee	Draper's manager	Worker	45 Kensington Road, Middlesbrough	Middlesbrough	None
Claude Pease	Vice-president	Estate agent, Middlesbrough Owner		Cliff House, Marske	Darlington, County Durham	12
Thomas F. Ward	Vice-president	Director and manager of ironworks		Park Villas, Middlesbrough	Banbury, Oxfordshire	2
Frederick P. Wilson	Treasurer	Mechanical engineer	Worker	1 Southfield Villas, Middlesbrough	Middlesbrough	2
Carl Winterschladen	Committee	Analytical chemist	Worker	Rhine Lodge, Grove Hill, Middlesbrough	Middlesbrough	1

a Unable to locate on census

b Kelly's Directory of North and East Ridings of Yorkshire, 1897 (London, 1897)

1 1901 census; Minute Book of Middlesbrough Amateur Boating Club (hereafter Minute Book of MABC), 15th April 1901; North Star, 16th April 1901

Table 5.2. Middlesbrough Golf Club officials, 1908[1]

	Role	Occupation	Employment Status	Address (1911 census)	Place of birth	Servants
John James Emerson	President	Barrister		Easby Hall, Easby	Stokesley, Yorkshire	7
Thomas Smales Calvert	Captain	Accountant		The Avenue, Middlesbrough	Middlesbrough	None
John Hedley	Vice-president	Doctor	Own account	Cleveland Lodge, Grove Hill, Middlesbrough	Ovingham, Northumberland	6
Amos Hinton	Vice-president	Grocer	Employer	26 Park Road North, Middlesbrough	Middlesbrough	2
William Henry Hinton	Treasurer	Grocer	Employer	The Homestead, Grove Hill, Middlesbrough	Middlesbrough	2
Carl Jervelund[a]	Vice-president	Merchant, vice-consul for Denmark and Netherlands		Zetland Road, Middlesbrough	Denmark	
Edmund Heppel Mason	Vice-president	Watchmaker and jeweler		Eastbourne Road, Middlesbrough	Stokesley, Yorkshire	1
George Scoby-Smith	Vice-president	Commercial manager at Bolckow Vaughan	Worker	Roman Road, Middlesbrough	Middlesbrough	1
Thomas Dormand Stewart	Secretary	Clothier	Employer	Tyneholme House, The Crescent, Middlesbrough[b]	North Shields, Northumberland	

[a] *Kelly's Directory of North and East Ridings of Yorkshire, 1909* (London, 1909)
[b] *Kelly's Directory of North and East Ridings of Yorkshire, 1909;* Address on 1911 census—Kenworthy's Hydropathic Establishment, Southport, Lancashire
[1] 1911 census; Minute Book of MGC, 20th November, 14th December 1908, 22nd January 1909; See also the composition of the club's officials in 1911—Minute Book of Middlesbrough Golf Club, 16th February 1911; *Sports Gazette*, 18th February 1911

Weastell[22] was engaged as Middlesbrough's professional for £1 a week, charging 1s per hour for teaching, 1s per hour for playing nine holes or 1s 6d for 18 holes.[23] Caddies were appointed through Weastell, with their fees paid through him rather than directly to the caddie; they were paid 4d for nine holes or 7d for 18 holes.[24]

The golf course opened a month after the club was formed, by which time it already had 150 members. The course was said to meet "a longfelt [sic] want in Middlesbrough . . . [it] would enable them to come and enjoy an hour or two of sport in the middle of the day, instead of having to spend the whole day in going to and from the other courses."[25] By 1910 there were four cups to compete for,[26] and it was decided that the course would be extended from nine to eighteen holes; subscriptions being increased to £1 10s for gentlemen and to 15s for ladies to finance it.[27] By early 1912 membership had reached 240. A year later a profit was reported of £30, including a fee of £7 10s received from Middlesbrough Football Club to allow their players to use the course during the football season.[28]

Three hundred and twenty-two new members are listed in the club's minute book between June 1909 and December 1914,[29] and details can be ascertained for 217 individuals. Four members were councillors, either before or during their membership, and one member had been mayor.[30] Thirty-nine members were listed as an employer in the 1911 census, and 131 members had domestic servants. The occupations of 148 male members can be identified (female members will be dealt with below), the majority of which were middle-class with a significant number of lower-middle class members (see appendix 3) who may have used membership of the club to confirm their place in middle-class society.[31] Of those 206 members (male and female) for whom it is possible to identify their birthplace, only sixty-six were born in Middlesbrough and thirty were born elsewhere in Yorkshire. Twenty members were born in Scotland, Wales, or Ireland, and seven were born overseas, reflecting the variety of birthplaces of the town's population in general.[32]

Jefferys points out that tennis was the preserve of the rich, being played "purely for pleasure, and always in a sportsmanlike way." As one contemporary stated, "it requires a stretch of the imagination to picture a working man playing tennis."[33] The sport's connection with the wealthy may have contributed to its decline in popularity in Middlesbrough, as at the turn of the century only a small number of individuals had the money and land to take part. However, in 1905 it was reported that the Grove Tennis Club was welcoming new members for their Wednesday section, there having been "such a run on the Saturday section that it has been found necessary to close the list," and there are mentions of nine tennis clubs in Middlesbrough during this period.[34] The Linthorpe Tennis Club was formed in 1906 and within a year had a membership of two hundred and five tennis courts. The club's first officials were undoubtedly middle class (see table 5.3). Similarly, the first president of the Excelsior Tennis Club was the manager and owner of a dental surgery, and other officials included two clerks and a coal merchant.[35] Though the number of tennis clubs increased, membership numbers were low. In 1910 the Linthorpe Avenue club only had thirty-five members, and the Grove club had sixty-eight members.[36] Lake argues that the behavioral conduct and prestige associated with tennis meant that it "provided a means for the most socially aspirant upper middle classes to enhance their social standing and to demarcate themselves from social inferiors."[37] This notion can be applied to those members of the lower-middle and middle-middle classes participating in Middlesbrough's tennis clubs, with aspirations of increased social status.

The costs involved in playing tennis enabled clubs to retain their exclusivity. The subscriptions of the Grove Club were increased in 1913 to 17s 6d for gentlemen and 12s 6d for ladies, on top of an entrance fee of 5s. Similarly subscriptions for female members of the Linthorpe club were increased from 10s 6d to 15s in 1913.[38] 'Old Bird' in the *Sports Gazette* suggested that more land should be made available for the sport, as interest was increasing. The inadequate facilities at the park meant that "clerks and others" were prevented from perfecting their game, but it did mean that they had to possess more enthusiasm than those members of clubs who were able to play on "well-tended courts and amid the luxuries of easily-obtained tea and lemon squash and basket chairs with cushions."[39] A proposal in 1914 to lay out tennis courts in Albert Park failed, and while it might be assumed that the increased participation this would have brought would have been welcomed, the *Teesside Weekly Herald* was pleased at the decision as the park was "intended for the people, not for small cliques and sections" of sports clubs. Tennis players should instead "pay for the ground they want," thus sustaining the clubability of the sport.[40]

Though not as elite as those clubs above, at the beginning of the twentieth century it is evident that Middlesbrough Cricket Club was also run by the town's middle and professional class. In 1903 the president was a doctor and other officials included two accountants, a jeweler, a surgeon, a bank manager, and a telephone superintendent. The vice-captain was the club's former professional who now worked as a sports outfitter and clerk.[41] In contrast the club's professional (Jack Newstead) was a butcher, replaced in 1904 by a plater's helper (J. L. Parkin).[42] That William Fox, the club's former professional, was able to take up the position of vice-captain would seem to confirm Hill's assertion that league professionals had more freedom and standing in the sport than their county equivalents. They could enjoy "status, esteem and (in some cases) a wealth that was impossible to match in the first class game."[43] The officials of the North Ormesby Cricket Club were far more diverse when compared to those

Table 5.3. Linthorpe Tennis Club officials, 1907[1]

	Role	Occupation	Employment Status	Address (1911 census)	Place of birth	Servants
Hans Casper	President	Ship broker	Employer	Marton	Denmark	3
Orla Casper[*]	Committee	Shipping clerk		New Grove Villas, The Avenue, Middlesbrough	Middlesbrough	1
George Jackson Curry	Committee	Land agent	Own account	Field House, Marton	Ormesby, Middlesbrough	1
Thomas Dove	Committee	Director of coal merchant	Employer	32 Eastbourne Road, Middlesbrough	Newcastle	2
Charles Sampson Ellington	Committee	Pharmaceutical chemist	Worker	1 Grosvenor Terrace, Middlesbrough	Rochester, Kent	None (lodger)
Frederick Ephgrave	Committee	Shipping clerk	Worker	Westwood Avenue, Middlesbrough	Middlesbrough	None
Frederick C. Hildreth[*]	Treasurer	Accountant	Worker	108 Granville Road, Middlesbrough	Middlesbrough	1
Carl Jervelund jr	Committee	Mineral stock keeper	Worker	9 Ryedale Terrace, Middlesbrough	Middlesbrough	None
Alfred Clive Mildred	Committee	Coal merchant	Worker	Newholme, Marton	Middlesbrough	1
Alphonso William Nitsch	Vice-president	Cashier	Worker	Marton	Hartlepool, County Durham	None
Harry R. Scoby-Smith	Secretary	Shipping manager	Worker	Wingfield, The Avenue, Middlesbrough	Norton, Lancashire	1
Hugh Wilson	Committee	Waterworks manager	Worker	Sycamore Road, Middlesbrough	Middlesbrough	2

[*] 1901 census

[1] 1911 census; *Sports Gazette*, 20th April 1907; See also the officials of the Nomads Tennis Club, *Sports Gazette*, 5th April 1913

of the Middlesbrough Cricket Club, and included a number of working-class men.

Hockey was "contentedly and unquestionably amateur," a sport that "retained Corinthian purity from top to bottom," and in Middlesbrough it was another middle-class sport.[44] The local press first reported on the Middlesbrough Hockey Club in 1902 with games against Darlington and the Nondescripts (West Hartlepool), and players included two wine merchants, a jeweler, a teacher, and a doctor.[45] Though the sport received little press coverage, by 1904 'Old Bird' in the *Sports Gazette* felt able to claim that "where football originally reigned supreme as the winter game hockey is rapidly coming to the fore . . . the games one may witness are both keen and enjoyable from all standpoints." Though it was pointed out that the game might appear brutal to the uninitiated, it would not have been "in accordance with our British traditions to have a pastime so utterly devoid of risk." This contrasts markedly with Lowerson's statement that self-control was important to this sport which had "a certain cachet of social distinction akin to bridge."[46]

Members of the lower-middle class had more involvement in cycling and swimming, and with the town's gymnasium. The officials of the Middlesbrough Amateur Gymnasium Society elected in 1907 had a variety of occupations, ranging from ironmaster to clerk (see table 5.5). The affluence of some of the officials was demonstrated by the idea that the club would "try to tap" the eleven vice-presidents in order to clear their debt of £12.

The Cleveland Roads Cycling Club's shrinking membership (attributed in part to the popularity of motor cycling) led the captain to suggest lowering the subscription from 1s entrance fee and 5s for membership as this was "somewhat beyond the reach of the working man." However, one committee member stated that "this would be impossible with their club, as it was a racing club, and if members' fees be reduced the prizes would consequently not be so valuable."[47] Although this club still undertook a number of road races, in contrast the RUFS club were regarded as a "mysterious body of cyclists whose social functions can always be reckoned on to reach the high water mark of excellence." There was rarely any reporting of clubs runs and unlike the majority of clubs, they did not hold a sports day.[48] The club's annual dinner, on the other hand, was "one of the social events which is talked about for weeks beforehand and lingers pleasantly in the memory."[49] At the beginning of the century the North Ormesby & Middlesbrough Cycling Club was regarded as "the principal club" in the town, and the club's officials were lower-middle and middle class, including a cement merchant, company accountant, shipping clerk, rent collector, and a teacher.[50] With its origins in Gjers Mills ironworks, the president of the Middlesbrough Ayresome Cycling Club was ironmaster Lawrence Farrar Gjers, and vice-presidents included three manag-

Table 5.4. North Ormesby Cricket Club officials, 1905[1]

	Role	Occupation	Employment Status	Address (1901 census)	Place of birth	Servants
James Worsley Pennyman[a]	President	Barrister and Lord of Ormesby Hall				
Henry Furmidge[b]	Committee	Laborer	Worker	40 Queen Street, North Ormesby	Ormesby, Middlesbrough	None
John William Hanks	Secretary	Teacher	Worker	Oakfield Road, North Ormesby	South Bank, Middlesbrough	None
Edwin Haslock	Committee	Foreman	Worker	3 South View, North Ormesby	Ireland	None
William Thomas Lawson	Selection and ground committee	Clergyman		North Ormesby Vicarage	Isle of Man	2
Walter Lloyd	Selection and ground committee	Laborer	Worker	6 James Street, North Ormesby	Brockmoor, Staffordshire	None
Herbert Nunn	Committee	Weigh lad	Worker	36 Queen Street, North Ormesby	North Ormesby, Middlesbrough	None
Matthew Thompson	Treasurer	Innkeeper	Own account	27 Smeaton Street, North Ormesby	Sadberge, Country Durham	1

[a] Unable to locate on census
[b] 1911 census
[1] 1901 census; *North-Eastern Daily Gazette*, 22nd December 1905

Table 5.5. Middlesbrough Amateur Gymnasium Society officials, 1907[1]

	Role	Occupation	Employment Status	Address (1911 census)	Place of birth	Servants
William A. Caddick[a]	Secretary	Brewer's clerk	Worker	158 Victoria Road East, Middlesbrough	Middlesbrough	None
Charles Coates	Vice-president	Manager of coal exporting house	Employer	Roman Road, Middlesbrough	York	2
Charles Dorman	Vice-president	Ironmaster	Employer	Rye Hill, Nunthorpe	Norton, County Durham	5
Benjamin Embleton	Committee	Teacher	Worker	121 Grange Road East, Middlesbrough	Carrington, Nottinghamshire	None
Walter Embleton	Instructor	Accountant		3 Gresham Road, Middlesbrough	Pudsey, Yorkshire	None
Horace Featonby	Committee	Draftsman	Worker	90 Granville Road, Middlesbrough	Middlesbrough	None
John Forbes	Vice-president	Baker		The Beeches, Marton	Scotland	2
Sir Samuel Sadler[b]	Vice-president	Chemical manufacturer		Southlands, Preston-upon-Tees	Oldbury, Worcestershire	4
Charles W. Sheppard[b]	Treasurer	Bank manager		Hudworth House, Coatham	Salford, Lancashire	
David Terrace	Vice-president	Gas engineer	Employer	1 St Hilda's, Grove Hill, Middlesbrough	Scotland	1
Walter Trevelyan Thomson	Vice-president	Iron merchant	Employer	Windsor Terrace, Middlesbrough	Stockton, County Durham	2

[a] 1901 census
[b] Kelly's Directory of North and East Ridings of Yorkshire, 1909
[1] 1911 census; Sports Gazette, 2nd February 1907; Teesside Weekly Herald, 9th February 1907

ers of the works. The committee included a foreman of the ironworks, and the secretary and treasurer was a commercial clerk.[51]

Despite the attention that Jack Hatfield had brought to swimming in the town (see below), it was suggested that this was not a pastime that many people could partake in. In a letter to the *Sports Gazette*, the headmaster of Denmark Street School, Joseph W. Wright, stated that although the "iron kings" provided prizes, "not one in 500 or 1,000 of his employees could be eligible to win the trophy he has given." Membership fees were too high and long working hours prevented men from attending club practices. Wright proposed that employers invite their workers to take part in galas, where events would be "the means of raising the standard right throughout the staff . . . what an enormous gain it would be to the community!"[52] Wright's suggestions are confirmed by the lower-middle- and middle-class officials of the Middlesbrough Amateur Swimming Club. The ironmaster Charles Dorman was president, and vice-presidents included the mayor, an accountant, and the manager of the cooperative society. In contrast, the secretary was a grocer, the assistant secretary was a warehouseman, and the treasurer was a draper's manager.[53]

Bowls proved a popular sport for those lower-middle-class men whose work "left little time for sports more greedy of time and physique . . . offering a gentle rather than strenuous manliness." Sir Samuel Sadler thought that bowling was "a most gentlemanly, a most philosophical, and [a] very proper and polite kind of sport." It was a sport that had "a placidity about it that did not accompany certain other forms of sport," and this contrasted directly with a sport such as professional football with its unruly spectators and associations with drink and bad behavior.[54] The secretary of the Cleveland & South Durham Bowling League thought that the sport should not become "a burden or a business," but should remain "a real pleasure and recreation." It was a sport of the workingman; bowlers were "men who have to work, and arrange for our pleasure for, perhaps, a week before hand."[55] The largely lower-middle-class makeup of the officials of Middlesbrough Bowling Club reflects this (see table 5.6).

The minute book of the club lists 118 members for 1901 and the occupations and/or places of birth for ninety-eight of the members can be identified (see appendix 4). The evidence suggests that most of the members were lower-middle and middle class, though there are a small number of members with working-class occupations. Five of the members were councillors,[56] and according to the 1901 census forty of the members employed domestic servants, and twenty-four members were employers. Of those ninety-seven members for whom it is possible to identify an occupation, ten worked in the drinks trade.[57] Only ten of the members were born in Middlesbrough, twenty-four were born elsewhere in Yorkshire, and twelve were born in Scotland.[58]

Table 5.6. Middlesbrough Bowling Club officials, 1901[1]

	Role	Occupation	Employment Status	Address (1901 census)	Place of birth	Servants
John Dean	President	Pawnbroker and builder	Employer	73 Southfield Road, Middlesbrough	Carlisle, Cumberland	None
Thomas Appleby	Treasurer	Fish merchant shopkeeper	Own account	84 Linthorpe Road, Middlesbrough	Scarborough, Yorkshire	None
Edward Bryant	Committee	Hosier and hatter	Employer	74 Linthorpe Road, Middlesbrough	Faversham, Kent	1
William J. Burton	Assistant secretary	Plumber	Worker	1 Acton Street, Middlesbrough	Lyng, Norfolk	None
John Davison	Vice-president	Licensed victualler	Own account	Station Dining Rooms, Middlesbrough	Hurworth, County Durham	5
John A. Dent	Vice-president	Brewery agent	Worker	13-15 Harris Street, Middlesbrough	Beverley, Yorkshire	2
William Hood	Committee	Manager of mineral water company	Worker	16 Southfield Road, Middlesbrough	Otterington, Yorkshire	None
John R. F. Readman	Secretary	Accountant's clerk	Worker	8 Oxford Street, Middlesbrough	Middlesbrough	None
Albert Scholes	Committee	Fishmonger	Employer	Imeson Terrace, Linthorpe Road, Middlesbrough	Radcliffe, Lancashire	1
John Boyd Spiers	Committee	Joiner	Worker	10 Oxford Street, Middlesbrough	Scotland	None (boarder)
William Thompson	Committee	Wiredrawer	Worker	111 Glebe Road, Middlesbrough	Sheffield	None
William Turnbull	Committee	Fruiterer	Employer	97 Newport Road, Middlesbrough	Gateshead, County Durham	1

[1] Minute Book of Middlesbrough Bowling Club (hereafter Minute Book of MBC), 7th, 29th November 1901; See also the officials of the Middlesbrough, Stockton & District Bowling League—*North-Eastern Daily Gazette*, 23rd December 1909; *Sports Gazette*, 5th April 1913

After the turn of the century steps were taken to improve standards and promote both the club and the game of bowls. The wages of the groundsman were increased in 1902 to 16s a week, rising to 18s in March 1903, followed by a further increase of 2s for "extra occasional labour" in June.[59] In 1905 it was decided that the club would arrange to buy their ground, and in 1914 the club could afford to double the size of their pavilion.[60] A municipal bowling green was opened in July 1914 and was thought to be "full value for the money spent"; the expense was entirely justified by "the large number of players who daily flock to the green."[61] 'Looker On' in the *Teesside Weekly Herald* thought this was long overdue, arguing that, "municipal bowling greens being a recognized institution in all parts of the country it does seem remarkable that . . . a town which is supposed to be governed in the most up to date progressive manner should be so woefully behind other towns." Indeed one councillor remarked that Middlesbrough "was backward in bowling greens; other towns of its size had eight or more."[62]

Though there were a number of cycling clubs with working-class members, bicycles remained relatively expensive during this period. In 1905, the most skilled blast furnace worker received 60s a week, while the lowest paid worker received 19s. In 1914, the weekly wage of steelworkers ranged from 18s to 37s a week, while skilled men in shipbuilding received 36s 2d a week.[63] Advertised prices of new cycles in 1903 ranged from £8 to £22 1s, and from £2 15s to £8 12s 6d for secondhand bicycles. A bicycle could also be purchased for payments of 3s 6d a week for 12 months (amounting to £8 8s).[64] An advertisement in 1909 for the Gloria Cycle Depot, offered bicycles from £5s to £12 12s, while Carling & Sons sold their "road racer" for £3 15s. In 1912 W. Evison's prices started at £5 15s.[65] In 1911 the officials of Middlesbrough Crescent Cycling Club were cross-class (see table 5.7). In 1913 the subscriptions for this club were "the small sum" of 1s 6d a year, and in the same year the club held 76 runs as well as a "record number of social events."[66] The officers of the Middlesbrough Gasworks Cycling Club in 1906 had various positions at the gasworks— two managers, a clerk, a joiner, a foreman, a gas fitter, and a maker of carburetted water gas.[67] Despite the proliferation of clubs in this period the 1913 annual report of the North Yorkshire & South Durham Centre of the National Cyclists' Union stated that, "attempts have been made to revive the small clubs that lapsed through the coal strike, but so far they continue to languish," demonstrating the vulnerability of clubs to fluctuations in the economy. Goodall has argued that as the bicycle became less of a novelty, "it became more a work horse;" there was no longer "a feeling of solidarity as with earlier cyclists; no more need to join a club."[68] This is borne out by the number of local clubs joining the Cyclists' Tour-

Table 5.7. Middlesbrough Crescent Cycling Club officials, 1911[1]

	Role	Occupation	Employment Status	Address (1911 census)	Place of birth	Servants
Thomas Brotton	Middle captain	Rolley [delivery] man		33 Wye Street, Middlesbrough	Stokesley, Yorkshire	None (lodger)
James Crone	Committee	Laborer	Worker	25 Gresham Road, Middlesbrough	Middlesbrough	None
James Jesse Fowler	Vice-president	Wine and spirit merchant	Own account	7 Waterloo Road, Middlesbrough	York	None
Charles Henry Kay	Vice-president	Hotel keeper	Own account	Miners Arms Hotel, High Street, Eston	Manchester	1
Fred Marwood	Secretary	Warehouseman	Worker	24 Milbank Street, Middlesbrough	Middlesbrough	None
Christopher McAdams	Vice-president	Motor and cycle engineer and dealer	Employer	10 Seaton Terrace, Middlesbrough	Middlesbrough	None
Thomas Herbert Milburn	Vice-president	Plater	Worker	180 Victoria Road, Middlesbrough	Middlesbrough	None
Philip Pinkney	Vice-president	Engineman	Worker	58 Gilkes Street, Middlesbrough	Middlesbrough	None
John William Randall	Committee	Machinist	Worker	30 Weastell Street, Middlesbrough	Sunderland	None
Edwin Turner	Vice-president	Master housepainter	Employer	371 Linthorpe Road, Middlesbrough	Middlesbrough	None

[1] 1911 census; *Teesside Weekly Herald*, 11th March, 16th December 1911; See also the diverse officials of Middlesbrough Tykes Cycling Club, presided over by Councillor Edwin Turner, "no mere figure head, but a real live 'sport'"—*Teesside Weekly Herald*, 11th November 1911; *Sports Gazette*, 9th November 1912, 26th November 1914

ing Club—one hundred in 1900 alone, but just forty-one from 1912–1914.[69] However, *Kelly's Directory* for 1913 lists twenty-seven cycle agents and dealers, three cycle manufacturers, three cycle repairers, and one cycle accessories dealer in Middlesbrough. The 1893 edition of the same directory listed only two cycle agents and dealers, and two cycle manufacturers.[70]

In contrast to many other sports in Middlesbrough, quoits had more working-class involvement. In 1908 the secretary of the Ayresome Quoits Club was a lead burner at a chemical works, the vice-president was a cooper, and one of the treasurers was a grocer.[71] The Middlesbrough & District Works Quoit League (formed in 1911), fulfilled a "long felt want" in the town for a league for "less proficient players." All nine clubs in the league were connected to large industrial works or factories.[72] The Erimus Quoit, Rifle & Social Club opened new premises in 1914. This club had "endeavoured with success to place healthy recreation in the way of the working-men of the district." One member stated that "they had no blue-blooded aristocrats among their members," instead they were "horny-handed sons of toil and business men." The sport was evidently viewed favorably and the facilities deemed important by the town's elite, as the mayor opened the premises, remarking that, "it reflected great credit on the working men who mainly composed the club that they had secured such excellent facilities." He thought that quoits should "appeal more to young people than it did. If some of them who lounged along Linthorpe Road and hung about street corners smoking cigarettes" joined such a club, "they would be much better off."[73]

Billiards was also played by working-class men, growing in popularity during the period and becoming more of a competitive sport. Holt attributes the game's popularity to a blend of "skill, drinking, banter and gambling,"[74] and in 1905 the *Sports Gazette* commented that billiards "very largely existed in connection with hotels and drinking taverns." Lady Florence Bell noted in "At the Works" that billiards was "the most popular of all indoor games . . . in all the public-houses and in nearly all the private clubs tables are to be found." Due to "very widespread demand" public billiard rooms ("which in no way rely on the sale of intoxicants") were opened.[75] The Teesside Catholic Billiard League was formed in 1909, to "draw together more closely the Catholics of the district and cement a friendship," followed in the same year by the formation of the Middlesbrough & District Billiard League.[76] That billiards could be divorced from drinking is further evidenced by the inclusion of billiards tables at the premises of a number of church organizations and other sports clubs, as well as the formation of the Church & Temperance Billiards League.[77]

THE STATUS OF CRICKET

For many Victorians and Edwardians, cricket was regarded as proof of their cultural supremacy. A national symbol, the sport "combined a sense of the bucolic increasingly sought after by a distinctly anti-urban indus-trial culture with a mode of social control of various levels of sophistica-tion." The notion of a desire for the "anti-urban" may account for the deference accorded to cricket in an overwhelmingly urban environment in this case, but may also account for the relative lack of success (when compared to football) for cricket in Middlesbrough. Holt states that cricket's attractiveness to both the middle and working classes, and to the north and south of the country meant that it was *the* national sport.[78] As Sandiford and Vamplew contend, it "represented all that many thought was best in the English way of life."[79]

Despite cricket's status in English society, Middlesbrough Cricket Club remained in a state of decline and new ways of increasing income were sought. A hockey club was established in 1902, paying the club £8 rent per year, and Middlesbrough hosted a match between a Yorkshire 2nd XI and Durham, with another match arranged for the following year between Yorkshire 2nd and Northumberland.[80] To further increase club funds, the price of admission was increased to 6d for the 1904 season.[81] By 1906 it was felt that the club were improving. The *Northern Athlete* noted that they had once possessed a "traditional exclusiveness" (as demonstrated by the club officials above) but that this had finally been done away with. "There isn't a shadow of doubt," stated the newspaper, "but that cricket is on the improve." However, the club failed to secure another visit by the Yorkshire 2nd team.[82] The club complained to the county that "our ground is second to none in this part of the world . . . our supporters cannot understand what they consider the unfair treatment the Middlesbrough CC received from the County Club."[83] However, the club's inability to attract spectators to Yorkshire 2nd versus Northumber-land in 1908 led to the cancellation of another fixture. Despite the desire to have Yorkshire matches played there, and the statements in the press that the quality of the cricket currently played by the Middlesbrough club was poor, it was suggested that the county would have to "get together a much better side before North Yorkshiremen will be found willing to lose half a day's work and plank down their nimble sixpences" to watch Yorkshire.[84] However, it was also stated by the *Teesside Weekly Herald* that, "the fact remains that only a very small percentage of the large crowds who attend the football matches, extend their patronage to local cricket in the summer."[85] The *Northern Athlete* asked what the committee intended to do to make the club worthy of its old traditions,

Surely it is time you did something to save the situation, and the club from going into oblivion, because the public, who pay the piper, will soon object to your perpetual calling of their ideas, and the general fitness of their ideas, and the general fitness of things. What they want is to see good cricket, and a win or two now and again. . . . Are you, as the responsible party, fulfilling the obligation your trust imposes on you? Are you giving us good cricket?[86]

When it was announced in 1910 that the club would have to leave their ground, the *Northern Athlete* argued that it was time that "some of the local monied men came forward and helped the committee . . . [to show] some little appreciation for the town in which they have made all their money, a town that has been an El Dorado for many." It was suggested that the Middlesbrough Owners reduce the amount of money they required for the land; this would be "the least they can do after all the years they have made money at the town's expense."[87] This attitude toward the Owners is rather different to the deference they had been treated with in the nineteenth century (see chapter 4). Only twenty–thirty people attended a public meeting to discuss the matter, and Alderman Alfred Mattison commented that elsewhere, "cricket was a game to which everyone gave their active or passive support, yet in Middlesbrough they did not seem to make any effort," which he attributed to the increasing number of works clubs in existence.[88] At the club's AGM in 1911, it was announced that having been in a "perilous condition" for several years, the club would be disbanded "owing to lack of public support and loss of ground."[89] "Free Lance" in the *Northern Athlete* asked,

Where is that boasted spirit of sportsmanship, and that deep-dyed love of amateurism we have heard so much of in the past? . . . The monied men in the place ought to be ashamed of themselves to allow the national pastime of the country to die . . . for want of a little help. All they think of in these days of hustle is the making of money, not the giving away of it.[90]

In contrast to the fortunes of Middlesbrough Cricket Club, North Ormesby prospered, due in no small part to the favorable terms by which they leased their field from the Pennyman family. In 1906 the club had been able to employ a professional and a groundsman, and a year later recorded their largest receipts of over £173.[91] However, by 1911 their income had decreased and the secretary attributed this to a lack of local competition since Middlesbrough had been disbanded. Instead, interest had to be maintained through social events and whist drives. In contrast to the complaints made about the lack of help offered to the Middlesbrough club, Pennyman stated, "in him cricket would always have a friend, and he could assure them that in the matter of the lease they would not find him hard."[92]

In late 1913 it was reported that North Ormesby would become "Middlesbrough Cricket Club" as it was now within the borough of Middlesbrough.[93] The club's secretary stated that they had become "the cricket club of Middlesbrough. . . . Middlesbrough never appreciated a town club until they lost it."[94] A year later the club changed its name to Middlesbrough, the secretary stating that it "had been urged upon them by many gentlemen in the town, including the Mayor," which might suggest that this more stable club would reflect well upon the town. The *Sports Gazette* hoped that the club would now be able to attract county matches, arguing that there was "no reason why Middlesbrough should lag behind other Yorkshire towns in its patronage of the great game."[95]

As Mattison had already claimed, the *Northern Athlete* stated that Middlesbrough had a "superfluity of athletic clubs each with its own cricket branch attached, which has much to do with the present poverty" of the Middlesbrough club.[96] The *Sports Gazette*'s 'Old Bird' suggested that the proliferation of clubs in the town was damaging to Middlesbrough Cricket Club. He argued that "many players prefer to indulge in their Saturday game with men with whom they associate in other directions during the week" where they could also be certain of getting a place in the team. 'Old Bird' felt that cricketers ought to feel duty-bound to play for the town club; "it should be the ambition of every player . . . to figure among the chosen eleven of his town."[97] As well as the multisport clubs of large employers (see below), there were also smaller clubs associated with places of work. New clubs formed at this time include Middlesbrough Passenger Station Cricket Club,[98] Bolckow & Vaughan's Middlesbrough Works Cricket Club,[99] and the Gazette Cricket Club.[100]

Church clubs also thrived. The Middlesbrough Church Cricket League was formed in 1910 with fourteen member clubs by the end of the first year. The *Northern Athlete* hoped that the League would not only promote the game, but also "cement good feeling between young men . . . and strengthen the bonds of universal brotherhood." Indeed, after the League's first year, the secretary (Thomas Dormand Stewart, owner of Stewart's Clothier Limited) remarked that "a most pleasing harmony existed among the teams, the games being fought in a spirit of friendly rivalry."[101] It is possible to identify some of the individuals involved in the running of such clubs, and professionals, clerks, and the lower-middle class were instrumental in their administration, though there were also a number of working-class men involved. For example, the captain, secretary, and a committee member of South Bank St John's Cricket Club in 1910 were all clerks, and other club officials included a member of the clergy, a chemist, an iron turner, and a laborer.[102] Linthorpe Parish Church Cricket Club's president was the church's vicar, the secretary was an inspector for the Board of Trade, the treasurer was a cashier and accountant, the assistant secretary and captain were both clerks, and the vice-captain was an inspector for the Tees Valley Water Board.[103]

Despite the problems encountered by Middlesbrough Cricket Club, in 1912 the Middlesbrough Church Cricket League stated that interest in cricket had been "fully sustained until the last match" of the season, and the Cleveland Minor Cricket League maintained that it was "still progressive and popular with the minor cricket clubs in Cleveland."[104] In contrast, the North Yorkshire & South Durham Cricket League felt it necessary to send a deputation to the *North-Eastern Daily Gazette* in an attempt to increase the popularity of the sport in the press.[105]

WORK-BASED CLUBS

Huggins has argued that at the end of the nineteenth century the "paternalistic influence" of Middlesbrough's elite decreased, leading to a growth of commercialised leisure.[106] However, the number of sports clubs attached to places of work suggests that this notion of elite withdrawal has been exaggerated. Middlesbrough Cricket Club attributed their own demise to works' clubs, but it was widely felt that these clubs fostered better working relationships between employers and workers. There was, according to the *Northern Echo*, less of a tendency on Teesside to view the workforce merely "as 'hands,' towards whom all responsibility ceases when their wages have been paid." Lady Bell noted that such clubs were indeed "eagerly used by those entitled to do so."[107] Munting argues that many larger employers increasingly regarded it as their duty to provide recreational facilities for their workers and the general population. The provision of such facilities was thought to help increase profits "through a contented labour force in an attractive working environment," and was also used to recruit and retain workers, and instil a wider company culture.[108] In his study of Crewe, Redfern notes that work "had a central role in determining the nature of local leisure," and Phillips's research on Boots shows that sport was viewed as "a valuable means of bringing employees together."[109]

In 1899 the iron and steel works of Dorman Long & Co contributed £500 to the newly formed Dorman Long & Co United Athletic Club.[110] Facilities for the workmen included a gymnasium, football and cricket grounds, six quoits pitches, and a bowling green. At the opening of the ground Sir Arthur Dorman stated,

> It was only right that they should do something for the benefit of the men who had done so much for them, and who by their steady and careful labour had made their firm famous throughout the world. . . . If the men only played

as well as they worked, they would soon make the name of the athletic club as famous as they had already made that of the firm.[111]

Arthur Dorman was elected president, and four of the vice-presidents were managers at the works. £2,500 was spent on the grounds and within a year the club had more than 1,800 members. Football teams were entered in the Northern League, the Cleveland Association, Teesside, and Middlesbrough leagues, but the club found that "the objects of the club were not being carried out" and a departmental league was inaugurated instead.[112] four thousand spectators attended the club's sports day in August 1900, the prize fund of which Dorman had "subscribed [to] handsomely."[113] The suggestion that such organizations could lead to greater productivity was asserted when Dorman remarked that "it was no doubt owing in great measure to the club that the men were able to work so well . . . owing to the good work they got out of the men the directors had been encouraged to spend a big sum of money" on the Britannia Works.[114] This statement may have been made in order to maintain productivity—greater results would be rewarded with improvements to the club.

Subscriptions were as low as possible—"it would be difficult to find another club in the country that would compare favourably with theirs." While the club's vice-presidents all had managerial or professional positions at the works, general committees were also elected for the eleven departments of the works, which included men from a range of roles including three clerks, two stock takers, two smelters, a foreman, a galvanizer, an engineer, a laborer, an iron rougher, a draftsman, and a roll turner.[115] In 1909 the club had 2,208 members. This accounts for a large proportion of the company's workforce, there being 4,361 employees in 1907.[116] In 1909 there was an increase in the number of members taking part in cricket, and a team was entered in the Cleveland Cricket League. A football team joined the Middlesbrough & District Works League and a cycling section was also formed.[117] Membership increased again in 1910, attributed to the distribution of a pamphlet "setting forth the many privileges afforded," and by 1913 membership reached 2,694.[118] Arthur Dorman extolled the benefits of the club, suggesting that it brought together employers and employees, "providing recreation which must be a benefit to all concerned." Indeed the club reported that "more interest and activity was shown in the [cricket] competition than any previous season," the position of the town's premier club evidently not affecting interest in the sport. Moreover, the cricket section of the Dorman Long club was far less elite than Middlesbrough Cricket Club, and it would therefore have been more accessible and more appealing to many of the works' employees.[119]

The North-Eastern Steelworks Athletic Club opened their recreation ground in 1903. The general manager of the company, Arthur H. Cooper, stated that "they were ambitious that their club should take the lead of all works athletic clubs . . . if anyone could make a club of that sort a success, it was the men employed by the North-Eastern Steel Company."[120] Though the company appeared benevolent in their provision of sporting facilities, they loaned rather than gave the club £200, which was duly repaid within two years. By 1906 the club had 1,700 members, and their Linthorpe ground was regarded as "a credit to the workmen who have contributed to making it the finest recreation ground in the Cleveland District."[121] Furthermore it was felt that it was an "extremely creditable state of affairs when after working hours both officials and men could join together and enjoy themselves in healthgiving recreations."[122] In 1908, the officials of the club were middle class. The president was a managing director of the steelworks, and vice presidents included another managing director, two managers, and two doctors. However, like the Dorman Long club, the thirty-six committee members elected a year later were diverse in their roles at the steelworks, ranging from clerks and assistant engineers to laborers and steelworkers.[123] By late 1908 the club had purchased six acres of land from the Middlesbrough Owners with space for a cricket ground, cycle track, gymnasium, rifle range, and a bowling green. There would also be "tables for games so that members can pass a quiet hour who do not wish to take part in the other more active games."[124] However, in 1911 certain sections of the club had proved unsuccessful. The sports day was "a great loss to the club," the cricket section suffered from a "laxity in practice," and the lack of success for the football team was attributed to the preference of the members for watching Middlesbrough FC.[125] This contrasts with the preference given to works cricket teams over the town club, and suggests a greater interest in *watching* rather than participating in football.

The Ayresome Athletic Club of Gjers Mills ironworks began in 1908, with the company being thanked for their "generous assistance and for the deep interest they had taken in the welfare of the club."[126] The clubhouse of the renamed Gjers Mills Club was opened in November 1910, including rooms for billiards, quoits, and reading and space for air-rifle shooting. At the opening, Lawrence Farrar Gjers commented on the "good feeling which it would promote between the masters and the men."[127] The *Teesside Weekly Herald* agreed that the existence of the club was conducive "to the harmonious conduct of the business and strengthening that bond of sympathy which should exist between employers and men;" when the employees felt that their well-being was being cared for, they would "respond with an increased interest in the performances of their duties."[128]

The Clarence Club, of Bell Brothers ironworks, was opened in 1903. Founded by Lady Florence Bell (the wife of ironmaster Sir Hugh Bell), it was "to serve as a resort, not only for the men employed at their works, but for their wives and families."[129] Lady Bell's Winter Gardens was also opened in 1907. Admission was 1d and the Gardens included a billiard table, reading and writing tables, a band platform, and refreshments.[130] Lady Bell stated that it was "a public institution for the benefit of the working classes," and as both alcohol and gambling were prohibited, her husband thought that it offered "a solution of many a difficulty with which they were oppressed."[131] Samuelson's ironworks opened their own social club in 1905 and the *Teesside Weekly Herald* again regarded this as further proof of the "bond of sympathy which exists between masters and men in some of the great industrial undertakings on Teesside." This club would "brighten the leisure hours of [the] workmen," and had reading, dining, and billiard rooms, as well as a rifle range. By 1913, the club had over one thousand members.[132] The North-Eastern Railway also possessed an athletic club, and a social club was added in 1907. Even though the club had been unable to secure a field, it still had 230 members paying 1d a week.[133] In 1910 a sports club was formed for employees of Stewarts's Clothiers Ltd. The club had their own cricket pitch, tennis court, and croquet lawn, and ran football and hockey sections, the latter in order to "find amusement for the non-footballers and ladies."[134]

OTHER SPORTING AND RECREATIONAL ORGANIZATIONS

It has been suggested that in other aspects of social life, the church did not play an active role in the town as it failed to provide charitable agencies or institutions.[135] However, the evidence shows that a number of sporting and social organizations were formed by various churches in Middlesbrough, providing further opportunities for people to partake in rational recreation and, through forms of muscular Christianity, assist in the maintenance of a "healthy, moral and orderly work-force." Churches were able to use recreation as a means of "facilitating evangelism, bolstering temperance and leading the battle against 'immorality.'"[136] Though it has been suggested that the socio-religious drive decreased at the end of the nineteenth century, Stubley argues that after the building of churches and schools, the chief concern of Middlesbrough's churches was "the provision of opportunities for harmless and uplifting activities out of work time."[137] In the mid-1890s the Seamen's Institute (or Tees Mission) offered a place where seamen could meet "for rational amusement and recreation." The aim was to make the men "more provident, religious and moral."[138] In 1897 an athletics club was formed in connection with St Peter's Mission Room with 175 members. Echoing the principles of muscular Christianity, members were called upon to use the facilities for religion and education, as well as for the "reasonable enjoyment of exercise and amusements so that they might have sound minds in sound bodies."[139]

Middlesbrough's YMCA opened new premises in 1904, providing "a more commodious and adaptable building for its great work—the uplifting of young men, not only in their spiritual life, but their physical, social and intellectual life." The building included a billiard room, gymnasium, reading room and a "social room,"[140] and the club possessed cricket, swimming, harriers, and cycling sections. The *Teesside Weekly Herald* commended the association as it was "free from temptations to drink intoxicants, and enveloped in a wholesome and elevating atmosphere."[141] With many other clubs competing for membership, it is perhaps not surprising that by 1909 the YMCA had only forty-four full members.[142]

St Patrick's Catholic Association was formed in 1906, and intended to have concerts, lectures, and social gatherings "if combination with our neighbouring Associations in defence of God and our children will not engage all our attention."[143] In 1909 the Association joined the Teesside Catholic Billiard League and took part in rifle shooting. However, membership was disappointingly low, it being stated that "there are still a large number of men and boys who have not been moved by our attractions to do more than praise us." The Association offered "many an hour of intellectual enjoyment and . . . innocent recreation," both of which were needed by those "whose toilsome nights and toilsome days give them a special zest for such relaxation."[144] Fluctuations in local trade did mean that membership suffered in 1911, but the Association was still "attractive, pleasant [and] alluring" to members.[145] The St Mary's Catholic Association and the St Thomas' Catholic Association were also members of the billiards league, the latter also having a quoits section and two football teams.[146] St George's Congregational Church had a men's social club and swimming section, a girls' club and a gymnasium, as well as a literary society and a reading room.[147] The objectives of the Cambridge House Club of St Paul's were "to provide such recreation and amusement as the Committee may allow" and "to promote social intercourse and good feeling amongst men of all denominations."[148] The club had the patronage of some of the members of Middlesbrough establishment, but the committee members of the club's football team also included a laborer, a bolt maker, and a plate layer.[149] As well as football, activities included billiards and shooting, and while in 1909 the club had ninety-nine members, a year later the existence of various works' clubs was said to have "reduced the membership very considerably."[150]

Some attempts were made to provide recreational facilities for boys. The Feversham Street Boys' Club was formed by Joseph Walton (barrister) and Councillor Walter Trevelyan Thomson (iron merchant) in 1906, and on opening had 250 members paying 2d a week. Walton stated that

the club was "entirely unsectarian and open to all denominations, preference alone being given to those living on the north side of the railway"
(the poorest part of the town). The club had a games room, billiard table,
swimming bath, gymnasium, and the club's football team joined the Middlesbrough Junior League in 1911.[151] "Physical efficiency" was advanced
through the gymnasium, shooting range, and "in a passive sense, by the
ban placed on smoking."[152] The *North-Eastern Daily Gazette* commended
Walton and Thomson for their "experiment in social work." The club's
members would "constantly have before them an object lesson in rational recreation and rational behaviour."[153] Run on similar lines, the Holy
Cross Mission started a boys' club in 1912. The Mission was in the "very
lowest district of the town . . . tenanted by the poorest class of labourers."
According to the Mission, this area had a great number of public houses
which was "terribly demoralising to the neighbourhood . . . especially to
the children who form an endless ragged procession of beer carriers."[154]
The boys' club possessed a billiard table, a football team was run in
winter, "opportunities for reading and games are afforded, and physical
culture is indulged in."[155]

HEALTH

As demonstrated by the formation of such organizations, the health of the
town's population had remained a concern since the nineteenth century.
As one contemporary stated, the town was "an example of how opportunities may be neglected, and an easy task turned into a difficult one,"
as the mortality rate was markedly higher in the oldest part of the town
where houses were neglected, ill-equipped, and unsanitary.[156] Indeed
Taylor points out that in many ways, housing and sanitary conditions
scarcely improved between 1870 and 1914. Poor health affected between
one-third and a half of the town's population, as blast furnaces and
factories continued to "belch forth clouds of smoke of varied hues." Furthermore, while wages increased, living and working conditions did not;
the rapid growth in population had exceeded facilities.[157] Many middle-
class reformers believed that sport was an antidote to the poor physical
health caused by urban squalor, as well as to the increased exertions of
work. It was also expected to lead to both a greater number of physically
fit men who were prepared for war, and to greater productivity in the
workplace.[158]

Better health was referred to in relation to swimming and gymnastics in
Middlesbrough, particularly with regards to the participation of children.
As Love states, advocates of swimming believed that water, cleanliness,
and swimming were clearly linked; swimming would promote cleanli-

ness among the lower classes, and increase health and physical fitness throughout society.[159] Praising swimming as a form of rational recreation, the *Sports Gazette* stated that it was,

> an art and an exercise superior to all others. It is health promoting, cleanly, recreative, mentally and morally philanthropic, and can be practised by both sexes at almost any age. It gives confidence, courage, readiness of resource, and self-reliance. No one could employ his leisure more usefully than in spreading knowledge of the art.[160]

Furthermore, in a letter to the *Sports Gazette*, headmaster Joseph W. Wright stated that "swimming helps the growth of the strong mind in the strong body," and in 1910, the Amateur Swimming Club held a schools' team competition and a contest for the Dent Shield for boys.[161] The Amateur Swimming Club had 166 members in 1904, and it was felt that their galas "brought the advantages of the club and of swimming generally before the public."[162] However, two years later membership had dropped to ninety-five and an appeal was made to parents to encourage their children to take up swimming. Since its formation, the club had been "persistently striving to stimulate public opinion in favour of a more general adoption of swimming and life saving, and bringing about a widespread and thorough practical knowledge of . . . the art of natation." The subscription was felt to be "nominal"—4s for juniors and 5s 6d for adults.[163] In contrast, the club of the Middlesbrough Seaman's Institute was said to be "of special benefit to tub-boatmen and others whose work is near the river and whose lives are therefore frequently dependent upon their ability to swim."[164]

In 1913, 'Teessider' in the *Teesside Weekly Herald* noted the increased popularity of swimming, stating that "if the pastime becomes much more popular the present Baths will have to be enlarged or a new building erected." The writer attributed this to the teaching of swimming to schoolchildren but also to local champion Jack Hatfield—"There is not one schoolboy who enters the Baths who does not mean to rival him if he can."[165] The response of the press, civic leaders, and the public to Hatfield's success suggests he was a local hero. His victories offered an opportunity to express feelings of civic pride, references being made to Hatfield's role in enhancing the town's sporting reputation. When Hatfield was selected to represent England at an event in 1911, the *Northern Athlete* commented proudly that, "We turn other things out of Middlesbrough besides pig-iron. . . . Amongst some of the smart men we have turned out of the Boro [sic] is this young man . . . who is a credit to the town." He was already the champion of Yorkshire for one hundred yards, quarter mile and one mile, the one hundred yards champion of Northumberland and Durham, and had taken third place in the English five hundred yard championship.[166] Hatfield was selected to represent Great Britain at the 1912 Stockholm Olympics and won silver medals for the four hundred and 1,500-meter races, and a bronze in the freestyle relay. The *Northern Echo* reported that Hatfield was "one of the principal themes of conversation in Middlesbrough," and the *North-Eastern Daily Gazette* remarked that he was "a credit to his country and the town of Middlesbrough is justly proud of him."[167] A crowd of thousands awaited his return at the railway station, where they were able to purchase photographs of the local champion. He was "hoisted shoulder high" while a band played 'See the Conquering Hero Comes,' and as the band played the 'Ironopolis March' he was driven to the baths for a formal reception. Councillor Edwin Turner stated that he had brought the town "to the top of the ladder," and Councillor Albert Edward Forbes described him as "a credit to the town."[168] Later in the year Hatfield won the national mile championship, took second place in the national one hundred-yard competition and won the 440-yard national salt water championship.[169] In 1913 he was invited to play in an international water polo match but was already engaged to swim in Dublin, and in "further proof of his wonderful versatility," Hatfield won the Amateur Swimming Association long-distance championship (5¼ miles) on the Thames, his first race in open water. The *Sports Gazette* reported that Teesside "rejoiced whole-heartedly for there is no more popular sportsman in the district."[170]

The Middlesbrough Amateur Gymnasium Society provided similar health-giving benefits to adults and children as swimming.[171] Parents were informed that "no roughness will be allowed" at classes, and "special care will be taken with boys who are in any way delicate." The *Sports Gazette* also advised "clerks, school teachers, shop assistants and those leading sedentary lives" to join in order to restore "lost tonicity to a healthy body and mind." By early 1905 the gymnasium had 134 members—eighty-five men, twenty-one ladies, ten boys, and eighteen girls.[172] At a gymnastic exhibition in 1906, Sir Samuel Sadler (evidently an adherent of muscular Christianity) remarked that the club had finally "got hold of that class of people who could appreciate the healthful exercise which it had promulgated"; the main purpose of the club was to "preach the gospel of muscle."[173] The club president (Walter G. Roberts) called on members to increase membership, and thus "not only make the competitions keener, but carry out the good work of the club, in a more emphatic manner." Roberts suggested that young people in the town "were apt to be mere spectators rather than partakers" in sport, particularly football, and thought that increased participation would "tell greatly against their physique in the future."[174] The *Sports Gazette* was particularly enthusiastic about the gymnasium, calling on parents to take their children to see "classes of happy-faced boys and girls, teeming with energy and health, and preparing for the arduous battle of life." The newspaper stated that new members were being enrolled every night at this establishment that was run "for the public good."[175] Indeed it was stated by the club in 1910 that it "did a very great deal for the health and the community . . . unostentatiously, but nevertheless effectively."[176] The backgrounds of those captains that can be identified suggest that the members of the gymnasium were more cross-class than those who were in charge of it. In 1910 the men's vice-captain was a steel billet dresser and the boys' captain was an apprentice engineer. The girls' vice-captain was the daughter of the manager of the steelwork's baths, and in 1912 the girls' captain was the daughter of a molder.[177]

NEW SPORTS AND FADS

A number of new sports were introduced to Middlesbrough during this period, some with more success and popularity than others. Some sports proved to be mere passing fashions, mirroring national patterns. Of the new sports, some involved elements of commercialism or were developed specifically with spectators or participants in mind, while others embraced technological advances.

The short-lived "commercial and competitive phenomenon" of Ping-Pong first appeared in 1902. The game had been aimed at the upper-middle classes, but had proved "too energetic and noisy" for most middle-class homes. It was also thought to be too overtly commercial, there being forty-nine models of Ping-Pong bat available to buy.[178] Nevertheless, the *Northern Echo* reported that, "as in other things, Middlesbrough has decided not to be behind in the matter of ping pong." A tournament was held at the Majestic Cafe in March 1902 with eighty-four competitors including eight women.[179] The Cleveland Ping Pong Club was formed a month later with a membership of fifty men and twenty women. Officials elected to the club a year later included a boot shop manager as secretary, a newspaper's sporting editor as treasurer, and a female stationery and fancy goods dealer as committee member.[180] By March 1903 the club were holding fortnightly tournaments, but it was also evident that they were keen on social events as was the case with so many of the town's middle-class sports clubs. Fifteen members cycled to Middleton-one-Row, where "a stroll was taken through the wood and the party were photographed . . . a game of football by the male members of the party produced great fun, and the ladies meanwhile had a walk." On the same day, twelve members also "had a very enjoyable outing to Redcar." The club's first annual picnic included a football match and a climb up Roseberry Topping. Male members competed in a cycle race, a three-legged race, and a sack race, while the women partook in an egg-and-spoon race, a footrace, and a blindfold race.[181]

There was no further mention of this sport in the local press until September 1909, when it was reported that the games committee of the Middlesbrough YMCA wanted to start a league, and the Middlesbrough & District Table Tennis League was subsequently formed.[182] However, the League received no further coverage in the press, until 1913 when "the champion player of the north" (Andrew Donaldson from Sunderland) visited Middlesbrough "to stimulate fresh interest in the game."[183]

The Middlesbrough & District Motor Cycling Club was formed in October 1906 with annual subscriptions set at 5s. This was relatively low, but the cost of purchasing and maintaining a motorcycle would have prevented the majority of people from joining. Advertisements from individual sellers in 1909 started at £6, increasing to £19 10s for a motorcycle with side car. Olliff's Garage's prices ranged from £8 10s to £10, and in 1912 prices from a number of sellers ranged from £10 to £65.[184] The club's first officials were lower-middle and middle class. The first president was a doctor (succeeded by an ironmaster), the vice-president was a mineral water manufacturer, the secretary was a housepainter and decorator, the treasurer was a hosier and hairdresser, and the captain was an electrical engineer.[185] "Club runs" were held on Wednesday and Saturday afternoons and Sunday mornings, and the first hill-climbing competition attracted sixteen participants, including one woman (Mary Considine, the wife of a doctor).[186]

'Teessider' in the *Teesside Weekly Herald* commented that "motor cycling is a form of sport which is beyond the reach of the vast majority," and congratulated the club on their success in spite of this fact. The members were "all united in a common bond of good fellowship which augurs well for the future prosperity of the club." Indeed by the end of 1907 the club had seventy members.[187] Club competitions in 1908 included a two hundred-mile reliability trial to Berwick-upon-Tweed and back, a flexibility hill climb, and an "old crocks race."[188] Membership had increased to ninety-nine by 1914. This increase may have been due to the number of events the club was now able to arrange. In July 1913 alone, the club held eight events, including a tour of the Lake District, and a visit to the Motorcycle Show in London.[189]

The Middlesbrough Skating Rink Ltd was formed in 1909, with the intention of building "the finest skating rink in the country."[190] The Olympia rink in Linthorpe was opened by the mayor and mayoress (their presence showing again the importance ascribed to the town's sports), and within a week it had become "a popular resort." There was thankfully "an entire absence of the rowdy element and the conduct of the visitors was most orderly." The *Teesside Weekly Herald* was keen that "every effort should be made to preserve the tone of the entertainment at its present level."

Admission to the rink was 6d, plus 1s for skating.[191] A gymkhana was held at Olympia in July, and included races for boys and girls, an obstacle race for men, an egg-and-spoon race and a balloon race for ladies, and a couples' race. The *North-Eastern Daily Gazette* suggested that, "skating has come to stay . . . visitors and regular patrons are unanimous in saying that it is in every way one of the finest and best-appointed rinks."[192]

The first rink hockey match at Olympia between Middlesbrough and Cleadon (Sunderland), was described in enthusiastic terms by the *North-Eastern Daily Gazette,*

> It was short, sharp, and strenuous. The 30 minutes were full of the fast chasing up and down the rink by eighteen perspiring young men of the diminutive football, the crash of meeting sticks, anon the tumbling about of players, the rasp of suddenly 'braked' skates, and the applause and shouts of encouragement of the spectators leaning over the upholstered barriers. A general whirl, in fact, of sticks and ball and limbs.[193]

The Middlesbrough Olympia Rink Speed Club was formed in 1910, and competitions at the club's sports included a mile handicap, a ladies' wool winding race, a four laps handicap for boys, a canoe race, and an obstacle race.[194] Another match in February 1910 between Middlesbrough and a traveling theater company was attended by "a large company, including many of the Middlesbrough footballers," and though it was pleasant enough, it was "marked by lustiness rather than science."[195]

Though a wide variety of sports were being watched and participated in at this time, the local press were not convinced that baseball would catch on again in Middlesbrough. Despite the position of Middlesbrough Cricket Club, in 1906 when baseball was being revived in London, one *Northern Athlete* writer thought that to try to restart the game in this "cricketing zone of England" would be "a suicidal policy because the game is dead as the proverbial door nail." However, in the same newspaper another writer thought that baseball was "a substitute for football, something that will be as brimful of excitement and incident as the great winter game."[196] Demonstrating the precarious position of cricket in Middlesbrough as a spectator sport, the *Sports Gazette* thought that "something more interesting than much of the present day cricket" was needed in the summer and baseball was ideal as the working classes would "find this exciting game just to their tastes."[197] When the game of pushball[198] was played at the ground of Middlesbrough Football Club in 1902, the *North-Eastern Daily Gazette* thought that there was very little interest in the game despite the "considerable curiosity" of the five thousand spectators. The *North Star* stated that the crowd had "found much cause for merriment and mirth," though "it was extremely doubtful whether it will 'catch on.'"[199] Indeed the game did not appear again until 1914 when a match between teams from Samuelson's and Eldon Workmen's Club was "pushed off" by Jack Hatfield.[200]

SPORTS DAYS

A wide variety of clubs continued to hold sports days in this period, the majority of which attracted large crowds, suggesting that such events may have been regarded as social as well as sporting occasions for the community. Moreover sports days were welcomed, as "there is nothing for the working man to do on a Saturday afternoon in summer."[201] As had been the case in the late nineteenth century, some clubs relied on the income such events generated. The *Teesside Weekly Herald* stated that without sports days, several clubs "would assuredly fail to make ends meet." Indeed, in 1910 the profits from Middlesbrough Cricket Club's sports day allowed them "to meet current expenses."[202] In 1905 the crowd of four thousand at the Grangetown sports day led the *Teesside Weekly Herald* to conclude that "the prospect of a good day's sport in the athletic field still forms an irresistible attraction." The Grangetown track was chosen by the Northern Counties' Athletic Association for the 440-yard race in 1906, which the *Northern Echo* regarded as "a fitting recognition of the endeavours put forth by the Grangetown sports managers to provide [the] best sport and talent possible for the public."[203] In 1906 Middlesbrough Football Club's sports day attracted seven thousand spectators and resulted in a profit of £45. That of Middlesbrough Cricket Club was regarded as "one of the most popular athletic events of the year in this district," attracting a crowd of four thousand in 1909 with eighty-one entrants for the sprint race alone.[204] The North-Eastern Steelworks hosted the half-mile championship of the North Yorkshire & South Durham National Cyclists' Union in 1909, and in 1913 the *Sports Gazette* reported a crowd of nine thousand spectators at the sports day of the Middlesbrough Medical Charities Organisation.[205]

The races and contests that took place, and the prizes available, varied from club to club. Competitions were open to various levels of ability, sometimes including women and children, and it is evident by the types of contests that sports days were not always serious occasions. The sports of the RUFS cycling club in 1901 included a "tortoise race," a costume-and-flag race, and an egg-and-spoon race, and that of the Samuelson's club a year later included the tug-of-war and an old men's race. In comparison, the championship sports of the North Ormesby & Middlesbrough Cycling Club in 1903 featured motor racing.[206] The sports of the Tees Conservancy in 1905 at the Thornaby cycling track included flat and cycling races, as well as a three-legged race, throwing a cricket ball, shying at a wicket, and a quoit handicap.[207] A walking race was held by the Eston Quoits Club at their sports for workmen "who had lost a leg whilst following their employment." The sports of the Dorman Long club included the usual foot and cycle races, as well as a "pig hunt" which "caused much amusement," the pig being presented to the winner. The prizes at Dorman Long's event in 1907 totaled £45 and included a threading the needle race for wives, daughters, and sisters of the workmen, and an ambulance competition for teams of five men.[208] Even though the event was designed to raise money, the North Ormesby Hospital Charity Sports also gave out prizes, including £6 for the mile flat race, £2 2s for the cycle parade, and prizes of 10s 6d for the best fancy costume.[209]

Some sports days were outings solely for club members but were still reported at length in the local press. The Ayresome Cycling Club held their event at nearby Nunthorpe in 1905 and it was attended by three hundred workmen of the Ayresome Ironworks and their wives and children. The sports of the Linthorpe Industrial School included a 120-yard footrace, boxing, the high jump, whistling, and a bun-and-treacle eating competition, and Mrs Lowthian Bell presented the prizes to the competitors at the sports of Middlesbrough High School.[210] The employees of the drapers Thomas Jones took part in a number of sporting contests at their annual picnic in 1907, including a 120-yard race for married men, a women's fifty-yard race, and cricket between ladies and gentlemen.[211]

WOMEN AND SPORT—INCREASING OPPORTUNITIES?

Growing female participation in sport occurred against a background of increasingly radical action in favor of female suffrage. The campaign for the vote had escalated from the "genteel and constitutional" to criminal damage and arson, leading to arrests, imprisonment, and hunger strikes, but in Middlesbrough there was little support among women or men for female enfranchisement.[212] It has been suggested that most sporting women were more concerned with "better health, enjoyment or a marriage partner" than with advancing their political status, but Kay argues that there was no reason why the "average" woman could not have been a feminist *and* a sportswoman.[213] Nevertheless, women's access to sport was still "constrained by the burdens of segregation and chaperonage, modesty and decorum." Women generally found it easier to make progress in individual, gentle sports than in those involving vigorous exercise or competitiveness.[214] It is evident however, that opportunities to play sport rarely existed for working-class women in Middlesbrough, being restricted by lack of free time and the cost of subscriptions to those clubs that admitted female members. Lady Bell stated that working women were unable to benefit from "the exhilaration of brisk recreative exercise in the open air," nor did they have any "possibilities of entertainment" which would give them "change of ideas and bring some relief to the monotony of their lives."[215] Nevertheless, in 1901 the *Northern Weekly Gazette* commented that,

> Physical culture is now a recognised part of the education of the modern girl. It is not enough that the mind should be trained and stored with knowledge; the body, too, must have a systematic course of training.[216]

One contemporary hoped that "instead of gossiping on doorsteps, or wandering . . . about the streets," women "would develop an interest in . . . appropriate games."[217] In contrast, in 1907 the *Teesside Weekly Herald* argued that sport presented "a great danger" to young women, suggesting that the sizes of shoes and gloves were increasing because of growing participation—"The dainty feet and hands which for so long have graced feminine beauty are doomed to disappear as a result of a too strenuous indulgence in athletics."[218] However, it was often reported that ladies were present at football matches, particularly in the grandstand. After complaining that "filthy ephithets" had been heard in proximity to women at a Middlesbrough match, the *North-Eastern Daily Gazette* remarked that ladies had "a restrictive influence over the coarser of the male sex."[219]

The *Northern Weekly Gazette* thought that "it is almost as usual a thing for a girl to take lessons in swimming as it is for her to go through a course of physical exercises for the benefit of her health." The Middlesbrough Ladies Swimming Club held a "water carnival" in 1904 that included racing and diving for girls, a display by Jack Hatfield and his sisters Mabel and Bertha, and "an excellent exhibition of life-saving" by the club's members. An event a month later also included ladies' water polo, "the first of its kind held in the Baths."[220] In contrast, Hilda Jefferson,[221] "the champion lady swimmer of Middlesbrough," swam 2¾ miles along the Tees from Newport to the Transporter Bridge in 1913. She was accompanied by two male swimmers and completed the distance in one hour, ten minutes. The *Teesside Weekly Herald* reported that a "considerable number of spectators lined the banks of the river, and gave her considerable encouragement by cheering her pluck effort."[222] She also appeared at a gala of the Ladies Club a month later alongside Jack Hatfield and a number of north eastern champion swimmers.[223]

Though the Cleveland Roads Cycling Club stated that the only clubs "that have good musters are those who have lady members to join in the runs,"[224] it is not clear how much cycling the female members actually undertook. While the Middlesbrough Crescent Cycling Club had a lady captain, and five women on the committee, the press reports of the Middlesbrough Ladies' Cycling Club refer mainly to social events. In 1902 it was reported that the members thought the club's outing to Carlton-in-

Cleveland had been "the most delightful picnic [they] have ever taken part in," though members also took part in a footrace, an egg-and-spoon race, a blindfold race, and a consolation race.[225] In contrast, the female members of the Cleveland Ping Pong Club did take part in competitions; for example in 1902 eight ladies entered the competition for a dressing case.[226] It was reported in 1911 that Middlesbrough Bowling Club was considering forming a ladies' section; women were reported to have "tried to find the 'Jack' and with a little more patience and practice they would no doubt prove useful members of the club."[227] The ladies section of Linthorpe Tennis Club had two female secretaries and the committee of the Avenue Tennis Club included four women, while in contrast the Grove Tennis Club had a tea committee of six women.[228] This club did not start a ladies' section until 1911 when a tournament for ladies' singles and doubles was introduced, and members were asked to "practise more together than previously, so as to increase the strength of the team put forward."[229]

By 1911, fifty thousand women had joined golf clubs in Britain.[230] Although Holt describes golf as "a kind of half-shared, half-segregated suburban activity,"[231] women gradually became increasingly active members of Middlesbrough Golf Club. In 1910 a committee was appointed to "ascertain the feeling of the ladies with regard to the competitions," though a year later the club debated whether female members should be allowed to vote on club matters as they did not pay full subscriptions. One male member suggested that to take the vote away from them amounted to "rather ungallant treatment," and another (Charles Coates, husband of Alice—see below) pointed out that the club "had ladies attempting and nearly succeeding in beating the champion of England." Ladies subsequently retained their voting privileges.[232] Despite restrictions on when women could take to the course, in 1912 eighty-six of the club's 241 members were female, increasing to 101 out of 274 members a year later.[233] The club's minute book records the names of ninety-four new female members from June 1909 to December 1914, and the details for sixty women can be found. Only seven of the female members were employed and only one of these seven women was married.[234] Of those not employed, twenty-eight were married and twenty-five were single; all of their husbands or fathers had a middle-class occupation. The fathers or husbands of twenty-seven of the female members were also members of the club. As a suffragette, golf club member Alice Schofield-Coates refused to supply information for the 1911 census.[235] She had spent a month in prison in 1909, having been arrested at Downing Street, and was the president of the Middlesbrough branch of the Women's Freedom League.[236] The *Suffrage Annual and Women's Who's Who* described her as "an active Suffragist" in the Northeast, and listed her recreations as walking, cycling, and golf. Schofield-Coates's involvement with sport contradicts Birley's statement that, "feminist politics rarely interested women golfers, who were engaged in a more traditional battle." Similarly, Tranter has also argued that "far from being revolutionaries," female golfers "were not even interested in challenging the subordinate status accorded to them in the sport they played."[237]

Though nationally there was only one cricket club for every fifty female hockey clubs, the *Cleveland Standard* thought that cricket was an ideal sport for young women to play. The newspaper preferred cricket over hockey and tennis; it had "such a number of advantages as a girls' game that it seems odd it should be so little encouraged." The writer felt that the sport was good "for the figure . . . the body, at least, is not liable to over-exertion." It is evident that this particular writer envisaged the sport being played by middle-class young ladies as he believed it was an ideal game for the summer holidays, adding "greatly to the possible list of pleasures in country homes."[238] Indeed the president of the Middlesbrough Ladies' Cricket Club in 1911 was the wife of a doctor (Mary Elizabeth Hedley, Chairman of the Board of Guardians), the treasurer was a teacher, and the secretary was a stenographer.[239] The *South Durham & Cleveland Mercury* thought that hockey offered the same benefits to women as football and cricket did to men, promoting "healthy activity, muscular development and moral discipline." Perhaps because of the novelty, when a ladies' hockey match was held at the Olympia rink in 1910 it was "lined with spectators, who gave the ladies a splendid reception as they entered the arena."[240] In contrast, "Free Lance" in the *Northern Athlete* regarded hockey as "essentially a masculine" game. Reflecting the idea that playing sport would make women more masculine and undermine their appearance, modesty, and femininity, he protested "against the encouragement meted out to the opposite sex to indulge" in the sport, suggesting that,

> if they would only try to realise how the majority of men detest the "mannish" women, they would think twice before they venture to indulge in games like hockey, which are entirely out of their sphere, and calculated to unsex them in more ways than one![241]

Since opening, the gymnasium had proved popular with women and girls. Female members were trained by the same instructor as the men, and exercises were said to be "smartly executed." The *Sports Gazette* suggested that if "ladies of the town who have respect for their physical welfare, would only look in some night, I am sure that they would soon become members,"

> A visit to the gymnasium . . . will show that physical training for women is coming more and more into vogue . . . a series of the most graceful, light and interesting marching and running movements are performed. The ladies all look very agile and graceful in their attractive gymnasium costume. . . . The

spectator is at once struck by the intensely conscientious and interested way in which the exercises are performed.[242]

The gymnasium was recommended in particular to female teachers, "who may have to drill the children at school" as they would learn "how to manoeuvre the class in a practical manner." In contrast to the remarks about hockey above, the *Sports Gazette* stated that ladies should not worry if they were "nervous, weak or have any fears about the result of moderate exercise," as exercise was "a beautifier in itself."[243] The *Middlesbrough Standard* suggested that the exercises had a refining effect on the working women who attended,

> It is to the credit of the working girl that she . . . chooses wisely and with discretion in her hours of recreation. After a long day in shop or factory these youthful people readily accept the opportunities offered by their clubs. There they are to be seen neatly and simply dressed, as clean and nice in their personal care as any dainty lady. Their manners, too, are pleasant, easy and gentle. That this refining influence is making its mark no one can dispute.[244]

However, the number of female members of the gymnasium was never very high. In 1905 there were only twenty-one members in the ladies' section, and eighteen in the girls' section. By 1909 this had only increased to twenty-six ladies and twenty-six girls.[245] It was also noted that "the ladies were not so well represented" at the AGM in 1906; "they thought that in leaving business details to the men they were leaving them in good hands."[246]

CONCLUSION

Despite the sheer number of sports clubs that existed in Middlesbrough prior to the First World War, it is clear that for the majority of men and women most sports were out of reach. The notion that leisure in the town was dominated by working-class and less respectable forms of leisure does not appear to be true.[247] Lady Bell stated that most workmen "have nowhere to go for change of thought and diversion but the streets, unless they turn into the ever-present, ever-accessible public house." There was nevertheless "an increasing and often unreasonable demand for pleasure."[248] Given that the costs of joining most clubs were steep, it is not surprising that for many people their only involvement in sport was through spectating or betting. The *Teesside Weekly Herald* remarked upon the number of people who visited the racecourse at Stockton in August race week. Even though this left some works temporarily idle, "there seemed to be no diminution in the thousands of Middlesbrough folk" attending the races, due to "the slavish fascination of betting."[249]

However, there was also a belief that sport could be beneficial. William James O'Neil of the Middlesbrough Church Cricket League believed that "the feeling of sportsmanship and good fellowship would spread not only among them in this town but in other towns all over the country, and thus keep England on its pedestal as a sporting nation."[250] The *Teesside Weekly Herald* praised the YMCA for "inducing young men to occupy their leisure hours in a manner spiritually, mentally and physically beneficial to themselves."[251] However, for the majority of sports clubs, membership remained low considering the size of the town. Only the clubs of works retained large memberships. The reasons such clubs were formed are unclear. There was evidently a belief among employers that participation in and provision of these clubs would foster good relations, retain workers, and increase productivity, but the reasons that so many men chose to join were never stated. That such clubs were the only ones that were affordable, was a key factor, and most workingmen would no doubt have preferred to spend their leisure time with their fellow workers. For many men, their only contact with sport was watching football. The game's increasing popularity and the role it played in Middlesbrough will be discussed in the following chapter.

NOTES

1. F. Bell, *At the Works: A study of a manufacturing town* (London, 1985 [first edition, 1907]), p. 131.

2. W. Lillie, *The History of Middlesbrough* (Middlesbrough, 1968), pp. 348–349, p. 474; The extension of the Borough meant that the town now included Acklam, Linthorpe, parts of Ormesby and the whole of North Ormesby.

3. D. Taylor, "The Infant Hercules and the Augean Stables: A century of economic and social development in Middlesbrough c.1840–1939," in A. J. Pollard (ed.), *Middlesbrough: Town and Community 1830–1950* (Stroud, 1996), pp. 61–64.

4. B. Doyle, "Managing and Contesting Industrial Pollution in Middlesbrough, 1880–1914," *Northern History* 47, 1 (2010), p. 138; Taylor, "The Infant Hercules and the Augean Stables," pp. 71–73; J. J. Turner, "Middlesbrough and the National Coal Strike of 1912," *Bulletin of the Cleveland & Teesside Local History Society* 43 (1982), p. 1.

5. *North-Eastern Daily Gazette*, 10th April 1906.

6. M. Huggins, "Second-Class Citizens? English middle-class culture and sport, 1850–1910: A reconsideration," *International Journal of the History of Sport* 17, 1 (2000), p. 15.

7. J. Lowerson, *Sport and the English Middle Classes 1870–1914* (Manchester, 1995), pp. 8–10.

8. In contrast, competitors in 1901 at a quarter-mile keelboat handicap promoted by the landlord of the Cross Keys Hotel, included a river keel man, a

general laborer, a sand wherry laborer and a shipyard laborer—*South Durham & Cleveland Mercury*, 31st May 1901.

9. Councillors—Thomas Baker, William J. Bruce, Thomas Gibson-Poole; MPs—Samuel Sadler, Joseph Walton; former MP—Sir Bernhard Samuelson; Aldermen—Thomas Carter, Samuel Sadler; former mayor—Thomas Baker, William J. Bruce, Thomas Carter, Sir Raylton Dixon, Samuel Sadler.

10. Minute Book of MABC, 4th June, 8th July, 8th August 1901; The new boathouse cost the club £130—Minute Book of MABC, 15th November 1901.

11. Minute Book of MABC, 13th June 1902; *Northern Echo*, 18th April 1902.

12. *South Durham & Cleveland Mercury*, 24th November 1905.

13. *Sports Gazette*, 8th June 1907.

14. *Teesside Weekly Herald*, 3rd August 1907.

15. *Sports Gazette*, 11th April 1914; *Teesside Weekly Herald*, 30th July 1910.

16. 1911 census; *Sports Gazette*, 11th April, 18th July 1914.

17. Minute Book of Middlesbrough Golf Club (hereafter Minute Book of MGC), 20th November 1908.

18. Quoted in W. Vamplew, "Successful Workers or Exploited Labour? Golf professionals and professional golfers in Britain 1888–1914," *Economic History Review* 61, 1 (2008), p. 67.

19. J. Hill, *Sport, Leisure & Culture, in Twentieth-Century Britain* (Basingstoke, 2002) p. 143.

20. J. Lowerson, "Golf," in T. Mason (ed.), *Sport in Britain: A social history* (Cambridge, 1989), p. 188.

21. N. L. Jackson, "Professionalism and Sport," *Fortnightly Review* 67 (1900), p. 156; Vamplew, "Successful Workers or Exploited Labour?," p. 68.

22. Weastell's three brothers were also golf professionals, and he had already been a professional at two other clubs before joining Middlesbrough—*Middlesbrough Golf Club Centenary 1908–2008* (Middlesbrough, 2010), p. 50.

23. The club also employed a groundsman for 25s a week, and Weastell's wife Isabel provided bread, teacakes, and jam twice a week, being paid 2s 6d per afternoon—Minute Book of MGC, 22nd January 1909, 23rd March 1911.

24. Minute Book of MGC, 22nd January 1909; Caddies were prevented from earning extra money when members were banned from purchasing golf balls from them, and in 1913 caddies were informed that "they must not wander about [the] course unless carrying"—Minute Book of MGC, 25th July 1910, 24th July 1913.

25. *Cleveland Standard*, 2nd January 1909; *Teesside Weekly Herald*, 2nd January 1909.

26. The cups were all presented by members of the club—Emerson Cup (for men over fifty-five years of age), Hinton Cup, Mason Cup, and Poole Cup—*Middlesbrough Golf Club Centenary*, p. 35.

27. *Sports Gazette*, 19th November 1910.

28. Minute Book of MGC, 21st December 1911, 30th January, 19th September 1912, unspecified date for January 1913.

29. It should be pointed out that were a number of resignations during the period, with members often rejoining later. Duplicates (i.e., those who left and re-joined) have been removed from this list.

30. David Almgill, Joseph Calvert, Patrick Considine, and Thomas Roddam Dent; the latter had been mayor and was an alderman from 1907–1924.

31. A further seven male members are listed in the 1911 census as being at school—Lawrence Gjers jr at Charterhouse School, Raymond Cooper at Uppingham School, and Raymond Wilkinson at Bede Training College for Schoolmasters. The occupations of the heads of household of the four other young members were iron agent, chief draftsman, pawnbroker, and clerk to the Guardians of the Poor Law Union.

32. Birthplaces of those born overseas—Germany (three), Cyprus, France, Trinidad, and "At Sea."

33. K. Jefferys, "The Heyday of Amateurism in Modern Lawn Tennis," *International Journal of the History of Sport* 46, 15 (2009), p. 2240; R. J. Sturdee, "The Ethics of Football," *Westminster Review* 59 (1903), p. 181.

34. *Sports Gazette*, 25th March 1905, 7th April 1906; Grove, Linthorpe, Nomads, Excelsior, Albert Park, Hugh Bell Teachers, Middlesbrough Shorthand Writers, Middlesbrough Wesley Guild, Bees.

35. *North-Eastern Daily Gazette*, 16th April 1913.

36. *Sports Gazette*, 9th April 1910; *Teesside Weekly Herald*, 26th March 1910.

37. R. J. Lake, "Social Class, Etiquette and Behavioural Restraint in British Lawn Tennis, 1870–1939," *International Journal of the History of Sport* 28, 6 (2011), p. 878.

38. *North-Eastern Daily Gazette*, 31st March 1913; *Sports Gazette*, 4th April 1914.

39. *Sports Gazette*, 13th April 1907.

40. *Sports Gazette*, 21st February 1914; *Teesside Weekly Herald*, 14th March 1914.

41. 1901 census; *North-Eastern Daily Gazette*, 4th November 1903.

42. 1901 census; *North-Eastern Daily Gazette*, 4th November 1903; *South Durham & Cleveland Mercury*, 22nd April 1904; Newstead joined the grounds staff at Lords in 1904.

43. J. Hill, "'First-Class' Cricket and the Leagues: Some notes on the development of English cricket, 1900–40," *International Journal of the History of Sport* 4, 1 (1987), p. 74.

44. J. Arlott, "Sport," in S. Nowell-Smith (ed.), *Edwardian England 1901–1914* (London, 1964), p. 469; D. Birley, *Land of Sport and Glory: Sport and British society 1887–1910* (Manchester, 1995), p. 252.

45. 1901 census; *North-Eastern Daily Gazette*, 17th January, 8th July 1902; *Northern Echo*, 13th January 1902; See also Linthorpe Hockey Club, formed in 1910—*Sports Gazette*, 15th April 1911.

46. *Sports Gazette*, 24th September 1904; Lowerson, *Sport and the English Middle Classes*, p. 86.

47. *North-Eastern Daily Gazette*, 1st March 1906; *Sports Gazette*, 28th March 1908; In 1901–1903 club officials included a shipowner, an accountant, a jeweler, a milk dealer, a builder, a hatter, a clothier and tailor, and a steelworker—1901 and 1911 census; *Middlesbrough & Stockton Morning Mail*, 12th January 1901; *North-Eastern Daily Gazette*, 21st January 1903.

48. *Teesside Weekly Herald*, 27th January 1907; The reference to the club being mysterious may refer to the name—the local press did not record what it stood for.

49. *Teesside Weekly Herald*, 28th December 1912; RUFS were the only cycling club to have their own musical director (John Henry Wilkinson, a musical instru-

ment dealer, appointed in 1912)—1911 census; *Teesside Weekly Herald*, 27th April 1912.

50. 1901 census; *North-Eastern Daily Gazette*, 19th December 1901; *South Durham & Cleveland Mercury*, 10th April 1903; See also Middlesbrough Rovers Cycling Club, *North-Eastern Daily Gazette*, 24th March 1903; *Teesside Weekly Herald*, 19th March 1904; See also Middlesbrough Cycling Club, *North-Eastern Daily Gazette*, 29th January, 2nd February 1901.

51. 1901 census; *North-Eastern Daily Gazette*, 4th March 1903; By 1911 the composition of the Ayresome club's officials had changed entirely, moving away from the ironworks, and included a house agent, assistant schoolmaster, a clerk, a doctor, and a relieving officer for the Middlesbrough Union—1911 census; *Kelly's Directory of North and East Ridings of Yorkshire, 1913* (London, 1913); *Sports Gazette*, 25th February 1911.

52. *Sports Gazette*, 28th December 1912.

53. 1901 census; *South Durham & Cleveland Mercury*, 13th February 1903; See also the officials of Middlesbrough YMCA Swimming Club—*North-Eastern Daily Gazette*, 11th February 1903, and the more diverse of officials of Middlesbrough Majestic Swimming Club—*North-Eastern Daily Gazette*, 13th October 1904.

54. *South Durham & Cleveland Mercury*, 24th November 1905; *Sports Gazette*, 25th November 1905; R. Holt, *Sport and the British: A modern history* (Oxford, 1989), p.157.

55. *Sports Gazette*, 3rd March 1906.

56. David Almgill, Thomas R. Dent, Foster Dodsworth, John H. Gunter and Thomas Gibson-Poole.

57. Two hotel managers, two licensed victuallers, a brewery agent, a hotel keeper, a publican, an off beer seller, a wine and spirit merchant's manager, a wine and spirit merchant. In comparison, none of the identifiable members of either Middlesbrough Golf Club or Middlesbrough Amateur Boating Club were employed in the drinks trade.

58. Only two of the members did not live in Middlesbrough—one in Redcar and one in Stockton-on-Tees; See also new members for 1906–07—Minute Book of MBC, 25th April, 3rd May 1906, 23rd April, 7th May, 8th July 1907.

59. Minute Book of MBC, 6th February 1902, 30th March, 23rd June 1903.

60. Minute Book of MBC, 3rd May 1905; *North-Eastern Daily Gazette*, 7th May 1914; *Sports Gazette*, 12th December 1914; *Teesside Weekly Herald*, 13th May 1905.

61. *North-Eastern Daily Gazette*, 15th September 1914; *Teesside Weekly Herald*, 23rd May, 18th July 1914.

62. *Sports Gazette*, 26th September 1914; *Teesside Weekly Herald*, 6th March 1909.

63. A. A. Hall, "Wages, Earnings and Real Earnings in Teesside: A reassessment of the ameliorist interpretation of living standards in Britain, 1870–1914," *International Review of Social History* 26 (1981), p. 208, p. 210; Taylor, "The Infant Hercules and the Augean Stables," pp. 71–72.

64. *North-Eastern Daily Gazette*, 3rd March, 31st March, 24th May, 23rd June 1903.

65. *North-Eastern Daily Gazette*, 18th May, 14th August 1909, 15th August 1912.

66. *Sports Gazette*, 6th December 1913.

67. *Sports Gazette*, 17th March 1906.

68. R. Goodall, "Cycling in North Yorkshire and South Durham, 1869–1914," unpublished MA thesis, Teesside Polytechnic, 1988, p. 68; R. Goodall, "Cycling Clubs of North Yorkshire and South Durham, 1876–1914," *Bulletin of the Cleveland and Teesside Local History Society* 57 (Autumn 1989), p. 27.

69. Goodall, "Cycling in North Yorkshire and South Durham," p. 73.

70. *Kelly's Directory of North and East Ridings Yorkshire, 1893* (London, 1893) p. 601; *Kelly's Directory of North and East Ridings Yorkshire, 1913*, pp. 764–765; Neither of these directories list sports outfitters in the "Trades and Professional" sections.

71. *Sports Gazette*, 25th January 1908; This club was located on North Road in one of the poorest and unhealthiest parts of the town, condemned by the Medical Officer of Health in 1900—L. Polley, "Housing the Community, 1830–1914," in Pollard (ed.), *Middlesbrough: Town and Community*, pp. 169–170; Taylor, "The Infant Hercules and the Augean Stables," pp. 73–74.

72. The members of the League were Shaw's (foundry), Sadler's chemical works, the North-Eastern Railway Company, Dorman Long, Samuelson's, North-Eastern Steelworks, Warners' (steelworks), Gjers Mills, and Ayresome, joined by Westgarth (engineers) and Crewdsons (tube manufacturers) a year later—*Sports Gazette*, 29th April 1911, 27th July 1912; In 1914 the vice-chairman of the League was a traffic manager at an iron and steel works, and the secretary was a chemical works clerk—1911 census; *Sports Gazette*, 19th September 1914.

73. *Sports Gazette*, 9th May 1914; *Teesside Weekly Herald*, 16th May 1914.

74. Holt, *Sport and the British*, p. 190.

75. Bell, *At the Works*, p. 128; Taylor, "The Infant Hercules and the Augean Stables," p. 65.

76. Members of the Middlesbrough & District Billiard League—Co-operative, Cycling, Albert, Dorman Long & Co United Athletic Club, North Ormesby Conservatives, Samuelson's, Artillery, Ironopolis, Liberal, Zetland Stockton—*North-Eastern Daily Gazette*, 15th September 1909; *Sports Gazette*, 6th February 1909.

77. Billiards tables were included at the following—Gjers Mills, Samuelson's, North-Eastern Railway Athletic Club, the Winter Gardens, YMCA, St Patrick's Association, St Mary's Association, Cambridge House, Feversham Street Boys' Club, and the Holy Cross Mission.

78. Holt, *Sport and the British*, p. 175; Lowerson, *Sport and the English Middle Classes*, p. 77; K. A. P. Sandiford, "Cricket and the Victorian Society," *Journal of Social History* 17, 2 (1983), p. 303.

79. K. Sandiford and W. Vamplew, "The Peculiar Economics of English Cricket Before 1914," *British Journal of Sports History* 3, 3 (1986), p. 311.

80. *North-Eastern Daily Gazette*, 5th November 1902; *Northern Echo*, 23rd August 1902; *South Durham & Cleveland Mercury*, 29th August, 7th November 1902; The appearance of the Yorkshire 2nd XI was viewed as important to the club's bank balance as the gate money was thought to account for 35 percent of the club's income for the year—*Teesside Weekly Herald*, 20th August 1904.

81. *North-Eastern Daily Gazette*, 29th April 1904.

82. *Northern Athlete*, 28th May, 23rd July 1906.

83. *Teesside Weekly Herald*, 19th January 1907.

84. *North-Eastern Daily Gazette*, 19th August 1908; *Northern Athlete*, 24th August 1908.

85. *Teesside Weekly Herald*, 11th May 1907.

86. *Northern Athlete*, 17th, 24th May 1909; The committee had allowed Steve Bloomer (a Middlesbrough and England footballer) to leave for the North Ormesby club, leading the *Northern Athlete* to comment that such a decision was "the kind of thing that has kept the Middlesbrough club in the background for 25 years"—17th May 1909.

87. The Middlesbrough Owners offered the land to the Corporation for £3,300, and it was suggested that the Corporation buy the ground and allow it to be used jointly by the cricket club and the High School—*North-Eastern Daily Gazette*, 9th May 1910; *Northern Athlete*, 27th June 1910; *Teesside Weekly Herald*, 9th April 1910.

88. *North Star*, 7th July 1910; *Sports Gazette*, 9th July 1910.

89. *Sports Gazette*, 11th March 1911.

90. *Northern Athlete*, 8th May 1911.

91. *Sports Gazette*, 22nd December 1906, 30th November 1907.

92. *Teesside Weekly Herald*, 9th December 1911, 7th December 1912.

93. *North-Eastern Daily Gazette*, 16th September 1913; *Sports Gazette*, 20th September 1913.

94. *Teesside Weekly Herald*, 6th December 1913.

95. *Sports Gazette*, 5th December 1914; *Teesside Weekly Herald*, 7th November 1914.

96. *Northern Athlete*, 21st June 1909.

97. *Sports Gazette*, 29th May 1909.

98. *North-Eastern Daily Gazette*, 3rd December 1902.

99. *North-Eastern Daily Gazette*, 28th May 1906.

100. *North-Eastern Daily Gazette*, 1st February 1904; Other work-based cricket clubs mentioned in the local press include Cleveland Asylum, Cleveland & Tees Dockyards, Middlesbrough Bank Clerks, Middlesbrough Butchers, Middlesbrough Hairdressers, Middlesbrough Police, Newhouse's Wednesday (drapers), North-Eastern Railway Staff, Westgarth's Boilershop, Westgarth's Foundry, and Winterschladen's (wine merchants).

101. The founding members of the League were South Bank Primitive Methodist, Ayresome Street Primitive Methodist, Lackenby Wesley, West End Wesley, Park Wesley and Eston Primitive Methodist, with Middlesbrough Parish Church, Middlesbrough Baptists, St Columba's, Thornaby St Luke's, South Bank Brotherhood, South Bank Baptists, and Linthorpe Road Primitive Methodists 2nd joining later—*Sports Gazette*, 15th October 1910; *North-Eastern Daily Gazette*, 9th April 1910; *Northern Athlete*, 16th May 1910; *Teesside Weekly Herald*, 28th October 1911.

102. *Sports Gazette*, 19th November 1910; *Teesside Weekly Herald*, 27th February 1909.

103. *Teesside Weekly Herald*, 2nd April 1910, 16th March 1912; See also Linthorpe Primitive Methodist Cricket Club, *Sports Gazette*, 15th January 1910, and the cricket club of the YMCA, *North-Eastern Daily Gazette*, 27th January 1908, *Sports Gazette*, 29th April 1911.

104. *Teesside Weekly Herald*, 19th October, 2nd November 1912.

105. Minute book of North Yorkshire Cricket League, 29th February 1912, U/NYSD/1, Teesside Archives.

106. M. Huggins, "Leisure and Sport in Middlesbrough, 1840–1914," in Pollard (ed.), *Middlesbrough: Town and Community*, p. 134.

107. *Northern Echo*, 27th January 1903; Bell, *At the Works*, p. 126.

108. R. Munting, "The Games Ethic and Industrial Capitalism Before 1914: The provision of company sports," *Sport in History* 23, 1 (2003), pp. 48–50.

109. S. Phillips, Industrial Welfare and Recreation at Boots Pure Drug Company 1883–1945, unpublished PhD thesis, Nottingham Trent University, 2003, p. 342; A. Redfern, "Crewe: Leisure in a railway town," in J. K. Walton and J. Walvin (eds), *Leisure in Britain, 1780–1939* (Manchester, 1983), p. 118.

110. Dorman Long & Co Ltd, Minute Book 1, BS.DL/1/2/2, Teesside Archives.

111. *Middlesbrough & Stockton Evening Telegraph*, 8th July 1899; *South Durham & Cleveland Mercury*, 14th July 1899.

112. 1901 census; *South Durham & Cleveland Mercury*, 23rd February 1900; The "objects of the club" are not explicitly stated. Membership of the football teams had declined, perhaps due to members preferring to watch Middlesbrough FC play, as was stated by the North-Eastern Steelworks Athletic Club in 1911.

113. *North-Eastern Daily Gazette*, 13th August 1900; *Northern Echo*, 21st August 1900.

114. *South Durham & Cleveland Mercury*, 27th March 1903.

115. 1901 and 1911 census; *North-Eastern Daily Gazette*, 27th March 1905; *Teesside Weekly Herald*, 8th April 1905; Separate secretaries were elected in 1908 for the each of the activities of the club—band, bowls, cricket (twelve teams), football (twelve junior teams and ten senior teams), gymnasium, quoits, and rifle club—*Teesside Weekly Herald*, 4th April 1908.

116. C. Shaw, "The Large Manufacturing Employers of 1907," *Business History* 25, 52 (1983), p. 53; *Teesside Weekly Herald*, 3rd April 1909.

117. *Teesside Weekly Herald*, 3rd April 1909.

118. *Sports Gazette*, 19th March 1910; *Teesside Weekly Herald*, 5th April 1913.

119. *Teesside Weekly Herald*, 6th April 1912.

120. *Teesside Weekly Herald*, 5th March 1904.

121. *South Durham & Cleveland Mercury*, 22nd June, 3rd August 1906; *Teesside Weekly Herald*, 11th March 1905.

122. *Sports Gazette*, 2nd March 1907.

123. 1911 census; *Sports Gazette*, 27th June 1908, 3rd July 1909.

124. *Sports Gazette*, 12th December 1908; Members were requested to contribute to the £105 spent on the new facilities and subscriptions were increased—*North-Eastern Daily Gazette*, 25th June 1909.

125. *Sports Gazette*, 24th June 1911; *Teesside Weekly Herald*, 24th June 1911.

126. *Teesside Weekly Herald*, 6th February 1909.

127. *North-Eastern Daily Gazette*, 14th November 1910; *Sports Gazette*, 19th November 1910.

128. *Teesside Weekly Herald*, 19th November 1910; With reference to the relationship between masters and men in Middlesbrough, Lewis states that in the later decades of the nineteenth century the iron and steel industry experienced "little sustained industrial conflict," most disputes being resolved through arbitration—R. Lewis, "The Evolution of a Political Culture: Middlesbrough, 1850–1950," in Pollard (ed.), *Middlesbrough: Town and Community*, p. 115.

129. *North-Eastern Daily Gazette*, 1st December 1903; *Northern Echo*, 27th January 1903.

130. J. J. Turner, "The People's Winter Garden, Middlesbrough," *Bulletin of the Cleveland and Teesside History Society* 46 (1984), pp. 31–34; J. Turner, "The Frontier Revisited: Thrift and fellowship in the new industrial town, c.1830–1914," in Pollard (ed.), *Middlesbrough: Town and Community*, p. 83; Lady Bell thought that working men would be prepared to pay the entrance fee as "they would prefer to have a share in the responsibility of its maintenance"—*North-Eastern Daily Gazette*, 25th October 1907.

131. *North-Eastern Daily Gazette*, 25th October 1907.

132. *Kelly's Directory of North and East Ridings of Yorkshire, 1909* (London, 1909), p. 183; *Kelly's Directory of North and East Ridings Yorkshire, 1913*, p. 193; *Teesside Weekly Herald*, 23rd September 1905 .

133. *North-Eastern Daily Gazette*, 23rd December 1907; Two years later, members were informed that the depression in trade "kept them from pressing the movement forward" to buy their own premises—*Sports Gazette*, 16th January 1909; For the club's officials see *Sports Gazette*, 16th January 1909.

134. *North-Eastern Daily Gazette*, 15th April 1910; *Sports Gazette*, 22nd October 1910; Other clubs also mentioned in the press included the Cargo Fleet Steel & Iron Works Athletic Club and Winterschladen's Athletic Club—*North-Eastern Daily Gazette*, 20th August 1913; *Sports Gazette*, 3rd October 1914.

135. Turner, "The People's Winter Garden," p. 30.

136. D. Erdozain, *The Problem of Pleasure: Sport, recreation and the crisis of Victorian religion* (Woodbridge, 2010), p.185; Holt, *Sport and the British*, p. 136.

137. Holt, *Sport and the British*, p. 144; P. Stubley, *Industrial Society and Church: Middlesbrouh, 1830–1914* (Bognor Regis, 2001) p. 9.

138. *Kelly's Directory of North and East Ridings of Yorkshire, 1897* (London, 1897), p. 184; *North-Eastern Daily Gazette*, 19th November 1895.

139. *North-Eastern Daily Gazette*, 23rd March 1897.

140. *North-Eastern Daily Gazette*, 23rd October 1903; *Teesside Weekly Herald*, 17th September 1904; Donations for the new facilities were received from Sir Christopher Furness (shipbuilder and MP for Hartlepool), Waynman Dixon (shipbuilder), Thomas Westgarth (of Westgarth English & Co engineering), Samuelson's, Dorman Long & Co and Bell Brothers—*North-Eastern Daily Gazette*, 23rd October 1903.

141. *Teesside Weekly Herald*, 25th March 1905; The concern with drink at this time was emphasized by the findings of the Middlesbrough Temperance Society who stationed enumerators outside the town's 106 public houses and thirty-six off-licences during the six hours they were open one Sunday in 1904. The premises were visited by 55,045 men, 21,594 women, and 13,775 children—Stubley, *Industrial Society and Church*, p. 83.

142. *North-Eastern Daily Gazette*, 19th October 1909.

143. *Teesside Weekly Herald*, 22nd February 1908.

144. *Sports Gazette*, 6th February 1909; *Teesside Weekly Herald*, 12th February 1910.

145. *Sports Gazette*, 4th February 1911.

146. *Teesside Weekly Herald*, 20th February 1909.

147. Stubley, *Industrial Society and Church*, p. 66; *North-Eastern Daily Gazette*, 25th October 1898; The *Northern Echo* had reported on this club as early as 1894, detailing the "capital entertainment" given by the girls' club—*Northern Echo*, 31st May 1894.

148. Cambridge House Club Rules, PR/M(P)/8/27, Teesside Archives.

149. 1911 census; Stubley, *Industrial Society and Church*, p. 63; *Sports Gazette*, 13th July 1907; In 1908, vice-presidents included three members of the clergy, three ironmasters and Sadler—*Teesside Weekly Herald*, 8th February 1908.

150. *Sports Gazette*, 6th February 1909, 12th February 1910.

151. P. Stephenson, *Joe Walton Community and Youth Club* (Middlesbrough, 2001), p. 4; *North-Eastern Daily Gazette*, 20th November 1906, 8th September 1911.

152. *Teesside Weekly Herald*, 29th February 1908.

153. *North-Eastern Daily Gazette*, 20th November 1906.

154. Holy Cross Mission, PR/M(P)/8/27, Teesside Archives.

155. *Teesside Weekly Herald*, 18th January 1913.

156. Polley, "Housing the Community," p. 169; F. Tillyard, "English Town Development in the Nineteenth Century," *The Economic Journal* 23 (1913), p. 559.

157. M. Heavisides, *Rambles by the River Tees* (Stockon-on-Tees, 1905); Taylor, "The Infant Hercules and the Augean Stables," pp. 71–76; D. Taylor, *Policing the Victorian Town: The development of the police in Middlesbrough c.1840–1914* (Basingstoke, 2002), p. 107.

158. N. Tranter, *Sport, Economy and Society in Britain 1750–1914* (Cambridge, 1998), p. 58.

159. C. Love, "Taking a Refreshing Dip: Health, cleanliness and the Empire," *International Journal of the History of Sport* 24, 5 (2007), p. 697, p. 701.

160. *Sports Gazette*, 14th September 1907.

161. *Sports Gazette*, 17th, October 1908, 16th April 1910.

162. *North-Eastern Daily Gazette*, 22nd March 1904; The gala in 1904 included a two lengths handicap for the Mascall Cup, a two lengths handicap for the Forbes Cup, a cork race, and a water polo match. This was followed a month later by the "speed swimming championships" where fourteen entrants raced over one hundred yards—*North-Eastern Daily Gazette*, 13th September, 3rd October 1904.

163. *Sports Gazette*, 10th, 24th March 1906; In comparison, the adult subscription for the YMCA club was 4s for adults—*North-Eastern Daily Gazette*, 28th April 1905.

164. *Sports Gazette*, 27th April 1907.

165. *Teesside Weekly Herald*, 1st November 1913.

166. *Northern Athlete*, 29th May 1911; *Sports Gazette*, 18th March 1911; The 1911 census lists Jack Hatfield as a baths attendant.

167. *North-Eastern Daily Gazette*, 17th July 1912; *Northern Echo*, 16th July 1912; Hatfield also swam in the 1920 and 1924 Olympics.

168. *North Star*, 20th July 1912; *Teesside Weekly Herald*, 27th July 1912.

169. *Sports Gazette*, 3rd, 31st August 1912; He also broke the world record for one thousand meters, though the time did not stand as it was not swum in open water—*North-Eastern Daily Gazette*, 12th October 1912.

170. *North-Eastern Daily Gazette*, 2nd September 1913; *Northern Echo*, 19th, 21st July 1913; *Sports Gazette*, 26th July 1913; Hatfield retained the long-distance title a

year later, with 15 years old George W. Leader from Middlesbrough taking fifth place—*Teesside Weekly Herald*, 1st August 1914.

171. *North-Eastern Daily Gazette*, 21st, 23rd January 1903; The Middlesbrough Gymnasium had been disbanded in January 1901, and the Middlesbrough Amateur Gymnasium Society was formed in January 1903—*Middlesbrough & Stockton Morning Mail*, 15th January 1901.

172. *North-Eastern Daily Gazette*, 17th January 1905; *South Durham & Cleveland Mercury*, 20th January 1905; *Sports Gazette*, 24th September, 29th October 1904.

173. *Teesside Weekly Herald*, 10th November 1906.

174. *Sports Gazette*, 15th February 1908; Such was the gymnasium's popularity, it could no longer accommodate all the boys who wanted to join, though there were only thirty-five members in the boys' section—*North-Eastern Daily Gazette*, 23rd March 1910; *Sports Gazette*, 19th March 1910.

175. *Sports Gazette*, 11th September, 16th October 1909.

176. *North-Eastern Daily Gazette*, 23rd March 1910 .

177. 1911 census; *North-Eastern Daily Gazette*, 15th March 1909; *Sports Gazette*, 19th March 1910; *Teesside Weekly Herald*, 12th October 1912.

178. Birley, *Land of Sport and Glory*, p. 205; Lowerson, *Sport and the English Middle Classes*, p. 25, p. 111.

179. *Northern Echo*, 11th 13th March 1902; The competition was promoted by William Allan (a stationer) and W. H. Proctor (proprietor of the Cafe)—*Northern Echo*, 13th March 1902.

180. *North-Eastern Daily Gazette*, 27th January 1903; *South Durham & Cleveland Mercury*, 25th April 1902; *Sports Gazette*, 9th August 1902.

181. *North-Eastern Daily Gazette*, 13th March, 4th, 11th, 25th June 1903; At a meeting later in the year, it was decided that once a month the club would hold an air-gun competition, a social, a whist drive, a concert, and a dance—*North-Eastern Daily Gazette*, 29th September 1903.

182. According to the *North-Eastern Daily Gazette* the League's members were Linthorpe Parish, St Cuthbert's, Thornaby St Luke's, Woodlands Road WG, and YMCA—*North-Eastern Daily Gazette*, 22nd September 1909; However the *Sports Gazette* stated that the members were Centenarians, Linthorpe, St Aidan's, St Cuthbert's, Thornaby St Luke's, and YMCA—*Sports Gazette*, 20th November 1909.

183. *Teesside Weekly Herald*, 4th October 1913.

184. *North-Eastern Daily Gazette*, 23rd July, 14th August 1909, 11th July, 16th August 1912.

185. 1901 and 1911 census; *Kelly's Directory of North and East Ridings of Yorkshire, 1909*; A. V. Buttress, The History of the Middlesbrough & District Motor Club, Part 1—http://homepage.ntlworld.com/dave.ransome/docs/Part1.pdf; *Northern Echo*, 25th October 1906; See also the club officials in 1914—*Teesside Weekly Herald*, 7th March 1914.

186. *Sports Gazette*, 10th, 17th November 1906.

187. *Sports Gazette*, 9th November 1907; *Teesside Weekly Herald*, 26th January 1907.

188. Buttress, The History of the Middlesbrough & District Motor Club; the club's summer program in 1910 included a paper chase, team trials, a ladies' picnic, and a competition of passenger machines—*Sports Gazette*, 9th July 1910.

189. Buttress, The History of the Middlesbrough & District Motor Club; *North-Eastern Daily Gazette*, 26th February 1914.

190. *Cleveland Standard*, 13th March 1909; *Sports Gazette*, 6th February 1909; The company was chaired by Councillor Edwin Turner, with John Durkin (a nautical instrument maker) and Horace G. Winney (timber merchant manager) as board members—1911 census; *Cleveland Standard*, 13th March 1909.

191. *Teesside Weekly Herald*, 29th May, 5th June 1909; Children paid 6d for admission and skating. Prices were the same as those at the skating rinks in Stockton and Darlington. One cycle depot advertised roller skates from 1s 9d—*North-Eastern Daily Gazette*, 23rd July, 25th August 1909.

192. *North-Eastern Daily Gazette*, 17th August 1909; *Sports Gazette*, 3rd July 1909; *Teesside Weekly Herald*, 3rd July 1909; Such was the popularity of skating that another rink was reportedly planned by the Park Arcadia Rink Skating Company opposite Albert Park that would accommodate 2,500 people—*Cleveland Standard*, 20th November 1909.

193. *North-Eastern Daily Gazette*, 25th October 1909.

194. *Sports Gazette*, 3rd December 1910; *Teesside Weekly Herald*, 12th November 1910.

195. *Teesside Weekly Herald*, 5th February 1910.

196. *Northern Athlete*, 16th, 23rd July 1906; In contrast, baseball became *the* summer sport in parts of South Wales. In 1906 there were thirty-six clubs in the South Wales & Monmouthshire Baseball Association, and the sport's popularity continued after the First World War—M. Johnes, "'Poor Man's Cricket': Baseball, class and community in South Wales, c.1880–1950," *International Journal of the History of Sport* 17, 4 (2000), p. 155.

197. *Sports Gazette*, 14th April 1906.

198. Pushball was invented in Massachusetts in 1894. The diameter of the ball was six feet, and it weighed between forty-eight and fifty pounds. Played between two teams of eleven, the aim was to push the ball to the goals at either end of the pitch—C. H. Allison, "Pushball, a Strenuous New Game," *National Magazine* 23, 1 (1905), pp. 47–49; F. W. Hoffmann and W. G. Bailey, *Sports and Recreation Fads* (Binghamton, New York, 1991), pp. 297–298.

199. *North-Eastern Daily Gazette*, 5th August 1902; *North Star*, 5th August 1902; *South Durham & Cleveland Mercury*, 8th August 1902.

200. *North-Eastern Daily Gazette*, 28th April 1914; *Northern Echo*, 29th April 1914.

201. *North-Eastern Daily Gazette*, 10th April 1906.

202. *Sports Gazette*, 9th July 1910; *Teesside Weekly Herald*, 11th May 1907.

203. *Northern Echo*, 16th April 1906; *Teesside Weekly Herald*, 13th May 1905.

204. *North-Eastern Daily Gazette*, 26th June 1908; *Northern Athlete*, 17th September 1906; *Sports Gazette*, 22nd June 1907, 26th June 1909.

205. *Northern Athlete*, 21st June 1909; *Sports Gazette*, 21st June 1913.

206. *North-Eastern Daily Gazette*, 25th July 1901, 6th May 1903; *Northern Echo*, 11th August 1902.

207. Programme of Tees Conservancy Commission, 7th October 1905, U/BL/25, Teesside Archives.

208. *North Star*, 21st September 1903; *Sports Gazette*, 17th August 1907; *Teesside Weekly Herald*, 20th August 1904.

209. Programme of North Ormesby Hospital Charity Sports, 17th September 1909, U/S/2073, Teesside Archives.

210. *North-Eastern Daily Gazette*, 24th July 1905, 16th July 1908; *South Durham & Cleveland Mercury*, 25th August 1905.

211. *Teesside Weekly Herald*, 6th July 1907; See also the picnics of Crewdson, Hardy & Co—*Sports Gazette*, 11th July 1908, and Dickson & Benson—*Teesside Weekly Herald*, 27th July 1912.

212. J. Kay, "It Wasn't Just Emily Davison! Sport, suffrage and society in Edwardian Britain," *International Journal of the History of Sport* 25, 10 (2008), p. 1339; Lewis, "The Evolution of a Political Culture," p. 122.

213. Kay, "It Wasn't Just Emily Davison!," p. 1351; Tranter, *Sport, Economy and Society*, p. 92.

214. C. Horwood, "'Girls Who Arouse Dangerous Passions': Women and bathing, 1900–39," *Women's History Review* 9, 4 (2000), p. 654; Tranter, *Sport, Economy and Society*, p. 87.

215. Bell, *At the Works*, p. 227, p. 236.

216. *Northern Weekly Gazette*, 18th May 1901.

217. C. E. B. Russell, *Social Problems of the North* (London, 1913), p. 78.

218. *Teesside Weekly Herald*, 10th August 1907.

219. *North-Eastern Daily Gazette*, 30th November 1903.

220. *Northern Weekly Gazette*, 27th July 1901; *South Durham & Cleveland Mercury*, 6th November 1903; *Sports Gazette*, 16th September, 28th October 1905; Day has noted a number of examples of swimming families like the Hatfields, pointing out that children were introduced to swimming early in their lives "as part of family aquatic displays." Day also states that teaching professionals generated "family dynasties" and the 1911 census records show Thomas Hatfield as baths superintendant, his wife Hannah as manageress, while Jack, his sister Mabel, and their uncle Septimus, were all baths attendants—D. Day, "London Swimming Professors: Victorian craftsmen and aquatic entrepreneurs," *Sport in History* 30, 1 (2010), p. 38.

221. Daughter of the captain of Middlesbrough Amateur Swimming Club.

222. *Northern Echo*, 15th September 1913; *Teesside Weekly Herald*, 20th September 1913.

223. *North-Eastern Daily Gazette*, 10th October, 13th November 1913; *Northern Echo*, 13th November 1913.

224. *Sports Gazette*, 28th March 1908.

225. *North-Eastern Daily Gazette*, 3rd July 1902.

226. *North-Eastern Daily Gazette*, 13th March 1902.

227. *Northern Athlete*, 15th May 1911.

228. 1911 census; *Sports Gazette*, 20th April 1907; *Teesside Weekly Herald*, 10th April 1909; Members of the tea committee included the wives of a secretary, draper, and printer and book manufacturer, with additions a year later of the wives of an oil manufacturer, a timber agent, and a boot dealer—*Sports Gazette*, 3rd April 1909, 9th April 1910.

229. *Teesside Weekly Herald*, 15th April 1911.

230. J. Kay, "'No Time for Recreations till the Vote is Won'? Suffrage activists and leisure in Edwardian Britain," *Women's History Review* 16, 4 (2007), p. 539.

231. Holt, *Sport and the British*, p. 132.

232. Minute Book of MGC, 16th March 1910; *Sports Gazette*, 18th February 1911 .

233. Minute Book of MGC, 30th January 1912, unspecified date for January 1913; In October 1912 it was decided that women would not be allowed to play after noon on Saturdays during the winter, amended five months later to restrict women from playing between 1 p.m. and 2:30 p.m., and changed again in October 1913 asking ladies not to play *before* noon on Saturdays—Minute Book of MGC, 17th October 1912, 20th February, 16th October 1913; That female members were still able to vote is unusual as McCrone states that "suggestions about equalising privileges almost inevitably produced stormy meetings . . . and negative results"—K. E. McCrone, *Sport and the Physical Emancipation of English Women, 1870–1914* (London, 1988) pp. 168–169.

234. Their occupations were "assisting in father's business" (butcher and inn keeper); assistant school mistress; assistant teacher; governess; doctor; masseuse; hotel manageress.

235. The form stated that, "No information can be given of the female residents in this house on April 2nd as they object to give such information until women are enfranchised." Only seventy women boycotted the census in the whole of Yorkshire, and in Middlesbrough only Schofield-Coates and her sister-in-law, Marion Coates-Hanson refused to comply. Amy Mahoney, the secretary of the Middlesbrough branch of the Women's Freedom League, did not boycott the census—J. Liddington and E. Crawford, "'Women do not count, neither shall they be counted': Suffrage, citizenship and the battle for the 1911 census," *History Workshop Journal* 71 (2011), pp. 98–127.

236. *The Times*, 19th February 1909; E. Crawford, *The Women's Suffrage Movement: A reference guide 1866–1928* (London, 1999), p. 130; E. Crawford, *The Women's Suffrage Movement in Britain and Ireland: A regional survey* (London, 2006), p. 54; Alice Schofield-Coates also became Middlesbrough's first female councillor in 1919.

237. A. J. R., *The Suffrage Annual and Women's Who's Who* (London, 1913), p. 351; Birley, *Land of Sport and Glory*, p. 199; Tranter, *Sport, Economy and Society*, p. 92.

238. *Cleveland Standard*, 6th August 1910; Tranter, *Sport, Economy and Society*, p. 83.

239. *North-Eastern Daily Gazette*, 19th May 1911; In contrast to Schofield-Coates, Hedley actively campaigned against female enfranchisement—Lewis, "The Evolution of a Political Culture," p. 122.

240. *South Durham & Cleveland Mercury*, 29th March 1901; *Sports Gazette*, 19th February 1910.

241. *Northern Athlete*, 26th November 1906.

242. *Sports Gazette*, 22nd October 1904, 25th February 1905.

243. *Sports Gazette*, 10th March 1906, 29th August 1908, 11th September 1909; McCrone states that gymnastic clubs often "catered to women who were eager to cultivate health as well as beauty"—McCrone, *Sport and the Physical Emancipation of English Women*, p. 104.

244. *Middlesbrough Standard*, 5th August 1911.

245. *North-Eastern Daily Gazette*, 17th January 1905, 15th March 1909.

246. *Teesside Weekly Herald*, 10th February 1906.

247. Huggins, "Leisure and Sport in Middlesbrough," p. 150.
248. Bell, *At the Works*, pp. 128–131.
249. *Teesside Weekly Herald*, 26th August 1905.
250. *Teesside Weekly Herald*, 2nd November 1912.
251. *Teesside Weekly Herald*, 19th October 1907.

SIX

"Going Football Mad"[1]

Football in Middlesbrough, 1895–1914

Although the number of sports played in Middlesbrough continued to expand, none could compete with football in terms of popularity among spectators and participants.[2] In 1908, one alderman remarked that football so greatly held the attention of young men in Middlesbrough that there were now one hundred teams in the town, and one councillor proclaimed that, "Middlesbrough is going football mad. I think the brains of the people are getting into their heels instead of their heads."[3] It was not difficult for football to become such a popular sport among much of Middlesbrough's male population. Not only was admission relatively inexpensive, there were a great number of clubs that suited the needs and interests of players and enthusiasts. Though some smaller clubs suffered because of the town club's success, new clubs and leagues were also formed throughout the period. Some clubs followed the same patterns of other sporting organizations in the middle-class backgrounds of their officials, with a member of the local elite acting as president or patron. For many clubs, however, there were far more opportunities for the workingman to be involved. Relations with Middlesbrough FC's directors were often strained, with shareholders and the local press being vocal critics, which may indicate the importance of football to those who watched the sport. This chapter examines the continued growth of football and will explain how the game came to hold such a strong position in the town's sporting culture, following the first failure of professionalism. Why was football able to attract the interest and attention of both working-class spectators and middle-class directors? What role did the Amateur Cup play for Middlesbrough, as well as, perhaps more importantly, for South Bank and Eston United? Did Middlesbrough's growth as a professional football club help or hinder other amateur clubs? Did football help Middlesbrough to find its identity within the North, Northeast, and Yorkshire?

AMATEUR SUCCESS

Despite the failure of Ironopolis FC and professionalism, at the beginning of 1895 the *South Durham & Cleveland Mercury* proclaimed that as far as amateur football was concerned, "interest in the winter pastime is not yet dead."[4] Indeed Middlesbrough proved the strength of the local amateur game when they reached the final of the English Amateur Cup in April, where they met the holders Old Carthusians at Leeds.[5] A crowd of three thousand–four thousand saw Middlesbrough win 2–1. Seizing on the opportunity to celebrate both the town and the North, 'Rover' in the *North-Eastern Daily Gazette* proclaimed that the victory represented "one of the most gladsome periods in the history of our comparatively young town." Furthermore, the "stamina and skill" on display was proof that "in the North players can be turned out who are well capable of overcoming exponents of the game in the South." Drawing attention to the difference between supporters in the North and South, and suggesting that those in the North were more passionate, it was pointed out that the "hearty, strong-lunged northerners mode of cheering" was "in direct contrast to that adopted by the Southerners' supporters." The *Athletic News* described the result as "a proud achievement for Northern as against Southern amateurism," one which had "strengthened the position of the unpaid form of the game in Tees-side." Indicating the importance of the match to some, 'Rover' also noted that many of the five hundred Middlesbrough supporters present had sacrificed "a day's work to cheer their favourites on to victory."[6] On their return, the players were greeted at the train station by crowds of supporters. The roads were said to be "densely packed with thousands who had congregated to do honour to the victors," and a band led the team to the Masham Hotel, where the club captain Thomas Bach was landlord. Bach "spoke like a born orator . . . and champagne and congratulations flowed in a continuous stream."[7] The club's chairman, Robert Forrester, remarked on the fact that the cup itself had not been brought to Leeds, suggesting that "it looks very much as though they were confident of the trophy remaining in the custody of the Southerners. Northern clubs will probably receive a little more consideration and respect in the future."[8]

Three years after their first success in the Amateur Cup, Middlesbrough played nearby Thornaby in the semifinal of the competition. However, the tie coincided with a small pox epidemic, and the match was played "with closed gates." The location of the game (at Brotton, fifteen miles east of the town) remained a secret, and it was reported that though "many keen footballists had been on the alert for the past few days, those who knew the location of the match were very limited in number."[9] Middlesbrough played Uxbridge at Crystal Palace to win the cup again,[10] and two matches were played at the club's Linthorpe Road ground at the same time, at which the half time score and final result were posted. Though London's *Daily News* suggested that the game lost "much of its interest" due to the final being played so late in the season, the *North Star* stated that in Middlesbrough,

> all were on the tip-toe of excitement, and when the half-time score arrived
> . . . everyone began to congratulate everybody else, and a heavy load seemed
> to be lifted off their minds. The final result was late in arriving, and many
> anxious individuals called at various places where the result might be known
> . . . when the result arrived . . . once again Middlesbrough breathed freely.[11]

As in 1895, the team was greeted by a large number of supporters on their return, on this occasion by a crowd of ten thousand–twelve thousand. The *North-Eastern Daily Gazette* stated "the scene both inside and outside of the Middlesbrough station was one which has never been witnessed before in the history of the town," the station yard being "filled with an excited and seething mass of humanity." The directors and "the principal supporters of the club" were also at the station to welcome the team, as were Milburn's Model Band, who played 'See the Conquering Hero Comes.' The team boarded brakes and "set off around town . . . the whole route was lined deeply with enthusiastic supporters, who loudly cheered at the sight of the cup." At the Masham Hotel, the chairman lifted up the cup for the crowds, who "gave vent to an ear-splitting cheer."[12] The two victories in the Amateur Cup justified the club's decision to retain their amateur status, and also gave the town opportunities to celebrate and build a sense of civic pride. That both victories were over teams from the south also allowed the town to assert its northern identity. The coverage given to the club in the local press confirms Russell's suggestion that the press "carried much of the daily burden of boosting sporting civic patriotism." Taylor's assertion that by the turn of the century, clubs relied on press coverage "to generate interest and stimulate demand" is borne out by the sheer number of column inches devoted to football in Middlesbrough.[13]

However, the local press was also quick to point out that there were drawbacks to Middlesbrough's latest victory. The *North-Eastern Daily Gazette* remarked that success had "only been secured at [a] heavy loss" and the club would need to attract big crowds in order to secure their financial future. The final had not attracted a very large crowd, and the *North Star* bemoaned the fact that the game had not been played in the North, where "the gate would doubtlessly have been considerably larger."[14] Indeed at Middlesbrough's 1898 AGM, the directors reported that the second half of the season "had been disastrous financially." Furthermore, winning the cup had attracted professional agents and three players had already left the club.[15]

THE RETURN TO PROFESSIONALISM,
THE FOOTBALL LEAGUE, AND AYRESOME PARK

In the 1890s professionalism was still met with a great deal of opposition. While amateur football was thought to embody "health, endurance, courage, judgement and above all a sense of fair play,"[16] critics wondered whether the principles underpinning the amateur ethos could coexist with partisan crowds that were only interested in victories for their own teams. Doubts were raised about the ability of footballers to reach the standards expected of them. As one contemporary stated, professionals played "to win at all costs . . . his strong desire to win . . . leads him to play up to the rules and to indulge in dodges and tricks which the public school man is apt to consider dishonourable."[17] N. L. Jackson (founder of the Corinthians) thought that football had become "a spectacle arranged for the enjoyment of those who pay to look on,"[18] but he conceded that by the end of the nineteenth century, football was "a business, pure and simple, and as such I respect it."[19] One of the motives behind the legalization of professionalism was the desire to control it, and remove the illegalities that pervaded the game. Mason has pointed out that those members of the lower-middle and middle classes that ran many professional clubs in the North and Midlands also thought that professionalism needed to be controlled; players were to be servants while the directors were their masters. Indeed, the *Athletic News*, a vocal supporter of the professional game, still believed that "money must be controlled and players must be servants." Such statements reflect the strained relationship between employers and workmen more widely, which despite changes in legislation saw the positions of masters and servants continue into the twentieth century.[20]

Money was now a fundamental part of football. John James Bentley, the president of the Football League, suggested that the game was "of such an important character as to render it compulsory that business-like methods must be absolutely observed." So long as football attracted a crowd, the game would have to be conducted as a business.[21] Nevertheless, this was not always viewed favorably. G. O. Smith was of the opinion that when sport "becomes a matter of pounds, shillings, and pence . . . the game must necessarily lose some of that keen enjoyment . . . which characterised it before the advent of such considerations." Elite amateur teams in the south objected so much to the growing influence of professional clubs on football's governing bodies that in 1907 it was found necessary to form the Amateur Football Association. Even in 1913 there was still a "concern that the game had been lost to monied interests."[22]

It is clear that the reasons behind the establishment of professionalism in Middlesbrough in the late 1890s were very different to the circumstances that led to the formation of Ironopolis. In 1889 it had been the club's supporters that had demanded better football. Now, it was the directors who recognized that if the club was to be successful they would have to join the professional ranks. Paying players would prevent them from being poached by other clubs, and the attention the amateur cup victories had brought to the town could be built on by playing in the Football League. It was not until 1897 that a meeting was held in Middlesbrough to discuss the possibility of turning professional. Given the club's experience of professionalism and the associated expenditure earlier in the decade, it is not surprising that the directors proceeded with a great deal of caution. It was decided that "as professional football is attended with so much financial risk, it would be exceedingly unwise again to enter upon it" without the assurance of support from two thousand individuals who could immediately pay for a £1 share. Evidence of a lack of interest, or at the very least major reservations, was demonstrated at the club's AGM when it was reported that "not one individual" intimated a willingness to subscribe to the fund toward professionalism.[23] Why then, when faced with such financial risks and the success already experienced without having to pay players, would the club turn to professionalism? The club had already lost players to professional teams and when it was rumored in early 1899 that the directors were again considering professionalism, the *North Star* pointed out that it would allow the club to have "the pick of the local players"; they would only need to be paid "such a remuneration as will give the committee absolute control over them." The newspaper reported that the club were loath to make any snap decisions, in case it was revealed that there was "an absurd misapprehension of the amount and of the financial value of football enthusiasm" in Middlesbrough.[24] Unlike the calls for professionalism in 1889, there was evidently little clamor for professionals among supporters, but there was an increasing realization that the club could only progress by paying players, and more important, little resistance to the idea of paying players. The *Middlesbrough & Stockton Sporting Telegraph* stated that local amateur players were being "snapped up much to the disgust, annoyance and impoverishment" of their clubs. A player could not be blamed for turning away from amateurism, as "he may as well be having his share of the plums while he has yet youth and activity on his side to barter for them."[25] At a meeting of the directors it was decided that so long as "sufficient capital is early subscribed," a professional team that would be "creditable to a town of the size and importance of Middlesbrough" should be formed. As the *Middlesbrough & Stockton Evening Telegraph* pointed out, the directors had "not forgotten their previous experience of professionalism and are not . . . disposed to take upon themselves the risk of repeating the experiment."[26]

A public meeting was subsequently arranged "to gauge the measure of public support," and anyone who has "taken the slightest interest in the club and desires a better class of football," were urged to attend.[27] Ahead of the meeting, the directors were asked to secure "promises of support," and the club's new director Councillor Alfred Mattison (of the Zetland Hotel), was asked "to use his influence with the licensed victuallers of the town."[28] The chairman (R. Forrester) informed those at the meeting of the directors' aspirations for the club and consequently, for the town,

> They felt that something must be done to rekindle that flame which once set the country on fire when they had two professional teams in the town. . . . They asked the public for the money so that they would be in a position not only to put a team in the field to win the Second League, but a team that would be able to play any team in England, and to lift the name of Middlesbrough to the highest pinnacle of fame, and be a credit and satisfaction to the town and the whole district.[29]

It was estimated that the cost of running a professional team was £2,267 7s a year, and that £1,000–1,500 would be required in subscriptions. Pointing out that 5s of each share would need to be paid within two weeks, Forrester stated that "should any working man not be able to meet the call no doubt the committee would make special arrangements." One member of the public suggested canvassing the tradesmen of the town to take up shares, stating that "there should not be a single tradesman who was not prepared to take shares" given the "great number of people that would be brought into the town if they had good professional matches." Two hundred forty-four shares were taken up at the meeting from eighty individuals, and a committee was duly appointed to canvass tradesmen and licensed victuallers.[30]

A week later "Old Bird" in the *North-Eastern Daily Gazette* reported that he had persuaded both the managing director (Sir James Clifton Robinson) and the chairman of the Imperial Tramway Company to take up one hundred shares between them. In return, the Company would "do everything that lies in their power to facilitate traffic, so that those desirous of seeing the home matches of the club will be conveyed cheaply and speedily to and from the ground," demonstrating that the purchasing of shares could be beneficial to both shareholder and club.[31] The minute book of the club states that the secretary was also requested to write to the following to ask them to take up shares—Sir Joseph Pease, Sir Christopher Furness,[32] licensed victuallers, "large employers of labour in the district," brewers, members of the council, and "others who might be influenced to interest themselves in the movement" such as the Marquis of Londonderry and Marquis of Zetland.[33] Shortly afterward 'Old Bird' confidently stated that "the success of the professional scheme has now been assured," the canvassers having gone about their work in "such a thorough and painstaking manner as to set at rest all doubts on the matter." Eight hundred fifty shares had been subscribed to either verbally or in writing within two weeks of the public meeting.[34] In a further example of what was felt to be a reciprocal relationship between shareholder and club, George Cathey, who had canvassed the town with fifteen others, suggested that club members should not patronize the publicans "who refused to support the team . . . within a week they would take up a couple of hundred shares."[35] On being admitted to the Second Division in May ("thanks to the influence of the Northern delegates" and the oratory skills of Henry Walker[36]), 'Linesman' in the *Middlesbrough & Stockton Sporting Telegraph* informed his readers of "the absolute necessity of loyally supporting the directorate." Placing the game at the heart of Middlesbrough, he thought that there was "no reason why a sporting town of the size and increasing prosperity and importance of the Teesside capital should not have a team in the premier division."[37]

The club already had twenty-three players prior to admittance to the Football League, and the *Middlesbrough & Stockton Sporting Telegraph* expected the signing of more players from "the Land of Cakes [Scotland], that bourne to which few football players return after they have had a sight of the money bags of England"; players were duly secured by the club's director Jack R. Smiles on a visit to Scotland. Wages ranged from 30s to 40s per week (though local players would be paid a maximum of 35s), and bonuses ranged from zero to £10. It was decided that no summer wages would be paid "except in the case of prominent players."[38] At the start of the 1899 season the *South Durham & Cleveland Mercury* thought that "the cream of local amateur talent will prove equal to that which older professional clubs can provide," but the *Middlesbrough & Stockton Evening Telegraph* suggested that the players would not "set the Tees on fire." Nevertheless, it would not matter as long as "the lads play with that determination which is characteristic of the youth of the North."[39]

Middlesbrough's first home match in the Football League drew a crowd of six thousand. The *Middlesbrough & Stockton Sporting Telegraph* reported that from an hour before the game began, "there was a constant stream of football spectators along Linthorpe Road, anxious to gain the best points of vantage . . . [the money takers] were unable to take the money fast enough."[40] Mattison stated that many in the town benefited from the return of professional football, arguing "from a tradesman's point of view . . . the club should be beneficial to the town," as "football enthusiasts" had previously left the town to watch matches at Sunderland or Newcastle instead. The *Middlesbrough & Stockton Evening Telegraph* stated that if the club was successful "there will be an inducement to keep football spectators in Middlesbrough on Saturdays . . . they will, as a matter of fact, spend their money in the town."[41] It is interesting to note the suggestion that spectators had been prepared to travel to see a good game, rather than watch a local amateur team, and justifies the directors' decision to join the Football League. The financial success of the first League match led the directors to pay a 10s bonus for a win and 5s for a draw to the players, with a further bonus if the team reached ninth position in the League. It is evident that some players continued to work in other jobs as well, as it was recorded in the club's minute book that the trainer should be informed that "some of [the] men allowed to work during [the] day were not exhibiting staying power," and he ought to "suggest a means of overcoming the weakness."[42]

Middlesbrough ended their first season in the Football League in fourteenth place and the *South Durham & Cleveland Mercury* hoped that the supporters would "insist upon engaging a capable manager of the team."[43] Mattison thanked the supporters as they "had rallied round that football club in a manner which was a credit to them, and also a lesson to the whole of England in that matter." £2,237 18s 7d had been spent on wages, bonuses, and transfer fees to players who had kept the club "out of that ignominious position of being at the bottom of the Second League."[44] Despite the necessity of spending money to remain competitive, *North Star's* 'Captain' criticized the club for the large amounts they were spending. Commenting on win bonuses of £3, he stated,

> It is but another proof of the deterioration of the game from the level of a sport to that of a business. . . . We hardly know whether to blame the Middlesbrough players for their grasping greed, or whether to blame the directors for being so foolish as to consent to such practices by showing their willingness to give big bribes to gain small ends.[45]

The club's trainer, Charlie Harper, was employed at a weekly wage of £2, and players' wages varied. Summer wages ranged from 30s to £3 10s, and most players were paid £3 in the winter. This would appear to be in keeping with the national average; the typical wage in the First Division in the late 1890s was £3–£4 a week.[46]

Enthusiasm for the club among spectators was demonstrated during efforts to secure promotion in 1902. Sixteen hundred Middlesbrough supporters travelled to a game in Preston and the *Northern Echo* reported that many of them "displayed the club's colours very conspicuously, and at frequent intervals 'made the welkin ring' with shouts of 'Play up the borough.'"[47] The victorious team were welcomed back at the train station shortly after midnight by "thousands of excited and enthusiastic people." The *South Durham & Cleveland Mercury* stated that the crowds divided up two different streets "each in charge [of] a number of the players, who were every now and then lifted shoulder high, to the accompaniment of 'He's a jolly good fellow.'"[48] Support for the team was demonstrated again when on winning their place in the First Division a few weeks later, the team were greeted by eleven thousand people at the station. A subscription list was opened "in order that some recognition may be made of the services of the players," Robson was rewarded with an increase to his salary, and the players were presented with new suits.[49] Ahead of the new season in the First Division the price of season tickets was increased and the Linthorpe Road ground was extended to accommodate a further eight thousand spectators. The expenditure was rewarded with a crowd of fifteen thousand for Middlesbrough's first practice game and an estimated crowd of seventeen thousand–twenty-three thousand for the first League match.[50] The *Northern Echo* also reported that three thousand Middlesbrough supporters travelled to a match in Newcastle, but in contrast, when Middlesbrough took on the elite amateur Corinthians team at the Linthorpe Road ground, the crowd totaled only one thousand, further proof of the popularity of professional, League football.[51]

When the club was unable to extend the tenancy for their Linthorpe Road ground, the existing grandstand was moved to land at Ayresome Park.[52] A new stand for two thousand spectators was to be erected which was said to be "of an elaborate character;" it was to include a gymnasium, billiard room, rooms for the secretary and directors, rooms and baths for home and visiting teams, and a room for referees.[53] £5,000 was needed to pay for the stand and twelve £100 shares were taken up by the directors, while Herbert Samuel (MP for Cleveland) took up £1,000 after a "deputation" had visited him in London. £3,000 of the total needed was soon subscribed, and a month later it was reported that Sir James Clifton Robinson had also agreed to subscribe a further £1,000 worth of shares.[54] £6,000 was spent on the thirty-two thousand-capacity Ayresome Park ground,[55] leading the *Athletic News* to proclaim that "the North Yorkshiremen are ready for big business." Charles Sutcliffe of the Football League management committee stated that prior to the First World War, there had been "an outcry for more comfortable accommodation," and that new grandstands were erected "in answer to popular clamour."[56] Although this contributed to the building of Ayresome Park, complaints were made later about the standard of the cheapest part of the ground, indicating that it was not built with the needs of all the supporters in mind. The directors were more concerned with the income that the new ground could bring in to the club.

The first League fixture at Ayresome Park against Sunderland attracted twenty-five thousand–thirty thousand spectators. The *South Durham & Cleveland Mercury* suggested that the club had been taken by surprise by the number of spectators present. The press gallery was "monopolised by the onlookers, much to the inconvenience of sundry knights of the pencil." No seats had been reserved in the grandstand, so that Herbert Pike Pease (MP for Darlington) "had a difficulty to find a seat at any price." The importance of the match was evidenced by the fact that hundreds of men had left work early in order to attend, and "went to the field dinnerless, many purchasing a democratic pork pie en route."[57] Furthermore, the importance of the match to local businesses was also in evidence as retailers and other commercial enterprises were able to take advantage of the numbers of people in the town that afternoon. The *North-Eastern Daily Gazette* reported that on the day of the match, Thomas Dent (a mineral water manufacturer) supplied "all comers with temperance drinks and sold refreshments on the ground at reasonable charges," and one of the club's directors, Arthur Barritt (a hatter), had a stock of red and white silk ties which "enthusiastic supporters" could purchase for a shilling.[58] The ground was opened by Sir James Clifton Robinson (of the Imperial Tramway Company) who remarked that it was "quite a revelation to him to see such an immense multitude gather to witness one of the finest games of football it was ever his privilege to witness." That his involvement could benefit the club was evidenced when he stated that he would "see if it was not possible to run the electric cars to the entrance of the new field."[59]

Despite the attendance at the first game at Ayresome Park, the large crowds did not continue. Receipts for the match against Sunderland had totaled £907, but the next home game against Small Heath resulted in only £498. The fixture against Wolverhampton Wanderers was kicked off by the mayor, Charles Dorman, and the *North-Eastern Daily Gazette* thought that this would be "heartily appreciated by the sportsloving [sic] public," but the game attracted a crowd of only eight thousand, the mayor evidently not being an attraction to spectators. The *Gazette* suggested that the directors should improve the accommodation by covering a section of one of the stands; the club "would promptly get back the cost in the increased attendance . . . when a person pays a shilling to see a football match he should be accommodated with ample protection."[60] Sufficient improvements were evidently not made, as a similar complaint was made seven years later when the *Northern Athlete* suggested that it was "a scandal and disgrace" that those in the cheapest section of the ground had to stand in "three inches of best juicy mud every time there has been a drop of rain." After all, it was those who paid just sixpence that "season after season prove themselves to be the backbone of the club."[61] In 1914 it was hoped again that the club's increased income would "enable certain required improvements" to be carried out at Ayresome Park. The *North Star* argued "on the principle that it is well to retain a strong grip on the splendid support which the team has obtained, it may be suggested that a modest outlay in this matter would be wise."[62]

In 1904 Middlesbrough did draw a crowd of thirty-four thousand for a FA Cup quarter-final replay. The attendance was surprisingly big given that the game was played on a Wednesday afternoon. The *North-Eastern Daily Gazette* suggested that "applications have been made at most of the works in the district for permission to have Wednesday afternoon off . . . [Work] will practically be at a standstill."[63] Harry Walker in the *South Durham & Cleveland Mercury* suggested that there were many at the game who had never attended a football match before, and his comments indicate that a cross section of people attended what was evidently regarded as an important event,

> The artisan and laborer, of course, are always there, and constitute the genuine reliable backbone of every important club in the kingdom. Even divinity had its representatives there. . . . Some of our manufacturing magnates were interested spectators, leading civic dignitaries from the neighboring towns cast off the cares and worries of local government for the time being . . . those learned in the law looked on with critical eyes, whilst the representatives of the drama and the instruments of musical culture lent countenance to the great contest.[64]

CRITICISM FROM SHAREHOLDERS AND SUPPORTERS

The importance of the club to supporters was demonstrated by the complaints that were made when results were poor. In November 1904 Middlesbrough had not won for eight games, and the club received a requisition signed by a number of shareholders requesting a vote of censure on six of the directors.[65] 'Old Bird' claimed that,

> Never in the history of the Middlesbrough Club . . . has there been such a general feeling of indignation as exists at present at the humiliating position the club has been permitted to drift into. . . . The thousands of loyal supporters of the club are heartily sick of the puerile exhibitions that have been given this season . . . the fate of the club hangs in the balance by such a very slender thread that it is only by straight talking and prompt action that the great danger that threatens may be averted.[66]

While the *Sports Gazette* thought the players should also take a share of the blame, given that they were "handsomely paid to give of their best," the *Teesside Weekly Herald* was keen to point out that "in spite of many loud-voiced protests," directors had been elected "who have plainly been most unpopular amongst the general body of shareholders, and whose acquaintance with football is of the most limited character."[67] At a shareholders' meeting in December 1904 there was further criticism of the directors. It was claimed that until recent weeks, Robson "had not had a free hand in the choice of players." Carter states that directors were often unwilling to hand over the responsibility of choosing the team to "salaried officials whom they regarded as socially inferior," but Middlesbrough's directors stated that they thought it was not fair "to throw all the responsibility on to the shoulders of one man." One shareholder told the meeting that they wanted "men on the Board who knew a player when they saw one, who knew how to negotiate terms, and who would discourage drinking and gambling amongst the players," indicating that poor behavior was a problem among the players. The vote of censure was withdrawn, and a temporary "consultative committee" was duly appointed.[68] The aim of this committee was to "improve the club's deplorable condition," but the directors would not comply with any of their requests for information, demonstrating that "there was no serious intention on the part of the directors to cooperate with the shareholders' representatives." One director retorted that they were being "hampered and bothered by meetings, letter writing etc., about their work." The director dismissed the shareholders' complaints and maintained that "if the squabbling is insisted upon we will go down, down in our talent, and down in our gate receipts."[69]

The report of the club in June 1905 showed that gate receipts had already decreased and a loss had been made of over £1,635. The directors attributed this to the "scarcity of money in the district, due to bad trade and the number of men out of work," and hoped that "better times are in store for the working classes."[70] It was pointed out that trade had been equally bad in Newcastle and Sunderland, but their balance sheets remained far superior. Indeed an article in the *Quarterly Review* stated that even when trade was poor, "thousands of operatives find enough money to attend a match." Despite previous statements about public interference, support was now requested in order to maintain "a first-class team and meet the expenses of the ground," and it was hoped that "the enthusiasm and love of sport on Teesside will raise them to a position equal to that of their neighbours on the Tyne and Wear."[71] One Middlesbrough shareholder remarked that "they would not grumble so much if they had had something for their money"; there had been some "disgraceful displays by men who were receiving presumably the maximum pay."[72] Supporters evidently wanted to see these well-paid footballers prove that they were worth their wages, given that most players were financially better off than the spectators. The maximum wage (introduced for the start of the 1901–1902 season alongside a ban on bonuses) was £4 a week and the majority of players in the First Division received the maximum.[73] In comparison, even the best-paid workers at a Middlesbrough blast furnace received only £3 a week, while other blast furnace workers were paid between 19s and 44s 2d a week. Lady Bell stated that ironworkers received between 18s and 80s a week, most of whom were paid between 20s and 40s. Shipyard laborers received just over £1 a week, and unskilled workers were paid 20s-22s a week.[74]

TRANSFERS, SCANDALS, AND CORRUPTION

The various scandals experienced by the club meant that the directors were in turn chastised for bringing undue attention to the club, or praised for attempting to progress the team in the League. The different types of relationships between the club and directors and their motivations, are also evident. In February 1906 Middlesbrough became the first club to pay £1,000 for a footballer when Alf Common was transferred from Sunderland.[75] Though the Middlesbrough director Lieutenant-Colonel Thomas Gibson-Poole thought that the attention on the club had had "an inspiring influence on the players," Harry Walker in the *South Durham & Cleveland Mercury* disapproved, suggesting that the directors were "determined to risk a good deal" in order to prevent relegation.[76] 'Old Bird' in the *North-Eastern Daily Gazette* felt that Common's transfer (alongside Green from Stockport County for £300) showed that there is "a unanimity of purpose being displayed that is almost bound to bring success in its train."[77] One contemporary stated that given the part Common subsequently played in saving the club from relegation, "he was a cheap man . . . his purchase was one of the best investments any club ever made," and another suggested that the transfer amounted to "a solid business arrangement." In contrast, the *Athletic News* suggested that "as a matter of commerce ten young recruits at £100 apiece might have paid better . . . the Second Division would be more honourable than retention of place by purchase."[78]

During this time, Middlesbrough was accused of breaching the rules ("as much through mismanagement as sheer ambition") on so many occasions that by the end of this period, they were thought to be lucky not to have been thrown out of the league. Middlesbrough were not the only club found guilty of such infringements, and the number of incidents escalated as clubs looked for ways to circumvent the restrictions of the maximum wage.[79] In mid-1905, Middlesbrough's auditor informed the shareholders that illegal payments had been made to players, and the shareholders informed the Football Association, seemingly unconcerned about the punishment the directors would incur. In November 1905, the directors admitted making illegal payments to players worth £400 (for winning or drawing cup ties and league matches) and fabricating accounts to conceal them. During the Football Association's investigation of the club, the directors made "very strenuous efforts" to avoid being exposed. The club were fined £250, eleven of the twelve directors were suspended until January 1908, and one former player was fined £10.[80]

Despite this, it was suggested that the directors had acted in the best interests of the club, just as they had done when signing Common. The *North Star* claimed that,

> but for the sacrifices which members of the directorate, inspired by a genuine enthusiasm for the game, and a commendable desire to keep the club alive, were prepared to make, Middlesbrough would long since have ceased to exist professionally.

Indeed, Mattison stated that

> It was done at a time when Middlesbrough were making a gallant fight
> for the English Cup . . . [and for their] very life in the League, and who in
> Middlesbrough should blame us. . . . If we had paid the men too little, if we
> had put the money in our own pockets, we might have deserved the severe
> criticism we have undergone, but who dare, amongst all our candid critics
> suggest that we have done anything but what any gentleman or body of
> gentlemen in the land would not have been tempted to do under the circum-
> stances?[81]

In contrast, the *Northern Echo* reported that supporters were pleased with
the punishment, "as it had been felt for some time that the directors had
not done what they ought in the way of signing new players." Furthermore, the *Sports Gazette* attributed the mismanagement of the club to the
fact that the shareholders had been "denied a popular representation."[82]
When the shareholders were called to select a new board, they were
urged to choose men "whose sole qualifications are business capacity,
football knowledge, and enthusiasm for the game and the club," and that
there should be "no enmities, no jealousies, no cliques, no favourites."[83]
With a view to "increased efficiency and to the simplification of work,"
an assistant secretary (George F. Allison, a *Northern Echo* journalist "well-
known on Teesside"), was appointed to work with the manager.[84] The
directors remained lower-middle and middle class. Smiles was appointed
vice-chairman, and Gibson-Poole chairman. Two former directors and
eight new directors were elected. In addition to Gibson-Poole and Smiles,
the occupations of four other can be identified—two clerks, a marine engineer, and a turf commission agent.[85]

By March 1906, Middlesbrough had only won six times during the season. Therefore the transfers of Steve Bloomer, William Frederick Brawn,
and Frederick J. Wilcox "served to restore confidence in the team." The
Sports Gazette stated that the "purchases do not look nice, but they are
lawful," and suggested that "the niceties of pure sport have now and
then to be disregarded, in view of the need for self-preservation," while
the *Northern Athlete* agreed that "desperate diseases require desperate
remedies." The *Athletic News* argued that the directors were "entitled to
unstinted support from all [of] Teesside," but questioned whether any
club ought to "buy the services of players at the eleventh hour." G. O.
Smith argued that buying players to avoid relegation was "contrary to
all ideas of sport." A club should be "content to rise or fall on its own
resources, and not owe its position to a body of men . . . who have and
mean to have no permanent connection with it."[86] The club's attempts at
self-preservation proved expensive. The price of admission for Middlesbrough's home matches at Easter had to be raised to pay for the trans-

fers, but the *Teesside Weekly Herald* thought this was entirely justified; it was not fair to ask the directors "to pay for the entertainment of several thousands."[87] Unfortunately for the directors, the Football Association chose to investigate the transfers of Bloomer, Brawn, and Wilcox, and the *Northern Athlete* stated that "the whole affair seems to smack of persecution." Despite Gibson-Poole's assertion that the directors had nothing to hide, the club were found to have paid Bloomer an improper bonus for re-signing. The club was fined £50 and had to agree to let the Football Association inspect their books at least twice over the next year.[88] Three months later, having failed to supply the Football Association with their books, the club was fined a further £50. The club also admitted to a "lack of proper control over expenditure," which had resulted in the loss of hundreds of pounds. Bloomer was suspended for two weeks, and the secretary and manager Alex Mackie (who had since left the club to manage the Star & Garter Hotel) was permanently suspended from football management.[89] A year later, Gibson-Poole stated that the directors had "been very careful indeed" as regards expenditure, and assured supporters that "he knew more about the club's affairs than any of the directors." Gibson-Poole's confidence was quickly shown to be misplaced as "owing to a slight error" he saw the club run out of money for hotels and other expenses while partway through their tour of Copenhagen, Prague, and Berlin in June 1908.[90]

The directors' elevated opinions of themselves were demonstrated at the AGM in June 1909. The directors were asked by a Mr Thompson why the meeting was held at the "unseasonable hour" of 6 p.m. Gibson-Poole replied that "several of the directors wished to get away for their holidays," and thought they "deserved some little consideration, seeing the time and money they devoted to the club." He hoped that the shareholders "would not stultify themselves by trying to harass the directors." Not surprisingly, Mr Thompson found this reply unacceptable, and suggested that more than 75 percent of the shareholders had been prevented from attending the meeting as the time did not fit in with their working hours.[91] The relationship between supporters and directors had evidently not improved a year later, as, when faced with "very strong criticism," the board threatened to resign. Gibson-Poole complained that there was "no justification for the criticism that [had] been levelled against them." In order to emphasize the amount of money put in by the directors and to show their disregard for supporters' criticism, a meeting was called at which shareholders and season ticket holders were asked to provide the same amount as the directors, £500, to pay summer wages. Only if the money was forthcoming would the directors be prepared to retain their positions.[92] The directors objected to being "talked about in every public house in the town, and called worse than murderers."[93] The *Northern*

Athlete sympathized with the directors, reminding supporters that those who criticized the board had "nothing at stake" in comparison to those running the club.[94]

It was unlikely that directors of professional football clubs took up their positions in order to make money for themselves. The limit of 5 percent for the payment of dividends meant that only men "who love football for its own sake" were involved. As the *Athletic News* stated, "no one who is out for a business return would look at football shares." William McGregor (the founder of the Football League) suggested that the position of director "carries with it an amount of work which, if a man looked at it through business spectacles, would call for heavy remuneration,"[95] while the secretary of the Football Association believed that there was in fact no desire among directors "to obtain any reward beyond the success of the club."[96] Kennedy notes that the football club boardroom was "locked into a network of civic organisations through which the cohesion of middle-class urban elite was maintained," a point which can be applied to many of Middlesbrough's sporting organizations, as well as to its football clubs.[97] Involvement with a football club could help promote a "civic and philanthropic image," as well as providing a means of enhancing the reputation of the town itself. Indeed, by 1899 "the potential of football had become obvious" to urban men of wealth and status. Profits could also be made from catering, building, providing the kit, and from advertising. A large number of directors were brewers or builders, but only a handful of clubs banned contracting with directors.[98]

Gibson-Poole's motivations for continuing his position with the football club may have been rather different to the club's other directors. In November 1910 Gibson-Poole was chosen as Middlesbrough's Unionist candidate for the forthcoming parliamentary election. He was, even according to the Liberal *Teesside Weekly Herald*, one of the best-known men in the town due to "his active business life, his long association with the civic life of the town, his honourable career as an officer of the volunteering forces and his success as the guiding spirit" of the football club. Indeed, when he had become mayor three years earlier, it was noted that he had always provided "valuable assistance and encouragement" in "clean, healthy sport."[99] However, it was alleged that the Middlesbrough players were pressured into helping with his election campaign. One member of the team, Fred Pentland, stated that though the players had not been coerced, some had spoken on their chairman's behalf. He believed that the players should have refrained "from any display of misguided enthusiasm" in order to prevent the football club from becoming a "political machine."[100] A leaflet was distributed which included photographs of Gibson-Poole and the captain Tim Williamson, alongside quotes from players. The *North-Eastern Daily Gazette* disapproved of the use of football for political gain, arguing that the players had "made a great mistake in appealing to their 'patrons' to support" Gibson-Poole; "as private individuals" the players "can do as they like . . . but as borough players their duty is to attend to their game."[101]

Two days before the election Middlesbrough played Sunderland at Ayresome Park. It was reported that "election fever was in the air"; political placards were carried around the pitch and there was "a lavish display of party colours" at the ground. When Gibson-Poole appeared in the grandstand he was reportedly greeted by "a roar of cheering that eddied its joyful way from one end of the ground to the other." Middlesbrough's subsequent victory over Sunderland was said to have had "a remarkable uplifting effect on the hopes" of Gibson-Poole's supporters, and the players attended a rally held after the match. The chairman remarked that he had been particularly anxious during the second half of the match, as "so much depended on it for me." He suggested that "the first thing my opponents would have done had the Borough not been successful would have been to say that the players were working for me the whole of the week, and they were unfit to play."[102] Despite the team's victory, Gibson-Poole lost the election; Penry Williams (an ironmaster) retained his seat, increasing his majority in the process.[103]

A month later, a Football Association commission was appointed to investigate the match after Sunderland's captain (Charles Thompson) alleged that Middlesbrough's secretary and manager (Andy Walker) had offered him £30 (£10 for himself and £2 each for the other players) to lose the match, as he wanted to win it for Gibson-Poole. Thompson had refused the bribe and informed his trainer and chairman.[104] Middlesbrough FC was said to be "largely under [Gibson-Poole's] domination," and he was "primarily responsible for the offence." The offer to Thompson had not been "made in the interests of, and on behalf of, the Middlesbrough club," but instead solely to assist Gibson-Poole in the election. Both Walker and his chairman were permanently suspended from football.[105] An editorial in the *North-Eastern Daily Gazette* failed to criticize Gibson-Poole, stating that the only explanation could be that "one or the other of the parties concerned lost his head" before the election. Walker stated that he was now deprived of making a living, but still defended his chairman, suggesting that it was "largely due to the excellent business methods he has introduced" that the club had been successful.[106] The *Athletic News* pointed out that somebody must have supplied Walker with the money to offer to Thompson—"who asked him to use the club as a political agency? . . . who prompted and suggested the scheme?" If it had not been Walker, then this writer pitied "the state of mind of those men who have so vilely, traduced him and robbed him of his character and calling."[107] At a public meeting, it was decided that a petition would be started to ask for

Walker's punishment to be decreased (but not that of Gibson-Poole), and it was "supported in a manner that even more than realises the sanguine anticipation of those who inaugurated it."[108] 'Free Lance' in the *Northern Athlete* claimed that "a certain high official" of the Middlesbrough Corporation spoke with an official of the Football Association "so as to avoid any further scandal, and to 'save the honour of the town.'"[109] However, the twelve thousand signatures (including those of directors, members, and supporters of Sunderland) could not persuade the Football Association to reduce Walker's sentence as he still denied the charge of bribery.[110]

The FA's commission also found that "there had been distinct and flagrant tampering with the books"; neither the minute books nor the gate book were kept in order, wage books were badly kept, and players' agreements had not been signed. Walker had also been engaged in football during his suspension (gate receipts having been altered in order to pay him). Having now admitted his part in the incident, Walker informed the commission that he had made the offer on Gibson-Poole's instructions, who in turn denied all knowledge. The club was fined £300 and five of the directors were banned from holding office at any Football League club, and the remaining three directors were also severely censured.[111] The *North-Eastern Daily Gazette* claimed that a relationship had been shown between expenditure and results that was "an inevitable product of professionalism." It was now the duty of the shareholders to "clean the Augean stable thoroughly, and to resolve that the club shall at least be above the average in its conduct."[112] Harry Walker in the *Northern Echo* regarded the fine as "a further tax upon the loyalty and long suffering patience of the shareholders and their football supporters."[113]

Despite the opportunity now given to the shareholders to elect new directors of their choosing, only four nominations were received from the 450 shareholders ahead of the AGM in 1911. It was felt that the management needed to be reformed in order to "guarantee future purity and re-establish Middlesbrough as a worthy entity in connection with British sport." Men were wanted who "will not be swayed by prejudice, or led away by partisanship; who will not treat the players as machines or merchandise to be bought and sold." The committee approached a number of men, "some had refused for business reasons, and some because they did not care to take a share of the liability at the bank." No doubt the preceding scandals dissuaded some men from getting involved with the club. Club officials remained lower-middle- and middle-class (see table 6.1).

That the club now wanted to proceed untainted by the worst aspects of professionalism was demonstrated during the next season. After Middlesbrough won their first home game of the new season in September 1911, the *North-Eastern Daily Gazette* was pleased to point out that the team were no longer receiving any further "incentive to exert themselves

Table 6.1. Middlesbrough Football Club officials, 1911[1]

	Role	Occupation	Employment Status	Address (1911 census)	Place of birth	Servants
Phil Bach[2]	Chairman	Hotel manager		Empire Hotel, Linthorpe Road, Middlesbrough	Ludlow, Shropshire	8
Cuthbert W. Beckwith*	Director	Retired engineer		38 Henry Street, Coatham	New Shildon, County Durham	None
James Colbeck	Director	Butcher	Own account	Vincent House, Orchard Road, Middlesbrough	Hemlington, Yorkshire	None
James J. Fowler*	Director and vice-chairman	Wine and spirit merchant	Own account	7 Waterloo Road, Middlesbrough	York	None
Thomas Herbert McIntosh	Secretary	Surveyor's assistant	Worker	11 Brook Terrace, Darlington	Sedgefield, County Durham	1
William Metcalf	Director	Traveling draper	Own account	37 Queen Street, Coatham	Yorkshire	None
John G. Pallister	Director	Shipyard foreman	Worker	10 Grove Road, North Ormesby, Middlesbrough	Hartlepool, County Durham	1
Edwin Turner	Director	Master housepainter	Employer	371 Linthorpe Road, Middlesbrough	Middlesbrough	None

* Former directors

[1] 1911 census; *North Star*, 4th, 6th July 1911; *Northern Athlete*, 17th, 24th July 1911; *Northern Echo*, 1st June 1911; *Sports Gazette*, 17th June 1911
[2] Brother of Frank and Thomas (see above). Phil Bach was a former Middlesbrough player and a member of the Football League Management committee from 1929–1937—Inglis, *League Football*, p. 393

as has been the case in certain games in the past."[114] The directors' determination to avoid corruption was demonstrated by the turning down of an offer from Stewarts Clothiers in November, who promised to award the players two "Famous Sovereign Overcoats" for every goal scored in the match against Newcastle. The goalscorer would receive one coat and the other would be given to "any spectator each successful player brings along with him." Stewarts declared that they wanted "to instil a healthy, hearty spirit of emulation" in the players but the directors stated that "such offers as these are not in the best interests of the game."[115] The *Middlesbrough Standard* applauded the decision, stating that such offers invited corruption and encouraged "individuality of that selfish nature, very despicable to the majority of spectators."[116]

The club's efforts to stay free of further scandals were rewarded with the Anglo-Scottish interleague match in February 1912. The Football League "wanted to prove to the Middlesbrough club and supporters that they had complete confidence in the gentlemen who were now managing the club's affairs." The game attracted a crowd of twenty-three thousand, and the *North Star* stated that the Scottish team had "a big following of sympathisers in the masses of folk" at the match due to the large number of Scots living on Teesside.[117] Middlesbrough also hosted England versus Ireland two years later, having hosted the same fixture for the first time in 1905. The crowd was estimated to be between twenty-six thousand and thirty thousand, and the *Northern Echo* reported that "the enthusiasm of the Teesside Irish was quite touching"; many of their supporters "wore green of some sort. Cabbage leaves and parsley were among the fantastic decorations worn."[118]

In contrast, other fixtures were affected by the state of trade in Middlesbrough. The League match against Aston Villa in 1912 drew a crowd of only nine thousand, which the *Football Mail* attributed to the coal strike and its "corresponding train of disasters to the iron workers of Middlesbrough." A month later, the game against Sheffield United had a crowd of eight thousand (nine thousand after half time). In "normal times" the match would have attracted sixteen thousand or eighteen thousand spectators, but "in such hard times . . . there is [not] a great deal of superfluous wealth about to satisfy the average man's craving for the most democratic of all sports."[119] At one match a number of "out of works" who had been admitted to the sixpence end of Ayresome Park for free "rushed across the ground" to the shilling end. They were not admitted to the next match but at half time, smashed a gate and "swarmed into the ground," and were excluded from future matches.[120] Middlesbrough's attendance was affected throughout the 1913–1914 season, averaging at 14,900. This was the third lowest in the First Division, the average attendance being 23,100.[121] The crowd for the first home game in September 1913 was fifteen thousand, but when Middlesbrough played local rivals Sunderland, the current champions, there was a crowd of twenty-seven thousand and three policemen had to "pacify a crowd of seven or eight thousand at the 'tanner' [sixpence] end."[122]

ELITE AMATEUR FOOTBALL

While some of Middlesbrough's smaller clubs suffered because of the professional football at Ayresome Park, South Bank and Eston United football clubs were both relatively successful, particularly in the FA Amateur Cup, and the status of such amateur clubs offers further evidence of the strength of the local football culture. The local press were full of praise for the two amateur teams, which contrasts with the various opinions for and against professionalism. South Bank FC had been run as a professional club for the 1891–1892 season, during which time they had spent £487, and had an income of £558. As they had been unable to arrange "home and home" matches "in consequence of the large sums required for guarantees," professionalism was abandoned in August 1892.[123] South Bank was very much in the shadow of Middlesbrough FC. In 1894 they had found it necessary to amalgamate with South Bank Blue Star as "slagdom [South Bank[124]] is not sufficiently big to maintain two clubs capable of competing on level terms with their big neighbour."[125] South Bank was able to maintain a rivalry with their neighbors in the mid-1890s. For example, when the two teams met on Christmas Day in 1894 it was to decide the issue of "local supremacy," and there was a crowd of four thousand.[126] The club was also able to attract local football enthusiasts to their own ground when Middlesbrough was not playing at home. When South Bank played Reading in the third round of the FA Amateur Cup in 1895, kick off was at 3:15 p.m., "so that followers of the game in Stockton and Middlesbrough who desire to see the match will be in time."[127] That particular season was considered successful, the team having reached the semifinal of the Amateur Cup, won the Cleveland Charity Cup, finished second in the Northern League, and reached the final of the Cleveland Senior Cup.[128] However, two years later, "they had lost every competition they had entered" and money was still owed to creditors following the club's yearlong experiment with professionalism.[129] The backgrounds of those involved in running the club at this time were diverse, and Taylor's assertion that many smaller clubs needed "some form of patronage from local institutions, wealthy individuals or fee-paying supporters"[130] is borne out by the role of Ward-Jackson (Lord of Normanby Hall and Justice of the Peace) as club president. In contrast, committee members included a clerk, a laborer, and a joiner, the secretary was a boilersmith, and the treasurer was a doctor.[131]

Despite the lure of the professional game, in 1899 the team remained "an exceedingly strong one." Some players had joined Middlesbrough, while others had left to play for Sheffield United, Millwall Athletic, and Nottingham Forest, which the committee thought "spoke well for the class of South Bank football."[132] However, in 1901 the *North Star* contended that "the counter attraction at Middlesbrough . . . has had its effect upon the patronage accorded to the club," so much so, that it was "the wish of the club management that . . . the fixtures should be so arranged as not to clash with those of Middlesbrough."[133] In 1906 the *Northern Athlete* stated that much of their support "is diverted into the coffers of Middlesbrough owing to the people naturally preferring League football"; Middlesbrough's gate receipts for that season were £9,797 in comparison to just over £370 at South Bank.[134]

In April 1907 the club enquired about the possibility of buying or leasing long-term the field that they rented from Bolckow Vaughan iron and steel works.[135] A rumor circulated two months later that the owner of the field wished to sell the land for building. In a letter from the commercial manager and secretary of Bolckow Vaughan, Walter William Storr, to the land owner's agent, Storr stated that the possibility of building "has caused the club a considerable amount of anxiety." The club had spent around £500 on the grounds and were "naturally very reluctant to lose their money." Storr wrote that, "I need scarcely say that the recreation of our workmen is a question that at all times appeals to us." He emphasized that the field "appears to have been always properly and well conducted and the behavior of the players and spectators is reported to me as having been exceptionally good."[136] Another letter from a local land agent stated that the club was endeavoring to get Bolckow Vaughan to buy the field for them.[137] It is hardly surprising that the club were not in a position to buy the field themselves as it was not until mid-1907 that the club had paid off the debts from "that foolish idea of running a professional team" fifteen years earlier.[138]

South Bank reached the final of the FA Amateur Cup in 1910. The final against RMLI Gosport was played at Bishop Auckland in County Durham (twenty-one miles away), and the North-Eastern Railway Company estimated that one thousand South Bank supporters would travel on "excursion" trains, with a further 200 passengers accompanying the team. The crowd totaled eight thousand–ten thousand and as it is safe to assume that few supporters would have travelled from Hampshire, the size of the crowd at this match (and that in 1913) suggests there was a great deal of local interest in seeing a potential victory for a northeastern team. Though South Bank was beaten, the income from the extra cup matches meant that they were able to pay for improvements to their ground.[139] However, a year later it was pointed out that the club would have been able to achieve a great deal more "had our team been left alone by the professional clubs." "No sooner does your committee get together a side to their liking," stated the club's annual report, "than round comes the professional agent and undoes all the work they had been planning."[140]

In 1913 South Bank reached the final of the Amateur Cup again and played Oxford City in Reading. The *Sports Gazette* remarked that since abandoning professionalism, the club's chief aim had been to win the Amateur Cup; it had been "tantalising to officials and supporters alike that at the very height of its ambition" they had failed to win it.[141] The *Northern Echo* reported on the team's journey from London to Reading. Having spent the morning sight seeing, the players traveled to Paddington on the tube,

> They entertained the crowded "tube" passengers with some of their special imported ditties and comic songs from the island of slag. They were a happy band, 40 in all, team, officials, and supporters and it was impossible to hear the stations being called out by the guard at each stopping place, his voice being drowned out by the Northerner's lusty voices asking him "who he was with last night."[142]

A crowd of 4,500 (including twenty South Bank supporters) attended the match, which ended in a draw. The replay at Bishop Auckland drew seven thousand spectators, this time including many from South Bank, "the cheap train being extensively patronised." South Bank's subsequent victory was greeted with "considerable rejoicing" when the team returned. The captain was "besieged by the crowd and carried shoulder-high through the town." Though the *Northern Echo* thought that once again "the evil of fame" would mean that "the Bankers will now be pestered by big clubs who are anxious to secure their players," it was also felt that the win more than made up for Sunderland's defeat in the FA Cup final on the same day.[143] This points toward a sense of a regional, north eastern identity, as those from Teesside could celebrate a victory elsewhere in the region and vice versa. As Russell asserts, "local rivalries were often suspended or ignored for long enough to allow various types of regional identity to emerge."[144]

Eston United, formed in 1905, were said to be composed "entirely of working lads" from the immediate area. However, this is not reflected in the occupations of those club officials that can be identified—the two presidents were a doctor and an MP (Herbert Samuel), the treasurer was a hotelkeeper, and the assistant secretary was an auction clerk.[145] The club attempted to achieve similar levels of success as South Bank. In 1909 Eston United were beaten by Clapton in the final of the Amateur Cup, won the Northern League at the first attempt in 1910, and reached the Amateur Cup final again in 1912. Even before the semifinal, the *Football Mail* was ready to proclaim that their success in the competition had had the effect of "strongly reviving interest in local amateur football." The *North Star* thought the selection of Ayresome Park for the final tie against Stockton was a good choice, given that "in the North of England amateur football still strongly appeals to a large following."[146] More important, the playing of the match in Middlesbrough resulted in a crowd of twenty thousand (when the average gate at Ayresome Park that season was 14,150) surpassing the previous record for an Amateur Cup final by eight thousand.[147] The match ended in a draw, and the replay was also played at Ayresome Park, at which there was a crowd of eight thousand at the start, increasing to twelve thousand after halftime. The *Teesside Weekly Herald* stated that,

> It was like old times to hear the bugles, rattles and other noisy instruments in the hands of well-meaning enthusiastic followers of the respective clubs. Thousands had walked from outlying villages and many from Stockton in order to see the contest. Many hundreds who were unable to afford even a "tanner" made their appearance at the turnstiles at the popular end at halftime, and had threepenny worth.[148]

These large crowds suggest that not only was there a great deal of interest in amateur football on Teesside, but also indicates that those who normally went to watch professional football at Ayresome Park also watched the amateur game. The *Sports Gazette* thought that the large attendances at these games proved that "amateurism in the North has a stronger hold on the public than even in the palmy days of the past." Though "professionalism has come to stay on Teesside . . . there is still a warm corner in the people's affections for a good display by amateurs."[149] Despite losing the replay, Eston United ended the season with a profit of over £442, but two years later it was reported that "football is in a sad way at Eston." The club's officials had "done all they can possibly think of to bring back again the popularity and success that was once attached to the team . . . the future of the United is far from secure."[150] The cup success had clearly been financially beneficial, but evidently it was more usual for an amateur club to struggle to make ends meet.

LOCAL LEAGUES

In 1914 Alfred Mattison noted that "it was pleasing to see the increasing number of local lads in the [Middlesbrough] side. . . . [While] he had nothing against the importation of costly players, it was better to have their own town products."[151] The "local lads" that played for Middlesbrough often began their playing careers with one of the other clubs in the town, and there was a large number of football leagues and competitions in the town and across the district, all vying for the public's attention. It has been pointed out by Taylor that recreational football was more highly concentrated in those areas with a Football League club, and Russell states that by the turn of the century, Britain was "criss-crossed by a network of leagues professional, semi-professional and amateur, providing the competitive structure that proved such a vital dynamic to the game's expansion."[152] It would certainly appear that the success of Middlesbrough FC was accompanied by an expansion in local clubs and leagues. Moreover, as will be demonstrated below, amateur league football included a great deal more involvement from the lower-middle and working classes.

In 1899 the *Northern Echo* remarked that the introduction of professional football had not had a damaging effect on local amateur teams. Furthermore, the large number of amateur clubs in Middlesbrough meant that "the senior club may feel assured there are dozens of diamonds in the rough . . . ready to be set in and promoted to the more brilliant professional rings."[153] Whether the smaller clubs would have regarded themselves as mere nurseries for Middlesbrough is doubtful. Middlesbrough were often accused of 'poaching' footballers. As early as 1888, the club were said to have poached players from Middlesbrough Albion FC, leading the *Northern Review* to point out that Albion "do not want to manufacture footballers for the benefit of other clubs."[154] The effect that Middlesbrough FC could have on other clubs and leagues in the district was often stated in the press. The *North-Eastern Daily Gazette* pointed out in 1901 that Middlesbrough's followers included "recruits from the whole of the surrounding towns and villages," while a year later the *Athletic News* suggested that should Middlesbrough secure promotion that season it would "cause the disbandment of certain of the Northern League clubs in the immediate vicinity." Indeed it was reported that Thornaby FC disbanded "owing to the advancement of Middlesbrough."[155] Harry Walker, writing in the *South Durham & Cleveland Mercury*, stated that Middlesbrough benefited from being more than thirty miles away from the nearest Football League club, and the club were able to draw on a "distinctly sporting" local population of half a million.[156] Demonstrating the attraction of good football, the *Northern Athlete* suggested in 1906 that large numbers of people "from the surrounding district" visited Ayresome Park "in order to see the best football and the leading teams of the country—they are not particular which side wins." Though it might be assumed therefore that the quality of football on display in Middlesbrough would have had a detrimental effect on other clubs, the *Northern Athlete* claimed that it was in fact "doing much good in fostering the game over a wide area . . . as it is not only stimulating local players, but likewise the public."[157] The sheer number of football clubs that continued to be formed throughout this period suggests that Middlesbrough FC's success did not always disadvantage smaller clubs.

The number of local leagues in existence before the First World War (see appendix 5) gives a clear indication of the popularity of football. Leagues included teams from Middlesbrough and across Teesside and East Cleveland, demonstrating the spread of football in the district, the attractiveness of the nonprofessional game, and the necessity of properly organized and administered fixtures. Both the Teesside League and Teesside Junior League were formed in 1891, and five years later the Middlesbrough League was formed for the "minor" clubs of the town. Its intention was to "improve the class of football played," and the league was extended in 1898 to include clubs from outside of the town.[158] It was felt that the amalgamation of the Middlesbrough and Teesside leagues a year later would garner "much greater interest,"[159] but in 1901 the secretary "expressed regret that their class of amateur football had not flourished in the Cleveland district." "The novelty of a professional team at Middlesbrough" meant that "young amateur players [prefer] to go and look on." Nevertheless the league was increased in 1904 to include two divisions of ten teams.[160] With a view "to fostering and developing local talent," in 1896 Gibson-Poole donated a cup for junior teams and the first final of the Poole Cup attracted three thousand spectators. The *North-Eastern Daily Gazette* pointed out the importance of such a contest, as "it is from the ranks of our junior organisations that the premier club of the town must look for its future players."[161] The aim of the Middlesbrough Junior League was "to purify junior football generally and to bring it under proper supervision and control." This league had had a great deal of success "in endeavouring to alleviate the condition of junior football," as similar leagues were subsequently set up elsewhere in the area.[162]

The South Bank & District Minor League was formed in 1899.[163] The first reported AGM was in 1903 when a joiner was listed as president and treasurer, and the secretary was a clerk. The AGM three years later lists fifteen clubs in the league, it having been extended to include teams from Stockton and across Middlesbrough.[164] The occupations of the League's officials were diverse (see table 6.2), and while the League had the patronage of some of the town's elite, it is unlikely that Walton and Williams would have had as much involvement as some of the other officials.

The Cleveland League was formed in 1909, with "a painstaking and energetic man" as secretary (John Gibbon, a clerk). The *Middlesbrough Standard* hoped that the league would prosper and that "the winter's sport will be enjoyed and invigorated by true amateurism."[165] The Eston & District League was also formed in 1914, with seventeen initial applications for membership.[166] The Cleveland Wednesday Football League (for clubs within a fourteen-miles radius of Middlesbrough) was established in 1910 for those men who were permitted to work a half-day on Wednesdays. Two of the founding member clubs were affiliated to Hinton's gro-

Table 6.2. South Bank & District Minor League officials, 1912–1913[1]

	Role	Occupation	Employment Status	Address (1911 census)	Place of birth	Servants
Jack R. Smiles	President	Owner of concrete works	Employer	71 Douglas Terrace, Middlesbrough	Newcastle	1
William Barnard	Vice-president	Jeweler	Worker	Malmesburn, Cambridge Road, Middlesbrough	Middlesbrough	1
Cecil Bevill Close	Vice-president	Clerk in Holy Orders[*]		18 Milton Street, Middlesbrough	Ealing, Middlesex	None
Thomas Priestley Cotton	Treasurer	Fitter	Worker	30 Milbank Street, Middlesbrough	Liverton Mines, Yorkshire	None
Giles Desmond Vandeleen Creagh	Vice-president	Assistant harbormaster	Worker	76 Palmerston Terrace, Middlesbrough	Norton Fitzwarren, Somerset	None (boarder)
Francis Harrison Dennis	Vice-president	Clerk	Worker	7 Belle Vue Road, Middlesbrough	Norton, Yorkshire	None
John Leith	Vice-president	Joiner	Worker	23 Gosford Street, Middlesbrough	Middlesbrough	None
James B. Morgan	Secretary	Laborer	Worker	75 Costa Street, Middlesbrough	Blackhill, County Durham	None
Joseph Walton Jr.	Vice-president	Barrister	Employer	Rushpool Hall, Saltburn	Saltburn, Yorkshire	6
Penry Williams	Vice-president	MP for Middlesbrough; Managing director of ironworks		Pinchinthorpe Hall, Great Ayton	Middlesbrough	7

[*]Curate of St Paul's—Kelly's Directory of North and East Ridings of Yorkshire, 1913 (London, 1913)

[1]1911 census; Sports Gazette, 31st May 1913; Teesside Weekly Herald, 8th June 1912; see also the diverse officials of the North Yorkshire & South Durham Thursday Football League, including Lord Londonderry—North-Eastern Daily Gazette, 27th November 1912; Sports Gazette, 18th June 1910; Teesside Weekly Herald, 15th June 1912

Table 6.3. Cleveland Wednesday Football League officials, 1910–1911[1]

	Role	Occupation	Employment Status	Address (1911 census)	Place of birth	Servants
Herbert Samuel	President	MP for Cleveland		31 Porchester Terrace, London	Liverpool	7
William Wright Archibald	Vice-president	Draper's manager	Employer	27 Clairville Road, Middlesbrough	Scotland	1
Richard Godolphin Walmesley Chaloner	Vice-president	MP for Liverpool Abercromby	Employer	90 Piccadilly, London	Wales	None
Cecil Bevill Close	Vice-president	Clerk in Holy Orders[a]		18 Milton Street, Middlesbrough	Ealing, Middlesex	None
Francis Harrison Dennis	Chairman	Clerk	Worker	7 Belle Vue Road, Middlesbrough	Norton, Yorkshire	None
Thomas Gibson-Poole	Vice-president	Retired jeweler		Roman Road, Middlesbrough	Dudley, Staffordshire	2
William Henry Hinton	Vice-president	Grocer	Employer	The Homestead, Grove Hill, Middlesbrough	Middlesbrough	2
John Leith	Secretary	Joiner	Worker	23 Gosford Street, Middlesbrough	Middlesbrough	None
John Thomas Pannell	Vice-president	General manager in Cooperative Society	Worker	Llenny, Cornfield Road, Middlesbrough	Exmouth, Devon	None
Thomas Dormand Stewart	Vice-president	Clothier	Employer	Tyneholme House, The Crescent, Middlesbrough[b]	North Shields, Northumberland	None
Arthur Tiplady	Vice-chairman	Shop assistant	Worker	36 Albany Street, Middlesbrough	Welburn, Yorkshire	None

[a] Curate of St Paul's—Kelly's Directory of the North and East Ridings of Yorkshire 1913

[b] Kelly's Directory of North and East Ridings of Yorkshire, 1909 (London, 1909); Address on 1911 census—Kenworthy's Hydropathic Establishment, Southport, Lancashire

[1] 1911 census; North-Eastern Daily Gazette, 10th August 1910; Sports Gazette, 9th July 1910, 27th May 1911; It was suggested that some players abused the fact that playing in the football team meant time away from work as it was proposed that "no players but those with only Wednesday afternoon off should be allowed to play in the League"—North-Eastern Daily Gazette, 29th May 1912

cers and Stewart's clothiers, and the formation of this league suggests that some employers were keen for their workers to engage in healthy recreation in order, perhaps, that they be more productive at work. Eight men were asked to take up the role of vice-president, all of whom accepted, though as with the South Bank league, some of those who took up the positions would have had little real involvement (see table 6.3).

The Middlesbrough & District Church Football League was founded in 1906, initially comprising eleven teams.[167] In 1910 it was decided to run a second division, and those intending to join either division were reminded that they needed to have a recommendation from the minister of their church. A year later the League was pleased to report that "never before had they had so many churches interested in [the] healthy recreation of young men," though players were also urged to remain with their teams rather than "bring their bible classes down to such a level that they would go to another place of worship because they had a better football team;" bible classes were not always the priority of the players.[168] In 1914 it was noted by the League's officials that from a playing point of view, the second division was "a failure . . . it had had a lengthy trial, but it had never been the success hoped for."[169]

William Johnson of the Hope & Anchor Hotel organized a medal competition for blast furnace men in 1898,[170] but it was another ten years before a league was formed for blast furnace men and coke men.[171] There was no further mention of this league, possibly due to the formation of the Middlesbrough Works League in the same year. Furthermore, the *Northern Athlete* thought that such a league would fail, as Middlesbrough's matches at Ayresome Park would "prove too powerful a magnet for those associated with such a league"; clubs would find that many of the players would be "found absent from duty without leave" on a Saturday afternoon.[172] It is not clear how successful this league was, there being no further mention in the press after 1909. This may indeed be attributed to the lure of football at Ayresome Park but also may be due to the number of other leagues in existence that included works teams. For example, members of the longer established South Bank & District Minor League included five works teams in 1910, and in 1912 the Teesside League included four works teams.[173]

RECREATIONAL FOOTBALL

There were a huge number of other clubs in existence during this period, and although information is only available for a small number of them, from club names alone (see appendix 5), we can examine the patterns of development of small amateur clubs. Prior to the establishment of the

Middlesbrough Works League in 1908, there were a small number of workplace-based clubs and only a slightly greater number of church-based clubs. For example, when the Middlesbrough & Teesside League expanded to two divisions in 1904, there were twenty members—two from the workplace and four from the church. Similarly, the South Bank & District Minor League included one work-based and three church-based clubs. More common are clubs whose names locate them in specific areas of Middlesbrough—most notably South Bank, Grangetown, Newport, and North Ormesby, areas with greater working-class populations. The limited evidence suggests that unlike many other sports in Middlesbrough, recreational football offered greater opportunities for working-class involvement. The evidence also demonstrates the continuation and importance of the voluntary tradition in the running of football clubs, as they remained "a vital feature of community life."[174] Many of those involved with Grangetown Athletic Football Club in 1903 can be identified, and aside from the president, the officials were all working class (see table 6.4). In 1908 the club's chairman stated that the committee had "endeavoured to do their best to keep together a gentlemanly team and play on sportsmanlike lines," pointing out that they "had done their best to purify the team,"[175] but three years later the club were said to be "passing through the most critical period of its somewhat chequered career." The committee had decided that the team would be composed entirely of players from Grangetown, but this "did not prove a success."[176]

After Middlesbrough turned professional in 1899, the chairman of Linthorpe Football Club, Rev John W. Dales (vicar of Linthorpe Parish Church), stated that he wanted to have "a really good amateur club" in Linthorpe. He emphasized that he took "great interest in amateur and not professional football," but there was a lack of interest among members and players.[177] Dales was also listed as the president of Linthorpe Parish Church Football Club seven years later, and as this club was located in a more affluent suburb, it is unsurprising that club officials included two clerks, an inspector for the Board of Trade, and a cashier and accountant.[178] It is debatable whether players joined church teams because of religious reasons. As already stated above, players for such teams were reminded to stay with the club of their church, rather than move to a different church simply because it had a better football team. The Linthorpe Parish Church club decided not to join either the Middlesbrough or Stockton Church Leagues in 1907 as the rules regarding church and Bible class attendance were not enforced. A year later, however, the club had to report that many members had left because of the subsequent lack of league football, suggesting that *this* was the priority for players rather than a connection to their church.[179] In 1906 the subscriptions of the

Table 6.4. Grangetown Athletic Football Club officials, 1903[1]

	Role	Occupation	Employment Status	Address (1901 census)	Place of birth	Servants
John Moss	President	Head teacher	Worker	Villa, Grangetown, Middlesbrough	Newcastle	2
John Burt	Committee	Vessel man	Worker	45 Bessemer Street, Middlesbrough	Middlesbrough	None
Robert M. Crane	Captain	Locomotive driver	Worker	28 Wood Street, Middlesbrough	Middlesbrough	None
Thomas Feeney	Vice-captain	Laborer	Worker	37 Laing Street, Middlesbrough	Middlesbrough	None (boarder)
Owen Murtha	Trainer	Laborer	Worker	4 Sea View Terrace, Middlesbrough	Yorkshire	None
Charles Phillipson	Committee	Stationary engine driver	Worker	44 Laing Street, Middlesbrough	Pickering, Yorkshire	None
Daniel Ramsay	Committee	Rougher	Worker	15 Vickers Street, Middlesbrough	North Ormesby, Middlesbrough	None
William Vasey	Committee	Laborer	Worker	2 Vickers Street, Middlesbrough	Guisborough, Yorkshire	None

[1] 1901 census; *South Durham & Cleveland Mercury*, 26th June 1903

Table 6.5. Middlesbrough YMCA Football Club officials, 1904–1906[1]

	Role	Occupation	Employment Status	Address (1901 census)	Place of birth	Servants
Herbert Samuel	President	MP for Cleveland		88 Gloucester Terrace, London	Liverpool	5
Thomas Burdon	Vice-president	Marine engineer	Worker	50 Linthorpe Road, Middlesbrough	Middlesbrough	1
Alexander Cargan	Committee	Stationary engine driver	Worker	13 Vickers Street, Middlesbrough	Witton Park, County Durham	None
Harold Crabtree	Secretary	Plasterer	Worker	21 Percy Street, Middlesbrough	Middlesbrough	None
Albert Edward Forbes	Vice-president	Articled clerk		20 Park Road North, Middlesbrough	Middlesbrough	1
Ernest Gilroy	Vice-president	Doctor	Own account	94-96 Corporation Road, Middlesbrough	Newcastle	2
John U. Millard	Secretary	Apprentice boilersmith	Worker	4 Myrtle Street, Middlesbrough	Middlesbrough	None
Stanley Aubrey Sadler[a]	Vice-president	Managing director of chemical works	Employer	Eastleigh, Eaglescliffe	Eaglescliffe, County Durham	3
Dr Steele[b]	Vice-president	Doctor				

[a] 1911 census
[b] Unable to locate on census, occupation taken from title
[1] 1901 census; North-Eastern Daily Gazette, 14th July 1904; Sports Gazette, 11th August 1906

YMCA football club were reduced from 5s to 2s 6d in a bid to attract more members.[180] The backgrounds of those involved in the football club of the YMCA were varied, dependent on the position held in the club (see table 6.5). A few details can also be found on those involved in other smaller clubs, and club officials ranged from laborers and blast furnace workers to clerks and other lower-middle-class occupations.[181]

A variety of football matches were reported involving smaller clubs that were not members of any local leagues. The *South Durham & Cleveland Mercury* detailed a match between officials from Dorman Long and Moor Steel & Iron Co in 1895 and teams playing under the heading "ordinary matches" in the *Middlesbrough & Stockton Sporting Telegraph* two years later included Malleable Fitters, Millwrights, and Imperial Swifts.[182] In 1903 clubs playing "ordinary matches" included Middlesbrough Wesley Guild, Middlesbrough Park Vale, Middlesbrough St Peter's and North Ormesby Erimus, and a match was reported on between the workmen of John Livingstone & Son's Brass Works and Theophilius Phillips Son & Co Brass Works.[183] In 1911 the *Sports Gazette* detailed a game between the East Otto and West Otto Coke Ovens at Samuelson's ground, which "owing to the friendly rivalry which exists" attracted a good crowd.[184] A number of charity matches were also held. The *North Star* reported on a match between teams representing topmen and enginemen employed at Eston jetty, "for the benefit of some of their unfortunate fellow workmen." A match took place in 1905 between Newport and Middlesbrough railwaymen with the receipts being donated to an orphan charity, and in 1910 a match between butchers and fruiterers was held at Ayresome Park for the benefit of those who had "suffered loss" on account of a fire at the butchers' market.[185] By 1905 the main competitions of the Cleveland Association were no longer deemed interesting to spectators. The Charity Cup final (Thornaby St Patrick's versus Cambridge House) drew a crowd of only five hundred, and the Cleveland Amateur Cup final attracted only two hundred spectators (Thornaby St Patrick's versus Darlington Friends' Adults). However, it may have been the case that the size of the crowds depended on which clubs were involved or the quality of the football on display, as when the Cleveland Chemical Works played Southfield Primitive Methodists in the 1911 Charity Cup there was a crowd of three thousand. Indeed the Chemical Works team "paraded the town in a brake with the cup held aloft."[186]

Kerrigan has pointed out that given the concerns about the health of the urban poor and the need for exercise, it is surprising that more time was not given over to football in schools as outdoor games were of "equal educational significance" to drill and other exercises.[187] One contemporary suggested that school football provided "youthful Britons with a healthy exercise in the open air."[188] The Middlesbrough Schools Football League was established in 1896, three years after the Sunderland Schools FA was formed.[189] Matches were organized between Middlesbrough schoolboys and those from Sunderland and Gateshead. It was reported in 1899 that all of the proceeds from the match against the Gateshead Schools' League at the Linthorpe Road ground would be given to Middlesbrough FC, as they had "at all times and in all ways done their best to promote the interests of the Schools' League," and therefore also benefited from another layer of local football.[190] Reflecting contemporary attitudes on both health and amateurism, the 1906 report of the League reminded participants that its aim was "the development of the boy physically and morally, and not the mere acquisition of medals or honour; these were the result not the aim." It was suggested that "it would be better both in regard to learning and sport if the means rather than the end were justly observed," emphasizing the importance of playing the game over winning the match.[191]

THE ROLE OF FOOTBALL IN MIDDLESBROUGH

The popularity of football in Middlesbrough was hard to deny. In a 1898 piece entitled "The Good of Football" the *North-Eastern Daily Gazette* pointed out the appeal of the sport,

> For the animated crowds who are the spectators the game . . . no doubt affords the means of an hour or two of pleasant, lively enjoyment. And any recreation, which without taxing the nerves and brain, takes the thoughts away from the carking cares and worries of every-day life, is not only a desirable interlude, but . . . a means of getting strength for the dreary battle to which we must always return. . . . [It is] a healthy stimulating sport, and for those who look on, an exhilarating pastime.[192]

One contemporary critic suggested that football offered an alternative to the "dull monotony of life in our large towns,"[193] and the *Northern Athlete* argued that football was "the characteristic recreation of the toilers and moilers of our land. It is their 90 minutes enjoyment after a laborious weeks' work." The Archdeacon of Cleveland, Rev T. E. Lindsay, also believed that football was "a magnificent game for men to play." The "keenness and rapidity of thought" necessary for training, self-discipline, and exercise, together with "the power of unselfish combination were elements which went to form the essence of man's life."[194]

It was also claimed, however, that on occasion, workingmen were prevented from attending matches. A letter in the *North-Eastern Daily Gazette* pointed out that some games started before the advertised time, and "there were many tradespeople [sic] who have no time to waste and always go to reach the field at the time advertised for the kick-off," and thus miss part of the match. Another letter complained about the times of the excursion trains for Middlesbrough's match in Nottingham over Christmas, as it left the traveling supporters little time before returning home—"It is not fairplay to the working class, who can only support the Borough away at holiday times."[195] There were also restrictions on where casual games of football could be played. In 1908 the sport was banned from Albert Park, it being declared that "there would be righteous indignation if they allowed football." If the Park was "destroyed by a few footballers [it] would be a great shame." However, at discovering that football was prohibited, one councillor wondered "where in the world were the boys to play football?" He could not imagine "such children doing any damage by playing football."[196] In contrast, there were complaints in 1914 that the police had failed to stop the "gangs of the rougher element from various works" playing football on the main approach to the North-Eastern Steelworks.[197]

It was often stated that playing or watching football helped to alleviate problems with alcohol in the town. Mattison stated that football had "made more men temperate and made more happy homes than all the preaching of temperance propaganda," while G. O. Smith suggested that "people who otherwise would spend their afternoon in the public house, to the detriment of their pocket" went to watch football instead.[198] In the *Gazette*'s "The Good of Football," it was stated that the sport was "highly preferable to many other ways in which young men are apt to spend their leisure time."[199] When Reverend Father Burns of Middlesbrough All Saints church complained that football was responsible for increases in drinking and poverty, 'Free Lance' in the *Northern Athlete* vociferously replied that "thousands of wives in England have good cause to be thankful for the coming of the day when their husbands took to the great national pastime, for where squalor, misery, and semi-starvation once reigned, we now have comfortable homes." 'Free Lance' suggested that two-thirds of those attending football matches "would probably be sitting in a public house making themselves lower than the swine" were it not for the sport. Indeed in 1910, the Chief Constable of Middlesbrough stated that a greater number of cases came before the magistrates when Middlesbrough FC were playing away on a Saturday.[200]

The growth and development of football on a number of levels, from a professional Football League team to the introduction of a local schools league, demonstrates the ways in which the sport had become an important and integral part of the recreational lives of many men. The reaction and celebrations to the involvement of Middlesbrough, South Bank, and Eston United in the Amateur Cup finals suggests that football could play a role in the shaping of local identities. Furthermore, the reactions of Middlesbrough FC's shareholders and of the local press to the mismanagement of the club, and the notion that those elected to run the club needed to act in its best interests, indicates the strength of feeling toward "their" football club. Expectations and support remained high, despite the scandals that affected the club, suggesting that supporters felt they had more invested emotionally and monetarily in the Middlesbrough club. The move from amateur club to a member of the national Football League allowed Middlesbrough to build their national profile, though the increased desire for success which accompanied this also led to the breaking of the rules.

NOTES

1. *North-Eastern Daily Gazette*, 13th January 1909.
2. Portions of this chapter were originally published as "'A healthy stimulating sport and an exhilarating pastime': Middlesbrough's amateur and recreational football clubs, c. 1880–1914," *Soccer History* 32 (2014), pp. 7–13.
3. *North-Eastern Daily Gazette*, 18th November 1908, 13th January 1909.
4. *South Durham & Cleveland Mercury*, 4th January 1895.
5. Prior to the match, it was reported that Old Carthusians were anxious about the game, having asked Middlesbrough's secretary to move the game to London. The *Sportsman* reported that Headingley had been chosen for the final "because of the support given by the local admirers to the semi-final tie." There had been three thousand spectators at the semifinal in Leeds; in comparison, the crowd at Middlesbrough's semifinal at Derby was only six hundred—*North-Eastern Daily Gazette*, 24th April 1895; *Sportsman*, 29th April 1895.
6. *Athletic News*, 29th April 1895; *North-Eastern Daily Gazette*, 29th April 1895.
7. *Athletic News*, 6th May 1895; *North-Eastern Daily Gazette*, 29th April 1895.
8. *North-Eastern Daily Gazette*, 29th April 1895.
9. *Middlesbrough & Stockton Evening Telegraph*, 2nd April 1898; *North-Eastern Daily Gazette*, 22nd March 1898; *North Star*, 19th March 1898.
10. Spectators were also able to watch some of the lacrosse final between Surbiton and Stockton on the adjoining "arena" which started thirty minutes before the football—*Daily News*, 23rd April 1898.
11. *Daily News*, 25th April 1898; *North Star*, 25th April 1898; *South Durham & Cleveland Mercury*, 29th April 1898.
12. *Middlesbrough & Stockton Evening Telegraph*, 26th April 1898; *North-Eastern Daily Gazette*, 26th April 1898; *North Star*, 26th April 1898; *Northern Weekly Gazette*, 30th April 1898.
13. D. Russell, *Football and the English: A social history of association football in England, 1863–1995* (Preston, 1997) p. 65; M. Taylor, *The Leaguers: The making of professional football in England, 1900–1939* (Liverpool, 2005), p. 263.
14. *North-Eastern Daily Gazette*, 25th April 1898; *North Star*, 26th April 1898.
15. *North Star*, 2nd June 1898.
16. M. Shearman, *Athletics and Football* (London, 1894), p. 392.
17. *Badminton Magazine* quoted in T. Mason, *Association Football and English Society 1863–1915* (Brighton, 1981), pp. 230–231.

18. Quoted in R. W. Lewis, "'Touched Pitch and Been Shockingly Defiled': Football, class, social Darwinism and decadence in England, 1880–1914," in J. Mangan (ed.), *Sport in Europe: Politics, class, gender* (London, 1999), p. 125.

19. Quoted in S. Tischler, *Footballers and Businessmen: The origins of professional football in England* (New York, 1981), p. 65.

20. N. Carter, *The Football Manager: A history* (Abingdon, 2006), p. 30; A. Harvey, *Football: The first hundred years, the untold story* (Abingdon, 2005), pp. 216–218; Mason, *Association Football*, p. 73, p. 241; *Athletic News* quoted in Tischler, *Footballers and Businessmen*, p. 69.

21. J. J. Bentley, "The Growth of Modern Football," in C. Leatherdale (ed.), *The Book of Football* (Westcliff-on-Sea, 1997 [first edition, 1906]), p. 12; J. J. Bentley, "Is Football a Business?," *World's Work* 20 (1912), p. 390.

22. Lewis, "Touched Pitch," p. 125; D. Porter, "Revenge of the Crouch End Vampires: The AFA, the FA and English football's 'Great Split,'" *Sport in History* 26, 3 (2006) p. 413; G. O. Smith, "Origin and Benefits of the League and the Effects of Professionalism on the Game," in M. Shearman (ed.), *Football* (London, 1899), p. 175.

23. Minute Book of MFC, 22nd March 1897; *Northern Echo*, 1st June 1897.

24. *North Star*, 21st January 1899.

25. *Middlesbrough & Stockton Sporting Telegraph*, 21st January 1899.

26. Minute Book of MFC, 3rd February 1899; *Middlesbrough & Stockton Evening Telegraph*, 6th February 1899; *Northern Echo*, 6th February 1899.

27. Minute Book of MFC, 20th February 1899; *Middlesbrough & Stockton Evening Telegraph*, 25th February 1899; *North-Eastern Daily Gazette*, 28th February 1899; The only disagreement over professionals within the club itself was expressed by the director, Samuel A. Glover, who tendered his resignation due to his opposition to professionalism. He agreed "not to press" his resignation immediately, though it was understood that he would "be glad to be relieved of the position at an early date"—Minute Book of MFC, 27th June 1899.

28. Minute Book of MFC, 27th February 1899.

29. *North Star*, 4th March 1899.

30. Minute Book of MFC, 3rd March 1899; *Middlesbrough & Stockton Evening Telegraph*, 4th March 1899; *North-Eastern Daily Gazette*, 4th March 1899; *North Star*, 4th March 1899.

31. *North-Eastern Daily Gazette*, 10th March 1899; The Imperial Tram Company had been involved in Middlesbrough's trams since 1878, and James Clifton Robinson was said to have had "a long and fairly happy association" with the town— W. Lillie, *The History of Middlesbrough* (Middlesbrough, 1968), pp. 242–245.

32. The MPs for Barnard Castle and the Hartlepools respectively.

33. Minute Book of MFC, 13th March 1899.

34. Minute Book of MFC, 17th March 1899; *North-Eastern Daily Gazette*, 17th March 1899.

35. *North Star*, 25th March 1899.

36. G. F. Allison, "The Rise of Middlesbrough Football Club," in Leatherdale (ed.), *The Book of Football*, p. 203; M. Taylor and J. Coyle, "The Election of Clubs to the Football League 1888–1939," *The Sports Historian* 19, 2 (1999), p. 3.

37. *Middlesbrough & Stockton Sporting Telegraph*, 29th May 1899.

38. Minute Book of MFC, 5th, 31st May 1899; *Middlesbrough & Stockton Evening Telegraph*, 21st June 1899; *Middlesbrough & Stockton Sporting Telegraph*, 30th May 1899.

39. *Middlesbrough & Stockton Evening Telegraph*, 25th August 1899; *South Durham & Cleveland Mercury*, 25th August 1899.

40. *Middlesbrough & Stockton Sporting Telegraph*, 11th September 1899; This was less than the seven thousand–eight thousand that had attended the club's first practice match, but the average home attendance of 5,925 was the highest in the Second Division—*North-Eastern Daily Gazette*, 25th August 1899; B. Tabner, *Football Through the Turnstiles Again* (Harefield, 2002), p. 96.

41. *Middlesbrough & Stockton Evening Telegraph*, 20th September 1899.

42. Minute Book of MFC, 18th, 25th September, 2nd, 9th October 1899.

43. *South Durham & Cleveland Mercury*, 30th March 1900.

44. Minute Book of MFC, Statement of Accounts 1899–1900; *Middlesbrough & Stockton Evening Telegraph*, 28th May, 1st June 1900; *North Star*, 1st June 1900; *Northern Echo*, 1st June 1900.

45. *North Star*, 8th January 1901.

46. Minute Book of MFC, 25th June, 2nd July 1900; M. Taylor, "Beyond the Maximum Wage: The earnings of football professionals in England, 1900–39," *Soccer and Society* 2, 3 (2001), p. 103.

47. *Northern Echo*, 10th March 1902.

48. *North Star*, 10th March 1902; *South Durham & Cleveland Mercury*, 14th March 1902.

49. *Athletic News*, 21st, 28th April 1902; *North-Eastern Daily Gazette*, 24th, 29th April, 2nd May 1902.

50. *North-Eastern Daily Gazette*, 22nd, 29th July, 27th August, 8th September 1902; *Northern Echo*, 8th September 1902.

51. *Northern Echo*, 20th October, 30th December 1902.

52. E. Paylor and J. Wilson, *Ayresome Park Memories* (Derby, 1995), p. 8.

53. *Northern Echo*, 21st April 1903.

54. *North-Eastern Daily Gazette*, 1st July 1903; *South Durham & Cleveland Mercury*, 3rd July, 14th August 1903.

55. Inglis states that the total cost of building Ayresome Park and rebuilding the old grandstand from the Linthorpe Road ground was £12,000—S. Inglis, *Engineering Archie: Archibald Leitch—football ground designer* (London, 2005), p. 66.

56. *Athletic News*, 24th August 1903; Sutcliffe quoted in Taylor, *The Leaguers*, pp. 255–256.

57. *Athletic News*, 14th September 1903; *South Durham & Cleveland Mercury*, 18th September 1903.

58. 1901 census; *North-Eastern Daily Gazette*, 11th September 1903.

59. *North-Eastern Daily Gazette*, 16th September 1903; *South Durham & Cleveland Mercury*, 18th September 1903.

60. *North-Eastern Daily Gazette*, 26th, 30th November 1903—The gate receipts for the following four home games were £419 (Stoke), £405 (Manchester City), £750 (Sheffield United) and £520 (Aston Villa). The average attendance at Ayresome Park was 13,475, tenth highest in the division, but this dropped during the the following two seasons. The highest season average during this period was

16,425 for the 1907–1908 season—Tabner, *Football Through the Turnstiles Again*, pp. 96–103.

61. *Northern Athlete*, 13th June 1910.

62. *North Star*, 28th April, 21st May 1914.

63. *North-Eastern Daily Gazette*, 7th, 8th March 1904; *North Star*, 10th March 1904; This was evidently not unique to Middlesbrough as H. F. Abell complained in 1904 that large establishments were often closed during the working week because "the whole body of workmen take it into their heads that their pets on the football ground require encouragement." If men are absent from work, "nobody asks where they are or if they are ill or dead, it being taken for granted that football somewhere has attracted them away"—H. F. Abell, "The Football Fever," *Macmillan's Magazine* 89 (1904), p. 281.

64. *South Durham & Cleveland Mercury*, 18th March 1904.

65. *North Star*, 23rd November 1904.

66. *North-Eastern Daily Gazette*, 22nd November 1904.

67. *Sports Gazette*, 26th November 1904 *Teesside Weekly Herald*, 3rd December 1904.

68. *North Star*, 9th December 1904; *Northern Echo*, 10th December 1904; Carter, *The Football Manager*, p. 26, p. 35.

69. *Sports Gazette*, 4th March 1905.

70. *North-Eastern Daily Gazette*, 30th June 1905; *Northern Echo*, 23rd June 1905

71. Newcastle had finished first, Sunderland fifth, and Middlesbrough had finished in fifteenth place; *North-Eastern Daily Gazette*, 30th June 1905; *Northern Echo*, 23rd, 30th June 1905; *Sports Gazette*, 24th June 1905; *Quarterly Review* quoted in Tischler *Footballers and Businessmen*, p. 127.

72. *North-Eastern Daily Gazette*, 30th June 1905.

73. Taylor, *The Leaguers*, pp. 102–103; M. Taylor, *The Association Game: A history of British football* (Harlow, 2008), p. 75.

74. F. Bell, *At the Works: A study of a manufacturing town* (London, 1985 [first edition, 1907]), p. 48; A. A. Hall, "Wages, Earnings and Real Earnings in Teeside: A re-assessment of the ameliorist interpretation of living standards in Britain, 1870–1914," *International Review of Social History* 26 (1981), pp. 211–212; D. Taylor, "The Infant Hercules and the Augean Stables: A century of economic and social development in Middlesbrough c.1840–1939," in A. J. Pollard (ed.), *Middlesbrough: Town and Community 1830–1950* (Stroud, 1996), pp. 71–72.

75. Before Common's transfer, the highest transfer fees were around £400. It was felt that "an uncontrollable surge" in fees might be set off and in March 1905 the Football Association decided that a maximum transfer fee would be set of £350 (though this proved impossible to control and was dropped after three months)— S. Inglis, *League Football and the Men Who Made It* (London, 1988), pp. 57–58.

76. *Northern Echo*, 28th February 1905; *South Durham & Cleveland Mercury*, 24th February 1905.

77. *North-Eastern Daily Gazette*, 15th February 1905.

78. *Athletic News*, 20th February 1905; W. I. Bassett, "Big Transfers and the Transfer System," in Leatherdale (ed.), *The Book of Football*, p. 162; Bentley, "Is Football a Business?," p. 392.

79. S. Inglis, *Soccer in the Dock: A history of British football scandals, 1900–1965* (London, 1985), p. 8, p. 22; Mason, *Association Football*, pp. 99–100.

80. *Athletic News*, 31st July 1905; *North Star*, 28th November 1905; Inglis, *Soccer in the Dock*, p. 24.

81. *North-Eastern Daily Gazette*, 11th December 1905; *North Star*, 29th November 1905.

82. *Northern Echo*, 28th November 1905; *Sports Gazette*, 2nd December 1905.

83. *Northern Echo*, 13th December 1905.

84. G. F. Allison, *Allison Calling: A galaxy of football and other memories* (London, 1948), p. 12; *Athletic News*, 5th, 12th February 1906.

85. 1901 census; *Athletic News*, 18th December 1905, 8th January 1906; *North-Eastern Daily Gazette*, 15th December 1905; The directors agreed that their predecessors should remain responsible for £1,000 of the club's debt, and were led to believe that they would pay the fine to the Football Association but it had to be paid by Gibson-Poole—*Athletic News*, 29th January 1906; *North Star*, 1st February 1906.

86. *Athletic News*, 19th March 1906; *Northern Athlete*, 7th May 1906; *Sports Gazette*, 21st April 1906; *Teesside Weekly Herald*, 24th March 1906; Smith, "Origin and Benefits of the League," p. 184.

87. *North-Eastern Daily Gazette*, 21st April 1906; *Teesside Weekly Herald*, 14th April 1906.

88. *North-Eastern Daily Gazette*, 31st May 1906; *Northern Athlete*, 14th May 1906; *South Durham & Cleveland Mercury*, 11th May 1906; It was later stated that the payment to Bloomer was to cover the costs of moving his possessions from Derby to Middlesbrough, and that the club should have asked the Football Association for permission to pay him—*Northern Athlete*, 11th June 1906.

89. Inglis, *Soccer in the Dock*, p. 26; *North-Eastern Daily Gazette*, 2nd November 1906; *South Durham & Cleveland Mercury*, 7th September 1906; For details see *Sports Gazette*, 3rd November 1906.

90. *North-Eastern Daily Gazette*, 27th June 1907; *Sports Gazette*, 22nd, 29th June 1907; *Teesside Weekly Herald*, 27th June 1908.

91. *Northern Athlete*, 31st May 1909; *Teesside Weekly Herald*, 5th June 1909; This complaint had also been made in 1901, when it was pointed out that by holding the AGM on a weekday evening rather than on a Saturday afternoon, 20–25 percent of shareholders would be unable to attend—*North-Eastern Daily Gazette*, 14th May 1901.

92. *North-Eastern Daily Gazette*, 3rd May 1910.

93. *North-Star*, 6th May 1910; *Sports Gazette*, 7th May 1910.

94. *Northern Athlete*, 6th June 1910.

95. Quoted in Mason, *Association Football*, p. 48; W. McGregor, "The £ s d of Football," in Leatherdale (ed.), *The Book of Football*, p. 60.

96. Quoted in Russell, *Football and the English*, p. 42.

97. D. Kennedy, "Class, Ethnicity and Civic Governance: A social profile of football club directors on Merseyside in the late-nineteenth century," *International Journal of the History of Sport* 22, 5 (2005), p. 856.

98. Mason, *Association Football*, p. 48, pp. 241–242; Russell, *Football and the English*, p. 42; Taylor, *The Association Game*, pp. 71–72; Tischler, *Footballers and Businessmen*, pp. 71–75; Middlesbrough decided in 1901 that in order that the club

could proceed "in a straight, honest and sound manner," that "all those who are holding pecuniary interests in the working of the concern of the Middlesbrough Football Club shall be asked to retire from its directorate"—*North-Eastern Daily Gazette*, 24th May 1901; *North Star*, 24th, 25th May 1901; *Northern Echo*, 24th May 1901.

99. *North-Eastern Daily Gazette*, 2nd November 1907; *Teesside Weekly Herald*, 19th November 1910; Since the mid-1880s Gibson-Poole had been involved with eight sports clubs as well as the football club. He was a councillor from 1896–1901, an alderman from 1910–37, was mayor in 1907, 1909 and 1927, and was made an Honorary Freeman of Middlesbrough in 1932. It has also been pointed out that when Samuel Sadler was elected as MP for Middlesbrough in 1900, he frequently alluded to his connections with the football club—R. Lewis, "The Evolution of a Political Culture: Middlesbrough, 1850–1950," in Pollard (ed.), *Middlesbrough: Town and Community*, p. 117.

100. *Northern Echo*, 1st December 1910; *Teesside Weekly Herald*, 3rd December 1910.

101. *North-Eastern Daily Gazette*, 1st December 1910.

102. *Athletic News*, 23rd January 1911; *North-Eastern Daily Gazette*, 5th December 1910; *North Star*, 5th December 1910.

103. Gibson-Poole received 6,568 votes, while Williams received 10,313—*The Times*, 6th December 1910.

104. *North-Eastern Daily Gazette*, 6th, 7th January 1911; *North-Star*, 7th January 1911; *The Times*, 17th January 1911.

105. *North Star*, 17th January 1911; *Teesside Weekly Herald*, 21st January 1911; *The Times*, 17th January 1911; Gibson-Poole's suspension did not prevent him from becoming a vice-president of Middlesbrough Golf Club a month later.

106. *North-Eastern Daily Gazette*, 17th January; *North Star*, 20th January 1911.

107. *Athletic News*, 23rd January 1911.

108. *North-Eastern Daily Gazette*, 25th January 1911; *North Star*, 14th February 1911.

109. *Northern Athlete*, 22nd May 1911; *Teesside Weekly Herald*, 27th May 1911.

110. *North Star*, 14th February, 14th March 1911.

111. *Middlesbrough Standard*, 3rd June 1911; *Northern Echo*, 30th May 1911; *Teesside Weekly Herald*, 3rd June 1911; *The Times*, 30th May 1911.

112. *North-Eastern Daily Gazette*, 30th May 1911.

113. *Northern Echo*, 1st June 1911.

114. *North-Eastern Daily Gazette*, 11th September 1911.

115. No such statements had been made in 1907 when it was reported in the *Northern Athlete* that Gill & Sons would give away a pair of boots (worth 10s 6d) each week to any Middlesbrough player scoring a hat trick, *Northern Athlete*, 14th January 1907; *North-Eastern Daily Gazette*, 8th, 15th November 1911.

116. *Middlesbrough Standard*, 25th November 1911.

117. *Football Mail*, 17th February 1912; *North Star*, 19th February 1912; *Sports Gazette*, 17th February 1912; The crowd may have been higher had an amateur international fixture not been taking place at Bishop Auckland at the same time.

118. *Northern Echo*, 16th February 1914; *Teesside Weekly Herald*, 21st February 1914; The North-Eastern Railway Company was criticized for not providing extra

trains to Middlesbrough from east Cleveland on the day of the match; the train due to arrive at Middlesbrough at 1:22 p.m. was too "early for working men who have to change and get their dinner"—*North Eastern Daily Gazette*, 12th February 1914.

119. *Football Mail*, 9th, 23rd, 30th March 1912.

120. *North-Eastern Daily Gazette*, 2nd April 1912.

121. H. Glasper, *Middlesbrough: A Complete Record* (Derby, 1993), p. 118; Tischler, *Footballers and Businessmen*, p. 84; W. Vamplew, *Pay Up and Play the Game: Professional Sport in Britain, 1875–1914* (Cambridge, 1988), p. 63.

122. *Football Mail*, 4th October 1913; *Sports Gazette*, 13th September 1913; *Teesside Weekly Herald*, 4th October 1913.

123. *Athletic News*, 15th August 1892; *North-Eastern Daily Gazette*, 8th August, 2nd September 1892; In 1901 the population of the parish of South Bank was 10,871, increasing to 15,630 in 1911—*Kelly's Directory of North and East Ridings of Yorkshire, 1909* (London, 1909), p. 258; *Kelly's Directory of North and East Ridings of Yorkshire, 1913* (London, 1913), p. 272.

124. South Bank was often referred to as "Slagdom" or "Slaggy Island" due to the large piles of slag in the area from the nearby iron and steel works.

125. *Northern Review*, 14th July 1894; The club had also amalgamated with South Bank Excelsior and South Bank Erimus in 1885, and with South Bank Black Watch a year later—B. Hunt, *Northern Goalfields Revisited: The millennium history of the Northern League, 1889–2000* (Shildon, 2000), p. 456; P. Joannou and A. Candlish, *Pioneers of the North: The origins and development of football in north-east England & Tyneside, 1870–93* (Derby, 2009), p. 219.

126. *South Durham & Cleveland Mercury*, 4th January 1895.

127. *North-Eastern Daily Gazette*, 8th, 11th March 1895.

128. *North-Eastern Daily Gazette*, 27th June 1895.

129. *Middlesbrough & Stockton Sporting Telegraph*, 19th July 1897.

130. Taylor, *The Association Game*, p. 78.

131. 1901 census; *Kelly's Directory of North and East Ridings of Yorkshire, 1897* (London, 1897); *Middlesbrough & Stockton Sporting Telegraph*, 23rd July 1897.

132. *Northern Echo*, 10th July 1899; *South Durham & Cleveland Mercury*, 1st September 1899.

133. *North Star*, 29th August 1901.

134. *North-Eastern Daily Gazette*, 2nd August 1906; *Northern Athlete*, 12th November 1906; *Sports Gazette*, 30th June 1906; *South Durham & Cleveland Mercury*, 29th June 1906.

135. Letter from O. O. Beadle to F. B. Punchard, 8th April 1907, U/STE/5/5, Teesside Archives.

136. Letter from W. W. Storr to F. B. Punchard, 13th June 1907, U/STE/5/5, Teesside Archives.

137. Letter from O. O. Beadle to F. B. Punchard, June 1907, U/STE/5/5, Teesside Archives.

138. *Northern Athlete*, 29th July 1907; *Teesside Weekly Herald*, 27th July 1907.

139. *North Star*, 15th, 16th, 18th April 1910; *Northern Athlete*, 25th April 1910; *Sports Gazette*, 23rd July 1910.

140. *North-Eastern Daily Gazette*, 19th July 1911; *Sports Gazette*, 22nd April 1911

141. *Sports Gazette,* 12th April 1913.

142. *Northern Echo,* 14th April 1913.

143. *Football Mail,* 26th April 1913; *North Star,* 14th April 1913; *Northern Echo,* 21st, 23rd April 1913; *Sports Gazette,* 19th April 1913.

144. Russell, *Football and the English,* p. 68.

145. 1911 census; *North Star,* 12th April 1912; *Sports Gazette,* 20th July 1907; In 1901 the population of the parish of Eston (including Grangetown) was 9,973, increasing to 11,476 in 1911—*Kelly's Directory of North and East Ridings of Yorkshire, 1909,* p. 91; *Kelly's Directory of North and East Ridings of Yorkshire, 1913,* p. 94.

146. *Football Mail,* 9th March 1912; *North Star,* 12th April 1912.

147. *Football Mail,* 13th April 1912; *North Star,* 15th April 1912; Tabner, *Football Through the Turnstiles Again,* pp. 96–103; In comparison, a crowd of only five thousand saw Eston United beaten in the 1909 Amateur Cup final at Ilford—*Northern Athlete,* 19th April 1909.

148. *Sports Gazette,* 20th April 1912; *Teesside Weekly Herald,* 20th April 1912.

149. *Sports Gazette,* 20th April 1912.

150. *Football Mail,* 11th April 1914; *Sports Gazette,* 6th July 1912, 24th January 1914.

151. *Sports Gazette,* 30th May 1914.

152. Russell, *Football and the English,* p. 34; Taylor, *The Association Game,* pp. 76–77.

153. *Northern Echo,* 24th August 1899.

154. *Northern Review,* 24th November 1888.

155. *Athletic News,* 31st March, 14th July 1902; *North-Eastern Daily Gazette,* 11th February 1901.

156. The area that the club could draw from included Stockton, Thornaby, Darlington, the Hartlepools, South Bank, Redcar, Saltburn, and the "numerous and thickly-populated mining villages of Cleveland," *South Durham & Cleveland Mercury,* 25th November 1904.

157. *Northern Athlete,* 28th May 1906, 25th February 1907.

158. *North-Eastern Daily Gazette,* 30th May 1896; *Northern Weekly Gazette,* 30th July 1898.

159. *North-Eastern Daily Gazette,* 9th August 1899; *Northern Echo,* 24th August 1899; *Sports Gazette,* 24th May 1913.

160. *North Star,* 25th July 1901; *Teesside Weekly Herald,* 20th August 1904.

161. *North-Eastern Daily Gazette,* 12th March, 30th April 1896.

162. The officials of this league included a number of prominent local individuals—an alderman and director of the Empire Theatre, an MP, an iron merchant, the owner of a concrete works, as well as an assistant harbor master, a joiner, and two clerks—1911 census; *North-Eastern Daily Gazette,* 28th June 1913; *Teesside Weekly Herald,* 8th June 1912.

163. *Northern Echo,* 12th September 1899.

164. 1901 census; *Teesside Weekly Herald,* 1st September 1906; *North Star,* 14th August 1903.

165. *Middlesbrough Standard,* 10th September 1910; *North-Eastern Daily Gazette,* 27th May 1909; See also the Cleveland Alliance and the Cleveland & South Durham Amateur Wednesday League—*North Star,* 17th October 1902; *Northern Echo,*

30th July 1900, 30th July 1901; *South Durham & Cleveland Mercury*, 10th August 1900.

166. *North-Eastern Daily Gazette*, 26th March 1914.

167. The secretary was a joiner and the treasurer was a plumber's clerk—*North-Eastern Daily Gazette*, 13th September 1906.

168. *North Star*, 15th June 1910; *North-Eastern Daily Gazette*, 13th June 1911; *Northern Athlete*, 13th June 1910; *Teesside Weekly Herald*, 8th June 1912.

169. *Football Mail*, 11th April 1914; *Sports Gazette*, 13th June 1914.

170. The competing teams were from Barry's Acklam Ironworks, Clarence Ironworks, Davy's Newport Ironworks, Linthorpe Ironworks, Murray's Newport Ironworks, Normanby Ironworks, Simpson's Newport Ironworks—*North-Eastern Daily Gazette*, 29th March 1898.

171. The league's secretaries can be identified as a blast furnace worker and an ironworker—1911 census; applications to join were received from Cargo Fleet, Dinsdale, Grangetown, Normanby, Port Clarence, Seaton Carew, Skinningrove, South Bank and Warrenby—*North-Eastern Daily Gazette*, 21st January 1908.

172. *Northern Athlete*, 29th June, 17th August 1908; A number of other leagues were also in existence which included teams from Middlesbrough, for example the Waller League, the Stockton Church League, the Haverton Hill League, the Guisborough Minor League, and the Marske League.

173. *Sports Gazette*, 1st January 1910; *Teesside Weekly Herald*, 16th March 1912.

174. J. Hill, *Sport, Leisure & Culture in Twentieth-Century Britain* (Basingstoke, 2002), p. 137.

175. *Teesside Weekly Herald*, 25th July 1908.

176. *North Star*, 17th August 1911; *Teesside Weekly Herald*, 17th June 1911.

177. *Middlesbrough & Stockton Evening Telegraph*, 18th July 1899.

178. 1911 census; *North-Eastern Daily Gazette*, 6th July 1906.

179. *Sports Gazette*, 15th June 1907, 20th June 1908.

180. *Sports Gazette*, 11th August 1906.

181. See for example Cleveland Chemical Works, Erimus, Middlesbrough Athletic, Middlesbrough Celtic and Middlesbrough United—*Athletic News*, 16th September 1889; *Football Mail*, 5th September 1908; *North-Eastern Daily Gazette*, 1st September 1898, 12th August 1909; *Northern Review*, 13th, 27th September 1890.

182. *Middlesbrough & Stockton Sporting Telegraph*, 2nd October 1897; *South Durham & Cleveland Mercury*, 8th March 1895.

183. *North-Eastern Daily Gazette*, 20th November, 4th December 1903.

184. *Sports Gazette*, 25th March 1911.

185. *North-Eastern Daily Gazette*, 19th April 1905, 21st April 1910; *North Star*, 2nd April 1904.

186. *North-Eastern Daily Gazette*, 28th April 1911; *Sports Gazette*, 29th April 1905

187. C. Kerrigan, *Teachers and Football: Schoolboy association football in England, 1885–1915* (Abingdon, 2005), p. 13, p. 50.

188. H. J. W. Offord, "Schoolboy Football," in Leatherdale (ed.), *The Book of Football*, p. 152.

189. *North-Eastern Daily Gazette*, 3rd September 1896; Mason, *Association Football*, p. 85.

190. *North-Eastern Daily Gazette*, 31st December 1896, 20th April 1897, 17th February 1899.

191. *Teesside Weekly Herald*, 28th July 1906.

192. *North-Eastern Daily Gazette*, 20th September 1898.

193. Ensor, "The Football Madness," *Contemporary Review*, 74 (1898) p. 752.

194. *North-Eastern Daily Gazette*, 27th January 1908; *Northern Athlete*, 14th May 1906.

195. *North-Eastern Daily Gazette*, 13th October 1903, 20th December 1910.

196. *North-Eastern Daily Gazette*, 18th November 1908, 13th January 1909.

197. *Teesside Weekly Herald*, 21st February 1914; Football constituted 5 percent of all street offenses from 1910–1913, while drunkenness made up 58 percent of the total—D. Taylor, *Policing the Victorian Town: The development of the police in Middlesbrough c.1840–1914* (Basingstoke, 2002), p. 157.

198. *Sports Gazette*, 2nd November 1912; Smith quoted in Lewis, "Touched Pitch," p. 134.

199. *North-Eastern Daily Gazette*, 20th September 1898.

200. *Football Mail*, 23rd April 1910; *Northern Athlete*, 14th May 1906; As Brian Harrison points out, those groups that opposed drinking rarely provided alternative recreations "as attractive as those they attacked"—"Religion and Recreation in Nineteenth-Century England," *Past and Present* 38, 1 (1967), p. 124.

Conclusion

By 1914 sport had become an integral part of Middlesbrough's culture, providing a form of entertainment that an increasing number of people could watch or participate in. In 1914 there was a far greater number and more diverse range of clubs, input from working-class and lower-middle-class men had increased, and professional football had become the most popular spectator sport. However, as had been the case in 1870, the town's middle class was still able to dominate much of the town's sport, and opportunities for women and the poorest members of the population remained limited.

The case study of Middlesbrough shows how sport developed in a late nineteenth- and early twentieth-century urban environment, demonstrating the ways in which a town's expansion and social structures impacted its sport. By examining Middlesbrough's sports clubs and organizations, it is evident that class was hugely influential on the growth of sport and determined participation. The case study of football in Middlesbrough explains how the game changed from an amateur pastime to a professional sport that was capable of attracting both thousands of spectators and producing numerous column inches. By exploring the contemporary debates surrounding professionalism and the circumstances which led to the establishment of professional football clubs in 1889 and 1899, it is clear that patterns of development differed from place to place—parts of the North were strongholds for amateur football while professionalism became the norm elsewhere. The strength of Middlesbrough's sporting culture is evidenced most clearly in the number and diversity of clubs, organizations, and leagues, while the importance attached to sport is demonstrated by the involvement of the town's elite as officials and by the establishment of clubs for workers by employers. Importantly, it is clear that the history of Middlesbrough should not be limited to its industry and economy, and that an examination of the town's sport not only sheds light upon its social and cultural history, but offers an insight into the interaction between different groups of people. In addition, the notion that the town was dominated by its uncivilized working class is not reflected in its sporting culture, which, for large sections of the population, was exclusive and inaccessible.

The dominant theme in the expansion of sport in Middlesbrough is the role played by members of the middle classes as participants, administrators, and providers of sport. It is evident that the majority of sports clubs were governed by the amateur ethos and the lower-middle and middle-middle classes. Football aside, much of the town's population was effectively excluded from sport. Organizations such as the boating and golf clubs were dominated by the middle class, and also included members of the upper-middle class. That Middlesbrough's clubs were characterized by the class of their members confirms Harris's assertion that during the period covered here, "all other social and cultural attributes became reducible to class categories."[1] The relationship between sport and the town's elite is shown explicitly on a number of occasions. In 1887 the *Northern Review* published a list of the "Twelve Most Popular Men in Middlesbrough," five of whom had roles with sports clubs. For example, Raylton Dixon was the president of the boating club, and John T. Belk was president of Middlesbrough Cricket Club, vice-president of the boating club, and vice-president of Middlesbrough Bicycle Club.[2] Samuel Sadler was described as a "lover and a generous supporter of all manly sports and pastimes," and the involvement of Arthur Dorman in the Dorman Long sports club was regarded as proof of "the interest he takes in the pleasures of his workpeople."[3] Furthermore, Sadler had roles in sixteen clubs and one association during this period. Similarly, the ironmaster Charles Dorman was involved with nine clubs, Jack R. Smiles, Alfred Mattison, Thomas Gibson-Poole and Lawrence Farrar Gjers had roles with ten clubs, and John Ellerton and Walter G. Roberts had involvement with eleven clubs or leagues. Briggs has argued that toward the end of the nineteenth century Middlesbrough's employers contributed less to "the life of the community" outside of the works, and were not as familiar with "daily life" as previous generations. Involvement with a sports club offered a way for them to show their commitment and connection to the town as well as a means of connecting with their employees and the wider community, even if sometimes this was in name only.[4] The way sport could be used to confirm a local leader's relationship with their community, and the necessity of being involved with sport, was further evidenced by the 1912 *Sports Gazette* headline, "The Tees-side Mayors— Sportsmen All," above photographs of the region's new mayors.[5]

While members of the town's elite continued to take up both titular and active roles in leagues and clubs, the changing social structure of the town was also mirrored in sport. The growth of the socially aspirant shopocracy and lower-middle class was reflected in the increasing number of roles taken up by this group as officials and members—emulating the memberships of their social superiors. Their involvement in sports clubs offered a means of attaining a higher social standing and confirms the suggestion that this group were concerned with "an obsessive pursuit of status and respectability."[6] The number of cross-class clubs also grew from the beginning of the twentieth century, and members of the middle classes were able to choose between membership of these clubs as well as the more elite clubs, and were therefore able to dominate all of Middlesbrough's sports.[7]

It is evident that in the last quarter of the nineteenth century, working-class leisure opportunities were limited, particularly when comparing the number of clubs that were open to the middle classes. The working-man was thought to be particularly susceptible to the "allurements of the public house . . . as he returns home after a hard day's toil . . . how sorely he is tempted to turn in the public house."[8] Local cricket and football also needed to be kept free from those "debasing entanglements" that were thought to result from the involvement of the workingman, and the responsibility was placed on the players to ensure that sport remained untainted by the "betting mania."[9] Middlesbrough has been described as a mere "dormitory for the men,"[10] indicating that its utilitarian and industrial nature left little room for the provision of facilities for the everyday comfort of its people, least of all, the provision of recreational and leisure facilities. The long working hours of many of the town's men precluded involvement in most sports, meaning that only on a Saturday afternoon could they "surrender unconditionally to [the] excitement" of football.[11] The leisure time of the working classes was often commented upon in the local press, which largely condemned the lack of provision made for their free time. It was after all, according to the *North-Eastern Daily Gazette*, during "the leisure hour that character is chiefly formed," and through recreation the "manysidedness [sic] of social life and character is more clearly displayed."[12] However, by 1914 the provision of leisure from larger places of work and the church, coupled with spectating at football matches, offered more respectable and controlled types of leisure. Alongside the profusion of clubs with middle-class membership, this contradicts Huggins's suggestion that Middlesbrough possessed "a very strong but predominantly less respectable pattern of working class leisure."[13]

Holt suggests that for those who wanted to encourage values of thrift, sobriety, and respectability in the working class, the task was sometimes too great.[14] Beaven has also argued that rapidly growing towns like Middlesbrough obstructed middle-class initiatives to improve the leisure of the working class,[15] and this has been demonstrated by the limited attempts at recreation in the town. It had been hoped that the Cleveland

and Middlesbrough Athletic Institute would assist in improving the leisure of workingmen, but it is perhaps *because* of the Institute's emphasis on altering the moral character of its members by prohibiting alcohol and gambling (and all for a membership fee), that it proved to be a failure. At the same time, football was encouraged by newspaper editorials and the likes of church clubs, as a character-building pastime, and there are a number of examples of the role of the church in forming clubs and providing facilities, it being felt that through "amusement and recreation," young people could become good Christians.[16] Such organizations were met with varying degrees of success, it being unclear whether members joined to worship or to play sport. It seems likely that in a place such as Middlesbrough that sport itself was the attraction, there being only limited forms of entertainment available.

One of the most important changes in the provision of sport from the start of the twentieth century was the establishment of clubs by large employers. These organizations allowed those in lower paid positions far greater involvement in running the club of their workplace, through the positions of secretaries. The large memberships of these clubs suggests that these organizations offered affordable facilities that were not available elsewhere and allowed men to play sports with their fellow workers. It also suggests that membership of such organizations was something that was desired by employers, particularly as a successful and popular club provided good publicity and may have helped to retain workers. The growth of such clubs should be viewed alongside developments in workplace paternalism in Britain in general. The provision of work-based clubs sheds light on the idea that paternalism was evidence of a reciprocal relationship between employers and workers, and that there existed "a benign regard . . . [among] capitalists for the well-being of their workforce." It also enables an exploration of the suggestion that workers' culture was dominated by the values of the employer.[17] Whether the popularity of such organizations was due to the sporting opportunities on offer, the chance for socialization, or because of a need to emphasize employer/employee relations, is difficult to ascertain. These clubs provide a clear example of philanthropy by Middlesbrough's major industrialists (though the amount of money put into the club by the works' owners varied from club to club) and offer further evidence that the notion of elite withdrawal has been exaggerated.

Though spectators at football matches were primarily working class, the lower-middle and middle-middle classes that were involved in clubs attempted to keep the game conducted in a respectable manner. However, Beaven has noted that much to the horror of rational recreationists, working-class spectators took the "'rational' dimension out of the game, adopting a mindless fanaticism for their team."[18] To a far greater extent than any other sport, football proved itself to be an attractive spectator sport which also offered increasing opportunities for working-class men to play in one of the numerous smaller teams. Taylor's suggestion that the growth of football can be attributed less to a desire to emulate a middle or upper class game, and more to "a genuine and largely autonomous popular enthusiasm for the game,"[19] can certainly be applied to football in Middlesbrough. In a town that offered little prospect of working-class sport, football offered an outlet for their "emotions and passions." Furthermore, football provided "a sober entertainment for the working man who might otherwise adapt himself to unwholesome exercises [in] the public-house."[20] More simply, football offered an alternative to work on a Saturday afternoon. Particularly after the turn of the century, the growing number of smaller clubs had a great deal more involvement from members of the lower-middle and working classes. This development ran alongside an increased desire for success by those supporters of the town's leading club. The decision by the Middlesbrough FC directors to turn professional in 1899 demonstrates a greater desire for victories, and thus large crowds and larger profits. It also suggests a rejection of the tenets of gentlemanly amateurism that had proved so strong ten years earlier, when it had been the spectators who had demanded better football.[21] This examination of Middlesbrough's football culture has also shown, as Taylor argues, that only "in the nature of its support and consumption rather than in the way it was organised and controlled" could football be considered a working-class game.[22]

It has been demonstrated that football was a popular form of entertainment in itself, but it is also apparent that it was capable of provoking strong feeling among spectators and officials, and within the local press. This is evidenced most clearly in the debates surrounding the professionalization of the sport and the breakaway formation of Ironopolis FC, as well as by the periodic criticism leveled at the officials of Middlesbrough FC. Supporters felt a sense of ownership over 'their' football club, and when results were poor or the directors were not thought to be acting in the club's best interests, disapproval was vehement. Though football clearly provoked strong emotions and a sense of *club* loyalty among spectators, it is unclear as to whether it played a role in the formation of *local* identities. Holt has argued that "the supreme appeal of football lay almost certainly in its expression of a sense of civic pride and identity."[23] In Middlesbrough, there was often support for more than one local team. During Ironopolis' existence, loyalties for the two town clubs were not divided on any definite lines of place, religion, or ethnicity, and spectators divided their time between the two clubs. Furthermore, as Middlesbrough was a new town, identities and loyalties were at an early stage of development as the population continued to change and grow. Middlesbrough's identity is complicated further by being uniquely part of both Yorkshire and part of the Northeast, references being made to the town's simultaneous membership of both regions throughout the period. Though victories for Middlesbrough (as well as for South Bank in the Amateur Cup) were celebrated, there is not enough evidence nor are there explicit references made to the direct role that football played in forming a local identity.

The achievements of local sporting heroes, professional rower Robert Boyd and Olympic swimmer Jack Hatfield, provided opportunities to promote Middlesbrough and boost civic pride. Both were celebrated as sons of the town, and that Boyd's birthplace was elsewhere was irrelevant to a population of migrants. The varied birthplaces of the population as a whole are reflected in the origins of officials and members of sports clubs. For example, only one of the first directors of Ironopolis FC was born in Middlesbrough, and only six of the eighteen boating club officials in 1901 were born in the town. This indicates that not only were clubs inclusive, but that the birthplaces of club officials were representative of those of the population in general. That the town was composed of migrants meant that sports clubs offered a means of integration for new arrivals, as well as opportunities to socialize with other men from their own social class.

Such was the increasing number of sports clubs in the late 1880s, that it was felt that "every athletic want is met."[24] An editorial in the *Northern Review* stated that "whatever requires the exercise of muscle and sinew is sure of a fair following,"[25] and clubs were formed for a wide range of sports. These comments and the column inches devoted to sporting activities are indicative of the increasing interest in sport in the press from the early 1880s. While interest and participation in clubs increased, the effects of the town's continued expansion were evidenced on a number of occasions, and the lack of available land proved particularly damaging to Middlesbrough's cricket, rugby, and boating clubs. Cricket and rugby also suffered from the ever-increasing popularity of football, yet in contrast other sports witnessed a growth in the formation of clubs. For example, the popularity of cycling rarely waned, assisted by the opening out of the sport beyond the middle class. In contrast, baseball, aimed squarely at the working class and competing directly with cricket, failed to find a place in Middlesbrough's increasingly crowded sporting culture. Furthermore, apart from football, the impact of commercialism and professionalism was small, evidence of the domination of the middle classes and attitudes toward amateur sport, and suggests a desire to encourage more respectable sports that would reflect well on a town that was perceived as tough and working class. The demand for sport as a form of entertainment is demonstrated further by the sustained popularity of sports days. From the 1870s until 1914, these events attracted considerable crowds and large numbers of participants, and sports were increasingly included at the picnics and events of places of work.

In general women's access to sport throughout this period was constrained not only by their gender, but also by their class. Those women who did participate in sport were almost entirely middle class, and it is clear that access to sport for both men *and* women was determined first and foremost by their class and thus their income and free time. Lady Bell's contention that Middlesbrough's working-class women had no opportunities for recreation is borne out by the middle-class membership of those clubs that did allow women to join. Lady Bell stated that Middlesbrough's working-class women were constrained by having "less health [and] less strength than her most prosperous sisters," and thus the demands on their "mental, moral and physical" resources were greater.[26] Middlesbrough had very low levels of female employment[27] and those work-based clubs that were aimed at working-class men inevitably excluded women as they were largely based in heavy industry where women did not work. It is unsurprising therefore that in a town dominated by its men (where at the start of twentieth century men still outnumbered women in the town), that opportunities for women's sport were extremely limited. Moreover, gambling and drinking, often associated with the town's working-class men, were also indulged in by working-class women.[28] Although there was a perceptible change in attitudes toward women's leisure between 1870 and 1914, most of the sports that were deemed acceptable for women to take part in involved only limited physical exertion, or revolved around opportunities to socialize.

Through an examination of Middlesbrough's sporting history, the social and cultural history of the town has also been explored. It has illuminated the relationships between employers and employees, and has allowed for an exploration of the recreational lives of individuals. The particular way in which professional football developed in Middlesbrough demonstrates the need for a closer examination of the professionalization of the sport in other towns and cities, and of the individuals involved. This study of Middlesbrough progresses our understanding of urban sport and urban history in a number of ways. It demonstrates how sport can be affected by urban growth, whether directly or indirectly, and equally, how sport can also affect the way in which a town develops. The time period covered here allows us to trace the growth of sport alongside the growth and expansion of the town, taking in Middlesbrough's exponential urban and industrial growth, to the start of the twentieth century when the sporting culture began to follow national patterns of development. A study of sport in a particular setting such as this provides another means of examining relationships between different social groups within a large urban landscape. As this case study has demonstrated, the ways in which sport was used by members of the elite to advance or maintain their position, points toward another means of examining urban elites. In addition, the detailed examinations of club involvement given here offer another means of showing the different ways in which people spent their free time in an industrial town. This study provides another approach to examining the different manifestations of civic pride and identity in urban environments. This examination of Middlesbrough demonstrates the variations in urban sporting cultures and allows for comparisons to be made with other case studies. By examining sport on a local level, we can see how sport developed within a specific environment and how the particular setting impacted on the sporting culture.

NOTES

1. J. Harris, *Private Lives, Public Spirit: A social history of Britain 1870–1914* (Oxford, 1993), p. 6.

2. John T. Belk, Raylton Dixon, Henry Morton Hedley, Samuel Sadler, Isaac Wilson—*Northern Review*, 23rd July 1887.

3. *North-Eastern Daily Gazette*, 13th August 1900, 29th November 1911.

4. A. Briggs, "Middlesbrough: The growth of a new community," in A. J. Pollard (ed.), *Middlesbrough: Town and Community, 1830–1950* (Stroud, 1996) p. 23.

5. *Sports Gazette*, 9th November 1912.

6. M. Huggins, "Second-Class Citizens? English middle-class culture and sport, 1850–1910: A reconsideration," *International Journal of the History of Sport* 17, 1 (2000), p. 15.

7. Though Harris suggests that "snobbery, class rivalry, and social differentiation" were common among groups that were similar in status, this does not appear to have been the case with the sporting activities of Middlesbrough's middle-class groups—Harris, *Private Lives, Public Spirit*, p. 8.

8. Bishop Lacy, Roman Catholic Bishop of Middlesbrough, quoted in P. Stubley, *Industrial Society and Church: Middlesbrough 1830–1914* (Bognor Regis, 2001), p. 82.

9. *North-Eastern Daily Gazette*, 28th February 1891.

10. D. W. Hadfield, Political and Social Attitudes in Middlesbrough 1853–1889: with especial reference to the role of the Middlesbrough ironmasters, unpublished PhD thesis, Teesside Polytechnic, 1981, p. 22.

11. *Sports Gazette*, 12th November 1904; Thomas McKenna, the secretary of the Cleveland Association of Blastfurnacemen stated in 1912 that furnace, men worked eleven hours during the day or thirteen hours at night, as well as a twenty-four-hour-long shift once a fortnight—Stubley, *Industrial Society and Church*, p. 32.

12. *North-Eastern Daily Gazette*, 24th October 1907.

13. M. Huggins, 'Leisure and Sport in Middlesbrough 1840–1914," in A. J. Polland (ed.), *Middlesbrough: Town and Community* p. 128.

14. R. Holt, *Sport and the British: A modern history* (Oxford, 1989), p. 144.

15. B. Beaven, *Leisure, Citizenship and Working-Class Men in Britain, 1850–1945* (Manchester, 2005), p. 27.

16. *North-Eastern Weekly Gazette*, 1st November 1890.

17. J. Melling, 'Employers, Workplace Culture and Workers' Politics: British industry and workers' welfare programmes, 1870–1920," in J. Melling and J. Barry (eds.), *Culture in History: Production, consumption and values in historical perspective* (Exeter, 1992), pp. 112–114.

18. Beaven, *Leisure, Citizenship and Working-Class Men*, p. 73.

19. M. Taylor, *The Association Game: A history of British football* (Harlow, 2008), p. 37.

20. *Sports Gazette*, 12th November 1904.

21. This suggests that Middlesbrough FC was governed by the "peculiar economics" of football as identified by Vamplew, being somewhere between profit and utility maximiser—W. Vamplew, *Pay Up and Play the Game: Professional sport in Britain, 1875–1914* (Cambridge, 1988), p. 77.

22. Taylor, *The Association Game*, p. 90.

23. Holt, *Sport and the British*, pp. 166–167.

24. *Northern Review*, 17th March 1888.

25. *Northern Review*, 27th May 1893.

26. F. Bell, *At the Works: A study of a manufacturing town*, (London, 1985 [first edition, 1907]), pp. 172–173.

27. Middlesbrough had the lowest proportion of employed women of all towns with a population of fifty thousand or more. As Lady Bell stated, there was "no organised women's labour"—Bell, *At the Works*, p. 178; D. Taylor, "The Infant Hercules and the Augean Stables: A century of economic and social development in Middlesbrough c.1840–1939," in Pollard (ed.), *Middlesbrough: Town and Community*, p. 61.

28. Bell, *At the Works*, pp. 254–258.

Appendix 1

Ironopolis Football Club Shareholders

Table A.1. Ironopolis Football Club Shareholders

Number of shareholders	Occupation	Number of shares	Percentage of share total (%)
29	Plater	74	8.32
11	Riveter	11	1.2
9	Blacksmith	27	3.03
7	Clerk	26	2.92
7	Grocer	11	1.2
5	Boiler smith	44	4.94
5	Butcher	17	1.91
5	Fruit merchant/fruiterer	17	1.91
5	Hotel proprietor/innkeeper	26	2.92
5	Married woman	37	4.16
5	Tailor	17	1.91
4	Commission agent	14	1.57
4	Hatter/hatter and hosier	23	2.58
4	Joiner	5	0.56
4	Molder	9	1.01
4	None	5	0.56
4	Painter	9	1.01
3	Accountant	13	1.46
3	Bicycle dealer	4	0.44
3	Contractor	22	2.47
3	Doctor	20	2.24
3	Draper	6	0.67
3	Engineer	9	1.01
3	Foreman plater	18	2.02
3	Jeweler	9	1.01
3	Laborer	7	0.78
3	Scholar	3	0.33
2	Angle smith	7	0.78
2	Bookmaker	4	0.44
2	Brewer*	45	5.06
2	Caulker	7	0.78
2	Driller	7	0.78
2	Engine driver	2	0.22
2	Fitter	7	0.78
2	General dealer	3	0.33
2	Machinist	4	0.44
2	Printer and/or stationer	11	1.23
2	Shipyard manager	52	5.84
2	Spinster	26	2.92
2	Stock taker	7	0.78
2	Wire drawer	4	0.44
2	Wireworks foreman	8	0.89
1	Architect	5	0.56
1	Athletic outfitter	6	0.67
1	Baker	5	0.56

Number of shareholders	Occupation	Number of shares	Percentage of share total (%)
1	Bank manager	29	3.26
1	Beer retailer	1	0.11
1	Boiler maker	1	0.11
1	Collector	1	0.11
1	Commercial traveler	1	0.11
1	Corn dealer	1	0.11
1	Draftsman	25	2.81
1	Electrician	1	0.11
1	Engineman	8	0.89
1	Galvanizer	2	0.22
1	Gentleman	4	0.44
1	Grocer's assistant	1	0.11
1	Herbalist	4	0.44
1	Ironmonger	1	0.11
1	Manager	2	0.22
1	Manager of aerated water factory	5	0.56
1	Marker	1	0.11
1	Medical student	1	0.11
1	Merchant	5	0.56
1	Miner	1	0.11
1	Mineral water maker	12	1.34
1	Music hall manager	3	0.33
1	News agent	1	0.11
1	Pattern maker	1	0.11
1	Pickle manufacturer	3	0.33
1	Plainer	1	0.11
1	Poor rate collector	3	0.33
1	Provision merchant	20	2.24
1	Saddler	2	0.22
1	Ship carpenter	2	0.22
1	Ship owner	10	1.12
1	Steam-boatsman	2	0.22
1	Steel smelter	2	0.22
1	Stevedore	2	0.22
1	Striker	1	0.11
1	Subcontractor	25	2.81
1	Tea merchant	2	0.22
1	Ticket porter	1	0.11
1	Traveler	2	0.22
1	Tripe merchant	1	0.11
1	Unknown	5	0.56
221		889	

*Includes Kirk Brothers (Stockton-on-Tees), twenty-five shares
Sources: 1891 census; Middlesbrough Ironopolis Football Company Limited, Memorandum of Association, BT 31/4608/30227, National Archives; Ironopolis Register of Members, U/S/1489, Teesside Archives

Appendix 2

Middlesbrough Amateur Boating Club members, 1899–1901

Table A.2. Middlesbrough Amateur Boating Club members, 1899–1901

5 Clerks	Engineering apprentice
3 Clergymen	Foreign correspondent
3 Iron and/or steel merchants	Iron and steel merchant's agent
3 Ironmasters	Ironworks manager
2 Brass founders	Jeweler
2 Doctors	Living on own means
2 Mechanical engineers	Member of Parliament
2 Retired	Oil merchant
2 Shipbuilders	Printer and stationer
Analytical chemist	Relieving officer
Assistant manager at shipyard	Secretary of employers association
Bank manager	Ship draftsman
Brewer	Shipstore merchant and sail maker
Chemical manufacturer	Solicitor
Correspondent	Solicitor's articled clerk
Draper	Steelworks foreman
Draper's manager	Stock and share broker

Sources: 1901 census; Minute Book of Middlesbrough Amateur Boating Club

Appendix 3

New members of Middlesbrough Golf Club, June 1909–December 1914

Table A.3. New members of Middlesbrough Golf Club, June 1909–December 1914

9 Doctors	Assistant managing engineer	Inspector of Nuisances
8 Clerks	Assistant medical officer of health	Iron founder
8 Teachers	Assistant salesman	Ironmaster
7 Accountants	Assistant Tees Harbour Master and certified master mariner	Jewelry dealer
7 Managers of shipbuilders, iron or steel works	Bank cashier	Lord of the Manor
7 Members of the clergy	Bookseller and stationer	Manager of aerated water works
5 Coal or iron merchants	Builder	Manager of coal exporting house
4 Dental surgeons	Civil engineer, borough engineer, and surveyor	Manager of dry color works
3 Headmasters	Clothier's assistant	Manager of jewelers
3 Pharmacist/Chemists	Collector of customs and excise	Manager of timber merchant
2 Assistant managers of works	Commercial manager	Master of the Workhouse
2 Assistant schoolmasters	Commercial traveler	Mechanical engineer's apprentice
2 Boot dealers	Constructional engineer	Organising secretary of Temperance Society
2 Cashiers	Costumiers, children's, and ladies outfitters shopkeeper	Pharmacist's apprentice
2 Chief draftsmen	Customs officer	Registrar of births and deaths
2 Clerks in Holy Orders	Dealer in tobacco	Secretary of Guild of Help
2 Company secretaries	Department manager of construction	Ship owner
2 Drapers	District superintendent North Eastern Railway	Ship surveyor for Lloyds Register of Shipping
2 Journalists	Draper's assistant	Shipbuilder
2 Managing directors	Electrical engineer	Shipping and commission agent
2 Oil or grease manufacturer	Electrician	Shop manager
2 Retired	Engineer	Solicitor
2 Rolling mill managers	Farmer	Solicitor's clerk and law student
2 Tailors	Foreman of steelworks	Superintendent of Industrial School
2 Wharfingers	Grocer and provision dealer	Tailor's cutter
Advertising contractor	Hatter and hosier	Town clerk
Analytical chemist's apprentice	House and estate agent	Understudy to buyer and seller of ironstone and coal bricks
Architect	Housepainter	

Sources: 1911 census; Minute Book of Middlesbrough Golf Club

Appendix 4

Middlesbrough Bowling Club members, 1901

Table A.4. Middlesbrough Bowling Club members, 1901

5 Clerks	Cigar merchant and commission agent	Master mariner
4 Drapers	Coal dealer	Master of the workhouse
3 Plumbers	Coal merchant	Master tailor
3 Builders	Collector of gas accounts	Naval architect
3 Butchers	Company's accountant	Off beer seller
2 Fishmongers/fish merchants	Constructional engineer	Pawnbroker and builder
2 Fruiterers	Contractor	Pawnbroker's manager
2 Grocers	Dental mechanic	Picture framer
2 Hotel keepers	Doctor	Plater
2 Hotel managers	Eating house keeper	Plumber's manager
2 House agents	Financial agent	Publican
2 Licensed victuallers	Financier	Railway porter
2 Living on own means	Gas and chemical engineer	Relieving officer
2 Managers for mineral water company	Herbalist shopkeeper	Retired milk seller
2 Slaters	Hosier and hatter	Shoeing smith
2 Steelworks managers	Joiner	Steam engine fitter
2 Tailors	Laborer	Town hall keeper
Accountant	Letterpress printer and stationer	Traveling draper
Assistant agent	Life assurance superintendent	Tug owner
Assistant schoolmaster	Manager at bridgeyard	Watchmaker and jeweler
Baker and confectioner	Manager at shipping office	Wharfinger
Blacksmith	Manager at steelworks	Wine and spirit merchant
Boot shop manager	Manager for wine and spirit merchant	Wire roller
Brewery agent	Marine engineer	Wiredrawer

Sources: 1901 census; Minute Book of Middlesbrough Bowling Club

Appendix 5

Local Football Leagues

Table A.5. Local Football Leagues

	Established	Founding Members
Teesside League	1891	Darlington Athletic, Darlington St Hilda's, Ironopolis Reserve, Middlesbrough Swifts, Port Clarence, South Bank Reserve, South Stockton, Stockton, Yarm
Teesside Junior League	1891	Middlesbrough Albert, Middlesbrough Albion, Middlesbrough Celtic, Middlesbrough Excelsior, Middlesbrough Grange, Middlesbrough Vulcan, Newport Olympic Stockton Reds
Middlesbrough League	1896	Acklam, Ayrton Rolling Mills, Cambridge, Cleveland Amateurs, East End, Grove Hill, Hill's Rovers, Linthorpe Crescent, Newport, North Ormesby Church Institute, Waterloo, West End
Middlesbrough Schools League	1896	Fleetham Street, Newport, South Bank, Southend, St Hilda's, St John's Victoria Road, Wesley
*Middlesbrough & Teesside League	1898	California, Cambridge House (Middlesbrough), Darlington St George's, Dorman Long, Hartlepool Temperance, Haverton Hill, Linthorpe, North Ormesby, Sedgefield, Thornaby East End
	1904 (expanded to two divisions)	First Division—Cambridge House (Middlesbrough), Cochrane's United, North Ormesby United, Nunthorpe, Preston & Eaglescliffe, South Bank St Peter's, Stockton Excelsior, Thornaby St Patrick's, West Hartlepool Reserve, Yarm & Eaglescliffe Second Division—Hope (Thornaby), Newport Ironworks, Port Clarence Celtic, Riley Bros (Stockton), Stillington Rovers, Stockton Blythewood, Stockton Brunswick Albions, Stockton Parish Church, Thornaby Old Boys, Thornaby St Patrick's A

League	Year	Clubs
South Bank & District Minor League	1899	Britannia Rovers, California Rangers, Eston Red Rose, Grove Hill, Middlesbrough Victoria, South Bank Juniors, South Bank Royal Oak, Warrenby United
	1906 (extends to include all of Middlesbrough and Stockton)	Eston United Reserve, Grangetown Albion, Grangetown St Mary's, Lackenby Ironworks, Middlesbrough Gilkes Street Primitive Methodists, Middlesbrough United Reserve, Newport Juniors, North Ormesby St Alphonsus, Riley Brothers Reserve, South Bank United, Stockton Celtic, Stockton Grange Estate, Stockton Grove, Stockton IOGT, Thornaby Parish Rovers
Cleveland Alliance	1900	Brotton, Eston Red Rose, Grangetown, Guisborough, Lingdale, Loftus, North Skelton, Skinningrove
Cleveland & South Durham Amateur Wednesday League	1902	Darlington, Guisborough, Hartlepool, Hinton's, Middlesbrough, Middlesbrough Exchange, Saltburn, Skelton
Middlesbrough & District Church League	1906	Gilkes Street, Holy Cross, Linthorpe Parish Church Reserves, North Ormesby Primitive Methodists, North Ormesby Parish Church, North Ormesby St Alphonsus Reserves, St Alban's Guild, South Bank Primitive Methodists Reserve, Wesley Guild, West End Wesleyan Reserve, Thornaby Baptist
Cleveland Schools League	1907	Eston, Grangetown Council Schools, Normanby, South Bank Council Schools, St Mary's, St Peter's
Middlesbrough Works League	1908	Ashmore Benson's, Ayresome, Bon Lea Foundry, Cleveland Chemicals, Dorman Long, North-Eastern Railways, North-Eastern Steelworks, Shaw's United
Cleveland League	1909	
Cleveland Wednesday League	1910	Cambridge House Wednesday, Cooperative Wednesday, Hinton's Erimus, Stewart's Wednesday, Warrenby Wednesday
Eston & District League	1914	
Middlesbrough Junior League		
North Yorkshire & South Durham Thursday Football League		

*Amalgamation of Teesside and Middlesbrough leagues
Sources: Athletic News, North-Eastern Daily Gazette, North Star, Northern Athlete, Northern Echo, Northern Weekly Gazette, South Durham & Cleveland Mercury, Sports Gazette, Teesside Weekly Herald

Appendix 6

Involvement of
Middlesbrough Councillors in Sport

Table A.6. Involvement of Middlesbrough Councillors in Sport

Name	Years	Sport involvement	Occupation
David Almgill	1893–1902	Vice-president of Middlesbrough Cycling Club Vice-president of Middlesbrough & District Motorcycling Club Vice-president and committee member of Middlesbrough Golf Club Member of Middlesbrough Bowling Club	Builder
Richard Archibald	1872–1881 1886–1889	Vice-president of Middlesbrough Schools Football League	Draper
Thomas Baker	1889–1908	Member and vice-president of Middlesbrough Amateur Boating Club President and vice-president of Middlesbrough Amateur Swimming Club	Oil merchant
Stephen Barron	1887–1899	Vice-president of Middlesbrough Magpies Cycling Club	Grocer
Charles Lowthian Bell	1885–1894	President and vice-president of Middlesbrough Amateur Swimming Club	Ironmaster
Hugh Bell	1870–1877	Vice-president of Middlesbrough Schools Football League	Ironmaster
George Hutton Bowes-Wilson	1906–1916	Committee member of Middlesbrough Golf Club	
Frederick Brewster	1889–1899	Captain of Middlesbrough Rovers Rugby Club	Solicitor
William Joseph Bruce	1886–1902	Vice-president of Middlesbrough Cycling Club Member and vice-president of Middlesbrough Amateur Boating Club	Cab proprietor
Joseph Calvert	1902–1919	President and vice-president of Middlesbrough YMCA	Coal, coke, and mineral merchant
Thomas Carter	1876–1901	Member and vice-president of Middlesbrough Amateur Boating Club	Retired picture frame maker
Matthew George Collingwood	1874–1883	Chairman of Cleveland & Middlesbrough Athletic Institute Treasurer and committee member of Middlesbrough Cricket Club	Watchmaker and jeweler

Name	Years	Positions	Occupation
Thomas Roddam Dent	1891–1907	Committee member of Middlesbrough Bowling Club; Vice-president of Middlesbrough Cricket Club; Member of Middlesbrough Golf Club	Wharfinger
Raylton Dixon	1868–1874 1879–1888	Member and president of Middlesbrough Amateur Boating Club	Shipbuilder
Foster Dodsworth	1901–1907	President of Middlesbrough Harriers; Vice-president of Middlesbrough Swimming Club; Member of Middlesbrough Bowling Club	Publican
Arthur Charles Dorman	1897–1912	Vice-president of Middlesbrough Amateur Boating Club; President of Middlesbrough Amateur Swimming Club; Vice-president of Middlesbrough & District Motorcycling Club; Vice-president and chairman of Dorman Long & Co United Athletic Club; Vice-president of Middlesbrough Amateur Gymnastic Club; President of Middlesbrough Cricket Club; Vice-president of Cambridge House Club; Vice-president of Nunthorpe Lawn Tennis & Bowls Club; Vice-president of Middlesbrough YMCA	Ironmaster
John Dunning	1872–1877	Vice-president of Middlesbrough Bicycle Club	Ironmaster and timber merchant
Charles Ephgrave	1883–1901	Vice-president of Middlesbrough Amateur Swimming Club	Grocer
Albert Edward Forbes	1910–1920	Director of Middlesbrough Football Club; Vice-president of Middlesbrough YMCA Football Club; Vice-president of Middlesbrough Amateur Swimming Club; Committee member of Middlesbrough Golf Club	Solicitor
John Forbes	1890–1904	Vice-president of Middlesbrough Amateur Swimming Club; Vice-president of Middlesbrough Magpies Cycling Club; Vice-president of Cleveland Roads Cycling Club; Vice-president of North Ormesby & Middlesbrough Cycling Club; Vice-president of Middlesbrough Amateur Gymnastic Club	Baker and confectioner

(continued)

Table A.6. *(Continued)*

Name	Years as Councillor	Clubs	Occupation
Thomas Gibson-Poole	1896–1901	Director, financial secretary, and chairman of Middlesbrough Football Club	Watchmaker and jeweler
		Member and vice-president of Middlesbrough Amateur Boating Club	
		Vice-president of Middlesbrough Cycling Club	
		Vice-president of Cleveland Roads Cycling Club	
		Vice-president of Middlesbrough Crescent Cycling Club	
		Honorary member of North-Eastern Steelworks Athletic Club	
		Vice-president of Middlesbrough Cricket Club	
		Vice-president of Middlesbrough Golf Club	
		President of Middlesbrough Harriers	
		Member and vice-president of Middlesbrough Bowling Club	
Randolph Gray	1907–1913	Vice-president of Cambridge House Club	House agent
		President of Middlesbrough Ayresome Cycling Club	
John H. Gunter	1899–1902	Director and secretary of Middlesbrough Football Club	Ironworks manager
		Vice-president, committee member and president of Middlesbrough Bowling Club	
		Vice-president of Dorman Long & Co United Athletic Club	
James Hansey	1902–1904	Vice-president of Middlesbrough Majestic Swimming Club	Master mariner
William Hanson	1872–1874	Vice-president of Middlesbrough Bicycle Club	Ironmaster
	1879–1882	Member and vice-president of Middlesbrough Amateur Boating Club	
		President of Newport Cricket Club	
		President of the Cleveland Club	
William Harkess	1901–1907	Officer of Middlesbrough Tennis Club	Shipbuilder
	1908–1921		

Name	Years	Roles	Occupation
John Hedley	1886–1904	Vice-president of Middlesbrough Baseball Club Vice-president of Middlesbrough Amateur Swimming Club President of Middlesbrough Cricket Club Vice-president of Middlesbrough Golf Club	Doctor
Joseph Henry Hill	1910–1919	Vice-president of Middlesbrough Amateur Swimming Club	Painter and decorator
Amos Hinton	1874–1879 1880–1883 1885–1892	Vice-president of Middlesbrough Golf Club	Grocer
James Innes Hopkins	1864–1868	Patron of Middlesbrough Cricket Club	
William Randolph Innes Hopkins	1863–1868	President and patron of Middlesbrough Cricket Club	Ironmaster
Theodore Hornung	1901–1906	Committee of Middlesbrough Cricket Club Vice-president of Middlesbrough Baseball Club Vice-president of Middlesbrough Amateur Boating Club	Iron merchant
Thomas James Kedward	1894, 1913– 1933	Committee member of Middlesbrough Football Club	Cashier
Alexander Main	1891–1906	Committee member, honorary instructor and vice-president of Middlesbrough Amateur Swimming Club Vice-president of Middlesbrough Magpies Cycling Club	Stationer
Alfred Mattison	1894–1907	Chairman of Ironopolis Football Club Committee member, chairman and director of Middlesbrough Football Club Committee member of Middlesbrough Cricket Club Vice-president of Middlesbrough Amateur Swimming Club Vice-president of Middlesbrough Magpies Cycling Club President of Cleveland Minor Cricket League Vice-president of Middlesbrough & District Motorcycling Club Vice-president of Cambridge House Club Vice-president of Tykes Cycling Club President of Middlesbrough Junior Football League	Licensed victualler

(continued)

Table A.6. *(Continued)*

Name	Years as Councillor	Clubs	Occupation
John McCreton	1909–1922	Vice-president of Middlesbrough St Patrick's Catholic Association Honorary vice-president of Middlesbrough St Mary's Catholic Association	House builder
Joseph McLauchlan	1880–1898	President and Wednesday captain of Middlesbrough Magpies Cycling Club Vice-president of Middlesbrough Amateur Boating Club Patron of Middlesbrough Harriers	Coal and coke merchant
John George Pallister	1913–1930	Director of Middlesbrough Football Club	Shipyard foreman
John Thomas Pannell	1899–1919	Vice-president of Middlesbrough Amateur Swimming Club Vice-president of Middlesbrough Cricket Club President of Middlesbrough & District Billiards League Vice-president of Cleveland Wednesday Football League	General manager of Cooperative Society
Theophilius Phillips	1884–1887	Captain of Linthorpe Tennis Club	Grease and oil manufacturer
	1889–1904	Vice-president of Middlesbrough Amateur Boating Club President and vice-president of Middlesbrough Amateur Swimming Club Vice-president of Middlesbrough Baseball Club President of Linthorpe Football Club President of Middlesbrough Football League President and patron of Teesside & Middlesbrough Football League	
William James Phillips	1910–1917	Vice-president of Cambridge House Club Member of Middlesbrough Bowling Club	Confectioner
Edward B. Pilkington	1901–1912	President of Middlesbrough Majestic Swimming Club	Coal merchant
Walter G. Roberts	1895–1910	reasurer of Middlesbrough Amateur Athletics Club Secretary of Middlesbrough Athletic Football Club Honorary secretary and treasurer of Cleveland & South	Architect and surveyor

Name	Dates	Occupation	Positions
Sir Samuel Sadler	1874–1880	Chemical manufacturer	Durham Baseball Association
			Honorary secretary of English National Baseball Association
			President of Northern Baseball League
			President of Middlesbrough Amateur Gymnasium Society
			Vice-president of YMCA Swimming Club
			Vice-president of Middlesbrough Amateur Swimming Club
			Vice-president of Cambridge House Club
			President of Middlesbrough YMCA
			President of Middlesbrough YMCA Cricket Club
			President of Middlesbrough Bicycle Club
			President and honorary vice-president of Middlesbrough Football Club
			President and vice-president of Middlesbrough Amateur Swimming Club
			President and patron of Middlesbrough Baseball Club
			Vice-president of Middlesbrough Amateur Athletic Club
			President of Cleveland & South Durham Baseball Association
			Honorary president and vice-president of Middlesbrough Harriers
			Member of Middlesbrough Amateur Boating Club
			Vice-president of North Ormesby Cricket Club
			President of Middlesbrough Rovers Cycling Club
			Vice-president of Cleveland Roads Cycling Club
			Member and vice-president of Middlesbrough Amateur Boating Club
			Vice-president of South Bank Football Club
			Vice-president of Middlesbrough Amateur Gymnastic Club
			Honorary member of North-Eastern Steelworks Athletic Club
			Vice-president of Cambridge House Club
			Honorary member of Middlesbrough Bowling Club
			Vice-president of Middlesbrough Golf Club

(continued)

Table A.6. *(Continued)*

Name	Years as Councillor	Clubs	Occupation
Stanley Aubrey Sadler	1906–1928	President of Middllesbrough Rovers Cycling Club Vice-president of Middlesbrough Golf Club Vice-president of Middlesbrough & District Motorcycling Club	Managing director of chemical works
Thomas Sanderson	1869–1888	Vice-president of YMCA Football Club Vice-president of North Ormesby Cricket Club	Slate merchant
Alfred Earnest Scanlan	1893–1896	Honorary vice-president of Middlesbrough Football Club Committee of Middlesbrough Bicycle Club Committee member of Middlesbrough Amateur Boating Club Vice-president of Middlesbrough Amateur Cycling Club President of Cleveland Roads Cycling Club Vice-president of Middlesbrough Magpies Cycling Club Member of Middllesbrough Bowling Club	Doctor
Albert Scholes	1912–1919	Committee member of Middlesbrough Bowling Club	Fishmonger
Richard Scupham	1875–1886	Vice-president of Middlesbrough Amateur Swimming Club Vice-president of Cleveland & South Durham Baseball Association	Draper
Joseph Smith	1881–1884 1885–1897	Vice-president, president, and chairman of Middlesbrough Bowling Club	Retired pawnbroker
Thomas Dormand Stewart	1911–1927	Vice-president of Cleveland Wednesday Football League Vice-president of YMCA Vice-president of Linthorpe Avenue Tennis Club President of Middlesbrough and District Church Cricket League Vice-president and secretary of Middlesbrough Golf Club	Clothier
William Lockwood Taylor	1877–1893	President of Middllesbrough Amateur Swimming Club	Housepainter

Walter Trevelyan Thomson	1904–1925	Vice-president of Middlesbrough Junior Football League Vice-president and president of Middlesbrough Amateur Gymnastic Club	Iron merchant
Edwin Turner	1908–1927	Captain and president of RUFS Cycling Club Chairman of Middlesbrough Skating Rink Ltd Director and vice-chairman of Middlesbrough Football Club Vice-captain of Park Side Cycling Club President of Middlesbrough Olympia Rink Speed Club President of Middlesbrough Tykes Cycling Club Vice-president of Crescent Cycling Club	Decorator
Theodore H. Ward	1883–1901	President of Middlesbrough Amateur Cycling Club	Solicitor
John F. Wilson	1878–1891	Honorary vice-president of Middlesbrough St George's Congregational Church Men's Club Vice-president of YMCA	Ironmaster
George Dean Wycherley	1901–1923	Vice-president of Middlesbrough Amateur Swimming Club	Hotel keeper

Sources: W. Lillie, *The History of Middlesbrough* (Middlesbrough, 1968), pp. 468–470; Minute Book of Middlesbrough Amateur Boating Club; Minute Book of Middlesbrough Bowling Club; Minute Book of Middlesbrough Golf Club; *Athletic News*, *Cleveland News*, *Daily Exchange*, *Middlesbrough & Stockton Evening Telegraph*, *Middlesbrough & Stockton Sporting Telegraph*, *North-Eastern Daily Gazette*, *North-Eastern Weekly Gazette*, *North Star*, *Northern Athlete*, *Northern Echo*, *Northern Review*, *South Durham & Cleveland Mercury*, *Sports Gazette*, *Teesside Weekly Herald*, *Weekly Exchange*

Appendix 7

Involvement of
Middlesbrough Mayors in Sport

Table A.7. Involvement of Middlesbrough Mayors in Sport

Years as Mayor	Name	Clubs	Occupation
1854	Isaac Wilson	Vice-president of Middlesbrough Amateur Athletic Club Patron of Middlesbrough Cricket Club	Ironmaster
1866–1867	William Randolph Innes Hopkins	President and patron of Middlesbrough Cricket Club	Ironmaster
1874, 1883, 1911	Hugh Bell	Vice-president of Middlesbrough Schools Football League	Ironmaster
1875	John Dunning	Vice-president of Middlesbrough Bicycle Club	Ironmaster and timber merchant
1877, 1896, 1910	Sir Samuel Sadler	President of Middlesbrough Bicycle Club President and honorary vice-president of Middlesbrough Football Club President and vice-president of Middlesbrough Amateur Swimming Club President and patron of Middlesbrough Baseball Club Vice-president of Middlesbrough Amateur Athletic Club President of Cleveland & South Durham Baseball Association Honorary president and vice-president of Middlesbrough Harriers Member of Middlesbrough Amateur Boating Club Vice-president of North Ormesby Cricket Club President of Middlesbrough Rovers Cycling Club Vice-president of Cleveland Roads Cycling Club Member and vice-president of Middlesbrough Amateur Boating Club Vice-president of South Bank Football Club Vice-president of Middlesbrough Amateur Gymnastic Club Honorary member of North-Eastern Steelworks Athletic Club Vice-president of Cambridge House Club Honorary member of Middlesbrough Bowling Club Vice-president of Middlesbrough Golf Club	Chemical manufacturer

Year	Name	Positions	Occupation
1884	John Frederick Wilson	Honorary vice-president of Middlesbrough St George's Congregational Church Men's Club Vice-president of Middlesbrough YMCA	Ironmaster
1886	Amos Hinton	Vice-president of Middlesbrough Golf Club	Grocer
1887	Thomas Sanderson	Honorary vice-president of Middlesbrough Football Club	Slate merchant
1888	Raylton Dixon	Member and president of Middlesbrough Amateur Boating Club	Shipbuilder
1889	Richard Scupham	Vice-president of Middlesbrough Amateur Swimming Club Vice-president of Cleveland & South Durham Baseball Association	Draper
1890	Matthew George Collingwod	Chairman of Cleveland & Middlesbrough Athletic Institute Treasurer and committee member of Middlesbrough Cricket Club	Watchmaker and jeweler
1891	Charles Ephgrave	Vice-president of Middlesbrough Amateur Swimming Club	Grocer
1892	Charles Lowthian Bell	President and vice-president of Middlesbrough Amateur Swimming Club	Ironmaster
1893	Thomas Baker	Member and vice-president of Middlesbrough Amateur Boating Club President and vice-president of Middlesbrough Amateur Swimming Club	Oil merchant
1894	William Lockwood Taylor	President of Middlesbrough Amateur Swimming Club	Housepainter
1895	Theophilius Phillips	Captain of Linthorpe Tennis Club Vice-president of Middlesbrough Amateur Boating Club President and vice-president of Middlesbrough Amateur Swimming Club	Grease and oil manufacturer
		Vice-president of Middlesbrough Baseball Club President of Linthorpe Football Club President of Middlesbrough Football League President and patron of Teesside & Middlesbrough Football League	
1897	Thomas Carter	Member and vice-president of Middlesbrough Amateur Boating Club	Retired picture frame maker
1899, 1913–1914	William Joseph Bruce	Vice-president of Middlesbrough Cycling Club Member and vice-president of Middlesbrough Amateur Boating Club	Cab proprietor

(continued)

Table A.7. *(Continued)*

Years as Mayor	Name	Clubs	Occupation
1900	Robert Mascall	Vice-president of Middlesbrough Amateur Boating Club	Slate merchant
1901	Joseph McLauchlan	President and Wednesday captain of Middlesbrough Magpies Cycling Club	Coal and coke merchant
		Vice-president of Middlesbrough Amateur Boating Club	
		Patron of Middlesbrough Harriers	
1902	John Hedley	Vice-president of Middlesbrough Baseball Club	Doctor
		Vice-president of Middlesbrough Amateur Swimming Club	
		President of Middlesbrough Cricket Club	
		Vice-president of Middlesbrough Golf Club	
1903	Arthur Charles Dorman	Vice-president of Middlesbrough Amateur Boating Club	Ironmaster
		President of Middlesbrough Amateur Swimming Club	
		Vice-president of Middlesbrough & District Motorcycling Club	
		Vice-president and chairman of Dorman Long & Co United Athletic Club	
		Vice-president of Middlesbrough Amateur Gymnastic Club	
		President of Middlesbrough Cricket Club	
		Vice-president of Cambridge House Club	
		Vice-president of Nunthorpe Lawn Tennis & Bowls Club	
		Vice-president of Middlesbrough YMCA	
1904	John Forbes	Vice-president of Middlesbrough Amateur Swimming Club	Baker and confectioner
		Vice-president of Middlesbrough Magpies Cycling Club	
		Vice-president of Cleveland Roads Cycling Club	
		Vice-president of North Ormesby & Middlesbrough Cycling Club	
		Vice-president of Middlesbrough Amateur Gymnastic Club	
1905	Thomas Roddam Dent	Committee member of Middlesbrough Bowling Club	Wharfinger
		Vice-president of Middlesbrough Cricket Club	
		Member of Middlesbrough Golf Club	

Year	Name	Positions	Occupation
1906	Walter G. Roberts	Treasurer of Middlesbrough Amateur Athletics Club Secretary of Middlesbrough Athletic Football Club Honorary secretary and treasurer of Cleveland & South Durham Baseball Association Honorary secretary of English National Baseball Association President of Northern Baseball League President of Middlesbrough Amateur Gymnasium Society Vice-president of YMCA Swimming Club Vice-president of Middlesbrough Amateur Swimming Club Vice-president of Cambridge House Club President of Middlesbrough YMCA President of Middlesbrough YMCA Cricket Club	Architect and surveyor
1907, 1909	Thomas Gibson-Poole	Director, financial secretary, and chairman of Middlesbrough Football Club Member and vice-president of Middlesbrough Amateur Boating Club Vice-president of Middlesbrough Cycling Club Vice-president of Cleveland Roads Cycling Club Vice-president of Middlesbrough Crescent Cycling Club Honorary member of North-Eastern Steelworks Athletic Club Vice-president of Middlesbrough Cricket Club Vice-president of Middlesbrough Golf Club President of Middlesbrough Harriers	Watchmaker and jeweler
1908	John Thomas Pannell	Member and vice-president of Middlesbrough Bowling Club Vice-president of Middlesbrough Amateur Swimming Club Vice-president of Middlesbrough Cricket Club President of Middlesbrough & District Billiards League Vice-president of Cleveland Wednesday Football League	General manager of Cooperative Society

(continued)

Table A.7. (Continued)

Years as Mayor	Name	Clubs	Occupation
1911	William Harkess	Officer of Middlesbrough Tennis Club	Shipbuilder
1912	Alfred Mattison	Chairman of Ironopolis Football Club	Licensed victualler
		Committee member, chairman and director of Middlesbrough Football Club	
		Committee member of Middlesbrough Cricket Club	
		Vice-president of Middlesbrough Amateur Swimming Club	
		Vice-president of Middlesbrough Magpies Cycling Club	
		President of Cleveland Minor Cricket League	
		Vice-president of Middlesbrough & District Motorcycling Club	
		Vice-president of Cambridge House Club	
		Vice-president of Tykes Cycling Club	
		President of Middlesbrough Junior Football League	

Sources: W. Lillie, *The History of Middlesbrough* (Middlesbrough, 1968), pp. 467; Minute Book of Middlesbrough Amateur Boating Club; Minute Book of Middlesbrough Bowling Club; Minute Book of Middlesbrough Golf Club; *Athletic News, Cleveland News, Daily Exchange, Middlesbrough & Stockton Evening Telegraph, Middlesbrough & Stockton Sporting Telegraph, North-Eastern Daily Gazette, North-Eastern Weekly Gazette, North Star, Northern Athlete, Northern Echo, Northern Review, South Durham & Cleveland Mercury, Sports Gazette, Teesside Weekly Herald, Weekly Exchange*

Appendix 8

Involvement of Members of Parliament in Middlesbrough's Sport

Table A.8. Involvement of Members of Parliament in Middlesbrough's Sport

Name	Clubs	Constituency
Richard Godolphin Walmesley Chaloner	Vice-president of Middlesbrough Junior Football League	Westbury, 1895–1900 Liverpool, 1910–1917
William Ernest Duncombe	Patron of Middlesbrough Cricket Club	North Riding, 1859–1867
Sir Christopher Furness	Vice-president of Middlesbrough Amateur Boating Club	Hartlepool, 1891–1896, 1900–1910
Henry Fell Pease	Vice-president of Middlesbrough Amateur Athletic Club	Cleveland, 1895–1897
Sir Robert Ropner	Patron of Teesside Football League	Stockton, 1900–1910
Samuel Sadler	President of Middlesbrough Bicycle Club	Middlesbrough, 1900–1906
	President and honorary vice-president of Middlesbrough Football Club	
	President and vice-president of Middlesbrough Amateur Swimming Club	
	President and patron of Middlesbrough Baseball Club	
	Vice-president of Middlesbrough Amateur Athletic Club	
	President of Cleveland & South Durham Baseball Association	
	Honorary president and vice-president of Middlesbrough Harriers	
	Member of Middlesbrough Amateur Boating Club	
	Vice-president of North Ormesby Cricket Club	
	President of Middlesbrough Rovers Cycling Club	
	Vice-president of Cleveland Roads Cycling Club	
	Member and vice-president of Middlesbrough Amateur Boating Club	
	Vice-president of South Bank Football Club	
	Vice-president of Middlesbrough Amateur Gymnastic Club	
	Honorary member of North-Eastern Steelworks Athletic Club	
	Vice-president of Cambridge House Club	
	Honorary member of Middlesbrough Bowling Club	
	Vice-president of Middlesbrough Golf Club	

Herbert Samuel	President of California Cricket Club	Cleveland, 1902–1918
	President of Cleveland Wednesday Football League	
	President of Eston United Football Club	
	President of Middlesbrough YMCA Football Club	
	President of Teesside Football League	
Sir Bernhard Samuelson	Vice-president of Middlesbrough Amateur Boating Club	Banbury, 1865–1895
Sir Joseph Walton	Vice-president of Middlesbrough Amateur Boating Club	Barnsley, 1897–1922
Penry Williams	Vice-president of South Bank Minor Football League	Middlesbrough, 1910-1922, 1923–1924
Isaac Wilson	Patron of Middlesbrough Cricket Club	Middlesbrough, 1897–1892
	Vice-president of Middlesbrough Amateur Athletic Club	

Sources: Minute Book of Middlesbrough Amateur Boating Club; Minute Book of Middlesbrough Bowling Club; Athletic News, Cleveland News, Daily Exchange, Middlesbrough & Stockton Evening Telegraph, Middlesbrough & Stockton Sporting Telegraph, North-Eastern Daily Gazette, North-Eastern Weekly Gazette, North Star, Northern Athlete, Northern Echo, Northern Review, South Durham & Cleveland Mercury, Sports Gazette, Teesside Weekly Herald, Weekly Exchange

Appendix 9

Subscriptions

Table A.9. Subscriptions

Club	Fees (per annum unless otherwise stated)	Year
Bolckow's Working-men's Club	2s per quarter	1873
Cleveland Club	£10 10s	1868
	£6 6s	1885
Cleveland and Middlesbrough Athletic Institute Lad's Club	1s 6d	1891
Erimus Club	£5 5s	1885
Feversham Street Boys' Club	2d per week	1906
Grove Tennis Club	17s 6d men	1913
	12s 6d ladies	
Linthorpe Parish Church Football Club	4s new members	1906
	3s 6d old members	
Linthorpe Tennis Club	15s ladies	1913
Middlesbrough Amateur Athletic Club	7s 6d seniors	1893
	2s 6d juniors	
Middlesbrough Amateur Boating Club	£1 1s	1888
	5s	1901
Middlesbrough Amateur Gymnasium Society	7s 6d ladies over 21	1905
	6s ladies 17-21	
	5s ladies under 17	
Middlesbrough Amateur Swimming Club	10s 6d	1886
	5s 6d policemen	1888
	5s 6d juniors	1889
	7s 6d juniors	1898
	5s 6d seniors	1906
	4s juniors	
Middlesbrough Baseball Club	5s seniors	1891
	2s 6d juniors	

(continued)

Table A.9. *(continued)*

Club	Fees (per annum unless otherwise stated)	Year
Middlesbrough Bowling Club	10s 6d	1893
	5s	1895
	10s	1896
	15s	1898
Middlesbrough Crescent Cycling Club	1s 6d	1913
Middlesbrough Cricket Club	10s 6d to play cricket or bowls	1894
	15s 6d to play cricket and bowls	
	5s under 18 and sons of members under 21	
Middlesbrough & District Motor Cycling Club	5s	1906
Middlesbrough Football Club	7s 6d	1890
Middlesbrough Golf Club	£1 1s men	1908
	10s 6d ladies/under 21	
	£3 3s vice-presidents	
	£1 10s men	1910
	15s ladies/under 21	
YMCA Football Club	2s 6d	1906
YMCA Swimming Club	4s	1905
	3s 6d for a season of 24 weeks	1912

Sources: A. Briggs, "Middlesbrough: The growth of a new community," in Pollard, A. J. (ed.), *Middlesbrough: Town and Community 1830–1950* (Stroud, 1996), p. 15; *Kelly's Directory of Middlesbrough, 1885* (London, 1885); Cleveland Club Rules and Regulations, U/CLB 1/1, Teesside Archives; Minute Book of Middlesbrough Amateur Boating Club; Minute Book of Middlesbrough Bowling Club; Minute Book of Middlesbrough Golf Club; *North-Eastern Daily Gazette, North-Eastern Weekly Gazette, Northern Echo, Northern Review, Sports Gazette, Weekly Exchange*

Bibliography

ARCHIVAL SOURCES

Teesside Archives

Cambridge House Club Rules, PR/M(P)/8/27.
Cleveland and Middlesbrough Athletic Institute Minute Book, 1891–1892, U/S/384.
Cleveland Club Rules and Regulations, U/CLB 1/1.
Dorman Long & Co Ltd, Minute Book 1, BS.DL/1/22.
Holy Cross Mission, PR/M(P)/8/27.
Ironopolis Register of Members, U/S/1489.
Lease and correspondence re South Bank Football Club, 1908, U/STE/5/5.
Middlesbrough Cricket Club membership cards, 1871–1940, U/S/820.
Middlesbrough Cycle, Motor Car and Accessories Exhibition, 1899, U/ML(3)8/18.
Middlesbrough Mechanic Institute, Rules for Cricket Club, 1849, U/MI/6.
Minute book of North Yorkshire and South Durham Cricket League, 1892–1936, U/NYSD/1.
North Ormesby Cricket Club, Correspondence between J. W. Pennyman and W. Lawson, U/PEN/5/332.
Programme for the Athletic Sports (boys) 1885, S/M/H/3/32.
Programme of North Ormesby Hospital Charity Sports, 17th September 1909, U/S/2073.
Programme of Tees Conservancy Commission, 7th October 1905, U/BL/25.
Rules and Regulations of the Cleveland Hunt Club, 1907, U/PEN/7/181.

National Archives

Middlesbrough Ironopolis Football Company Limited, Memorandum of Association, BT 31/4608/30227.

Privately Held Material

Minute Book of Middlesbrough Amateur Boating Club, 1895–1902.
Minute Book of Middlesbrough Bowling Club, 1893–1908.
Minute Book of Middlesbrough Football & Athletic Company Limited, 1892–1900.
Minute Book of Middlesbrough Golf Club, 1908–1918.

Census Returns

1861, 1871, 1881, 1891, 1901, 1911—www.findmypast.co.uk.

DIRECTORIES

Kelly's Directory of Middlesbrough, 1885 (London, 1885).
Bulmer's History, Topography and Directory of Yorkshire 1890 (Ashton-on-Ribble, 1890).
Kelly's Directory of North and East Ridings of Yorkshire, 1893 (London, 1893).
Kelly's Directory of North and East Ridings of Yorkshire, 1897 (London, 1897).
Kelly's Directory of North and East Ridings of Yorkshire, 1909 (London, 1909).
Kelly's Directory of North and East Ridings of Yorkshire, 1913 (London, 1913).

NEWSPAPERS

Athletic News
Cleveland News
Cleveland Standard
Cycling
Daily Exchange
Daily Gazette
Falcon
Middlesbrough & Stockton Evening Telegraph
Middlesbrough & Stockton Sporting Telegraph
Middlesbrough Morning Mail
Middlesbrough Standard
Newcastle Courant
North Star
North-Eastern Daily Gazette
North-Eastern Weekly Gazette
Northern Athlete
Northern Echo
Northern Review
Northern Weekly Gazette
South Bank Advertiser
South Durham & Cleveland Mercury

Sporting Gazette
Sporting Life (USA)
Sporting Telegraph
Sports Gazette
Sportsman
Teesside Weekly Herald
The Times
Weekly Exchange
Weekly Gazette

CONTEMPORARY BOOKS AND ARTICLES

A. J. R., *The Suffrage Annual and Women's Who's Who* (London, 1913).

Abell, H. F., "The Football Fever," *Macmillan's Magazine* 89 (1904), pp. 276–282.

Allison, C. H., "Pushball, a strenuous new game," *National Magazine* 23, 1 (1905), pp. 47–49.

Allison, G. F., "The Rise of Middlesbrough Football Club," in Leatherdale, C. (ed.), *The Book of Football* (Westcliff-on-Sea, 1997 [first edition, 1906]).

Anon., "The Popular Pastime—Cricket," *Blackwood's Edinburgh Magazine* 140 (1886), pp. 755–763.

Anon., "Cricket and Cricketers," *Blackwood's Edinburgh Magazine* 151 (1892), pp. 96–113.

Bassett, W. I., "Big Transfers and the Transfer System," in Leatherdale, C. (ed.), *The Book of Football* (Westcliff-on-Sea, 1997 [first edition, 1906]).

Bell, C., "Eight Teetotal Mayors of Middlesbrough," *The Temperance Worker* 46 (1899), pp. 41–55.

Bell, F., *At the Works: A study of a manufacturing town* (London, 1985 [first edition, 1907]).

Bentley, J. J., 'The Growth of Modern Football," in Leatherdale, C. (ed.), *The Book of Football* (Westcliff-on-Sea, 1997 [first edition, 1906]).

Bentley, J. J., "Is Football a Business?," *World's Work* 20 (1912), pp. 383–393.

Budd, A., "Past Development in Rugby Football, and the Future of the Game," in Marshall, F. (ed.), *Football—The Rugby Union Game* (London, 1892).

Burnett, W. H., *Middlesbrough and the District: Being notes, historical, industrial, scientific* (Middlesbrough, 1881).

Bury, Viscount, "Cycling and Cyclists," *Nineteenth Century* 17 (1885), pp. 92–108.

Bury, Viscount, and Lacy Hillier, G., *Cycling* (London, 1891).

Edwardes, C., "The New Football Mania," *Nineteenth Century* 32 (1892), pp. 622–631.

Ensor, E., "The Football Madness," *Contemporary Review* 74 (1898), pp. 753–760.

Gibson, A., and W. Pickford, *Association Football and the Men Who Made It* (London, 1905).

Goodall, J., *Association Football* (London, 1898).

Heavisides, M., *Rambles by the River Tees* (Stockon-on-Tees, 1905).

Jackson, N. L., "Professionalism and Sport," *Fortnightly Review* 67 (1900), pp.154–161.

McGregor, W., "The £ s d of Football," in Leatherdale, C. (ed.), *The Book of Football* (Westcliff-on-Sea, 1997 [first edition, 1906]).

Offord, H. J. W., "Schoolboy Football," in Leatherdale, C. (ed.), *The Book of Football* (Westcliff-on-Sea, 1997 [first edition, 1906]).

Praed, L., *History of the Rise and Progress of Middlesbrough* (Newcastle, 1863).

Ravenstein, E. G., "The Laws of Migration," *Journal of the Statistical Society* XLVIII (1885), pp. 167–235.

Reid, H. G., *Middlesbrough and its Jubilee: A history of the iron and steel industries, with biographies of pioneers* (Middlesbrough, 1881).

Russell, C. E. B., *Social Problems of the North* (London, 1913).

Shearman, M., *Athletics and Football* (London, 1889), *Athletics and Football* (London, 1894).

Smith, G. O., "Origin and Benefits of the League and the Effects of Professionalism on the Game," in Shearman, M. (ed.), *Football* (London, 1899).

Steel, A. G., "Bowling," in Steel, A. G., and Lyttelton, R. H., *Cricket* (London, 1904).

Sturdee, R. J., "The Ethics of Football," *Westminster Review* 59 (1903), pp. 180–185.

Tillyard, F., "English Town Development in the Nineteenth Century," *The Economic Journal* 23 (1913), pp. 537–560.

Wilberforce, H. W. W., "The Four-Handed or Double Game," in Heathcote, J. M., and Heathcote, C. G., *Tennis* (London, 1890).

Secondary Sources

Allen, J., and Allen, R. C., "Competing Identities: Irish and Welsh migration and the north-east of England, 1851–1980," in Green, A., and Pollard, A. J. (eds.), *Regional Identities in North-East England, 1300–2000* (Woodbridge, 2007).

Allison, G. F., *Allison Calling: A galaxy of football and other memories* (London, 1948).

Appleton, A., *Hotbed of Soccer: The story of football in the north-east* (London, 1960).

Arlott, J., "Sport," in Nowell-Smith, S. (ed.), *Edwardian England 1901–1914* (London, 1964).

Bailey, P., "'A Mingled Mass of Perfectly Legitimate Pleasures': The Victorian middle class and the problem of leisure," *Victorian Studies* 21, 1 (1977), pp. 7–28; *Leisure and Class in Victorian England: Rational recreation and the contest for control, 1830–1885* (London, 1978); "The Politics and Poetics of Modern British Leisure," *Rethinking History* 3, 2 (1999), pp. 131–175.

Baker, N., "Whose Hegemony? The origins of the amateur ethos in nineteenth century English society," *Sport in History* 24, 1 (2004), pp. 1–16.

Baker, R., "The Formative Years of Middlesbrough Cricket Club," *Bulletin of the Cleveland and Teesside Local History Society* 54 (1988), pp. 6–24, *Iron and Willow: A history of Middlesbrough CC, volume one 1855–1911* (Middlesbrough, 1989).

Baker, W. J., "The Making of a Working-Class Football Culture in Victorian England," *Journal of Social History* 13, 2 (1979), pp. 241–251.

Beaven, B., *Leisure, Citizenship and Working-Class Men in Britain, 1850–1945* (Manchester, 2005).

Beck, P. J., "Leisure and Sport in England 1900–1939," in Wrigley, C. (ed.), *A Companion to Early Twentieth Century Britain* (London, 2003).

Benning, D., and D. Bloyce, "Baseball in Britain 1874–1914," in Svoboda, B., and Rychtecky, A. (eds.), *Physical Activity for Life: East and West, South and North: The Proceedings of 9th Biennial Conference of International Society for Comparative Physical Education and Sport at the Charles University, Faculty of Physical Education and Sport, Prague, Czech Republic* (Prague, 1995).

Beynon, H., R. Hudson, and D. Sadler, *A Place Called Teesside: A locality in a global economy* (Edinburgh, 1994).

Birley, D., *Sport and the Making of Britain* (Manchester, 1993), *Land of Sport and Glory: Sport and British society 1887–1910* (Manchester, 1995).

Bloyce, D., "'Just Not Cricket': Baseball in England, 1874–1900," *International Journal of the History of Sport* 14, 2 (1997), pp. 207–218, "'That's Your Way of Playing Rounders': The response of the English press to American baseball tours to England, 1874–1924," *Sporting Traditions* 22 (2005), pp. 81–98, "The English Response to American's National Pastime: American baseball tours to England, 1874–1924," in Tolleneer, J., and Renson, R. (eds.), *Old Borders, New Borders, No Borders: Sport and physical education in a period of change* (Oxford, 2000).

Bloyce, D., and P. Murphy, "Baseball in England: A case of prolonged cultural resistance," *Journal of Historical Sociology* 21, 1 (2008), pp. 120–142.

Brake, L., and M. Demoor, (eds.), *Dictionary of Nineteenth-Century Journalism in Great Britain and Ireland* (Gent, Belgium, 2009).

Briggs, A., *Victorian Cities* (London, 1963), "Middlesbrough: The growth of a new community," in Pollard, A. J. (ed.), *Middlesbrough: Town and Community 1830–1950* (Stroud, 1996).

Bromhead, J., "George Cadbury's Contribution to Sport," *Sports Historian* 20, 1 (2000), pp. 97–117.

Bullock, I., "The Origins of Economic Growth on Teesside 1851–81," *Northern History* 9 (1974), pp. 79–95.

Cannadine, D., *Class in Britain* (London, 1998).

Carson, R., *A Short History of Middlesbrough* (Redcar, 1977).

Carter, N., *The Football Manager: A history* (Abingdon, 2006).

Chase, M., "The Teesside Irish in the Nineteenth Century," *Cleveland History* 69 (1995), pp. 3–22.

Chinn, C., *Better Betting with a Decent Feller: A social history of bookmaking* (London, 2004).

Clark, P., *British Clubs and Societies 1580–1800* (Oxford, 2000).

Cleveland and Teesside Local History Society, *Saints Alive!* (Middlesbrough, 1994).

Collins, T., *Rugby's Great Split: Class, culture and the origins of rugby league football* (Abingdon, 2006); *A Social History of English Rugby Union* (Abingdon, 2009).

Collins, T., and W. Vamplew, "The Pub, the Drinks Trade and the Early Years of Modern Football," *The Sports Historian* 20, 1 (2000), pp. 1–17.

Colls, R., and B. Lancaster, (eds.), *Geordies: Roots of Regionalism* (Newcastle, 1992).

Conboy, M., *The Press and Popular Culture* (London, 2002), *Journalism: A critical history* (London, 2004).

Crawford, E., *The Women's Suffrage Movement: A reference guide 1866–1928* (London, 1999); *The Women's Suffrage Movement in Britain and Ireland: A regional survey* (London, 2006).

Croll, A., *Civilizing the Urban: Popular culture and public space in Merthyr, c.1870–1914* (Cardiff, 2000).

Davies, A., *Leisure, Gender and Poverty: Working-class culture in Salford and Manchester, 1900–1939* (Buckingham, 1992).

Day, B. J., *Lost for a Hundred Years* (Middlesbrough, 1996).

Day, D., "London Swimming Professors: Victorian craftsmen and aquatic entrepreneurs," *Sport in History* 30, 1 (2010), pp. 32–54.

Dixon, D., "New Town, New Newspapers: The development of the newspaper press in nineteenth-century Middlesbrough," in Isaac, P., and McKay, B. (eds.), *The Moving Market: Continuity and Change in the Book Trade* (Delaware, 2001).

Dixon, P., and N. Garnham, "Drink and the Professional Footballer in 1890s England and Ireland," *Sport in History* 25, 3 (2005), pp. 375–389.

Dixon, P., N. Garnham, and A. Jackson, "Shareholders and Shareholding: The case of the football company in late Victorian England," *Business History* 46, 4 (2004), pp. 503–524.

Donajgrodzki, T., "An Even Vision: The ideology of 'At the Works,'" *Cleveland and Teesside Local History Society Bulletin* 55 (1988), pp. 30–44.

Doyle, B., "Rehabilitating the Retailer: Shopkeepers in urban government, 1900–1950," in Couperus, S., Smit, C., and Wolffram, D. J. (eds.), *In Control of the City: Local elites and the dynamics of urban politics, 1800–1960* (Leuven, 2007); "Managing and Contesting Industrial Pollution in Middlesbrough, 1880–1914," *Northern History* 47, 1 (2010), pp. 135–154.

Dunning, E., "The Development of Modern Football," in Dunning, E. (ed.), *The Sociology of Sport* (London, 1971).

Dunning, E., and K. Sheard, *Barbarians, Gentlemen and Players: A sociological study of the development of rugby football* (Abingdon, 2005 [first edition, 1979]).

Edwards, K. H. R., *Chronology of the Development of the Iron and Steel Industries of Tees-side* (Wigan, 1955).

Erdozain, D., *The Problem of Pleasure: Sport, recreation and the crisis of Victorian religion* (Woodbridge, 2010).

Fishwick, N., *English Football and Society, 1910–1950* (Manchester, 1989).

Garnham, N., "Both Praying and Playing: 'Muscular Christianity' and the YMCA in north-east County Durham," *Journal of Social History* 35, 2 (2001), pp. 397–407.

Garnham, N., and A. Jackson, "Who Invested in Victorian Football Clubs? The case of Newcastle-upon-Tyne," *Soccer and Society* 4, 1 (2003), pp. 57–70.

Glasper, H., *Middlesbrough: A complete record* (Derby, 1993).

Goodall, R., "Cycling Clubs of North Yorkshire and South Durham, 1876–1914," *Bulletin of the Cleveland and Teesside Local History Society* 57 (1989), pp. 20–34; "Women a Wheel Around Cleveland: Cycling pioneers," *Cleveland History* 68 (1995), pp. 40–43.

Griffiths, J., "'Give my Regards to Uncle Billy . . .': The rites and rituals of company life at Lever Brothers, c.1900-c.1990," *Business History* 37, 4 (1995), pp. 25–45.

Gunn, S., *The Public Culture of the Victorian Middle Class: Ritual and authority and the English industrial city, 1840–1914* (Manchester, 2000).

Gwynne, T., and Sill, M., "Welsh Immigration into Middlesbrough in the Mid-nineteenth Century," *Bulletin of the Cleveland and Teesside Local History Society* 31 (1976), pp. 19–22.

Hall, A. A., "Wages, Earnings and Real Earnings in Teesside: A re-assessment of the ameliorist interpretation of living standards in Britain, 1870–1914," *International Review of Social History* 26 (1981), pp. 202–219.

Halladay, E., *Rowing in England: A social history—the amateur debate* (Manchester, 1990).

Hampton, M., "Rethinking the 'New Journalism,' 1850s-1930s," *Journal of British Studies* 43, 2 (2004), pp. 278–290, *Visions of the Press in Britain, 1850–1950* (Chicago, 2004).

Hardy, S., *How Boston Played: Sport, recreation and community 1865–1915* (Boston, Massachusetts, 1982).

Harris, J., *Private Lives, Public Spirit: A social history of Britain 1870–1914* (Oxford, 1993).

Harrison, B., "Religion and Recreation in Nineteenth-Century England," *Past and Present* 38, 1 (1967), pp. 98–125.

Harvey, A., *Football: The first hundred years—the untold story* (Abingdon, 2005).

Hayes, W., "Sport as Spectacle: Swimming in Victorian and Edwardian Britain," *Cahiers Victoriens et Édouardiens* 59 (2004), pp. 101–116.

Hill, J., "'First-Class' Cricket and the Leagues: Some notes on the development of English cricket, 1900–40," *International Journal of the History of Sport* 4, 1 (1987), pp. 68–81; "British Sports History: A post-modern future?," *Journal of Sport History* 23, 1 (1996), pp. 1–19; "Rite of Spring: Cup finals and community in the north of England," in Hill, J., and Williams, J. (eds.), *Sport and Identity in the North of England* (Keele, 1996); *Sport, Leisure & Culture in Twentieth-Century Britain* (Basingstoke, 2002); "Anecdotal Evidence: Sport, the newspaper press, and history," in Phillips, M. G. (ed.), *Deconstructing Sport History: A postmodern analysis* (Albany, 2006).

Hoffmann, F. W., and W. G. Bailey, *Sports and Recreation Fads* (Binghamton, New York, 1991).

Holt, R., "Working Class Football and the City: The problem of continuity," *British Journal of Sports History* 4 (1986), pp. 5–17; "Football and the Urban Way of Life in Nineteenth-Century Britain," in Mangan, J. (ed.), *Pleasure, Profit and Proselytism: British culture and sport at home and abroad 1700–1914* (London 1988); *Sport and the British: A modern history* (Oxford, 1989); "Heroes of the North: Sport and the shaping of regional identity," in Hill, J., and Williams, J. (eds.), *Sport and Identity in the North of England* (Keele, 1996); "Sport and History: The state of the subject in Britain," *Twentieth Century British History* 7, 2 (1996), pp. 231–252; "The Amateur Body and the Middle-class Man: Work, health and style in Victorian Britain," in Porter, D., and Wagg, S. (eds.), *Amateurism in British Sport: It matters not who won or lost?* (Abingdon, 2008).

Holt, R., and R. Physick, "Sport on Tyneside," in Colls, R., and Lancaster, B. (eds.), *Newcastle upon Tyne: A modern history* (Chichester, 2001).

Horrall, A., *Popular Culture in London c.1890–1918* (Manchester, 2001).

Horton, M. C., *The Story of Cleveland: History, anecdote and legend* (Middlesbrough, 1979).

Horwood, C., "'Girls Who Arouse Dangerous Passions': Women and bathing, 1900–39," *Women's History Review* 9, 4 (2000), pp. 653–673.

Huggins, M., "Social Tone and Resort Development in North-East England: Victorian seaside resorts around the mouth of the Tees," *Northern History* 20 (1984), pp. 187–206; "'Fashionable Watering Place' or 'Popular Resort': Residential visitors and day trippers to Redcar and Coatham, 1865–90," *Journal of Regional and Local Studies* (December 1983), pp. 51–62; "'Mingled Pleasure and Speculation': The survival of the enclosed racecourses on Teesside, 1855–1902," *British Journal of Sports History* 3, 2 (1986), pp. 158–172; "Stockton Race Week 1855–1900: The growth of an unofficial holiday," *Journal of Regional and Local Studies* 6, 1 (1986), pp. 47–55; "The Glory Years: An early north-east football club 1878–1887," *Bulletin of the Cleveland and Teesside Local History Society* 51 (1986), pp. 28–40; "The Spread of Association Football in North-East England, 1876–90: The pattern of diffusion," *International Journal of the History of Sport* 6, 1 (1989), pp. 299–318; "Leisure and Sport in Middlesbrough, 1840–1914" in Pollard, A. J. (ed.), *Middlesbrough: Town and Community 1830–1950* (Stroud, 1996); "More Sinful Pleasures? Leisure, respectability and the male middle classes in Victorian England," *Journal of Social History* 33, 3 (2000), pp. 585–600; "Second-Class Citizens? English middle-class culture and sport, 1850–1910: A reconsideration," *International Journal of the History of Sport* 17, 1 (2000), pp. 1–35; "Sport and the Social Construction of Identity in North-East England, 1800–1914," in Kirk, N. (ed.), *Northern Identities: Historical interpretations of 'the north' and 'northerness'* (Aldershot, 2000); *The Victorians and Sport* (London, 2004).
Hughson, J., "The Modern City and the Making of Sport," *Sport in Society* 12, 1 (2009), pp. 103–117.
Humphreys, R., "Spending Leisure Time in Teesside During the mid-Nineteenth Century," *Bulletin of the Cleveland and Teesside Local History Society* 24 (1974), pp. 4–9.
Hunt, B., *Northern Goalfields Revisited: The millennium history of the Northern Football League, 1889–2000* (Shildon, 2000).
Inglis, S., *Soccer in the Dock: A history of British football scandals, 1900–1965* (London, 1985), *League Football and the Men Who Made It* (London, 1988), *Engineering Archie: Archibald Leitch—football ground designer* (London, 2005).
Jackson, A., "Football Coverage in the Papers of the Sheffield Telegraph, c1890–1915," *International Journal of Regional and Local Studies* 5, 1 (2009), pp. 63–84.
James, G., and D. Day, "The Emergence of an Association Football Culture in Manchester 1840–1884," *Sport in History* 34, 1 (2014), pp. 49–74; "FA Cup Success, Football Infrastructure and the Establishment of Manchester's Footballing Identity," *Soccer & Society* 16, 2–3 (2015), pp. 200–216.
Jefferys, K., "The Heyday of Amateurism in Modern Lawn Tennis," *International Journal of the History of Sport* 46, 15 (2009), pp. 2236–2252.
Jewitt, F., and Oakey, S., *100 Not Out: The history of the Cleveland and Teesside Cricket League, 1885–1985* (Stockton-on-Tees, 1985).
Joannou, P., and A. Candlish, *Pioneers of the North: The origins and development of football in north-east England & Tyneside, 1870–93* (Derby, 2009).
Johnes, M., "'Poor Man's Cricket': Baseball, class and community in South Wales, c.1880–1950," *International Journal of the History of Sport* 17, 4 (2000), pp. 153–166; "Great Britain," in S. W. Pope and J. Nauright (eds.), *Routledge Companion to Sports History* (Abingdon, 2010).

Jones, A., "Local Journalism in Victorian Political Culture," in Brake, L., Jones, A., and Madden, L. (eds.), *Investigating Victorian Journalism* (Basingstoke, 1990).

Jones, S. G., *Sport, Politics and the Working Class: Organised labour and sport in inter-war Britain* (Manchester, 1988).

Joyce, P., "In Pursuit of Class: Recent studies in the history of work and class," *History Workshop Journal* 25, 1 (1988), pp. 171–177; *Visions of the People: Industrial England and the question of class 1848–1914* (Cambridge, 1991).

Joyce, T., "Sport and the Cash Nexus in Nineteenth Century Toronto," *Sport History Review* 30 (1999), pp. 140–167.

Kay, J., "'No Time for Recreations till the Vote is Won'?: Suffrage activists and leisure in Edwardian Britain," *Women's History Review* 16, 4 (2007), pp. 535–553; "It Wasn't Just Emily Davison! Sport, suffrage and society in Edwardian Britain," *International Journal of the History of Sport* 25, 10 (2008), pp. 1338–1354.

Kay, J., and W. Vamplew, "Beyond Altruism: British football and charity, 1877–1914," *Soccer & Society* 11, 3 (2010), pp. 181–197.

Kennedy, D., "Locality and Professional Football Club Development: The demographics of football club support in late Victorian Liverpool," *Soccer & Society* 5, 3 (2004), pp. 371–391; "Class, Ethnicity and Civic Governance: A social profile of football club directors on Merseyside in the late-nineteenth century," *International Journal of the History of Sport* 22, 5 (2005), pp. 840–866; "And Then There Were Two: Everton and Liverpool football clubs, 1892–1902," *Soccer & Society* 12, 4 (2011), pp. 523–537.

Kerrigan, C., *Teachers and Football: Schoolboy association football in England, 1885–1915* (Abingdon, 2005).

Lake, R. J., "Social Class, Etiquette and Behavioural Restraint in British Lawn Tennis, 1870–1939," *International Journal of the History of Sport* 28, 6 (2011), pp. 876–894; *A Social History of Tennis in Britain* (Abingdon, 2015).

Lancaster, B., "The North East, England's Most Distinctive Region?," in Lancaster, B., Newton, D., and Vall, N. (eds.), *An Agenda for Regional History* (Newcastle, 2007).

Le Guillot, M., *A History of the River Tees* (Middlesbrough, 1978).

Lee, A. J., *The Origins of the Popular Press in England 1855–1914* (London, 1976).

Leonard, J. W., "Lady Bell's Survey of Edwardian Middlesbrough," *Bulletin of the Cleveland and Teesside Local History Society* 29 (1975), pp. 1–19.

Lewis, R., "The Evolution of a Political Culture: Middlesbrough, 1850–1950," in Pollard, A. J. (ed.), *Middlesbrough: Town and Community 1830–1950* (Stroud, 1996).

Lewis, R., and D. Ward, "Culture, Politics and Assimilation: The Welsh on Teesside, c.1850–1940," *Welsh History Review* 17, 4 (1995), pp. 550–570.

Lewis, R. W., "'Touched Pitch and Been Shockingly Defiled': Football, class, social Darwinism and decadence in England, 1880–1914," in Mangan, J. (ed.), *Sport in Europe: Politics, class, gender* (London, 1999).

Liddington, J., and E. Crawford, "'Women do not count, neither shall they be counted': Suffrage, citizenship and the battle for the 1911 Census," *History Workshop Journal* 71 (2011), pp. 98–127.

Lillie, W., *The History of Middlesbrough* (Middlesbrough, 1968).

Love, C., "Swimming and Gender in the Victorian World," *International Journal of the History of Sport* 24, 5 (2007), pp. 586–602; "Social Class and the Swimming World: Amateurs and professionals," *International Journal of the History of Sport* 24, 5 (2007), pp. 603–619; "Local Aquatic Empires: The municipal provision of swimming pools in England, 1828–1918," *International Journal of the History of Sport* 24, 5 (2007), pp. 620–629; "Taking a Refreshing Dip: Health, cleanliness and the Empire," *International Journal of the History of Sport* 24, 5 (2007), pp. 693–706.

Lowerson, J., "Joint Stock Companies, Capital Formation and Suburban Leisure in England, 1880–1914," in Vamplew, W. (ed.), *The Economic History of Leisure; Papers presented at the 8th International Economic History Congress, Budapest* (Adelaide, 1983); "Golf," in Mason, T. (ed.), *Sport in Britain: A social history* (Cambridge, 1989); *Sport and the English Middle Classes 1870–1914* (Manchester, 1993).

Mandle, W. F., "Games People Played: Cricket and football in England and Victoria in the late nineteenth century," *Historical Studies* 15, 60 (1973), pp. 511–535.

Mason, T., *Association Football and English Society 1863–1915* (Brighton, 1981); "Football and the Workers in England, 1880–1914," in Cashman, R., and McKernan, M. (ed.), *Sport: Money, morality and the media* (Queensland, 1982); "All the Winners and the Half Times . . . ," *Sports Historian* 13, 1 (1993), pp. 3–13; "Football, Sport of the North?," in Hill, J., and Williams, J. (eds.), *Sport and Identity in the North of England* (Keele, 1996); "When Professional Baseball Nearly Came to Britain," *Revue Française de Civilisation Britannique* 10, 4 (2000), pp. 37–46.

McCord, N., *North-East England: An economic and social history* (London, 1979); "Some Aspects of Change in the Nineteenth-Century North-East," *Northern History* 31 (1995), pp. 241–266.

McCord, N., and D. J. Rowe, "Industrialisation and Urban Growth in North-East England," *International Review of Social History* 22 (1977), pp. 30–64.

McCrone, K. E., *Sport and the Physical Emancipation of English Women, 1870–1914* (London, 1988); "Class, Gender and English Women's Sport, c.1890–1914," *Journal of Sport History* 18, 1 (1991), pp. 159–182.

McDowell, M. L., *A Cultural History of Association Football in Scotland, 1865–1902: Understanding sports as a way of understanding society* (Lewiston, New York, 2013).

McKibbin, R., *Classes and Cultures, England 1918–1951* (Oxford, 1998).

Meller, H. E., *Leisure and the Changing City, 1870–1914* (London, 1976).

Melling, J., "Employers, Workplace Culture and Workers' Politics: British industry and workers' welfare programmes, 1870–1920," in Melling, J., and Barry, J. (eds.), *Culture in History: Production, consumption and values in historical perspective* (Exeter, 1992).

Metcalf, S., "Albert Park: A place for the recreation of the people," *Bulletin of the Cleveland and Teesside Local History Society* 38 (Spring 1980), pp. 14–23.

Metcalfe, A., *Leisure and Recreation in a Victorian Mining Community: The social economy of leisure in North-East England, 1820–1914* (Abingdon, 2006).

Middlesbrough Golf Club Centenary 1908–2008 (Middlesbrough, 2010).

Middlesbrough Rugby Union Football Club Eightieth Anniversary 1872–1952 (Middlesbrough, 1952).

Milne, G. J., *North-East England, 1850–1914: The dynamics of a maritime-industrial region* (Woodbridge, 2006); "Business Regionalism: Defining and owning the industrial north-east 1850–1914," in Green, A., and Pollard, A. J. (eds.), *Regional Identities in North-East England, 1300–2000* (Woodbridge, 2007).

Moorsom, N., *The Birth and Growth of Modern Middlesbrough* (Middlesbrough, 1967); *Middlesbrough's Albert Park—History, heritage and restoration* (Barnsley, 2002); *The Story of Middlesbrough Dock in Greater Middlehaven* (Middlesbrough, 2006).

Morris, R. J., "Clubs, Societies and Associations," in Thompson, F. M. L. (ed.), *Cambridge Social History of Britain, 1750–1950: Social agencies and institutions* (Cambridge, 1990).

Munting, R., "The Games Ethic and Industrial Capitalism Before 1914: The provision of company sports," *Sport in History* 23, 1 (2003), pp. 45–63.

Nicholson, T., "'Jacky' and the Jubilee: Middlesbrough's creation myth," in Pollard, A. J. (ed.), *Middlesbrough: Town and Community 1830–1950* (Stroud, 1996); "Masculine Status and Working-class Culture in the Cleveland Ironstone Mining Communities, 1850–1881," in Laybourn, K. (ed.), *Social Conditions, Status and Community 1860-c.1920* (Stroud, 1997).

North, G. A., *Teesside's Economic Heritage* (Margate, 1975).

Orde, A., *Religion, Business and Society in North-East England: The Pease family of Darlington in the nineteenth century* (Stamford, 2000).

Parker, C., "Swimming: The 'ideal' sport for nineteenth-century British women," *International Journal of the History of Sport* 27, 4 (2010), pp. 675–689.

Parratt, C. M., "Athletic 'Womanhood': Exploring sources for female sport in Victorian and Edwardian England," *Journal of Sport History* 16, 2 (1989), pp. 140–157; *"More Than Mere Amusement": Working-class women's leisure in England, 1750–1914* (Boston, Massachusetts, 2001).

Paylor, E., and J. Wilson, *Ayresome Park Memories* (Derby, 1995).

Phelps, N. A., "Professional Football and Local Identity in the 'Golden Age': Portsmouth in the mid-twentieth century," *Urban History* 32, 3 (2005), pp. 459–480.

Phillips, M. G., "Deconstructing Sport History: The postmodern challenge," *Journal of Sport History* 28, 3 (2001), pp. 327–343.

Phillips, S., "'Fellowship in Recreation, Fellowship in Ideals': Sport, leisure and culture at Boots Pure Drug Company, Nottingham c.1883–1945," *Midland History* 29 (2004), pp. 107–123.

Polley, L., *The Other Middlesbrough: A study of three nineteenth century suburbs* (Middlesbrough, 1993); "Housing the Community, 1830–1914," in Pollard, A. J. (ed.), *Middlesbrough: Town and Community 1830–1950* (Stroud, 1996); "To Hell, Utopia and Back Again: Reflections on the urban landscape of Middlesbrough," in Faulkner, T., Berry, H., and Gregory, J. (eds.), *Northern Landscapes: Representations and realities of north-east England* (Woodbridge, 2010).

Pooley, C. G., and J. C. Doherty, "The Longitudinal Study of Migration: Welsh migration to English towns in the nineteenth century," in Pooley, C. G., and Whyte, D. I. (eds.), *Migrants, Emigrants and Immigrants: A social history of migration* (London, 1991).

Ponting, K. G., "Lawn Tennis: The formative years 1880–1914—some social and economic consequences," in Vamplew, W. (ed.), *The Economic History of Leisure;*

Papers presented at the 8th International Economic History Congress, Budapest (Adelaide, 1983).

Porter, D., "Revenge of the Crouch End Vampires: The AFA, the FA and English football's 'Great Split'," *Sport in History* 26, 3 (2006), pp. 406–428; "Entrepreneurship," in Pope, S. W., and Nauright, J. (eds.), *Routledge Companion to Sports History* (Abingdon, 2010).

Redfern, A., "Crewe: Leisure in a railway town," in Walton, J. K., and Walvin, J. (eds.), *Leisure in Britain, 1780–1939* (Manchester, 1983).

Riess, S. A., *City Games: The evolution of American urban society and the rise of sports* (Chicago, 1991); "From Pitch to Putt: Sport and class in Anglo-American sport," *Journal of Sport History* 21, 2 (1994), pp. 138–184; *Sport in Industrial America 1850–1920* (Illinois, 1995).

Rosenzweig, R., *Eight Hours for What We Will: Workers and leisure in an industrial city, 1870–1920* (Cambridge, 1983).

Rowe, D. J., "The Economy of the North-East in the Nineteenth Century: A survey," *Northern History* 6 (1971), pp. 117–147, "The North-East," in Thompson, F. M. L. (ed.), *Cambridge Social History of Britain, 1750–1950: Regions and Communities* (Cambridge, 1990).

Rubinstein, D., "Cycling in the 1890s," *Victorian Studies* 21, 1 (1977), pp. 7–28.

Russell, D., *Popular Music in England, 1840–1914 — A social history* (Manchester, 1987); "Sport and Identity: The case of Yorkshire County Cricket Club, 1890–1939," *Twentieth Century British History* 7, 2 (1996), pp. 206–230; *Football and the English: A social history of association football in England, 1863–1995* (Preston, 1997); *Looking North: Northern England and the national imagination* (Manchester, 2004); "Culture and the Formation of Northern English Identities from c.1850," in Lancaster, B., Newton, D., and Vall, N. (ed.), *An Agenda for Regional History* (Newcastle, 2007).

Sandiford, K. A. P., "Cricket and the Victorian Society," *Journal of Social History* 17, 2 (1983), pp. 303–317.

Sandiford, K., and W. Vamplew, "The Peculiar Economics of English Cricket Before 1914," *British Journal of Sports History* 3, 3 (1986), pp. 311–326.

Savage, M., and A. Miles, *The Remaking of the British Working Class, 1840–1940* (London, 1994).

Seddon, P., *Steve Bloomer: The story of football's first superstar* (Derby, 1999).

Shaw, C., "The Large Manufacturing Employers of 1907," *Business History* 25, 52 (1983), pp. 42–60.

Stephenson, P., *Joe Walton Community and Youth Club* (Middlesbrough, 2001); *Ormesby Urban District* (Middlesbrough, 2003); *The Grove Hill "Aristocracy": Marton Road* (Middlesbrough, 2003).

Stubley, P., "Churchmen in a Late Victorian Town," *Theology* 83, 695 (1980), pp. 346–354; *Industrial Society and Church: Middlesbrough 1830–1914* (Bognor Regis, 2001).

Szymanski, S., "A Theory of the Evolution of Modern Sport," *Journal of Sport History* 35, 1 (2008), pp. 1–32.

Tabner, B., *Football Through the Turnstiles Again* (Harefield, 2002).

Taylor, D., "The Infant Hercules and the Augean Stables: A century of economic and social development in Middlesbrough c.1840–1939," in Pollard, A. J. (ed.),

Middlesbrough: Town and Community 1830–1950 (Stroud, 1996); *Policing the Victorian Town: The development of the police in Middlesbrough c.1840–1914* (Basingstoke, 2002); "Bearbrass or Ballarat? Asa Briggs' Middlesbrough and the pattern of nineteenth century urbanisation," *Journal of Regional and Local Studies* 22, 2 (2003), pp. 1–19; "Conquering the British Ballarat: The policing of Victorian Middlesbrough," *Journal of Social History* 37, 3 (2004), pp. 755–771; "Melbourne, Middlesbrough and Morality: Policing Victorian 'new towns' in the old world and the new," *Social History* 31, 1 (2006), pp. 15–38.

Taylor, H., "Sporting Heroes," in Colls, R., and Lancaster, B. (eds.), *Geordies: Roots of Regionalism* (Newcastle, 1992).

Taylor, M., "Labour Relations and Managerial Control in English Professional Football, 1890–1939," *Sport History Review* 31, 2 (2000), pp. 80–99; "Beyond the Maximum Wage: The earnings of football professionals in England, 1900–39," *Soccer and Society* 2, 3 (2001), pp. 101–118; "Work and Play: The professional footballer in England, c.1900–c.1950," *The Sports Historian* 22, 1 (2002), pp. 16–43; *The Leaguers: The making of professional football in England, 1900–1939* (Liverpool, 2005); *The Association Game: A history of British football* (Harlow, 2008).

Taylor, M., and J. Coyle, "The Election of Clubs to the Football League 1888–1939," *The Sports Historian* 19, 2 (1999), pp. 1–24.

Tischler, S., *Footballers and Businessmen: The origins of professional football in England* (New York, 1981).

Trainor, R., "Urban Elites in Victorian Britain," *Urban History* 12 (1985), pp. 1–17, "The Middle Class," in Daunton, M. (ed.), *The Cambridge Urban History of Britain, volume III, 1840–1950* (Cambridge, 2000).

Tranter, N. L., "The Patronage of Organised Sport in Central Scotland, 1820–1900," *Journal of Sport History* 16, 3 (1989), pp. 227–247; *Sport, Economy and Society in Britain 1750–1914* (Cambridge, 1998).

Turner, J., "The Frontier Revisited: Thrift and fellowship in the new industrial town, c.1830–1914," in Pollard, A. J. (ed.), *Middlesbrough: Town and Community 1830–1950* (Stroud, 1996).

Turner, J. J., "Middlesbrough and the National Coal Strike of 1912," *Bulletin of the Cleveland and Teesside Local History Society* 43 (1982), pp. 1–12; "The People's Winter Garden, Middlesbrough," *Bulletin of the Cleveland and Teesside Local History Society* 46 (1984), pp. 30–41.

Vamplew, W., "Playing for Pay: The earnings of professional sportsmen in England 1870–1914," in Cashman, R., and McKernan, M. (eds.), *Sport, Money, Morality and the Media* (Queensland, 1980); *Pay Up and Play the Game: Professional sport in Britain, 1875–1914* (Cambridge, 1988); "Sport and Industrialization: An economic interpretation of the changes in popular sport in nineteenth-century England," in Mangan, J. (ed.), *Pleasure, Profit and Proselytism: British culture and sport at home and abroad 1700–1914* (London 1988); "Successful Workers or Exploited Labour? Golf professionals and professional golfers in Britain 1888–1914," *Economic History Review* 61, 1 (2008), pp. 54–79; "Theories and Typologies: A historical explanation of the Sports Club in Britain," *International Journal of the History of Sport* 30, 14 (2013), pp. 1569–1585.

Vertinsky, P., *The Eternally Wounded Woman: Women, doctors and exercise in the late nineteenth century* (Manchester, 1990).

Walker, A., "Reporting Play: The local newspaper and sports journalism, c.1870–1914," *Journalism Studies* 7, 3 (2006), pp. 452–462.

Walker, H., "Lawn Tennis," in Mason, T. (ed.), *Sport in Britain: A social history* (Cambridge, 1989).

Waller, P. J., *Town, City and Nation: England 1850–1914* (Oxford, 1983).

Walton, J. K., and J. Walvin, "Introduction," in Walton, J. K., and Walvin, J. (eds.), *Leisure in Britain, 1780–1939* (Manchester, 1983).

Wiener, J. H., "How New Was the New Journalism?," in Wiener, J. H. (ed.), *Papers for the Millions: The new journalism in Britain, 1850s to 1914* (New York, 1988).

Wigglesworth, N., *A Social History of English Rowing* (London, 1992).

Williams, J., "'One Could Literally Have Walked on the Heads of the People Congregated There': Sport, the town and identity," in Laybourn, K., (ed.), *Social Conditions, Status and Community 1860-c.1920* (Stroud, 1997).

Yasumoto, M., *The Rise of a Victorian Ironopolis: Middlesbrough and regional industrialization* (Woodbridge, 2011).

Unpublished Works and Theses

Bartley, C., Evolution of a Football Culture in Cleveland, unpublished MA thesis, University of Teesside, 2007.

Crump, J., Amusements of the People: The provision of recreation in Leicester, 1850–1914, unpublished PhD thesis, University of Warwick, 1985.

Curran, C., Why Donegal Slept: The development of Gaelic Games in Donegal, 1884–1934, unpublished PhD thesis, De Montfort University, 2012.

Galligan, F., The History of Gymnastic Activity in the West Midlands, with special reference to Birmingham, from 1864 to 1918: With analysis of military influences, secular and religious innovation and educational developments, unpublished PhD thesis, Coventry University, 1999.

Goodall, R., Cycling in North Yorkshire and South Durham, 1869–1914, unpublished MA thesis, Teesside Polytechnic, 1988.

Hadfield, D. W., Political and Social Attitudes in Middlesbrough 1853–1889: with especial reference to the role of the Middlesbrough ironmasters, unpublished PhD thesis, Teesside Polytechnic, 1981.

Hobbs, A., Reading the Local Paper: Social and cultural functions of the local press in Preston, Lancashire, 1855–1910, unpublished PhD thesis, University of Central Lancashire, 2010.

Hunt, T., The Development of Sport in County Westmeath 1850–1905, unpublished PhD thesis, De Montfort University, 2005.

James, S., Growth and Transition in the Cleveland Iron and Steel Industry, 1850–1914, unpublished PhD thesis, Durham University, 2013.

Leonard, J. W., Urban Development and Population Growth in Middlesbrough 1831–71, unpublished PhD thesis, University of York, 1975.

Parker, C., An Urban Historical Perspective: Swimming a recreational and competitive pursuit 1840 to 1914, unpublished PhD thesis, University of Sterling, 2003.

Phillips, S., Industrial Welfare and Recreation at Boots Pure Drug Company 1883–1945, unpublished PhD thesis, Nottingham Trent University, 2003.

Roberts, B. K. O., Civic Ritual in Darlington and Middlesbrough in Comparative Perspective, c.1850–1953, unpublished PhD thesis, Teesside University, 2013.

Turnham, M. H., Roman Catholic Revivalism: A study of the area that became the Diocese of Middlesbrough 1779–1992, unpublished PhD thesis, University of Nottingham, 2012.

Warwick, T., Middlesbrough Steel Magnates 1880–1934: A philanthropic elite?, unpublished paper presented at the Voluntary Action History Conference, 14–16 July 2010, University of Kent; Middlesbrough's Steel Magnates: Business, Culture and Participation: 1880–1934, unpublished PhD thesis, University of Huddersfield, 2014.

Index

Sunderland Albion Football Club, 56, 58, 76n35, 78n90

Sunderland Football Club, 45–46, 63, 76n35

Swimming, 33, 106–108, 141, 153, 154–156; health benefits, 154–155; public baths, 33, 107, 155; women, 114–115, 162

Tees Amateur Boating Club, 131

Tees Amateur Rowing Regatta, 29, 31, 104–105

Tees Conservancy, 160

Tees Oil Works Cricket Club, 91

Tees Sailing Club, 85–86

Tees Wanderers Rugby Club, 28

Teesside Catholic Billiard League, 145, 153

Teesside Cricket League, 91

Teesside Football League, 206

Teesside Junior Football League, 206

tennis, 85, 94–95, 101, 116, 135–136; equipment and clothing, 95; women, 113–114, 163

Thomas, William H., 50, 58, 72, 78n88

Thornaby, 92, 160, 182, 223n156

Thornaby Football Club, 205

Walton, Sir Joseph, 153–154, 206–*207*

water polo, 107, 124n168, 156, 162, 174n162

Westmeath, 4

Wilson, Isaac, 68, 112, 234n2

Williams, Penry, 197, *207*

Winter Gardens, 152

Women, 11, 113–115, 161–165, 233; athletics, 106, 115; amateur sports days, 160–161; bowling, 163; cricket, 90, 164; cycling, 115, 162, 163; as football spectators, 50, 162; girls, 106, 115, 153, 156–157, 158, 162, 164–165, 174n147; golf, 163–164; gymnastics, 156, 164–165; hockey, 152, 164, 165; Ironopolis shareholders, 56; Middlesbrough Ladies Cricket Club, 164; Middlesbrough Ladies Cycling Club, 162–163; Middlesbrough Ladies Wednesday Club (cycling), 115; Middlesbrough Ladies Swimming Club, 162; motorcycling, 158, 175n188; ping pong, 157, 163; rink hockey, 159; skating, 158–159; St George's Congregational Church girls club, 153; suffrage, 161–164; swimming, 114–115, 162; tennis, 113–114, 163;

water polo, 162; work, 233, 235n27

workplace sport, 7, 11, 129, 149–152, 166, 227, 229, 233; cricket clubs, 148, 171n100; football clubs, 206, 209, 210, 213

Yorkshire County Challenge Cup (rugby), 28

Yorkshire County Cricket Club, 146

About the Author

Dr. Catherine Budd is an associate lecturer in history at De Montfort University, Leicester.

CPSIA information can be obtained
at www.ICGtesting.com
Printed in the USA
BVOW08*1948310317
480016BV00003B/7/P

9 781498 529433